Northern Ireland: Can Sean and John Live in Peace?

An American Legal Perspective

MORE PRAISE FOR
NORTHERN IRELAND...

"Marvelous descriptions of the political and religious factions now operative in Northern Ireland.... Prof. Rasnic's devotion and love for all of Ireland is infectious in her narratives and her commentaries... her lucid writing captures the essence of the educational problems caused by discrimination in Ireland and the U.S.A. A superior piece of insights!"

The Right Reverend Robert P. Atkinson
retired Bishop of the Dioceses of West Virginia and Virginia

"In this scrupulously fair and balanced study, Professor Rasnic combines the objectivity of an outsider with the empathy of a native."

David Capper
Faculty of Law, Queen's University Belfast

"Professor Rasnic's research is meticulous and her narrative is characteristically warm and engaging. This is no mere recounting of events: it is a troubled tale, told in a tranquil voice."

Eoin Quill
School of Law, University of Limerick

"Utilizing a narrative style that is at once trenchant and fluid, Professor Rasnic has produced a work that blends impeccable scholarship with a palpable affection for all of Ireland."

Al Stauber
Professor of Business Law, Florida State University

"Her well-researched, thoughtful treatment of the Troubles in Northern Ireland is extremely interesting and a great aid in understanding the depth and complexity of these problems. I heartily recommend this book!"

The Honorable William R. Wilson
Judge of the Federal District Court, Eastern District of Arkansas

Northern Ireland: Can Sean and John Live in Peace?

An American Legal Perspective

By Carol Daugherty Rasnic

Brandylane Publishers, Inc.

Richmond, Virginia

❊ Brandylane Publishers, Inc.
1711 East Main Street, Suite 9
Richmond, Virginia 23223
804.644.3090 or 1.800.553.6922
e-mail: *brandy@crosslink.net*

Library of Congress Cataloging-in-Publication Data

Rasnic, Carol Daugherty, 1941-
   Northern Ireland: can Sean and John live in peace? an American
legal perspective / By Carol Daugherty Rasnic.
       p. cm.
Includes bibliographical references and index.
   ISBN 1-883911-55-9 (pbk.)
   1. Law--Northern Ireland--History. 2. Northern
Ireland--History--1969-1994. 3. Northern Ireland--History--1994- I.
Title.

   KDE88.R37 2003
   320.9416'09'045--dc21

                                                    2003008066

Table of Contents

Map of the island of Ireland with a dark line separating the 6 counties of Northern Ireland from the 26 counties in the Republic of Ireland.

Foreword

I can still remember my first meeting with Carol Rasnic. We were all sitting having coffee in the old staff common room in the basement of the Law School here in Belfast, when it was announced that our new Fulbright Visiting Fellow was to join us. I must say that some of us were a little apprehensive. We did not doubt but that this Ms. Rasnic would have distinguished academic qualifications—were it otherwise, she would not be a Fulbright Fellow at all—but how well would she fit in to the School? After all, most of those who frequented the coffee lounge in those days were fairly easygoing, without pretensions to great academic distinction. We took to heart the rather acid comment of Kevin Myers in the pages of the *Spectator*, which were to the effect that being on the staff of the Queen's University of Belfast was "hardly evidence of Copernican brilliance." Would our new Visiting Fellow expect the sort of conversation to be found in the Senior Common Rooms of Oxford or Cambridge – or, even worse, of Harvard or Yale? All of these doubts were dispelled at a stroke when Carol herself put in an appearance a few minutes later. Half an hour later, it was as if we had known her all our lives. Academic distinction there most certainly was, as we were to find out over the months to come. But here was one who wore her laurels lightly. From that day on, Carol was not just a colleague but a good friend to myself and to any others in the School who got to know her.

Carol has not been the first person to puzzle over the apparent contradiction between the easygoing and friendly nature of those who live in Northern Ireland and the terrible sectarian hatreds which have sullied the fair name of our province for centuries past. The question whether there can be peaceful co-existence between Seamus and Jimmy is one which has taxed many distinguished minds down the ages, and especially in the last thirty years. Some of the comments from outsiders have tended to rankle in local minds, but there are a number of reasons why Carol's thoughts on the subject are well worth reading in the pages which follow.

The first of these is her undoubted academic distinction. We have here no mere saloon-bar pundit, but one who is ideally qualified by background to speak on such affairs. Anyone who takes the trouble to read Carol's long and distinguished *curriculum vitae* will see an impressive record of international scholarship, including two Fulbright Fellowships (most of us would never even hope to qualify for one), a long list of publications (she has lost count of the number of articles she has written) and membership of some of the most select and prestigious societies in the academic legal world. Moreover, she has travelled widely, and has worked in many different countries. This gives her not only academic expertise but the breadth of experience that gives rise to sound and balanced scholarship.

The second reason for taking this book very seriously indeed is the work that has gone into it. Carol developed an interest in the local political situation during her visit here in the spring of 1998—a time when, as she so rightly points out, momentous events were taking place. During the summer of 2000—another rather eventful period, it is fair to say—she returned to Belfast and spent several weeks interviewing major political figures in the "peace process" and studying in the libraries of Dublin and Belfast. As well as this, Carol's natural friendliness and approachability have earned her many contacts among the ordinary people of Ireland, both North and South. All of this has enabled her to gain the broad perspective on our local affairs which many of us who live here often lack. Hampered by the constraints of our background and of our daily routine, we only see the trees. In this book, Carol is trying to show us the wood.

Last but by no means least, there is Carol's undoubted affection for Northern Ireland and its people. "I truly love Ireland and Northern Ireland", she wrote to me in an e-mail yesterday. "I would move there IN A MINUTE if I could!" One of the least attractive characteristics of some of those who criticise us from outside is that they clearly neither know nor care what makes us tick. But one does not resent criticism from a friend. The prophet Jeremiah, whose name has become a byword for savage and gloomy prognostications, wished that his head were all water, and his eyes a fountain of tears, so that he might weep day and night for his people. Such is a natural sentiment for those who see those whom they love being led into disaster by their own folly and ignorance. And there is no doubt that Northern Ireland has a great appeal for those who come to its shores. My own story may not be out of place in this context. An Englishman born and bred, with no family or other connections with this part of the world, I applied for and was offered a post teaching law in the Queen's University of Belfast. My interview took place on 2nd May 1977 – almost exactly a quarter of a century ago. I did not particularly want to come here. The only reason why I took the job was that there was nobody else willing to employ me. My original plan was to move on at the earliest possible opportunity. Yet here I am still! There are many others of my acquaintance who have shared this experience.

The poet Burns once penned the following lines:
>"I wad some Pow'r the giftie gie us
>To see oursels as others see us!
>It wad frae mony a blunder free us
>And foolish notion"

In this book, Carol has provided us with a mirror in which we can discern some of our characteristics, both good and bad. If this helps us to free ourselves from some of the blunders and foolish notions which hinder us on the road to peace in Northern Ireland, she will have done a worthwhile job.

John E. Stannard
QUEEN'S UNIVERSITY OF BELFAST, *24th April 2002*

Preface

Perhaps my personal interest in all things Irish is a congenital one, since both my father and mother were of Irish origin. Daddy was Edward Rogan Daugherty (originally Doherty), and his County Donegal family came to America during the 1798 rebellion. Mama was Mary Margaret Murphy, whose people left County Wexford during the potato famine in the 1840's.

Consequently, my brother and I were reared in what I later figured to have been in "good Irish stock" fashion. We were taught (whether or not it "took" is probably yet debatable) to be humble, industrious, faithful and honest. Complaining was not something which would endear us to Daddy, and Mama's unending sense of humor complemented his relative seriousness to result in something quite close to a perfect union: that very special mix of reality and levity which I was to learn is characteristically Irish. One need only see Irish dramatist J. M. Synge's wonderful play "The Well of the Saints" to experience this combination.

My red-haired Granddaddy Murphy took his grandchildren under his wing at our early ages. He taught me the same love of sports which he had engrained in Mama, who was truly a natural athlete. We would all revel and delight in Granddaddy's talks of his experiences as mayor of a small West Virginia coal mining town before the family moved to Virginia, and as owner and operator of several movie theaters while Mama and her four siblings were growing up. His stories were always laced with that unique form of Irish wit, and I loved watching baseball games, horse racing, and even boxing matches with him on television.

When my Grandmother Murphy died, Mama and her sister were ages nine and eleven, respectively. (The three brothers were fifteen, seventeen, and nineteen.) My Protestant granddad then sent Mama and my Aunt Juanita to a Catholic boarding school near Cincinnati, Ohio, for two years, and they both had fond memories of this time and talked about it to us frequently. Thus, my brother and I were raised to appreciate and to be familiar with both Protestant and Catholic traditions.

When I later was to visit County Donegal, I understood better the differences in demeanors of our Daughertys and our Murphys. Donegal is probably the most rugged locale on the entire island, and the Atlantic seaside winds and craggy mountain terrain make for harsh weather. There are literally no operable trains in all of Donegal, and there is little industry other than fishing. Because of its relative inaccessibility, most visitors to Ireland miss what is arguably the island's most impressive scenery.

When in Donegal, one truly feels as though time stopped a century ago. The largest *Gaeltacht* (Irish speaking region) in Ireland is in Donegal, and the largest of the workhouses was located in the small Donegal village of Dunfanaghy. The "workhouse" was an institution established by the British government to house the poor Irish when the potato famine virtually either killed or impoverished the greater part of the Irish people. The only function of these involuntary residents was to labor in a form of indentured servitude.

Donegal folks are a bit distant and at times even dour, but nevertheless, they are people of complete integrity and dependability. In contrast, folks along the southeast of the island where Wexford is situated exhibit an exuberance and cheer which seems to accompany the milder weather, typical of the coast along the southern part of the Irish Sea. Wexford and its adjacent counties of Kilkenny and Wicklow are the sites of Johnstown Castle with its sweeping gardens, an agricultural gem; island seabird sanctuaries; Kilkenny castle and Kilkenny Town's abundance of historic pubs; the imposing Powerscourt mansion, Sally Gap and the "garden of Ireland"; and St. Kevin's 6th century spiritual oasis, Glendalough. The region literally buzzes with tourists, particularly during the summer months.

It was a revelation for me to realize that the two sides of our family so obviously reflected these two distinctly different regions. My brother has noted that the Murphys could suddenly become quite angry, but that this same anger faded just as quickly. To the contrary, a fairly consistent trait among our Daughertys was a reasoned resistance to anger, but once their anger surfaced, it generally simmered and remained a while.

Furthermore, all our Murphys seemed always to be living for the moment and laughing in true *carpe diem* style, the Daughertys were more frugal and cautious with regard to the future. Granddaddy Murphy once laughed to me about how much money he had earned and how much he had spent (quite close to like figures). He concluded, "I didn't come into this world with any wealth, and nobody should expect me to leave it by giving any to them." Granddaddy Daugherty, on the other hand, assiduously maintained a sufficient savings, and he was always cognizant of the merit of a good education. My brother and I were always proud of both sides of our Irish heritage.

After my graduation from law school, I became more curious from a legal perspective about our Irish background. The onset of the so-called "Troubles" of Northern Ireland in the late 1960s and early 1970s was widely published in the U.S.A. The general nature of a lawyer is to view these events according to the law, in this case perhaps especially so when the lawyer has an Irish background. I was intrigued by the legislative, judicial and executive responses to the Troubles and their respective efforts to abate the escalating violence.

The apex undoubtedly was my semester as a Fulbright Visiting Professor at the School of Law at Queen's University in Belfast. Fate—and surely a touch of the proverbial luck of the Irish—allowed for this time to be set during the spring of 1998. It was on April 10, of that year that the Belfast Agreement was signed and on May 22, that the subsequent referenda on the Agreement in both the Republic of Ireland and Northern Ireland were held. (This agreement is commonly referred to as the "Good Friday Agreement" for the day on which it was executed, and this book will use that term.) My husband and I were in Kilkenny at the time the Agreement was executed, and my cousin was visiting me in Belfast at the time of the vote which resulted in substantial margins of approval on both sides of the border. Being able to share the euphoria over this chance for peace with part of my family was the highlight of a wonderful semester during which so many lasting friendships were forged.

These good friends included members of the law faculty, secretaries (Eleanor, Fiona, Gina, Janice, Karen, Meave, and Sandra), and domestic workers (Gloria and Phyllis) at the Queen's University School of Law; my charming landlady, Jean, and her neighbors; and the very special Sunday morning congregation of the Church of St. Nicholas and the Very Rev. Frederick J. Rusk, all who truly gave me a *de facto* "dual citizenship" and a "second home."

In Summer 2000, I returned to the island of Ireland and to the law schools of Queen's University Belfast, Trinity College Dublin, and University College Dublin for more in-depth legal research into Northern Ireland's problems and the post-Good Friday Agreement events. This book is the story which has evolved from this research and from my own experiences of living in Northern Ireland. The purpose is two-fold: (1) to explain objectively the critical legal aspects of the several issues, comparing Northern Ireland's difficulties to some parallel ones under U.S. law where there are similarities; and (2) to provide a personal, and thus at times quite subjective, perspective of the Troubles. The latter has been shaped not only by the research and teaching in Northern Ireland, but also by my contemporaneous daily living experiences in Belfast (and, for a shorter while, in Dublin) during this work.

It was my privilege to have interviewed more than twenty principals involved either directly or indirectly in this peace process, as well as others with vested interests in the future of the province of Northern Ireland, both personally and professionally. This group crossed the occupational, religious, and political spectrum, including clergy, both Catholic and Protestant; jurists; elected legislators on the New Northern Ireland Assembly and leading spokespeople from all major political parties; personnel in the office of the *Taoiseach* (prime minister) and Attorney General of the Republic of Ireland; mediators; and academics.

Augmenting these scheduled interviews was the indispensable "glue" which made sense of the disparity of positions: comments of persons on the streets, in pubs, groceries, and shops, and on trains and buses. The people of Ireland and Northern Ireland are surely the island's singularly most remarkable asset, and their assessments and opinions have been both insightful and invaluable.

My personal thanks go to all those who enlightened me about the Troubles: Father Peter Ward, Clonard Monastery Belfast; the Right Reverend James Moore, Bishop of the Church of Ireland, Diocese of Connor; Northern Ireland Assembly Members Monica McWilliams, Alex Atwood, David Ervine, Mitchel McLaughlin and Mark Robinson; David Trimble, First Minister of the Assembly; Sir Ronnie Flanagan, Chief Constable of the Royal Ulster Constabulary (now Police Service of Northern Ireland); the Honorable John Martin, Chief Judge for Social Security and Child Commissioners of Northern Ireland; Jackie Johnston, Office of Secretary of State for Northern Ireland; Stephen Farry, Policy Director of the Alliance Party; Human Rights Chief Commissioner Brice Dickson; Paul Mageean, Committee for the Administration of Justice; Claire Archbold and Neil Lambe, Northern Ireland Office of Law Reform; Professor Dennis Kennedy and Professor John Lynch, both on faculties at Queen's University; Professor Seamus Dunn, University of Ulster Coleraine; Professor Jerry Tyrell, University of Ulster Derry (Magee); Eoin O'Brion, *Sinn Féin* Party; Caoimhghín O'Murchidh; Eamon McKee of the Press Service of Ireland (New York Office); Dave Wall of Northern Ireland Association for the Care and Resettlement of Offenders; Dr. Martin Mansergh, Special Assistant to the *Taoiseach* (Prime Minister of Ireland); and Caitlín Ní Fhlaitheartaigh, Office of the Attorney General of Ireland.

I am especially grateful to Olivia Lloyd for her expertise in editing and to my own "personal board of editors and critics." These patient folks include my husband, R. Jackson Rasnic; my clergy friends, the Right Rev. Robert P. Atkinson, retired Bishop of the Episcopal Diocese of West Virginia, the Rev. Dr. Robert M. Watson, Calvary Episcopal Church, Memphis, Tennessee, and the Rev. Robert G. Hetherington, my rector at St. Paul's Episcopal Church, Richmond, Virginia; my brother, Roger A. Daugherty; my cousins, Mary Molly Murphy Flanders and Prof. James K. Murphy; my former student at Queen's University School of Law, David A. Bredin; Professors Norma Dawson, Sean Doran, John Jackson, and John Stannard of Queen's University School of Law; Virginia H. Cogger and Professor Dr. Barbara L. Peery, all of Richmond, Virginia. Their rigorous critiques and comments were of immense help.

The research and the data are factual, but the story that has unfolded is my own. I hope that it conveys something of the Northern Ireland and her people whom I love, folks who so deserve "peace in [their] own land"* and for whom my prayer each day is *"Go mbeannai Dia dhuit."***

    *The prayers of the people in the Book of Common Prayer
    of the Church of Ireland includes a prayer for "peace in
    our own land."

   ** *"Go mbeannai Dia dhuit"* is the Irish (Gaelic) phrase for
    "May God bless you."

Introduction

In 1920, the island of Ireland was partitioned by British government, and the twenty-six counties of the South and the far Northwest became (in 1922) the *Saorstát Éireann* (Free State of Ireland). The remaining six counties in the small Northeast segment of the island became the province of Northern Ireland of the United Kingdom (including also England, Scotland and Wales). The former Free State of Ireland gained full independence from Great Britain and the United Kingdom in 1949, when it became the Republic of Ireland.

The entire island of Ireland is only a bit over 32,400 square miles. The Republic of Ireland is about 27,000 square miles, an area smaller than the American state of South Carolina. Northern Ireland covers about 5,400 square miles, just a little bit larger than the state of Connecticut, one of the smallest American states. The relative smallness of the island as a whole is perhaps best perceived by the American by comparing the size with that of one of our largest states. The island of Ireland would fit into the state of Texas more than eight times.

The tragedy of Northern Ireland is universally familiar. However, not so well understood by the "man-on-the-street" are the causes and the responsive political and legal measures, both prior to and after the unofficial onset of the "Troubles"[1] in 1969. The division within Northern Ireland carries with it much historical baggage, and there are understandable (if not seemingly illogical) reasons for strife. It is actually possible to appreciate both sides of the conflict, albeit perhaps not without personally aligning oneself with one side or the other.

The struggle has been a virtual undeclared war, and the violence on the streets of this British province has continued sporadically, even after the 1998 Belfast Agreement (the so-called "Good Friday Agreement," in reference to the day on which it was signed.)

To view the problem as fundamentally a Catholic versus Protestant one is an oversimplification, although somewhat true. The gulf was created by an amalgam of areas of differences in identities and ideologies of which religion is only one. These areas of identification include also national cultures and political alignments.

To the uninitiated, the current dispute is between Unionists, those who advocate a perpetuation of the current political affiliation of the region of Northern Ireland with the United Kingdom[2] and Nationalists, who yearn for a reunited thirty-two-county Ireland. The goal of the latter group, then, is to terminate the provincial status of Northern Ireland as being part of and subordinate to the British government.

For the most part, Nationalists are Roman Catholic, and Unionists—which are in the majority—are generally Protestant. These religious identities at times become peripheral to the basic dispute, since underlying these denominational identities are the two distinct cultures and political philosophies.

Nationalists claim an allegiance to a national culture for all of Ireland. This is a culture that embraces the music and dance generally associated with the Irish, a pride in history of the Irish struggle for independence, and revitalization of the Irish (Gaelic) language. The designation as "Nationalist," then, infers the perception of the island of Ireland as a nation. The term "Republican" carries with it a somewhat negative connotation, referencing the paramilitary groups of those who unapologetically fight for their cause. The most well known and publicized of these is the Irish Republican Army, or IRA, but there are several other Republican groups that promote the use of violence.

About 2/3 of the Protestant majority is Presbyterian. The proximity by sea to Scotland, where the Presbyterian Church is the official state church, made the migration of many Scots to Northern Ireland throughout the years a natural one. (The many Scottish surnames in the region are apparent to the visitor.) This accounts for the considerable Scottish influence on religion in Northern Ireland. The second largest numbers of Protestants are the members of the Church of Ireland (the counterpart to the Episcopal Church in the United States), and Methodists are a close third. To be sure, there are many Protestant denominations throughout Northern Ireland, a fact that seems to come as a surprise to most Americans who generally expect the Church of Ireland to be the dominant one.

The "Unionist" label refers to continued unity of the province with Great Britain. Unionist paramilitary groups are "Loyalists," which—similarly to Republicans on the Nationalist side—achieve their desired end. It is probably fair to say that the vast majority on both sides deplores violence and terrorism. With regard to Loyalist groups, it is this writer's opinion that Americans are typically familiar with the Republican IRA, but not with the several Loyalist paramilitary groups, such as Ulster Volunteer Force (UVF) and Ulster Freedom Fighters (UFF).

Population-wise, Unionists presently make up about 55% of Northern Ireland, and Nationalists, about 45%.[3] Thus, although a minority, Nationalists are a strong— and growing— minority.

Below is a general summary of terminology:

General Political Term	Unionist	Nationalist
Usual Religious Affiliation	Protestant	Catholic
Military Component	Loyalists	Republicans
Political Stance	For remaining with the United Kingdom	For a United Ireland

The reader should remember that many on both sides of this divide are not religious people and the Catholic-Protestant identity is not necessarily a spiritual one. It is axiomatic that Christians, by doctrine, do not kill other Christians simply because they worship the same God and the same Christ in a somewhat different manner.

A popular novel and motion picture in the United States during the late 1990s, "The Devil's Own," is illustrative. The film stars Harrison Ford as a New York policeman with Irish ancestry and Brad Pitt as an Irishman, and a member of the IRA, in the U.S.A. solely to obtain weapons for his paramilitary group (unbeknownst to Ford). When the Ford character and his family took Pitt to the confirmation of Ford's daughter in a Catholic Church, Pitt scarcely knew the procedure. He commented that it had been many years since he had been in a church, but yet, he identified himself as Catholic. His involvement in the Republican movement was intense indeed.

The reader should be familiar with another term used frequently in Northern Ireland. One may hear the comment, "He is not 'involved.'" This means that the person to whom the speaker is referring is not concerned about the political status of Northern Ireland, at least not in a politically active sense. Despite this, the usual nature of the Irish seems to this writer to be to attach oneself emotionally to a cause, and the result for one growing up in Northern Ireland is a sort of inbred identification with one side or the other.

The author is a professor of law who formerly practiced law, and this book is about the law. Nonetheless, the facts that provided the impetus for the laws, orders and regulations controlling Northern Ireland are critical, for they give a sense and fabric of an unfolding drama. The story is about a conflict, a struggle that has given birth to much hatred carefully nourished through the years and thereby not permitted to diminish. The legal references are official, but the underlying story is influenced by the author's personal interviews, conversations, and experiences of living and working in Northern Ireland, a region whose people I have come to love as family. These personal commentaries are interspersed throughout.

Because each chapter is written so as to facilitate reading separately, some material is necessarily repeated summarily on occasion.

The three chapters in Part I outline the history of Ireland and Northern Ireland, the significance of parades in the region and the influence of religion on the strife.

The chapters in Part II are analyses of the major segments of the 1998 Belfast Agreement (referred to hereinafter as the Good Friday Agreement, or the GFA), the implementing legislation, and subsequent events which have shaped—or which will likely shape—the future of Northern Ireland.

Much of the book contains parallels which compare British laws adopted in response to the Troubles in Northern Ireland to the body of American law which has addressed racial conflict on the other side of the Atlantic Ocean.

The necessary conclusion must be of the "to-be-continued" sort, since there is truly no crystal ball which permits one to foresee what ultimately will transpire for the good people of this wonderful region.

Endnotes to Introduction

[1] The "Troubles" is the term used in Ireland and the United Kingdom to refer to the strife in Northern Ireland.

[2] The United Kingdom is a political entity which includes England, Scotland, Wales, and Northern Ireland. It should be distinguished from Great Britain, a geographical term, which refers to the island containing England, Scotland and Wales. Northern Ireland lies across the Irish Sea on a separate island, which it shares with the Republic of Ireland. In this sense, Northern Ireland might be compared to the proverbial "ugly stepsister," not as much a part of the "family" as are the other members. In this case, the difference is geographical, but also one which the author has sensed to be the position of many persons in Great Britain with regard to Northern Ireland.

[3] These statistical figures vary according to the source. Some report a closer ratio.

Part I

Pre-Good Friday Agreement Ireland and Northern Ireland

Chapter 1:

A Historical Background (or: Why the Irish in Northern Ireland Might Understandably Dislike the British)

"For gold is tried in the fire, and acceptable men in the furnace of adversity."

Ecclesiasticus 2:5, The Apochrypha

Michael was our cheerful tour bus guide on my very first trip to Ireland, a man so delightful that he endeared himself to everyone on the bus. While we traveled from the West coast to Dublin through Michael's home county of Kerry and Counties Limerick, Tipperary, and Kildare, he made repeated references to the pernicious Oliver Cromwell, the powerful British military ruler of England in the mid-17th century. Atrocity after atrocity committed by Cromwell was described by an atypically angry Michael, mile after mile, and it was apparent that, to him, Cromwell had been the devil incarnate. When someone asked, "Michael, didn't Cromwell ever do *anything* right?" his adamant response was, "Not on *this* bus, he didn't!" My thought was that it would be a rare mother on the island of Ireland who would name her son "Oliver," after the ignominious Cromwell.

Today, Irish-English relations are amazingly amicable, at least with respect to the two governments. Ireland has been a Free State (*Saorstát Éireann*) since 1922, and a fully independent Republic (*Éire*) since 1949, so only those devotees of history (such as Michael) hold the English of the past in such disdain. It is in Northern Ireland—which remains a part of the United Kingdom and whose allegiance thus is to the Crown of England—where this bitterness is still so patent. Moreover, this antipathy for Britain is absent among most Protestants and all those who regard themselves as Unionists. It is the Irish Catholics—Nationalists—who feel as though they are pariahs, strangers in their own land.

The British government partitioned the island of Ireland in 1920, and Northern Ireland Catholics have ever since deemed themselves cast in the role of illegitimate children, treated by the majority as an unwanted and inferior breed. Yet it is not entirely about religion, and the story of two different cultures pre-dates partition and Reformation by centuries.

A Panoramic View of Ireland vs. England
From the Celts to 1366

Probably the 'Troubles'—the term which refers to the division and attendant violence which characterized Northern Ireland for much of the 20th century, especially during its last thirty years—germinated as long ago as the first British presence on the island of Ireland in 1169. These were the Anglo-Normans, originally Scandinavian Vikings who had conquered England in 1066.

In 1171, only two years after the arrival of these Anglo-Normans in Ireland, England's King Henry II came to the island. He achieved a lordship not only over the recent Norman colonists (who were his subjects), but also over the Gaelic kings who had conquered the island in the first few centuries after the birth of Christ. The Celtic Gaels were victorious over all the other Celtic groups which had fought for control of the island. By 400 A.D. their conquest had been complete.[1] The semi-official geographical division of the island into four areas— Ulster (North), Leinster (Mid- and Southeast), Munster (Southwest), and Connaught (the Midwest)—dates from the Celtic era. Henry II's entry onto the island which transferred power from the Celts is generally regarded as the beginning of the British crown's governmental involvement in Ireland.[2]

Praising the king's assumption of control over Ireland, Pope Alexander III wrote to him, referring to the Irish in the most unflattering of terms. The pontiff wrote of the "enormities of vice with which [the Irish] are infected, and how they have departed from the fear of God and the established practice of the Christian faith...." He described Henry II as "our dearest son in Christ...[who has] subjugated this barbarous and uncouth race...[which is] ignorant of divine law...[and an] undisciplined and untamed people...."[3] Pope Alexander's contempt for the Irish was not the first such statement from Rome. His forerunner, Adrian IV, had issued a papal edict in 1156, authorizing Henry II to enter Ireland and to "subject [the] people to law and to root out from them the weeds of vice.... [and to] increase... the Christian religion."[4]

Apparently, both pontiffs had suffered memory lapses with regard to one of the most renowned of saints, the venerable St. Patrick, who had brought Christian-

3

ity to the Irish people back in the 4th century. It is difficult to find a spot on the island within a twenty-five-mile radius which does not have a St. Patrick's Church. [Any reader who may have grown up in Virginia must be reminded of George Washington, since there are a multitude of inns, houses, and sites where buildings once stood with signs reading, "George Washington slept here." I can recall wondering as a child whether our first president might have had narcolepsy, since he seemed to have fallen asleep everywhere he went.]

Interestingly, arguments over whether Patrick was a Catholic or a Protestant recur. There are St. Patrick's churches which are Catholic, and those which are Protestant (usually Church of Ireland). Of course, Patrick was neither Protestant nor Catholic, since he lived more than 1,000 years before the Reformation.

Despite this 12th century overpowering of the Celtic people, the Celtic-Gaelic language and culture are still characteristic of what the world perceives as "Irishness."[5] This English control seemed only to toughen their resolve to preserve all that is Irish.

Why was there an English interest in the island of Ireland? Some historians have reasoned that the assumption was that it would be simple to dominate the Irish because of the absence of an Irish monarchy, and that the potential of increased power was too tempting to resist. To be sure, Ireland had its kings, approximately 150 at a time. However, there was never one single ruler. Indeed, the term "high king" (*e.g.*, the legendary Brian Boru, killed at the Battle of Clontarf in 1014) is somewhat misleading, since the holder of this title did not exercise island-wide authority.[6] It is likely that this internecine squabbling for power among these Irish kings, or *chieftains*, made a unified defense against the invading Anglo-Normans from England unlikely, if not impossible. A second, and perhaps more important, reason is that Ireland contained fertile farmland and was an overall picturesque site for the castles and churches the Anglo-Normans would build.

The role of these Irish kings was somewhat similar to that of an American court, since one of their functions was to interpret laws. The actual creators of the law—a legislature of sorts—were the *brehons*, or the lawyers. Hence, the term "*Brehon* law" was used.[7] This legal system was to change with the Anglo-Normans in power.

There was yet another reason for the English invasion in addition to the lack of cohesion among the kings, one which concerned the Church in Rome. The early Irish churches did not have a centralized structure, to the chagrin of the popes during the area of the first conquest. The clergy did, however, hold power among the people. Next to the *brehons* on the hierarchy of authority were the abbots, church leaders who were monks and who lived in monasteries scattered throughout the island. The kings comprised the third rung of this power structure, a sort of triarchy, rather than a monarchy.

The power vested in the abbots was significant because there were no bishops. This localization of the church had been of considerable concern to Adrian IV, who became pope in 1154, the same year that Henry II ascended to the English throne. Moreover, he was troubled by the absence of ritual in the services. There were neither canonical marriages nor celibacy among clergy and no enforcement of tithing.[8] Rome was not happy with the church in Ireland.

These Anglo-Normans were a completely alien breed to the Irish and their rural way of life. With them came military expertise, feudalism to the extreme, and a legal system based on primogeniture (*i.e,* the status of royalty, lordship, or the position of chancellor—or judge—attained by way of inheritance). To their credit (particularly in the eyes of modern tourists), these Anglo-Norman colonists built many of the magnificent fortified castles remaining in Ireland (such as St. John's Castle in Limerick) and many of the most impressive of churches and cathedrals (*e.g.*, Christ Church Cathedral and St. Patrick's Cathedral in Dublin, and St. Canice's in Kilkenny) during the 12th and 13th centuries. By 1250, the Anglo-Normans had ownership by conquest of three-fourths of the entire island, including the most prime tracts of land.[9]

The Statutes of Kilkenny

The aspiration of the new colonists was to eradicate Irish culture and to superimpose an English legal system, church structure, and manner of living. In 1366, the British Parliament met in Kilkenny (in the South) and enacted a series of laws known collectively as the Statutes of Kilkenny. The purpose was to obliterate all vestiges of Gaelic/Celtic influence. Prohibited were the speaking of Irish-Gaelic, the wearing of Irish clothing, and the use of any of the old *Brehon* laws. The spirited Irish simply ignored these mandates and continued as though the English had never arrived.[10]

With the Statutes of Kilkenny came the concept of "the Pale." "Outside the Pale" or "beyond the Pale" (hence, the origin of this phrase) was the term used for all the areas from Dundalk (the most northerly town in the Republic of Ireland on the road/train route from Dublin to Belfast) southward through the Boyne Valley and Dublin, down to Wexford in the far Southeast and Waterford in the Mid-South. The significance was that this "Pale" area was English-speaking, and thus superior to the rest of Ireland, where people were officially titled the "Irish enemies." Another statute ordered all Irish landowners to return to their estates "beyond the Pale."[11] The most visible English landlords, the royal family of England, remained absent, however, a fact which was quixotic indeed. Journalist and historian Paul Johnson has written that the reluctance of the monarchy to be in Ireland during this era was the most central weakness of English policy on the island.[12]

15th Century to 1829
The House of Kildare

During the 15th century, England was otherwise occupied, attending to warfare on its own turf. The royal House of York (whose symbol was a white rose) and the House of Lancaster (whose symbol was a red rose), two factions of the dynasty of Plantagenet, became engaged in a series of royal battles, a war which history has labeled the Wars of the Roses. The relevance for Ireland was the split support of its people between York and Lancaster.

The effect on Ireland was a lasting one. King Edward IV of the House of York had defeated the Lancasters in 1461, and he appointed the Earl of Desmond as Governor of Ireland. However, Desmond proved far too Gaelic to suit the king, who, in typical 15th-16th century England fashion, simply had Desmond peremptorily beheaded. Thus, Ireland was in need of an English Governor.

Sir John Butler, Earl of Ormond, was a dark-horse because of his Lancaster leanings. Richard, Duke of York, became Governor of Ireland in 1449, but Richard was a serious problem for the king, since he was a challenger to Edward as monarch. Richard was held in high esteem both by the Anglo-Irish and the Irish, but he was killed in battle in 1485. [His place in history is one not envied: Richard is the last British monarch to have met his demise on the battlefield.[13]]

The House of Kildare remained as the most likely possibility to provide a Governor, and by 1478, Gearold Mor Fitzgerald, Earl of Kildare, was named to the helm of Ireland. He, too, boasted support from among both the Irish and the Anglo-Irish, but his power was far greater than had been Richard's. Unlike Richard, Fitzgerald also had many relations among Anglo-Normans. He became known as the Great Earl, so complete and sweeping was his power.

Even when Henry VII (House of Tudor, and a Lancastrian) ascended to the English throne in 1485, Fitzgerald retained the governorship except for a brief hiatus in the 1490s. He was succeeded by his son, the 9th earl, who ruled in Ireland until 1534.[14] The Fitzgeralds remain one of the benchmarks of Irish history.

Poynings' Law

Meanwhile, the British Parliament had enacted Poynings' Law.[15] Although Ireland had its own Parliament in Dublin, the island was, of course, subject also to Acts of the Parliament in Westminster. Poynings' Law added another layer of control over the Irish Parliament. This statute required approval of the Parliament in London before any Act of the Irish Parliament could be effective.

This British stamp of approval proved not to be taken for granted. W.N. Osborough, Professor of Jurisprudence and Legal History at University College Dublin, has written of one occasion in 1692 when Irish Lord Ormond forwarded several pending bills to London for approval. Some were perfunctorily signed, but several were refused because the king found some displeasure in the language. When Ormond wrote to the Secretary of the English Privy Council to ask the reasons for the disapproval (his express reason for the inquiry was to avoid any future such choice of wording which might be distasteful to the king), the reply was curt. The Secretary responded that there was neither precedent nor acceptable rationale which obligated the Council to offer an account of their—or the king's— reason(s).[16] Obviously, the British government had issued a reminder to the Irish lords that their superior, the Parliament in Westminster, had the upper hand.

Henry VIII and His Successors

The reign of English King Henry VIII (1502-1553) was pivotal for Ireland. If Richard's claim to historical fame is his death in battle, surely Henry VIII's is his ruthlessness in disposing of those among his six wives who had failed to provide him with a male heir. He separated the Church of England from the Catholic Church in Rome in order to divorce the first such unfortunate wife, Catherine of Aragon. Of Catherine's five children, only a daughter, later to become Queen Mary I, survived. When his subsequent marriage to young Anne Boleyn produced yet another girl, he had Anne beheaded (the fabricated charge was infidelity) in 1536. This event post-dated his having shoved two acts through Parliament in 1534, which (i) declared that the pope had no authority over the Church of England, and (ii) established the King of England as the head of the newly independent Church of England. His third wife, Jane Seymour, did bear her husband a son, Edward VI, but she died shortly after his birth. He next divorced his fourth wife, Anne of Cleves, and had his ill-fated fifth wife, Catherine Howard, executed for misconduct. The last "Mrs. Henry VIII," Catherine Paar, did have one stroke of good fortune: she managed to outlive her husband before he was able to dispense with her.[17]

Why was Henry VIII of such significance in Irish history? First, he had demanded Ireland's full allegiance in 1521 and declared himself King of Ireland in 1541. His intent was to achieve a comprehensive and complete colonization of Ireland. An obedient Irish Parliament acquiesced, both to his denunciation of the Catholic Church and to his presumptive extension of his kingdom.[18] This usurpation of the Catholic Church, the church of most residents on the island of Ireland, was his second lasting legacy, one of seismic proportions.

Henry's plan to control Ireland did not subside with his death in 1553. He was succeeded on the throne by his only son, ten-year-old Edward VI, who suffered from ill health and who lived to serve (primarily through surrogates) only six years.[19] When young Edward died, Henry's oldest child, the daughter of Catherine of Aragon, became Mary I. Mary kept her Catholic faith and married a Catholic, Philip of Spain. Indeed, she was despicable for her persecution of Protestants, and in 1555, she repealed her father's laws announcing the Church of England would separate from the Church in Rome and the pope.

Mary initiated a plantation system in Ireland, beginning a confiscation of lands and vesting ownership in the Crown. Her murders of those with whom she had differences (*e.g.*, the O'Moore and O'Connor *chieftains* with lands in Counties Laois and Offaly) earned her a title of dubious distinction, "Bloody Mary." [20]

Additionally, this professed devout Christian had more than 300 persons burned at the stake, including many high-ranking Protestant clergymen. She died in 1558 at the age of forty-two, saddened at the prospect of her Protestant half-sister Elizabeth I's rule as Queen of England and Ireland.[21]

If Mary was no blessing for Ireland, she was a veritable Mother Teresa in contrast to her younger sister. Elizabeth's forty-five-year reign remains the longest in English history. She constantly sent new English colonists to Ireland, extending the plantation southward to Munster. She died childless and unmarried (hence her nickname, the "Virgin Queen") in 1603,[22] but not until after she had literally beaten Ireland into submission.[23]

James I followed, and with him, an expulsion of the Jesuit priests. The Earl of Tyrone, Hugh O'Neill, and the O'Donnells had achieved a powerful victory over British forces in Ulster in 1598, while Elizabeth was still on the throne. However, James' plan to empower the Protestant Church in Ireland included the requirement that all earls take an oath to him, a man who had been excommunicated from the Catholic Church. The pope denounced such oaths as sinful, and the earls in Ulster feared arrest because they could not follow the king's command. Their quick departure to Rome in 1607 is known by every Irish school child as the "Flight of the Earls." [24] It became clear indeed that the Catholic Church was targeted by England for extinction.

Oliver Cromwell

John Lynch, Professor of History at Queen's University Belfast, has observed that the "English didn't try to convert the Catholics, they simply tried to control them." [25] This observation is especially profound when considering the military reign of Oliver Cromwell, the nemesis of our bus driver-guide, Michael.

Cromwell's coming to power in England was an aberration. Charles I, who had become King of England in 1627, was frustrated over the government's financial difficulties which had so plagued Elizabeth. Determined to obtain a greater cash flow from Ireland, Charles' solution was to negotiate a deal with the Catholic peerage in Ireland. Upon their payment to the British government of 120,000 pound sterling (at today's exchange rate, approximately $190,000, a substantial sum in the 17th century) over a three-year period, much of the land in Ireland would revert to them, and England would permit Catholics to practice law. This ambitious plan backfired, however, when the Protestant Parliament in Dublin refused to pass the necessary legislation.[26] This was the antithesis of Poynings' Law, with the Irish government's balk now impeding the goal of the British government.

Charles' lack of control over both governments gave rise to a rebellion in 1641. Cromwell assumed military leadership over a crownless England, and the results for Ireland were devastating. Cromwell landed in Ireland on August 15, 1649, a date which likely appears on many a history examination in Irish schools.[27]

To say that Cromwell was lacking in sensitivity is the greatest of understatements. Religious in the same vein as Mary I had been, Cromwell was a Protestant full of twisted religious fervor. Just prior to departing England, he told his troops that they were on a godly mission, Israelites about to enter Canaan in order to exterminate all the idolators. Cromwell had three burning passions: (i) to avenge the 1641 massacres when Ulster Catholics had risen in arms against the English; (ii) to establish Protestant "freedom of conscience"; and (iii) to preclude Ireland's being a foreign island hostile to England.[28]

He began with an attack on Drogheda, just South of Dundalk in the Northeast of what is now the Republic of Ireland. Cromwell did not believe in "casual slaughter," and he maintained such a grip on his own troops that he had two of his own men hanged for stealing hens from the Irish. If civilians were in the line of fire, his "siege-train" would nonetheless proceed. Sir Arthur Aston, the Catholic governor of Drogheda, avowed that he and his men would "perish rather than to give up the place" (reminiscent of Jim Bowie and Davy Crockett's band of Texans who were slaughtered at the Alamo by Mexican General Santa Ana rather than surrender). When Cromwell's forces took the town, he ordered all those who had been armed against the army from England to be executed. Aston himself was beaten to death with his own wooden leg.[29]

Cromwell's only serious obstacle came at Clonmel, when Irish *chieftain* Hugh O'Neill had managed to escape. Nonetheless, Ireland had effectively been overtaken by this ruthless military officer. Historian Johnson credits Cromwell with bearing a distinction among other English fighters in that he was the first one to take stern measures to enforce against the masses the strict laws making Ireland subservient to England.[30]

The Post-Cromwell era

Legal recourse against the Irish rebels was draconian. In August 1652, the Parliament at Westminster adopted a law which listed ten categories of Irishmen. The first five included those engaged in active rebellion (about 100,000), who were ordered to be hanged. Those in the remaining five categories would not be killed, but would lose all rights to their property. The preamble is unambiguous: because the English had lost "so much blood and treasure" by suppressing the rebellion, a "total reducement and settlement" of Ireland was necessary.[31] A statute passed concurrently provided that any English officers who were due back pay would be paid in land, but that such land would be that formerly owned and occupied by the displaced rebels.

In September 1653, the method of separation was formalized. Legislation divided the island into two parts, but in a manner totally dissimilar to the division effected by the later partition, which was North/South. The areas of Clare and Connaught (the Midwest coast of Ireland) was left for Irish gentry and landowners (the Anglo-Irish), and the remainder was to be occupied by British troops and those who had subscribed to the earlier law requiring forfeiture of land by those who had participated in the rebellion.[32] This separation of Connaught from the rest of Ireland was the origin of the phrase "To hell or Connaught," which infers that these people had no choice.[33] The result of enforcement of these and other laws enacted during the 1640's to the 1660's was the increase of Protestant ownership of Irish land from 41% to 78%.[34]

By 1661, the Church of Ireland had become the official state church. Oddly, of the 1,100,000 in Ireland, 800,000 were Catholic. Moreover, of the 300,000 Protestants, only slightly over one-half were Church of Ireland.[35]

Mention should be made of poor Oliver Plunkett, a Jesuit man-of-the-cloth who was destined to become the Catholic Archbishop of Armagh Primate of All Ireland in 1654. Plunkett was arrested for treason. The charge was having plotted to import French soldiers into Ireland and to levy a tax on Catholic clergy to support a 70,000-soldier rebellion against the Crown. Because an acquittal in Ireland was practically assured, he was moved to England for trial. He was convicted, hanged, disemboweled, and quartered in 1681. Plunkett was removed from the gallows while still alive, and beheaded.[36] The message was loud and clear that there were to be no special favors for Catholic clergy by English juries.

"King Billy": The Siege of Derry and the Battle of the Boyne

Meanwhile, Charles II was succeeded by James II as King of England. The year was 1685, and a serious difficulty was James' Catholicism. In February, 1689, Parliament voted in favor of the joint rule of James' daughter Mary and her Protestant husband, William of Orange, a Dutchman and a Protestant, to displace James. Poor James, trumped for the first time by his rambunctious son-in-law, found himself no longer King when he returned to England from Kinsale (South Ireland) on March 12.[37]

Acting "king-like," James nonetheless called a meeting of the Parliament in Dublin in May, 1689. Those present were nearly entirely Catholic, since the majority—Protestants—refused to honor James as King and did not attend the session. This skeleton Parliament "repealed" Poynings' Law and the 1653-54 Acts of Settlement, essentially removing all impediments to Catholics with regard to holding public office and owning land. Moreover, the makeshift Parliament—albeit over the objection of the probably fearful James—adopted another statute which stripped some 2,400 Protestants in Ireland of property ownership.[38]

James proved to be a weak opponent for William. When William landed in Derry, the then-Protestant majority gave him their allegiance. James' army then attacked the city, ensconced inside its ancient city walls. William and the people of Derry were virtually imprisoned inside the walls, but a young group of men and boys later known as the Apprentice Boys were able to close the city gates to prevent James' troops from entering. This famous "Siege of Derry" lasted 105 days until more British troops arrived to save the day for William.[39]

One year later, William—affectionately known by loyal Protestants in Northern Ireland as "King Billy"—trounced his father-in-law once again at the Battle of the Boyne in County Meath (in the North of the now-Republic of Ireland). This July 1, 1690, victory is the event which is celebrated each July 12, and is the source for the many parades throughout Northern Ireland.[40] It is this event which ultimately led to the creation of a Parades Commission in Northern Ireland whose purpose is to contain the violence between parading Protestants and offended Catholics. [See Chapter 2 on parades.]

It is important to note that the majorities in the six counties which are now the province of Northern Ireland were Protestant, having come largely from Presbyterian Scotland just across the Irish Sea. The Catholic minority, then, had played the role of "underdogs" long before partition in 1920.

The Penal Laws

From 1695-1727, a series of harsh statutes were passed to diminish Catholicism in Ireland, the so-called "Penal Laws." For example, a 1704 act (the Tory Act) required all public office-holders to participate in the rite of Holy Communion in the Church of Ireland. Notably, this also affected a group which labeled itself the "Dissenters." Although Protestants, they were Presbyterians, rather than members of the Church of Ireland. This statute also prevented Protestants from selling or devising land to Catholics, who therefore could own land only via of sale or inheritance from another Catholic. The result was a blackmail which actually caused many Catholics to convert in order to avoid the effects of the law.[41]

Another act adopted in 1703 banished all Catholic bishops and clergy and created the "modern Irish problem," one which was to last for more than 100 years. This "problem" was, in the words of historian Paul Johnson, the creation of a "landless Catholic peasantry governed by a legally exclusive Protestant ruling class.... with a predominately Protestant middle class sandwiched in between, and a multi-class Protestant enclave in Ulster."[42]

The Irish became relegated to farming, working in the linen industry, and in brewing (the Irish profession par excellence). My friend Father Peter Ward, priest at Clonard Monastery in Belfast, told me that his father had been a "spirit grocer" in Belfast. Father Peter explained that a "spirit grocery" is a small grocery store licensed to sell off-premise alcoholic beverages. He added that this was one of the few occupations in which a poor Irish Catholic could engage in mid-20th century Belfast.[43]

Other such laws prohibited Catholics from being members of Parliament (MPs), owning any horse valued at more than 5 Irish punt (in today's currency, about $6), holding a military commission, leaving Ireland to be educated (remember that Catholics did not attend Trinity College, established in the 16th century by Elizabeth I and the only university in Ireland), practicing law, or voting in any parliamentary election.[44]

Interestingly, one of the most respected and well-known of Church of Ireland clerics, Jonathan Swift, supported the Ascendancy, the term referring to the resentment among Irish Protestants of their subservience to England. [The American reader is reminded of the late 18th century rebellions by colonists, largely from England, which led to American independence.] Swift was the first Irishman to state in the English language the position promoting an "Irish consciousness of a separate identity, lit by a burning indignation at English injustice."[45] Another Protestant viewed the Ascendancy in a much more negative light. Edmund Burke called this movement an effort of one group (the Anglo-Irish Protestants) which presumed itself to be the only true citizens of Ireland to dominate the other group (Irish Catholics) by reducing them to a state of slavery.[46]

The dreaded Penal Laws gradually were repealed, but most Catholics were by then impoverished and excluded. In the 1790's, Westminster Parliament, led by William Pitt the Younger, adopted legislation permitting Catholics to bear arms and to obtain degrees from Trinity College, hold rank in the British Army, and sit on grand juries.[47] However, Catholics still were not eligible for membership in Parliament or governmental office, nor did they have the right to vote.

Struggles for Irish Independence
1798 and 1803

The first well-orchestrated revolt for independence took place in the late 18th century. Theobold Wolfe Tone, a politician-lawyer born in County Kildare, felt passionately about the issue of independence and non-sectarianism for Ireland. He joined a newly formed group known as the United Irishmen and sought the help of the French in staging an uprising. The United Irishmen plotted a rebellion which was not centralized, but which took place simultaneously, largely in Wexford and Antrim. The legendary Cornwallis, anathema to all Americans, was instrumental in defeating the rebels, whose promised aid from France been well below what they had anticipated. Wolfe Tone was taken to Dublin where he was tried by court martial, convicted, and sentenced to death. His suicide in prison preempted his execution.[48]

The losses were a critical point for Ireland. In 1801, the Westminster Parliament responded by officially abolishing the Irish Parliament and making Ireland

To Matt, my golden boy,
Andy, the child of my heart,
and Jack, who tries to keep me sane and healthy.

(and Scotland) part of the United Kingdom.[49] A small rising initiated by Protestant Anglo-Irishman Robert Emmet in Dublin was soundly defeated by British forces in 1803. Emmet's death sentence for treason was brutal. He (together with twenty-six of his colleagues) was hanged, drawn, and quartered.[50]

Daniel O'Connell and Catholic Emancipation

It was a dashing Kerry-born lawyer and Member of Parliament (despite his being Catholic, he had been elected) who became The Great Emancipator. Daniel O'Connell was able to push the Catholic Relief Bill [51] through Westminster Parliament, with the unlikely aid of the pompous Arthur Wellesley, Duke of Wellington. Wellesley, who had been so ashamed of his birth in Ireland that he had once stated, "Even though one is born in a stable, this does not make him a horse." Nonetheless, the Duke realized as well as anyone in Parliament the looming of another massive revolt if Catholics were not granted some freedom. The law repealed nearly all vestiges of legalized discrimination against Catholics in Ireland, with only ineligibility to the very highest offices of government and state remaining.[52]

Most towns and cities in Ireland now have an O'Connell Street or Avenue, and there are multitudes of statutes to this Irish hero. The widest intra-city avenue in Europe is Dublin's O'Connell Street, the site of the annual St. Patrick's Day parade and an imposing monument to the "Great Emancipator" facing the River Liffey.

The Great Famine

The Great Famine (*An Gorta Mor* in Gaelic) of 1845-49 was devastating for Ireland, particularly for its poor Catholics. Already, Westminster had enacted a law which established workhouses.[53] Such buildings would provide housing and some manual labor for those who were so destitute that they had been forced off their land because of high rents (despite Emancipation, there remained a *de facto* non-ownership of land by Catholics). Others were impoverished because of crop failures or because the yield was too low to make them economically able to sustain themselves.

These workhouses could accommodate as many as 1,000 persons, and by 1844 (before the onset of the famine), ninety-eight workhouses had taken in 86,000. The largest was in the coastal Donegal village of Dunfanaghy, and a visit to that grim prison-like structure is sobering indeed. Families were separated in order to make maximal use of work output and to house persons where there was room available.[54]

Then came the famine, a devastation which exacerbated the already dire economic conditions. Potatoes were the absolute staple of Ireland, and when the fungus which had swept through the potato crops in Europe reached Ireland, the effect was physically and economically catastrophic. By 1846, the wipeout of the entire potato crop on the island was total.[55]

Workhouses were already teeming, and there was virtually nothing to do for the Irish farmers. The English government responded by setting up various work schemes and putting men, women, and children to work. Even Daniel O'Connell could not help his people. His last speech in Britain's House of Commons was in 1847, a plea for assistance for the Irish. Sadly, O'Connell died three months later.[56]

Anglo-Irish landlords were not sympathetic to their tenants' plights. This altered the by-then camaraderie and good will between landlords and their wards into a genuine sense of hatred of the landlords by their Irish tenants. Moreover, the British government exported the only remaining Irish product, wheat, to England. Britain also sent English foods to other countries, but it neglected this island which was a part of its own Commonwealth.[57] The neglect of the Irish by the English during the famine is well documented, and the gruesome effects make for painful reading.

I have often heard the question asked as to why the Irish could not have survived by fishing. It is an island, after all, surrounded by water. The answer has always been that fishing in the sea or the ocean requires sturdy boats equipped to venture miles out. The Irish had neither the boats nor the equipment, strength, or expertise to build them.

The pre-famine population of Ireland was over 8 million, a figure from a census taken in 1841. One estimate of the count at the beginning of the famine was 9 million. The famine and emigration because of the conditions making abject poverty unavoidable decreased that number by nearly one-half.[58] [The current population is around 5.5 million for the entire island.]

One often hears of the Diaspora of the Irish, a term referring to dispersion of a people over a number of countries or regions. Those poor Irish who survived the famine left in great numbers, relocating in America, Canada, Australia, and even England. The devastation had left them a beaten people, unable to subsist in their homeland.

Gladstone, Home Rule, and Parnell

In 1869, William Gladstone (later to become Prime Minister of the United Kingdom) sponsored a bill which led to removing the Church of Ireland as the official state church.[59] This, together with the 1829 Emancipation of the Catholic Church, paved the path to freedom of religion in Ireland, at least *de jure*.

Lessening of domination over Catholics continued. An Irish statesman of considerable note, Charles Stewart Parnell, was one of the founders of the Irish Land League. The goal of this group was to facilitate the acquisition of ownership of land by occupants and, in the meantime, to reduce the rent. Parnell, a Protestant, was arrested several times for his activities with the Land League (which the British Parliament had made illegal). His negotiation with Gladstone for the 1881

Treaty of Kilmainham solved the high rent problem, and he was rewarded with release from jail. Parnell then became an instant hero in Ireland,[60] affectionately known thereafter as the "uncrowned king of Ireland."

Parnell was a Protestant in the political mold of Wolfe Tone, and he also strongly advocated Home Rule for Ireland. A member of the Anglo-Irish aristocracy, he had been elected to Parliament in 1875 and became leader of the Irish Parliamentary Party (IPP). He seemed destined for greatness.

His downfall was an extra-marital affair with Kitty O'Shea. Parnell's choice of paramour was not wise, since she was married to one of his party colleagues. Captain O'Shea, himself a notorious philanderer, filed for divorce in 1889 and named Parnell co-respondent. This scandal essentially terminated Parnell's career.[61] Parnell died in 1891, a likely frustrated man with unfulfilled goals, but still dear in the hearts of the Irish. Some 200,000 people of both faiths stood in a typical Dublin downpour to watch his funeral cortege.[62]

In addition to Gladstone's Home Rule bill, there was a second such effort in 1912. This bill, which was predicted to have passed, was suspended because of World War I.[63] The next significant event in the efforts for Irish independence occured in 1916, one of the true turning points in the Irish struggle to end their bondage under England.

1916: The Easter Rising

Planning for this *crème de la crème* of all Irish fights for independence was nearly two years in the making. Opposition to Home Rule was confined largely to Ulster, and Protestant Sir Edward Carson found the idea particularly abhorrent. For Ulster Protestants, becoming a minority in a Catholic state was unthinkable. A majority in the South advocated Home Rule, as did as many as 40% of the people in Ulster. Carson's fear was that Home Rule would divide his beloved Ireland, and he delivered a speech in Larne, County Antrim, on July 12, 1912, pleading for the people of Ulster to take a strong stance against Home Rule. His prediction of a division into two Irelands proved to be prescient, since this split that he dreaded ultimately occurred.

As Carson spoke, a revolt was already underway. Sir Roger Casement, a former British diplomat, was striking a deal with German forces, hoping to gain their assistance if Ireland remained neutral during the war. Although he was a Protestant born in County Antrim, Casement was a Republican who supported Home Rule for Ireland.

The logic underlying the timing was simple. England's priority had to be fighting the Germans, and the war effort would clearly take precedence over any struggle to keep Ireland. One often hears from an Irishman talking about the Rising that England's difficulty was Ireland's opportunity. Obviously, however, the English military was able to take care of both.

Germany promised to send munitions to assist the Irish, but the soldiers and sailors delivering arms failed to reach their destination. The English Royal Navy had intercepted them on the Saturday before the Rising, the German soldiers were captured, and their arms, confiscated. Casement was tried for treason in London, convicted, and hanged on August 3, 1916, three and one-half months after the Rising.

The scheduled date for the reading of the proclamation establishing a provisional government for Ireland was April 24, Easter Monday, a bank holiday in Ireland. Lawyer turned scholar Patrick H. Pearse was the orator, and the site was the steps in front of the General Post Office (GPO). This one-page declaration of independence for Ireland was signed by seven of the organizers: Pearse, Thomas J. Clarke, Sean MacDiarmada, James Connolly, Thomas MacDonagh, Eamonn Ceannt, and Joseph Plunkett. About 2,500 copies were printed and distributed not only in Dublin, but throughout Ireland. Laminated copies are still available for purchase in most gift shops in Ireland. The huge Ionic building on O'Connell Street, the GPO became the headquarters, fortified and taken over by the rebels. The rebellion had officially begun.

British troops already stationed in Ireland numbered about 2,500, and more arrived from England later in the week. Checkpoints were established throughout the city by the Irish fighters, and one goal of the Irish Citizens Army was to take Dublin Castle. This was not to be.

The GPO was gutted by British shelling, and Dublin Castle remained under British control. The over-soldiered, over-armed Irish rebels had been beaten. On Saturday, April 29, at 3:45 pm, Pearse surrendered in the name of the Irish Volunteers, the Citizens Army. Approximately 500 had been killed during the five days of fighting, and about 3,000 Irishmen were sent by ship to England to be tried without being charged. Joe Plunkett had been killed, and Connolly, gravely wounded.

It is the proverbial "rest-of-the-story" which makes this effort so poignant in Irish history. Several of the rebels were immediately court martialed. Except for a few who were permitted to call a witness, the only evidence in the "trials" was a single witness for the prosecution against each, who testified that he or she had seen the accused fire a weapon during the Rising. There was no chance to cross-examine, no defense counsel, and no chance to rebut. Indeed, the prisoners pleaded guilty only to the charge of causing disaffection among the population of Ireland against British rule. Convictions were summarily determined, and there was no avenue of appeal.

All were imprisoned at Kilmainham Jail except for Connolly, whose injuries required hospitalization after his summary trial. By order of British General Maxwell, fifteen of the leaders were executed (Roger Casement's execution in England was the sixteenth), each shortly following the judgment of the court. It was necessary to strap the ailing Connolly to a chair, supported by pillows, in order for him to be shot.[64]

Writer Peter de Rosa concluded his excellent book on the Easter Rising with the following words: "That final bullet exploding in Connolly's brain broke the last of Ireland's chains." [65] de Rosa's statement alluded to the real legacy of the Rising, that it did not quell the Irish determination for independence. Indeed, it actually inspired those who might have been theretofore complacent.

[Author's note: The killings of those convicted took place in the yard at Kilmainham Jail. Although it requires a bus trip from downtown Dublin, a visit to Kilmainham is most informative regarding the Easter Rising. At any rate, the GPO is directly on O'Connell Street, just North of the Liffey. The plaques and monuments to the martyrs summarize the events.]

The eastern rail station in Dublin, Connolly Station, is named for one of the martyrs for Irish freedom. (Interestingly, Connolly was a Marxist.) The western station in the city is Heuston, named for Sean Heuston, unit commander of the Irish Volunteers. A DART (Dublin Area Rapid Transit) station South of the Liffey in the middle of the city is Pearse Station.]

1920 Partition and Civil War

The end of World War I in November 1918 was followed by the forming of the *Dáil Éireann* (Parliament of Ireland), as Ireland's MPs elected to Westminster refused to take their seats.[66] Britain's problem of what to do with Ireland re-emerged. The two Irish communities—those for independence and those wanting to retain political affiliation with the United Kingdom—only grew wider apart. Sir Winston Churchill, then British War Secretary, said, "We saw the flames of orange and green flash out from the Irish furnace." [67]

The Westminster Parliament drafted a third Home Rule Bill, proposing two Irish Parliaments: one in the North comprised of fifty-two members (MPs, or Members of Parliament), and one in the South, with 128. The representation in Westminster Parliament would be twenty for each of the two parts and forty-two all-Ireland MPs. The two legislatures would be self-ruling, except that Westminster would keep control of peace and war, foreign affairs, customs and excise, land and agricultural policy and law and order. [Note: For the American accustomed to the Tenth Amendment's reservation clause granting abundant areas of power to the states, this transfer of power to the two Parliaments seems relatively meager.]

On March 4, 1920, the Ulster Unionist Council reluctantly accepted the proposal, but the Irish *Dáil* (in particular, *Sinn Féin* party), overwhelmingly rejected it. One month later, *Sinn Féin* virtually commenced guerilla warfare and raided tax offices throughout Ireland.[68]

More British troops were sent to Ireland. Meanwhile, Michael Collins had been given the title of Director of Organizations for the Volunteers, the *Sinn Féin* body pledged to attain independence for Ireland. This group was officially named

17

the Irish Republican Army, the beginning of the IRA paramilitary group which was later to gain notoriety in Northern Ireland. Collins had been an aide to Joseph Plunkett and had himself been interned for his participation in the Easter Rising.

Ulster Unionists and surviving Home Rulers would not take part in the new *Dáil*, so it was an exclusive *Sinn Féin* institution. At its first meeting on January 21, 1919, the session was conducted in the Irish language, and a provisional constitution was adopted. This *Dáil* ratified the republic proclaimed in 1916, and the situation was back to square one.[69]

Aid for the Volunteers came from the United States, and the British government was expending an inordinate amount on suppression, an effort which was not completely effective. The result was the passage by Westminster Parliament of the statute which effectively partitioned Ireland,[70] dividing it into the two parts which exist today. Undaunted, the Volunteers initiated the Civil War.

The signing of the Treaty of 1921, adopted by a split *Dáil* on January 22, 1922,[71] was a mutually acceptable settlement between the British government and the Irish legislature. The provisional government's constitution went into effect, and the name of the portion of the island to be represented by the *Dáil* became the *Saorstát Éireann* (Free State of Ireland). A Boundary Commission was established to determine the exact line between the two Irelands. However, the hardline *Sinn Féiners* voted against the treaty, holding out for a fully independent Ireland.

What did Home Rule mean? The Free State would have dominion status, rather than complete independence, a fact unacceptable to those opposed to the treaty. Although the *Dáil* was its official legislature, Ireland remained within the Commonwealth. The Civil War waged by the anti-treaty group actually lasted less than a year, but it had engendered a bitterness which was to last for years.

Michael Collins had been the primary negotiator during deliberations for the treaty, and those who were disappointed with "half a loaf" were angry. Collins' genuine belief was that dominion status was the best Ireland could achieve at this point, and he felt he had attained victory. His opponents did not agree, and Collins was ambushed and killed in a convoy while on an official journey. The site was *Béal nam Bláth* in his home county of Cork, and the killers were anti-Treaty forces that had once been aligned with Collins. Ironically, this soldier-politician who had fought so passionately for the Ireland he loved so much lost his life at the young age of 31, precisely because of what he had achieved for his country.[72]

The Free State attained full independence in 1949,[73] and its Constitution already adopted in 1937 became its official basic document. The province of Northern Ireland never achieved the Free State status of its neighboring counties to the South (and Donegal in the Northeast, which remained a part of *Saorstát Éireann* when the Boundary Commission established the dividing line). It remains a part of the United Kingdom, and the true Irish Catholics who reside within its borders still nurse the hatred which began when Henry II first declared England's sovereignty over Ireland in 1171, a hatred which is understandable, even if not condoned or supported.

Partition to the Present

The political events of post-partition Northern Ireland are recounted in Chapters 4 and 5, so they are not a part of this chapter on history. It is important, however, to relate some of the strife, which has arisen out of allegations against occupying British military and the Royal Ulster Constabulary, designated the Police Service of Northern Ireland since November, 2001, in compliance with the Good Friday Agreement. The desire to be a part of the Ireland with which they affiliate themselves is a zeal for Irish Catholics/Nationalists. This zeal becomes an obsession when they feel suppressed—indeed *oppressed*—and subjected to discriminatory treatment by those who are charged with maintaining their very security.

Any chapter the purpose of which is to explain with some logic the existing antagonism between Northern Ireland's Catholics and anything British must include some elaboration on examples of the more publicized such charges. Every man, woman and child in Northern Ireland is familiar with "Bloody Sunday," and most recall the incidents leading to the Lee Clegg trial for murder.

The Use of "Excessive Force" Issue

Which situations call for the use of force by security personnel, and what is to be deemed "excessive" force are legal issues. Charges in Northern Ireland that excessive force was unwarranted generally are founded upon allegations of discriminatory use of force against Catholics. The parallel in the United States—*i.e.*, charges of police discrimination against blacks—makes an instructive comparison.

This has been a volatile issue in both the U.S.A.[74] and Northern Ireland. Professors Anthony Jennings of Oxford University,[75] Sean Doran, of Queen's University School of Law[76] and John Stannard,[77] also of Queen's School of Law, have written extensively on the development of the law in Northern Ireland on this issue.

THE VIEW OF AMERICAN COURTS

In the United States, whether or not force used by police was excessive traditionally was governed by 14th Amendment Due Process standards. For example, in *Johnson v. Glick*,[78] the Second Circuit Court of Appeals used four factors to determine whether a victim's constitutional due process rights had been violated: (i) was there a need for any use of force at all, (ii) if so, was there any relationship between the need for force and the amount of force used, (iii) what was the extent of the resulting injuries, and (iv) was the force applied in good faith, or was it used maliciously and sadistically to cause harm?

In 1989, the United States Supreme Court modified the rule in *Graham v. Connor*[79] to gauge the lawfulness of excessive force by Fourth Amendment search-and-seizure standards. The measure became whether one had been "reasonable officer" under the circumstances. The relevant factors under the revised rule are (i) the severity of the crime in question, (ii) the immediacy of the threat the suspect presented, (iii) any active resistance to arrest by the suspect, and (iv) any attempt to flee. There was a possible significant distinction from the two major incidents in Northern Ireland which will be discussed: the officer in *Graham* had used *non-deadly* force, so the question there arose as to whether any use of force at all was appropriate.

Most Americans above the age of 25 will recall the Rodney King incident in March of 1991. King was a black man who had led police on a high-speed chase on the infamous Los Angeles freeway. When four white policemen were eventually able to stop him, they handcuffed King and pushed him to his knees, then completely onto the ground, and beat him severely with night sticks. The word "allegedly" is intentionally not used, since the prosecution was bolstered with some unique evidence. The entire occurrence was captured on a video recorder by an amateur hack who apparently whiled away his evening hours by filming highway incidents. The film was broadcast on network television, and public indignation was aroused. A ten-member commission established to study rampant charges of racism within the ranks of the Los Angeles Police Department concluded that racist and violent behavior of L.A. policemen had long been a serious problem. The commission recommended that thirteen-year Chief of Police Darryl Gates resign immediately.[80]

All officers pleaded not guilty to common law assault and battery charges in a California state trial court. Their defense was that their actions were reasonable and justified because (i) the chase had taken place on a crowded freeway, (ii) King had actively resisted arrest, and (iii) the officers had reasonably suspected King of being under the influence of illegal drugs. This defense paled when contrasted with the evidence on the film viewed by the jury. King had been mercilessly beaten by an angry "gang of four." Incredibly, in April of 1992, the all-white jury acquitted all four. Civil rights riots ensued, not only in Los Angeles, but in other major large cities, such as Atlanta, Las Vegas, and San Francisco.

Retaliation was inevitable, reminiscent of the "pay-back" mentality so evident among paramilitary groups in Northern Ireland. In a predominately black section of Los Angeles, militant blacks pulled Reginald Denny, a white truck driver, from his driver's seat and clubbed him in full view of television camera crews. He sustained serious head injuries. His "whiteness" was the provocation.

President George Bush then directed the Justice Department to determine whether federal charges of civil rights violations might be filed against the officers who had beaten King.[81] [For the non-lawyer reader, this is not a violation of the Fifth Amendment's prohibition of double jeopardy, *i.e.*, precluding one from being "twice tried for the same crime." In this case, the same act constituted viable charges both under California state common law and federal statutory law.] Two of the same men who had been acquitted in the California state court were found guilty by the federal jury and sentenced to thirty months in federal prison. The remaining two were acquitted. The length of the sentences seemed a mere slap-on-the-wrist, but the convictions were a retribution of sorts.[82]

King himself had the last hurrah. He sued the City of Los Angeles and the four policemen in a deprival-of-rights civil action in federal court[83] and on April 19, 1994, he was awarded a verdict of $3.4 million. Interestingly, no punitive damages were awarded.

Another such incident occurred in the early morning hours of October 1, 1998. Christopher DiPasquale, a white Philadelphia policeman, fatally shot Donta Dawson, a nineteen-year-old black man. The victim had stopped his still-running car in the middle of a North Philadelphia street, under an overpass. Several officers arrived at the scene to investigate. After a twenty-two-minute standoff, DiPasquale shot Dawson when the young man tried to jerk another approaching officer into his car. Dawson had been sitting on one hand, and the officer had yelled to his colleague DiPasquale that the suspect had a gun. The racism charges stemmed from the evidence that DiPasquale did not shoot Dawson until *after* he had raised both hands. There was no evidence that Dawson had in fact been armed.[84]

An internal investigation determined that the officer had not had reason to shoot Dawson, and DiPasquale was consequently terminated. Dawson's surviving family sued the officer and the City of Philadelphia, and the claim was settled in July, 1999, for $700,000. The proverbial fat lady has not sung for this case, however. Some black elected officials in Philadelphia responded to the dismissal of manslaughter charges by a (white) judge filed a private criminal complaint under an old statute permitting "private justice," charging DiPasquale with murder. This time, the judge is black.[85]

As a quagmire of allegations of racism, the DiPasquale case is one to watch. The president of the Philadelphia Lodge of the Fraternal Order of Police sees a "strong dose of racism" in this act by a group of legislators "with utter contempt for the justice system...."[86]

Another such incident occurred in Cincinnati. Black leaders were enraged when a grand jury returned charges of mere misdemeanors rather than felonies against a white police officer who had fatally shot an unarmed black man. The May 7, 2001 indictment resulted in both riots and peaceful protests in this Southern Ohio city.

The police officer was twenty-seven-year-old Stephen Roach. He had shot and killed nineteen-year-old Timothy Thomas as he fled down an alley. Roach

21

contended that he thought that Thomas, who was being sought for fourteen outstanding warrants, was reaching for a gun. Evidence revealed that Thomas was wearing oversized pants and ran with his hands at his waist, which might explain the grand jurors' belief that the defendant policeman had acted in self-defense.

Compounding the supposed racist element was the fact that fifteen blacks had been killed by Cincinnati policemen since 1995, and no whites had suffered this same fate during that time. Kweisi Mfume, president of the National Association for the Advancement of Colored people (NAACP), described Cincinnati (with a 43% black population) as "ground zero for race relations" in the country.[87]

Substitute the word "religion" for "race" in these cases, and one might well be in Northern Ireland.

From the other side, some police officers themselves are subject to across-the board disdain, even at times by elected officials. At least one such American has advocated the ultimate punishment for police officers "when they cross the line." Tom Alciere, elected to the New Hampshire state House in November, 2000, went so far as to declare on his Internet Webpage that "[n]obody will ever be safe until the last cop is dead." Alciere was elected as a Republican, having run unsuccessfully twice as a Libertarian and once as a Democrat. The state GOP chairman has called upon him to make a public renunciation of his extremist anti-police views or to resign his legislative post. Alciere has said that he will do neither, contending that he "loves it when someone kills a police officer."[88] If Alciere's opinion were to become a popular one, it would be reasonable to expect that whatever has been deemed by the judiciary as "excessive force" will be judged by a more lenient standard by the courts.

"Excessive Force" in Northern Ireland

The DiPasquale facts appear inapposite to the theory which is advocated by many among the criminal bar in Northern Ireland: *i.e.,* to allow for a manslaughter verdict when murder is not deemed applicable. The DiPasquale protagonists pursue the reverse: to charge murder when even manslaughter has not been proven.

This is a type of "unhappy medium" when an officer who has killed in the line of duty is not technically guilty of murder because of his defense of self-defense, but the sense is that there should be some redress for his having resorted to killing a suspect. The manslaughter alternative allows for a conviction, albeit one based on fictitious grounds. This is the law in the Republic of Ireland,[89] but Northern Ireland's courts have not accepted it.[90]

The common law rule regarding whether use of force can be justified as self-defense was stated in the leading case of *Palmer v. Regina.*[91] When one is faced with an unjustified attack and must defend himself, others, or his property, force is permissible, according to what is "reasonable" under the circumstances. This rule was adopted in a 1967 Westminster statute applicable to Northern Ireland with wording which seems uniquely suited to the province's difficulties. This law permits a "person" to use "such force as is reasonable under the circumstances in the prevention of crime or in effecting or assisting in the lawful arrest of offenders or suspected offenders or of persons unlawfully at large." [92]

Professor Sean Doran of Queen's University School of Law has pointed to three sources of law in determining the propriety of the use of force, and the extent of such force: (i) the common law self-defense doctrine, as stated in *Palmer*; (ii) section three of the 1967 Criminal Law; and (iii) the so-called "Yellow Card" drafted and used by British Army forces in Northern Ireland. [93]

The Yellow Card directions are to avoid the use of force if possible, and to use only "minimum" force when necessary; to warn before firing; and to use force only against a person about to use a firearm, throw a bomb or attack property, if the circumstances indicated that this was likely to endanger life. Force is also permitted under the Yellow Card's regulations against someone who has killed or seriously injured a member of the security forces or someone whom the army or police officer's duty it is to protect. No warning would be necessary if the officer is facing direct gunfire or an impending bomb attack. In 1980, an addition to the Yellow Card required security officers to take a pledge committing them to use firearms only as a last resort. [94]

Professor Anthony Jennings has noted that between 1969 and 1985, 270 persons were killed by security forces in Northern Ireland, 155 not being affiliated with a paramilitary group, police or other security services, including prison personnel. Of the twenty-one of these security force members who had killed while on duty and who were prosecuted, only two had been found guilty (either of murder or manslaughter). Professor Jennings has interpreted these figures as evidence that to a "large degree," security forces have been granted by the courts the unilateral authority to determine whether those suspected of unlawful paramilitary activity are guilty or not, without permitting these victims (or their survivors) access to the courts. [95]

As a signatory nation, the entire United Kingdom is also bound to comply with the standard set by the European Convention on Human Rights. Article 2 of this document states that

(1) Everyone's right to life shall be protected by law. No one shall be deprived of life intentionally save in the execution of a sentence of a court following his conviction of a crime for which this penalty is provided by law; [Author's note: This is moot, since the U.K. abolished capital punishment in 1969].

(2) Deprivation of life shall not be regarded as inflicted in contravention of this Article when it results from the use of force which is no more than absolutely necessary (a) in defence of any person from unlawful violence;

(b) in order to effect a lawful arrest or to prevent the escape of a person lawfully detained; or (c) in action lawfully taken for the purpose of quelling a riot or insurrection.[96]

Notably, a civil complaint filed in 1971 against the U.K. government by a widow in Newry (County Down, near the border with the Republic of Ireland) was settled in a substantial amount.[97] The terms of the settlement included an assurance by the U.K. that Article 2 would be respected. The plaintiff's husband had been fatally shot by British soldiers, and the settlement inferred that the government would thereafter act in good faith, even if domestic legislation fell short of the European Convention standard.

The applicable law in Northern Ireland, then, is that any lethal force must be used only if "absolutely necessary." This differs significantly from the more lenient "reasonable police officer" standard approved by the U.S. Supreme Court in *Graham v. Connor.*[98]

"Bloody Sunday"

January 30, 1972, was actually the second date in Irish history labeled "Bloody Sunday," and, ironically, both involved fourteen killings. The first was November 21, 1920, a reversal of sorts from the 1972 incident. The post-partition law massacre was an orchestrated series of retaliatory murders *of* security officers, rather than killing of civilians *by* them. Seven officers and three former officers of the Black and Tans (an auxiliary unit of the Royal Irish Constabulary [the RIC, precursor of the Royal Ulster Constabulary, now the Police Service of Northern Ireland] whose khaki uniforms and black belts gave them this nickname), two RIC officers, and two civilians were murdered by the IRA. All occurred in the early morning hours while the victims were at home and still asleep. Most were witnessed by their horrified spouses.[99]

The second Bloody Sunday virtually put Northern Ireland on the world map, so to speak. It was probably the single most publicized instance from the difficulties in the province aired and viewed on the international scene to date.

The Northern Ireland Civil Rights Association had been formed in 1967 for the purpose of eliminating what was deemed the official governmental stance of ignoring Catholics' civil rights. [The inspiration came from the black civil rights movement in 1960's America.[100]] This group planned a peaceful march in Londonderry/Derry to protest internment of Republicans without trial. [Note the alternate names for this city and county. The official name is the British one – Londonderry. However, the more generally used name is Derry, its title prior to King Billy's victory in 1689 at the Siege of Derry. This is because Catholics command a strong majority in Derry today.]

Significantly, such a parade had been prohibited by a statute recently enacted by the Northern Ireland Parliament shortly before the march.[101] This is another reminder of the contrast between laws applicable to the scene in Northern Ireland and those in First-Amendment-America, where such a peaceful protest would be constitutionally protected. In spite of the fact that it was illegal, from all reports the march in Derry began peaceably.

Because their duty was to assume compliance with the law, British Army troops had been instructed by superiors to make as many arrests as possible and to attempt to block the march. The route for the march would be from the Creggan Estate area, a Catholic housing project in Southwest Derry, and through the adjacent Bogside—a Catholic section which even today is striking for its poverty—to Guildhall Square in Northeast Derry, just outside the city walls. The compact town center lies inside the walls.

The large crowd (estimates have ranged from 5,000 in the first inquiry[102] to 10,000 by the BBC [103]) was confronted with several stone barriers erected by British Army troops, in accordance with their orders. Marchers made the collective decision to go around the barricades and to avoid a confrontation with any of the officers. It has not been disputed that there were several mavericks among marchers who threw stones at and yelled profanities to the soldiers. However, there was no evidence produced that any of the victims was armed.

The Army opened fire when marchers reached the Bogside, allegedly in self-defense. Thirteen Catholic men were killed (a fourteenth died shortly thereafter from his wounds), and thirteen were wounded. The list of the dead is heartbreaking, for most were twenty years of age and under. Only five were over the age of twenty, and the oldest was forty-one. The fatalities included John Frances Duddy (17); Patrick Joseph Doherty (31); Hugh Pius Gilmore (17); Bernard Guigan (41); John Pius Young (17); Michael McDaid (20); William Noel Nash (19); Michael Kelly (17); Kevin McElhinney (17); James Joseph Wray (22); Gerald McKinney (35); Gerald Donaghy (17); and William McKinney (26).

The Widgery Tribunal

To the credit of Westminster Parliament, an investigatory tribunal was established immediately in accordance with statutory law.[104] However, to the discredit of the tribunal was the haste and, most concluded, perfunctory nature of the inquiry. Headed by Chief Justice Lord Widgery, the body known as the Widgery Tribunal began its task on February 21, 1972, after only six weeks. After seventeen sessions during which the three members of the tribunal heard evidence from 114 witnesses, this work was concluded on March 14, and the tribunal's report was filed on April 10, 1972. [Ironically, the date coincided with the day of the signing of the Good Friday Agreement twenty-six years later.]

The Widgery Tribunal unequivocally absolved the British Army of any wrongdoing, concluding that culpability lay with the marchers. The report concluded that the soldiers had acted defensively in response to shots from marchers. The tribunal had even conceded the fact that none of those killed or injured carried weapons, but nonetheless held that the Army's suspicion of their complicity and the support of some marchers who were armed exculpated the British soldiers. Moreover, the Tribunal reminded that the officers were acting in accordance with their orders and with the legendary Yellow Card.[105]

The Widgery Tribunal report is regarded by many as having become the greatest single cleft between Nationalists and Unionists. Moreover, it hardened the resolve of Nationalists to disparage all British governmental efforts to appear neutral when the actions of its own soldiers are subject to question. None of those injured, nor any eyewitnesses other than persons from the media and priests, were called to testify from among the 500 potential witnesses. Testimony came primarily from British soldiers, and, importantly, counsel for the survivors inexplicably were not given access to the statements made by soldiers to Military Police immediately following the shootings. These statements conflicted significantly from their testimony before the Tribunal, which had also read the first statements.[106]

Notably, Bloody Sunday was the impetus for the resumption of Britain's direct control over Northern Ireland and the dissolution of its Parliament on March 25, 1972.

Was Widgery fair? Even Unionists generally concede that indeed it was not. There was conclusive forensic evidence that those killed not only were unarmed, but they were shot in the backs while fleeing from the British officers, evidence which the Widgery Tribunal ignored. The 36-page report seemed hastily drafted, lending the appearance of a conclusion reached prior to the taking of evidence. Moreover, the three and one-half weeks devoted to this hearing were woefully inadequate.

An American law student, Kara Irwin, has taken the position that had Bloody Sunday occurred twenty-five years later, the survivors of victims and those who were injured would have redress against the British officers who fired the shots. The forum would be the European Court of Human Rights.[107] She cites *McCann and Others v. U.K.*[108] as controlling. *McCann* also concerned British soldiers, Special Air Services (SAS) officers who shot and killed three unarmed IRA members on March 6, 1988, whom they thought were going to detonate a bomb on the peninsula of Gibraltar.

The European Commission on Human Rights held that the soldiers' use of violence was necessary under the circumstances, but the European Court on Human Rights reversed. The linchpin in *McCann* was Article 2 of the European Convention on Human Rights,[109] the provision which grants an exception to the general rule that no one should be deprived of life. No violation occurs when death is the result of the use of force which is "no more than absolutely necessary" and is either in defense of any person from unlawful violence; [or] in order to affect a lawful arrest or to prevent the escape of a person lawfully detained; [or] in action lawfully taken for the purpose of quelling a riot or insurrection."[110] The Court held that the killings in *McCann* did not fall within any of these exceptions, and the soldiers were thus liable to survivors in damages.

Ms. Irwin writes that Article 2 has been interpreted by the European Court on Human Rights to create more than a "negative individual right," also imposing upon member nations (among which is the U.K.) certain positive duties to assure compliance with the general rule of protecting the right to life.[111] Reportedly, the *McCann* decision so angered the British government that Westminster Parliament considered withdrawing from the jurisdiction of the European Court on Human Rights.[112]

The Saville Tribunal

Prime Minister Tony Blair was not insensitive to continued charges that Widgery had been a mockery. Eamonn McKee of the Irish government's Press Office was among those who drafted a formal rebuttal to Widgery, arguing that it was flawed on its face. McKee approached his chore by attacking the Widgery Report paragraph by paragraph and to pose some viable alternatives, primarily to establish a second tribunal.

Blair's response was his January 2, 1998 (just a little more than three months before the signing of the Good Friday Agreement), appointment of such a tribunal. Named as chair was Lord Saville of Newdigate, a Law Lord. The other two members were from outside the United Kingdom, Sir Edward Somers (former Judge of the Court of Appeal of New Zealand) and William Hoyt, Chief Justice of the highest court in the Province of New Brunswick, Canada. [Sommers resigned in summer, 2000, and was replaced by former Chief Justice of the High Court of Australia, John L. Toohey.] The Prime Minister's charge to the new tribunal was to determine the facts by considering "new evidence," even though the passage of time would be problematic.[113]

The Saville Inquiry began its work on March 27, 2000, and has continued to meet in morning and afternoon sessions. Blair did not set a date for the filing of its report, but projections have been that it will last for three years (*i.e.*, until the end of 2003).[114] This is a vivid contrast to the three and one-half week existence of Widgery. Moreover, Saville is reviewing 122 volumes of information, including 12 volumes of photographs; 30 audiotapes; and 59 videotapes. As of early November 2001, the Tribunal had already taken testimony from 1,500 witnesses.[115]

Tellingly, these and additional persons who will be called to testify include eyewitnesses and survivors who were injured. This overwhelms the mere 114 persons interviewed by the Widgery Tribunal, when 500 had been willing to testify. Compared with its predecessor, the Saville Inquiry is thorough indeed. The opening statement alone was an approximate 1.25 millions words,[116] and the cost to the British government has been estimated at 33.8 million pound sterling (approximately $50 million).[117]

Whether the Saville Tribunal will be able to determine what actually happened on Bloody Sunday, its very existence represents an olive branch from the British government to Nationalists, one which has likely accomplished much in the way of allaying thoughts among Northern Ireland's Catholics that the United Kingdom is their enemy.

There has been some criticism that the Blair government has, by establishing the Saville Tribunal, lent an aura of its giving more significance to the loss of fourteen civilian lives because of the actions of British Army officers that day than to the remaining 3,000 persons killed in the Troubles. Professor Paul Bew is one of the two historical advisors to the Saville Tribunal. He has pointed to statistics which have fueled such opposition to Saville: Republican terrorists have caused 58.8% of these 3,000 violent deaths; Loyalists terrorists, 28.9%; the British Army, only 6.6%; and the RUC, 1.4%.[118]

According to Professor Bew, one message is that the government sets a higher standard for the "forces of a liberal, Democratic state than the standard terrorists set for themselves." His fear is that the combination of the failure to respond with "moral seriousness to the scale of the tragedy" for Northern Ireland's "ordinary people," and the "all too obvious sensitivity to paramilitary demands" could well undermine the people's support for the GFA. He terms this "selective amnesia" on the part of the British government.[119] The Prime Minister must feel caught between the proverbial "rock and hard place" on this issue.

Some Personal Recollections on Derry
and the Site of Bloody Sunday

I chanced upon an unexpected tour of the walls of Derry and the Bloody Sunday site while in town for one night and one full day. One interview was scheduled, and the charming owners of the bed-and-breakfast where I stayed, Joan and Dr. Peter Pyne, suggested that I check with the Irish language teaching institute next door for a meeting with one of Derry's *Sinn Féin* MLAs (Members of the Legislative Assembly).

The owner-manager of the language center was Gerry O'Hara. I could not help but think of Scarlett O'Hara's father in *Gone With the Wind*, but this Gerald O'Hara was a much younger version. He called Mitchel McLaughlin, who immediately agreed to sandwich me in after my scheduled meeting at University of Ulster. The ease with which these Northern Irelanders could facilitate such meetings and their genuine delight to meet with an American who was interested in their problems was a source of continued amazement to me.

The entire staff were charmers indeed. We decided that we must be all interrelated, since all seemed to have the surname "Doherty" (my maiden name, and a common one in Counties Derry and Donegal) or "Murphy" (my mother's maiden name, the most common surname in the entire island of Ireland). The difference, however, was that their spellings were the Irish Gaelic ones—"O'Dochartaigh" and "O'Murchada." One of them was Caoimhghín O'Murchada, who almost insisted that he show me the *real* Derry and the Bloody Sunday site, after I had told him that I had walked around the walls on a prior visit. "But you didn't know what you were seeing," he remarked. So, after my meeting with McLaughlin, Caoimhghín and I met to begin our jaunt. [His first name is pronounced somewhat, but not precisely, as "Kee-vuhn," but he kindly indulged my inability to master the mysteries of the Irish Gaelic language and permitted me to call him "Kevin."]

I asked the reason for his English accent. Caoimhghín explained that, although he was (clearly) Irish, he grew up in England. An avowed Republican and a dedicated Nationalist, he did not reside in Derry at the time of Bloody Sunday. This was amazing, since the event seemed so personal to him. My own explanation is that Derry is a small city in which everybody seems to know each other. Thus,there likely are few—Protestant or Catholic, Unionist or Nationalist—who did not know someone who had been personally pained by this tragedy. A sort of empathetic and unified pain is probably as natural for those in Derry as is breathing.

We walked around part of the wall past the mural of Raymond McCartney, the young imprisoned IRA member who had survived a hunger strike in 1980 in protest of prison conditions. [Note that it was one year later that a much publicized hunger strike involving ten prisoners took place in the invidious Maze Prison outside Belfast. One striker, Bobby Sands, died, and his mural is one of the largest and most visible in West Belfast.] Once we were near Glenfada Park in the Bogside, I began to appreciate the fact that I was with a virtual walking and talking history book. Caoimhghín pointed to two bullet holes in the exterior wall of a large ugly building, and he took me to the memorial erected to memorialize the fourteen who had died on Bloody Sunday. As a mother of two boys, the line-up of names, alongside their young ages, lingers with me still.

Earlier that afternoon, between my meeting with Mitchel McLaughlin and before Caoimhghín and I began our personalized tour, I had met three young Catholic boys in a park just across from St. Eugene's Catholic Cathedral, about one-half block from the bed-and-breakfast and the Irish language center. [These are the three young men who appear with me in the photograph at the end of this book.] My "mother instinct" takes over when I'm with boys, since I usually see in them my own two at the same ages.

Conor, Gavin, and Jason, they were, and we struck up a real friendship. Gavin said, with eyes as big as saucers, "Gawsh – yer the first real American I've ever talked to." They bombarded me with questions: "Is ever'body thar rich? Are yuz rich? Do yuz know Bill Clinton?" Rather than making me feel like a creature from outer space, these cute kids made me feel special. I have kept up with them sporadically, and I sent each a copy of the photograph and some "real American" dollars. They have a standing invitation to visit us, and I hope someday that they do. While in the Bogside with Caoimhghín, it occurred to me that, had they lived twenty-five years earlier, they might have been among these young men shot in 1972.

Back to our walk, Caoimhghín pointed to a British Army post. He explained that "they're watching us" through a telescopic lens. My reaction was, "Goodness, should we really be here?" He laughed and assured me that I would not likely be shot dead in Derry that day. [I envisioned a by-line in my hometown newspaper reading "Reckless American loses life on the site of Northern Ireland's Bloody Sunday," and my husband's having to explain to friends who had been concerned about my going to that "awful place" the circumstances of my untimely demise. Prior to my going to Belfast for several months in 1998, he was asked if he were not worried about me. The American perception seems to be that everybody in Northern Ireland walks around wearing a flak jacket, with a gun—and perhaps a hand grenade or two—in his or her pocket.]

Caoimhghín spoke in graphic detail about where each of the victims had been shot and how each had been attacked while unarmed and trying in vain to flee from the British soldiers. A captivating speaker, he almost seemed to have known each of them personally. I realized that his telling this story to an interested "foreigner" was a catharsis for him, and he had indeed found a mesmerized listener. A historian, he peppered his remarks with facts such as the origin of the well-known hymn "There is a Green Hill Far Away." The author of those lyrics—followed by "without a city wall…where the dear Lord was crucified"—was Cecil Frances Alexander, the wife of a Church of Ireland bishop, and she had penned these words about Derry. Caoimhghín explained that the "green hill" referred to the fields beyond the Bogside, and that Mrs. Alexander quite likely wrote of the wall as the separation it had become. I understood his nuance to be that the "crucifixion" in the hymn's lyrics might now be a simile for those buried on that hill, killed senselessly on Bloody Sunday.

He pointed on my city map to the location of the Catholic Church and graveyard in the Creggan area where the fourteen funerals and burials had taken place. "My" three boys—Conor, Gavin, and Jason—lived in the Creggan and, most likely, this was their church. "We're like child abusers – we become abusers ourselves," mused Caoimhghín. Apparently, he was referring to the retaliations from the Republican community born in the tragedy that was Bloody Sunday.

Lest I should think that impoverishment and second-class living standards are reserved for Catholics in Derry, Caoimhghín then took me to The Fountain, a cramped and despondent-looking Protestant residential enclave that veritably clings to the city walls. The Fountain is separated from the Bogside only by a concrete and fenced wall, apparently erected to "keep the peace" between the two and to deter them from mingling. [Author's note: "Mingling" in this context means "fighting."] The only splash of color amidst the gloom was a gloriously bright mural to "King Billy," the "saviour" of Protestants in 1689 Derry.

Journalist Susan McKay has written a wonderfully perceptive and compelling book about religion in Northern Ireland, *Northern Protestants.* In her opinion, the disturbing division in Derry is likely being perpetuated through its children. She quotes some school-age residents of The Fountain as saying to her, "We don't speak to Catholics. Certainly not. Would you speak to people that has broke twenty-eight windows, broke into your cars, stolen them?.... We do fight wi' them. But there's not enough of us to go after them. There's a whole swarm of them. They call us Orange bastards...." They explained to Ms. McKay that a favorite activity against the youngsters in the neighboring Bogside is 'brickin,' throwing bottles and paint bombs. "My brother is eight and he throws bricks," the latter having been a remark of great sibling pride.[120] Again, I wondered if "my" Conor, Gavin, and Jason could be engaged in similar manifestations of hatred. Caoimhghín is a Catholic and a devoted Nationalist, but his eyes were sad when he commented upon the cycle of poverty that is the fate of the children we watched playing in the streets of this depressingly downtrodden area. Hope breeds hope, but there was no hope here to breed.

There is an irony in Derry. Protestants had been the ones who first fought for and were victorious over King James' Catholic forces when the famed Apprentice Boys successfully closed the gates of the walls of Derry, leaving James powerless against King Billy. Now, the city is overwhelmingly Catholic, and The Fountain is conclusive evidence that poverty is no respecter of religions in Derry, indeed in all of Northern Ireland. The Bogside reeks of poor conditions, but The Fountain somehow seems worse. The (Catholic) Creggan's relatively middle- or upper-lower class 11,000 inhabitants dwarf the 500 residents crowded into The Fountain.[121]

Caoimhghín explained that in Derry, "90% live in an area where 90% are one [religion] or the other." This was yet another stunning reminder of the black *vis-a-vis* white residential districts which remain in parts of the United States, *de facto* segregation. Probably because he saw that I was on the verge of tears, Caoimhghín reminded me that life is not so bleak for people here as it might seem. "For them, it's normal," he said, describing this as the "absorption of abnormality into normalcy." I had found not only a genuine philosopher-historian in Derry, but a new friend in Caoimhghín, a friend who had taught me much about the realities of Bloody Sunday and the Troubles.[122]

The Lee Clegg Case

The killings of teenage joy riders Karen Reilly and Martin Declan Peter McPeake in West Belfast on Sept. 30, 1990, garnered much notoriety in Northern Ireland. [Author's note: A "joy-rider" is one who has stolen a vehicle and who thereafter drives it, often at high speed, primarily for his/her own entertainment.] Ms. O'Reilly was eighteen years of age, and McPeake, only seventeen. They were shot by British soldiers ordered to patrol the area, expressly to deter and stop joy riders.

Two Army privates, Lee William Clegg and Barry Wayne Aindow, were charged with murder, Clegg for Ms. Reilly's, and Aindow, for that of young McPeake. Clegg was convicted and sentenced to life in prison.[123] [Because Aindow's conviction was for lesser charges (attempted murder, perverting the cause of public justice and conspiracy to pervert justice) and his respective sentences of seven, two and three years (to be served concurrently) were relatively minor, Clegg was the one who received the abundance of coverage by the press.]

The British media immediately condemned the Northern Ireland court system for having deprived Clegg of the basic rights which the English legal system provides simply because he was tried in Northern Ireland. Paradoxically, Westminster Parliament itself had established the trial without jury in certain situations in Northern Ireland. [See Chapter 7 for an explanation of these so-called "Diplock trials."] Newspapers stressed the fact that Clegg was only the second British soldier to be convicted during some 25 years of violence in the province, an indictment which was pursued during the height of sectarian killings. The more cautious (or at least conservative) among the media emphasized that although he was entitled to an appeal, his freedom should not be "won at the expense of a far greater loss," *i.e.,* he did in fact take part in a killing which should be treated as are all killings in the province.[124]

Nonetheless, Clegg seemed to have inspired a veritable fan club in Britain, and he became almost a poster boy for the Boy Scouts.[125] On January 19, 1995, a five-member panel of the House of Lords unanimously affirmed the conviction on a procedural point,[126] but on February 27, 1998, the Court of Appeals in Northern Ireland granted him a new trial, based on newly presented forensic evidence.[127]

The opinion by Justice Carswell (who is currently Chief Justice of the Supreme Court of Northern Ireland) actually quashed the conviction, in British terminology, finding the first judgment to have been "unsafe." [128] [To the American lawyer, this simply means that there had been shown on appeal a reasonable doubt.]

This "unsafeness" [doubt] came from the corroboration of medical evidence that the fatal bullet possibly had not been fired by Clegg. There had been a total of thirty-six shots fired by the four men in Clegg's unit, nineteen which had hit the vehicle as it raced past the soldiers. Clegg had stated that he had fired four shots. The Court had delved through a mound of evidence regarding the number of bullets which had hit each part of the car, the point of entry of the fatal shot into the deceased's body (her back), and expert opinions about possible angles of contact by each bullet. The sheer volume was enough to tire even the most passionate criminal justice theorist.

Why was there a remand rather than a single reversal? There were several reasons offered by the Court. First, Clegg might well have found himself back in prison because of his convictions of the lesser charges. Second, he had requested a second trial in order to clear his name of any criminal record. Finally, Justice Carswell noted the general public interest in assuring that, if he in fact *had* fired the fatal shot, justice would have been served for Karen Reilly and Martin McPeake.

Clegg was acquitted in this second trial. Many in Northern Ireland bemoaned the travesty visited upon the two dead young people, determined that a guilty but clever Lee Clegg had averted justice.

A Final Comment on Two Murders of Officers of the Court

Because they resemble the type of "vigilante justice" advocated by Tom Alciere of the New Hampshire state House,[129] two killings of lawyers who fought for justice and peace in Northern Ireland bear comment. [Recall that Alciere had proposed simply killing all police officers because they too often "cross(ed) the line."]

Pat Finucane

Pat Finucane was a Catholic solicitor, one with a high-profile reputation for his frequent defending of Republicans. While having dinner with his family in his affluent Belfast home, Finucane was shot and killed. Evidence pointed to a Loyalist paramilitary group, the Ulster Defence Association (UDA). Because of the loss of critical evidence in the late 2001 trial of a suspect, the presiding judge (Lord Chief Justice Carswell, who had earlier ordered the new trial in the Lee Clegg case) was forced to declare a verdict of not guilty. A journalist to whom UDA William Stobie, being tried for the solicitor's murder, had confessed was determined to be too emotionally ill to testify.

Rosemary Nelson

Although the second murder occurred subsequent to the signing of the GFA, it is properly mentioned along with the Finucane case because of the similarity of circumstances. Rosemary Nelson, another Catholic solicitor, was killed in the late morning hours of March 25, 1999. A booby-trap style bomb planted in her car exploded when she was leaving the driveway of her home in Lurgan, County Down. An active Loyalist group known as the Red Hand Defenders claimed responsibility.

Ms. Nelson was a forty-two-year old mother of three who had represented the Garvaghy Road Residents' Coalition, a Catholic group which opposes the July 12 Orange Order marches through their Catholic residential area in Drumcree, on the outskirts of the predominately Protestant town of Portadown, just a few miles from Lurgan. [See Chapter 2 on parades for an explanation of the Drumcree marches.]

The Nelson murder has been publicized for another reason. There have emerged charges of RUC complicity with the terrorists who killed her. These suspicions arose from Ms. Nelson's own statements the prior September 29 that the RUC had "question(ed) my professional integrity, making allegations that I am a member of a paramilitary group and…making threats against my personal safety including death threats;" and statements from witnesses who had been in the general area just after the explosion that RUC men were "sniggering," and "laughing and smirking" at the bomb scene, and were "jubilant, jovial, almost celebratory" when news later that afternoon that she had died from her injuries reached them in mid-afternoon that day.[130]

Despite these charges of collaboration between the police and the Loyalist paramilitary, the former RUC launched immediate full-scale investigations in both the Finucane and Nelson killings. There is no indication that the force headed by Sir Ronnie Flanagan has not conducted this work other than to "ensure and to demonstrate honesty of purpose, professionalism and integrity in this investigation," as Flanagan stated just after the Nelson murder.[131] One person was arrested in December 2001, and others have been questioned.

The poignancy of the Finucane and Nelson killings comes from the fact that both were committed to human rights, equitable treatment, and justice in Northern Ireland.

Some Concluding Remarks

When did this divide—the 'Troubles'—begin? The most common date cited is 1969, when the civil rights movement was organized and when Catholics took to the streets, inspired by American blacks.

Perhaps it became a palpable reality in 1972, with Bloody Sunday and the resumption of British control over the province. It could have been 1920, when partition officially divided the country of Ireland.

Others say the inception was the Penal Laws imposed by the British upon Irish Catholics in the 18th century. Some refer to King Billy's victories in Derry and Boyne in the late 17th century as the actual starting point. Many are of the opinion that Oliver Cromwell's 17th century devastation of the island, or Henry VIII and the plantation program of his progeny, were the real beginnings, particularly when Henry declared himself King of Ireland in 1541.

It could have been the enactment by the British Parliament of the Statutes of Kilkenny in 1366, aimed to stifle all that was "Irish." Perhaps the Troubles actually date back to the 12th century when the English first conquered the island of Ireland.

Historian J.C. Beckett once discerned that there is another partition in Ireland, one beyond the geographical boundary. Such a physical line might be removed by simple political action, but the partition of Ireland is characterized by far more. Beckett has been quoted as having classified the separation as one marking "the very important differences in outlook between two groups of people…[and a]

partition…not on the map, but in the minds of men." [132]

More importantly, did the Troubles die a natural death when the GFA was signed in 1998? Apparently not, for there remains yet life in those in the province of Northern Ireland who are committed to violence.

One must remember that tagging the division a "religious" one is far too simplistic. It is, rather, a dispute that is "religious-plus," one where the wounds are deep, with origins which have survived centuries. The hope of the proponents of the GFA is that it will enable the two segments to take the steps necessary to work in tandem to achieve peace, not by removing their differences, but together working in spite of these differences.

Former Vanderbilt University football coach Dan McGuigan, an Irish-American himself, reportedly said, "Don't live on the fading memories of your forefathers. Go out and make your own records and leave some memories for others to live by." [133] One of Sir Winston Churchill's maxims could be appended to McGuigan's statement: "Nourish your hopes, but don't overlook realities." [134] The gridiron great and the old British statesman could well be speaking to those living in Northern Ireland today. The success of the GFA is not dependent upon mutual fondness, but it will require at least a modicum of determination to live together compatibly.

Endnotes to Chapter 1

[1] Richard Killeen, A SHORT HISTORY OF IRELAND 8 (Gill & MacMillan Ltd., Dublin, Ireland, 1994).

[2] *Id*. at 15.

[3] Paul Johnson, IRELAND: A CONCISE HISTORY FROM THE TWELFTH CENTURY TO THE PRESENT DAY 18 (Academy Publishers Chicago, Chicago, Illinois, 1984)

[4] *Id*. at 16.

[5] *Celts,* Vol. 3 THE WORLD BOOK ENCYCLOPEDIA 254 (1978).

[6] Johnson, *supra* note 3, at 13.

[7] *Id.* at 2.

[8] *Id*. at 15.

[9] Killeen, *supra* note 1, at 15.

[10] Séamas MacAnnaidh, MICROPEDIA: IRISH HISTORY 68-69 (Parragon Publishing, Bath, England, 1999).

[11] Act of Absentees 1368.

[12] Johnson, *supra* note 3, at 25.

[13] MacAnnaidh, *supra* note 10, at 74-75.

[14] Killeen, *supra* note 1, at 18-19.

[15] 10 Henry VII, c. 4.

[16] W.N. Osborough, *Mysteries and solutions: experiencing Irish legal history*, from MYSTERIES AND SOLUTIONS IN IRISH LEGAL HISTORY, a Volume of Irish Legal History Society Discourses and Other Papers, 1996-1999, at 234-235 (Norma Dawson and D.S. Greer, editors, Four Courts Press, 2001).

[17] *Henry VIII*, Vol. 9, THE WORLD BOOK ENCYCLOPEDIA 181 (1978).

[18] MacAnnaidh, *supra* note 10, at 80, and Johnson, *supra* note 3, at 30.

[19] *Edwards of England*, Vol. 6, THE WORLD BOOK ENCYCLOPEDIA 76 (1978).

[20] MacAnnaidh, *supra* note 10, at 91.

[21] *Mary I,* Col. 13, THE WORLD BOOK ENCYCLOPEDIA 192 (1978).

[22] Killeen, *supra* note 1, at 21, 26.

[23] MacAnnaidh, *supra* note 10, at 99.

[24] Johnson, *supra* note 3, at 36-40.

[25] Conversation with Dr. John Lynch, July 31, 2000, Duke's Pub, Belfast. This view is one shared by M.W. Hislinga, in his book, THE IRISH BORDER AS A CULTURAL DIVIDE (Van Gorcum and Comp. N.V. [the Netherlands], 1971), at 147. Hislinga added that the English Prayer Book was never even published in the Gaelic language. In his opinion, it was this neglect on the part of the British which led to the religious issue.

[26] Johnson, *supra* note 3, at 44, 46, 49.

[27] *Id.* at 49.

[28] *Id*. at 30.

[29] *Id*. at 50-52.

[30] *Id*. at 53-54.

[31] Act for the Settling of Ireland 1652.

[32] Act of Satisfaction 1653.

[33] Johnson, *supra* note 3, at 55.

[34] *Id*. at 57.

[35] *Id*. at 58.

[36] MacAnnaigh, *supra* note 10, at 116.

[37] Johnson, *supra* note 3, at 60-61.

[38] Act of Attainder 1689.

[39] MacAnnaigh, *supra* note 10, at 118-119.

[40] Note that the date was changed in 1752 from the actual July 1 date when the battle actually took place to July 12. This was to comport with the change from the Julian to the Gregorian calendar. *Id.* at 120.

[41] Johnson, *supra* note 3, at 62-63.

[42] *Id.* at 63-64.

[43] Interview with The Reverend Peter Ward, C. Ss. R., July 5, 2000, Clonard Monastery, Belfast.

[44] Johnson, *supra* note 3, at 62-63.

[45] *Id.* at 67. An excellent biography of the enigmatic Jonathan Swift, Dean of St. Patrick's Cathedral in Dublin from 1713 until his death in 1745, is Victoria Glendenning, JONATHAN SWIFT (Pimlico, London, England, 1999).

[46] *Id.* at 69-70.

[47] Catholic Relief Acts 1792 and 1793. These statutes are discussed in Johnson, *id.*, at 75, 77.

[48] MacAnnaidh, *supra* note 10, at 138-139, 142-145.

[49] Act of Union 1801.

[50] When he was sentenced, Emmet made a speech which is often quoted as the epitome of the bravery and determination of the Irish to attain independence from England. His words, in part, were: "Let no man write my epitaph.... When my country takes her place among the nations of the earth, then and not until then, let my epitaph be written." This last statement is included in Gretta Curran Browne, TREAD SOFTLY ON MY DREAMS: ROBERT EMMET'S STORY, 579 (Wolfhound Press, Dublin, Ireland1998).

[51] Roman Catholic Relief Act 1829 (10 Geo. 4).

[52] MacAnnaidgh, *supra* note 10, at 155.

[53] Poor Law 1836.

[54] MacAnnaigh, *supra* note 10, at 160-161.

[55] *Id.* at 166-167.

[56] *Id.* at 168-169.

[57] Johnson, *supra* note 3, at 103-105.

[58] MacAnnaigh, *supra* note 10, at 168, Killen, *supra* note 1, at 50, and Johnson, *id.*, at 107-109.

[59] Church Disestablishment Act 1869.

[60] MacAnnaigh, *supra* note 10, at 188-193.

[61] *Id.* at 200-201, and Johnson, *supra* note 3, at 147-148.

[62] *Id.* at 201.

[63] Johnson, *supra* note 3, at 164-173.

[64] This summary of the Easter Rising was extracted from scattered portions of one of the finest works on the subject the author has found, Peter de Rosa, REBELS: THE EASTER RISING OF 1916 (Fawcett Columbine, New York City, New York, 1990).

[65] *Id.* at 503.

[66] MacAnnaidh, *supra* note 10, at 257.

[67] Johnson, *supra* note 3, at 187.

[68] *Id.* at 187-188.

[69] MacAnnaidh, *supra* note 10, at 258-259.

[70] Government of Ireland Act 1920.

[71] Anglo-Irish Treaty 1921 and Irish Free State (*Saorstát Éireann*) Act of 1922, 10 & 11 Geo. 5, ch. 67 (Eng.).

[72] A chronicle and forensic account of Collins' murder is detailed in Meda Ryan, THE DAY MICHAEL COLLINS WAS SHOT (Poolbeg Press Ltd., Dublin, Ireland, 1989).

[73] The *Dáil* passed its own legislation making this break, and in 1949 the 26 counties of the Free State became the Republic of Ireland (*Éire*). The British government did not resist, except for having already responded to the Irish Constitution's claim of sovereignty over all 32 counties, including those in Northern Ireland, by adopting the Atlee Declaration in 1947. This action on the part of the Labour government guaranteed that, "in no event will Northern Ireland or any part thereof cease to be part of the United Kingdom without the consent of the parliament of Northern Ireland." *See* Johnson, *supra* note 3, at 206-207.

[74] *See,* e.g., Geoffrey R. Albert and Michael R. Smith, *Police Use of Force data: Where we are and where we should be going*, 2 POLICE QUARTERLY 57 (March, 1999). Michael R. Smith, Associate Professor of Criminal Justice at Virginia Commonwealth University, has earned both the Ph.D. in Criminal Justice and Juris Doctor degrees and is considered an expert in the area of excessive force in the police field. He has written widely on the subject. For example, *see also Michael R. Smith, Police Use of Deadly Force: How Courts and Policy-Makers Have Misapplied Tennessee v. Garner,* Vol, VII THE KANSAS JOURNAL OF LAW AND PUBLIC POLICY 100 (spring, 1998).

[75] *See*, e.g., Anthony Jennings, *Shoot to Kill: the Final Courts of Justice* 104, and Anthony Jennings, *Bullets above the Law* 131, Jennings *et al.*, JUSTICE UNER FIRE AND CIVIL LIBERTIES IN NORTHERN IRELAND (London, 1998).

[76] *See* Sean Doran, *The Doctrine of Excessive Defence: Developments Past, Present, and Potential*, 36 NORTHERN IRELAND LEGAL QUARTERLY 314 (1985), and *The Use of Force by Security Forces in Northern Ireland: a Legal Perspective*, 7 LEGAL STUDIES 291 (1987).

[77] *See* John Stannard, *Excessive Defence in Northern Ireland*, 43 NORTHERN IRELAND LEGAL QUARTERLY 147 (1992).

[78] 481 F.2d 1028, 1033 (2d Cir. 1973).

[79] 490 U.S. 386 (1989).

[80] *Los Angeles,* THE 1992 WORLD BOOK YEARBOOK 290 (1992).

[81] *Civil Rights,* THE 1993 WORLD BOOK YEARBOOK (1993).

[82] *Civil Rights,* THE 1994 WORLD BOOK YEARBOOK 138 (1994).

[83] The statute is one of the post-Civil War statutes enacted from 1865-1870 to provide a procedural vehicle for enforcement of the civil rights ensured by the 13th, 14th, and 15th Amendments to the United States Constitution. 42 U.S.C. sec. 1983.

[84] Terry Carter, *Cops in the Cross Fire,* AMERICAN BAR ASSOCIATION JOURNAL 58 (October, 2000).

[85] *Id.* at 58.

[86] *Id.* at 62.

[87] *Cincinnati policeman is indicted,* RICHMOND TIMES-DISPATCH (The Associated Press), May 8, 2001, at A-1.

[88] *'I view cops as enemy officers,'* RICHMOND TIMES-DISPATCH, January 3, 2001, at A-5, col. 1-3.

[89] Dwyer [1972] IR 416.

[90] *See* Doran, *supra* note 76, at 301, citing *Palmer,* [1971] AC 814, and P.C. and R. v. *McInnes* [1971] 3 All ER 295, CA.

[91] Palmer, *id.*

[92] Sec. 3 Criminal Act (Northern Ireland) 1967.

[93] Doran, *supra* note 76, at 292, 3-4-305. [The official title of the "Yellow Card" is *Instructions for Opening Fire in Northern Ireland* (Army Code No. 70771). It was also used by the RUC, the police force in Northern Ireland.]

[94] *Id.*

[95] Jennings, *Shoot to Kill, supra* note 75, at 104-105.

[96] Article 2, Convention for the Protection of Human Rights and Fundamental Freedoms, Nov. 4, 1950, art. 19, 213 U.N.T.S. 222, 234.

[97] Farrell v. United Kingdom (5 E.H.R.R. 466).

[98] *Graham, supra* note 79.

[99] Johnson, *supra* note 3, at 188, 192.

[100] McAnnaidh, *supra* note 10, at 304.

[101] Act of 9 August 1971, Northern Ireland Parliament.

[102] Report of the Tribunal appointed to inquire into the events on Sunday, 30th January, 1972, which led to the loss of life in connection with the processions on that day by the Right Honorable Lord Widgery, O.B.E., T.D. at 8 (Her Majesty's Stationery Office, H.L.101, H.C. 220).

[103] *The Bloody Sunday Inquiry*, British Broadcasting Company (BBC), "Northern Ireland," December 5, 2001.

[104] Tribunals of Inquiry (Evidence) Act 1921.

[105] Widgery Report, *supra* note 102.

[106] 29 January 1998 House of Commons Official Report, Parliamentary Debates (Hansard). This is the document containing Prime Minister Tony Blair's speech to the Parliament when he appointed the second tribunal to conduct an inquiry into Bloody Sunday.

[107] Kara E. Irwin, *Prospects for Justice: the Procedural Aspect of the Right to Life under the European Convention of Human Rights and its Applicability to the Investigation of Northern Ireland's 'Bloody Sunday,'* 22 FORDHAM INTERNATIONAL LAW JOURNAL 1822, 1858 (1999).

[108] 324 Eur. Ct. H.R. (ser.A), paragraph 161 (1995); App. No. 18984/91, Eur. Commission of H.R. (March 4, 1994), paragraphs 191-193).

[109] *Supra* note 96.

[110] *Id.* Article 2, at 224.

[111] Irwin, *supra* note 107, at note 88.

[112] *Id.* at note 138.

[113] *Supra* note 106.

[114] David Pallister, *Lives of 400 ex-soldiers would be put at risk in Derry, says QC,* THE GUARDIAN, November 6, 2001.

[115] Suzanne Rodgers and Ciaran O'Neill, *Families fear Bloody Sunday delay,* BELFAST TELEGRAPH, August 2, 2000, at 2, col. 7.

[116] *Id*

[117] Bloody Sunday webpage, http://www.bloody-sunday-inquiry.org.uk

[118] Paul Bew, *Opening the Bloody Sunday can of worms,* THE TIMES, August 4, 2000, at 18, col. 3-6.

[119] *Id.*

[120] Susan McKay, NORTHERN PROTESTANTS 306 (The Blackstaff Press, Belfast, Ireland, 2000).

[121] *Id.*

[122] Conversation and walk through Derry with Caoimhghín O'Murchadh, July 26. 2000.

[123] The Queen v. Lee William Clegg and Barry Wayne Aindow, March 30, 1994, In Her Majesty's Court of Appeals in Northern Ireland, Hutton, Lord Chief Justice.

[124] *See, e.g., Comment: The high price of instant justice,* THE GUARDIAN, January 25, 1995, at 19, col. 1.

[125] David Sharrock, *Campaign to free Clegg sickens victim's family,* THE GUARDIAN, January 25, 1995, at 5, col. 1-3.

[126] R. v. Clegg, House of Lords, January 19, 1995, *per curiam* opinion.

[127] The Queen v. Lee William Clegg, In Her Majesty's Court of Appeal in Northern Ireland, February 27, 1998, Carswell, Lord Chief Justice.

[128] *Id.* at 33.

[129] *Supra* note 88.

[130] *Rosemary Nelson: the life and death of a human rights defender* 23, 24 (published by the Pat Finucane Centre, 1999). The Pat Finucane Centre was established in 1989, shortly after Finucane was murdered.

[131] *Id.* at 11.

[132] *See* M.W. Hislinga, *supra* note 25, at 204, *quoting from* A SHORT HISTORY OF IRELAND (Hutchinson, London, 1958, 2d ed.).

[133] THE WISDOM OF SOUTHERN FOOTBALL 28 (Criswell Freeman, compiler and editor, Walnut Grove Press, 1995).

[134] THE WIT AND WISDOM OF WINSTON CHURCHILL 44 (James C. Humes, editor, Harper Perennial, 1994).

Chapter 2

Parades, Politics and Religion

We think the starting point is competing identities [rather than] competing rights, or competing interests.... [a competition which has] become sharper and more focused due largely to political events.

Tony Holland, Chair of Parades
Commission, July 2, 2000[1]

Perhaps the spirit underlying Northern Ireland's demonstrations and parades season long pre-dated the first such parade. The centuries-old struggles of the Irish against England reached an apex in the days of Oliver Cromwell, with his efforts to abolish—or least to overcome—anything "Irish" in nature. (See Chapter 1.)

The concept of parades in Northern Ireland is most often associated with Unionists and, commensurately, with Protestants. The official "Marching Season" encompasses the major parades—thirty-five in all. Beginning on Easter Monday, the last of these is held on October 18.[2] Because "parade" in the province is synonymous with "demonstration," these two terms will be used interchangeably.

The most parade-saturated time during Marching Season is the week preceding and including July 12. On this date in 1689, William of Orange overwhelmingly defeated Catholic troops at the Battle of the Boyne in County Meath. This most significant of British victories over the Irish is regarded by Unionists much as Americans regard July 4. A one-sided patriotism unique to Northern Ireland is evident throughout the province during this period.

The Beginning

The majority of Unionist parades are organized and participated in by members of the Orange Order, a group of Protestants known as the "Orangemen," founded in 1795. The very first Orange Order parade was in 1796, only a year after the group's beginning. Probably portending events to come, one man was killed,[3] and a proud tradition has since been accompanied by the sad one of violence. The emotions and counter-emotions which are the fabric of the idea of parades probably make this a natural consequence.

A parliamentary response was not immediate. The first statute addressing the issue of parades violence was the Party Procession Act of 1832. Although Parliament decided in 1845 not to enforce this law, the repeated violence led to its reintroduction in 1850. Inexplicably, it was repealed in 1872.[4]

Partition

Then came partition of the island of Ireland in 1920. Unionist-Protestants were concentrated in the six counties constituting the province of Northern Ireland, and a majority joined a Protestant order which pledged support to unity with Great Britain. In a classic use of power of the majority, the British government actually encouraged Protestant parades. When Nationalist Catholics organized parades of their own, police routinely required that they be held only in predominately Catholic areas. Faced with the possibility of a violent counter-reaction to such discriminatory oversight, the British Parliament (Westminster) approved legislation in 1922 which vested authority in the Minister for Foreign Affairs to ban any meeting or procession.[5] The Public Order Act was later made effective in Great Britain to control the eruption of fascist, communist, and anti-Semitic violence in North London,[6] and Parliament later adopted similar legislation for Northern Ireland, this time to curb sectarian violence.[7]

The Civil Rights Movement and the Troubles

During the 1960's, the civil rights movement for equality for Nationalist Catholics in Northern Ireland took its inspiration from the contemporaneous civil rights movement for blacks in the United States.[8] The newly formed Northern Ireland Civil Rights Association, comprised of Nationalists, began to organize parades on their own as a means of objecting to suppression. Unionists strenuously objected to Catholic parades in predominately Protestant areas, and Catholics in return presented a more overt defiance to Protestant parades in Catholic areas.[9] Thus began a tit-for-tat position which is characteristic of both sides' refusals to make concessions, and the chasm only grew wider. The onset of the Troubles in 1969 was a watershed event for political demonstrations. To say that emotions over the political division intensified is roughly comparable to describing Michelangelo's David as a nice little piece of sculpture.

The consensus was that, for a while at least, Catholics tolerated Protestant marches, with some exceptions. Perhaps the most memorable such exception in the embryonic days of the Troubles was the so-called Battle of the Bogside in Londonderry ("Derry" to Nationalists) on January 30, 1972. At a peaceful Catholic civil rights protest, British Army forces entered and killed fourteen unarmed men and boys. Forever referred to as "Bloody Sunday," this incident has twice been investigated by the British government. (See Chapter 1.) Here, Northern Ireland experienced her worst riots since the partition.[10] This was the incident which led to the entry of British troops into Northern Ireland.

A visit to Derry City provides a mini-education in the history leading to the Troubles. In Londonderry/Derry, the famous Apprentice Boys Association was formed to memorialize the brave young apprentices who closed the gates of the walls of Derry in 1689 to prevent the advancing forces of King James II of Scotland from overtaking the city. A sound victory for the king's son-in-law, Protestant King William II (William of Orange, or "King Billy"), this battle is commemorated each year by Protestant marching groups throughout Northern Ireland, but particularly in Londonderry/Derry. Surprisingly small with a population of only about 70,000, the official name is the British one, Londonderry, as is the County. Whether one is speaking with a Nationalist Catholic or a Unionist Protestant is imminently and immediately obvious. His reference to the town as either "Londonderry" (the official term, used by Unionists) or "Derry" (used by Nationalists) is the first indicator. Moreover, the section of town in which he lives makes one certain as to his affiliation. The Bogside, a poor Catholic section lying just outside the city walls, was the place where co-Nobel Peace Prize winner John Hume[11] spent his boyhood and school days.

Londonderry/Derry city itself is somewhat of an anachronism. On the edge of the Bogside is a large statue in the middle of the road with the caption "You are now entering Free Derry," confusingly—and falsely—seemingly announcing that the area is part of the Republic of Ireland. Actually, the introduction of this label followed Bloody Sunday (see Chapter 1), when the Westminster Parliament assured the Bogside residents that it would remain "free" from the presence of RUC and British Army forces. Situated on the banks of the Foyle River, the small city seems more to lie in County Donegal, the most northeastern of the twenty-six counties of the Republic of Ireland, than in the province of Northern Ireland. The distance to County Donegal is only about ten miles, and the city of Londonderry/Derry is located on the Donegal side of the river. Indeed, Donegal in the Republic, not County Londonderry/Derry in Northern Ireland, actually contains the most northerly parts of the entire island, and the southern border of the county barely touches the next county in the Republic to its south, Sligo. One has the sense that, geographically, either Donegal should be part of Northern Ireland, or Londonderry should be a part of the Republic. The border followed strictly religious lines, however, with Donegal remaining predominately Catholic and Derry containing the mix that has caused the city so much strife.

To their credit, post-Battle of the Bogside Orange Order march participants voluntarily refrained from playing politically charged songs, shouting political slogans to Catholics, using profanity or consuming alcoholic beverages during parades. The music for a while consisted solely of Protestant hymns.[12] Unfortunately, this moderation was short-lived, and the sectarian music and slogans which were so irritating to Catholics soon resumed.

This time Parliament did not deliberate long as to whether the Bogside event was an aberration. In 1970, the Public Order Act[13] required that seventy-two hours notice of any parade or demonstration be given to the designated governmental authority, the British Home Secretary. This law was altered a year later, when the required notice period was extended to five days. Furthermore, this new statute gave the Home Secretary considerably more guidance in determining whether or not to ban a planned parade. Such a ban would be permitted if the parade imposed an "undue hardship" on those who conducted business or worked in the area, or if the parade made "undue demands" on the police or on military forces.[14]

In 1987, the Westminster Parliament enacted legislation that empowered the Royal Ulster Constabulary (RUC, Northern Ireland's police force) to alter parade routes and to impose conditions on marching. This law vested the Home Secretary with broader authority than in the previous statutes, permitting him the discretion as to whether to ban a parade entirely.[15] The statute followed the government's initial approach of permitting localities rather than the centralized government of the province to impose their own constraints, making the intervention of the Home Secretary a sort of last resort. The legislature's purpose was to excise the RUC from the political role that had been forced upon it and superimposed upon its usual law enforcement and security duties. However, this 1987 law's returning of decision-making power to localities had the result of throwing back to the RUC the discretion of deciding parade issues on the local level. This clearly placed it in an unenviable role. Any re-routing would likely be assessed by Unionists as caving in to Nationalist demands, and any decision not to re-route or ban would be viewed by Nationalists as giving preferential treatment to Unionist marchers.

The 1987 statute required only forty-eight hours notice to the local police of a planned parade. This provision was partially swallowed by its exception, however. No notice was necessary for parades "customarily held" on a specific route. This exception, of course, applied to Orange Order parades which generally had followed the same path for many years. Note that the prior laws regulating parades that were subsumed into the 1987 statute were seemingly stricter on parade participants than was the law as amended with regard to the now more lenient required notice period. However, the 1970 law had empowered the Home Secretary to prohibit only specific marches, whereas the 1987 statute permitted a general ban. In this latter sense, the later legislation was a tighter means of parades control, a fact that did not endear it to Orangemen and other Unionists.

The Lower Ormeau Road

The volatility accompanying the parades worsened in the mid-1990's. In Belfast, the Lower Ormeau Concerned Community was formed in 1995 in order to strengthen the mounting protest against the July 12, Orange Order parade down this street in southeast Belfast. This July 12, march on the Lower Ormeau remains a bone of contention for security personnel.

To the first-time visitor, Belfast seems surprisingly compact, with the actual downtown being confined to an area beginning just south of the classic city hall and extending only a couple of blocks westward. The eastern boundary of downtown looks to the dock area of the River Lagan, where ships carry foot-passengers and vehicles across the Irish Sea to southwest Scotland (the small seaside village of Stanraer), the Isle of Man, and to points in northwest England. Downtown continues north from city hall several short blocks to St. Anne's (Church of Ireland) Cathedral. Essentially, downtown forms a near-perfect square.

The northeast section beyond downtown is primarily Unionist Protestant, with headquarters of some of the Unionist political parties (such as Progressive Unionist Party, or PUP), the RUC headquarters, and Stormont, location of the first Northern Ireland government and the post-GFA New Northern Ireland Assembly. Some of East Belfast is low-to-middle class, but much of it is upper class, with lovely homes surrounded by sweeping lawns. North of St. Anne's is North Belfast, a working-class Unionist Protestant section which Clair Archbold, one of my Queen's School of Law friends and colleagues, referred to as a "hot-bed of Protestantism." Sidewalks are painted the red, white, and blue royal colors of the Union Jack flag of the United Kingdom, and the flag is flown from outside most storefronts, houses and/or apartments. This, too, is a Loyalist sector, with many paramilitary murals on sides of buildings. Similarly, southwest of city hall and behind the Grand Opera House is Sandy Row, a Unionist-Loyalist area which has seen its share of violence. Between the Grand Opera House and the combined train-bus station on Great Victoria Street is the Europa Hotel which, as the site of many pre-peace talk sessions and overnight accommodation for many members of the press as well as governmental principals, holds the dubious distinction of being known as the "most bombed hotel in the world."

Beyond the western edge of downtown Belfast lies West Belfast's Falls Road, one of the city's most Nationalist Catholic-concentrated sections. (Other Catholic areas extend to the south of the Falls area, such as Andersontown.) The Falls is the antithesis of East Belfast. Many buildings are adorned with Nationalist murals. The Irish tri-color flag—green for Catholicism, orange for Protestantism, and white in the middle which ironically stands for unity between the two—flies virtually everywhere. Some pubs are strictly Gaelic speaking, and signs in Gaelic (Irish) are paramount. Headquarters of *Sinn Féin*, the more extreme of the two National-ist political parties (SDLP is the more moderate party) are on the Falls, and *ceilis* and *saisons* (Irish music) frequent its pubs. There are virtually no Protestant churches, and the Falls is home to one of the longest established monasteries in the area, the Redemptorist fathers' Clonard Monastery. The Falls is mostly a poor area, and unemployment is high. Just north of the Falls is the Shankill Road, an area as passionately Unionist Protestant as the Falls is Nationalist Catholic, and equally poor, or at least working class. If ever there was a misnomer, it is the name of the barbed-wire stone edifice separating the Falls and Shankill areas, the Peace Line.

Belfast is indeed a divided city, comprised of Catholic, Protestant, and so-called "neutral" residential areas. Even the newspapers are political. The *Belfast News Leader* is blatantly Unionist Protestant, while the *Irish News* is Nationalist Catholic to the core in perspective. The exception is the *Belfast Telegraph* which apparently attempts to achieve a more balanced and unbiased position.

Belfast's Lower Ormeau Road is a long diagonal road running southeast from downtown Belfast, slightly east of the so-called "royal mile" running south be-tween downtown and the Tudor-styled Queen's University founded by Queen Victoria in 1849. In general, South Belfast is regarded as a "neutral" area, an alien-sounding term to American ears. Usually, the word "neutral" connotes a buffer in the middle of a war zone, and this is very much what the city of Belfast was for many years.

I lived in the upstairs apartment of a lovely house owned by my wonderful landlady, Jean. Scottish by birth and still stubbornly so by nature, Jean had been the manager of the Queen's University student housing for many years before her retirement. She lived in this house owned by her parents since her engineer-father brought his family to Northern Ireland when she was eight years old. Jean is exemplary of the non-religious connotations of the conflict. She insists that she is not religious or spiritual, but she is very much a Unionist, and one who was op-posed to the GFA. Located in Marlborough Park, an upper-middle to upper class area in South Belfast, Jean's house is approximately one-and-a-half miles south of Queen's University. All the local residents referred to this area as "neutral."

The Lower Ormeau, while without the style and residential class of the area slightly to its south and west, is also generally considered "neutral." To be sure, if one must classify this section, it would be leaning toward Unionist-Protestant. Slightly east of the Lower Ormeau and in the same general area is situated Raven Hill Road. Only a few buildings from each other on this road are the headquarters of the Democratic Unionist Party (DUP), the most extreme of the Unionist politi-cal parties (very anti-GFA), and the Martyrs' Memorial Free Presbyterian Church, where the Rev. Ian Paisley has preached for some fifty years. When I asked one of my favorite friends and colleagues at Queen's School of Law about this "non-

Presbyterian-ish Presbyterian Church" (at least not a Presbyterian church in the American sense), he explained that "Presbyterian" in this case was with a small "p," used to designate the form of church government rather than its doctrine. He continued with his analogy to the Holy Roman Empire which he viewed as "neither 'holy' nor 'Roman'," adding his characterization of Paisley's church as "neither 'free' nor 'Presbyterian.'" The significance of this close proximity is that the Rev. Dr. Paisley heads the DUP and is one of the most vocal opponents of the GFA because of, in his words, its "pro-Roman" provisions. (See Chapter 4.)

There is a wonderful parody that alludes to the Rev. Paisley's legendary sanctimoniousness and fundamentalism. The story goes that he and Gerry Adams, *Sinn Féin* leader, were driving in opposite directions on the same road on the outskirts of Belfast late one night, and they had a horrible collision. Although both vehicles were totaled, miraculously neither man was even injured. When they alighted from their mangled cars and recognized each other, Adams pulled out from his back seat a bottle of Irish whiskey (presumably undamaged, another miracle). He insisted that Paisley, a teetotaler, have a drink to praise God for having saved their lives. Because of his staunch anti-booze position on which he had regularly preached, Paisley adamantly refused. Adams persisted, however, so he finally wavered and had a drink. Since Paisley's first taste of alcohol was surprisingly good, he asked for another. Adams then offered him another, and yet another, and so on, each which Paisley accepted "in praise of Almighty God." Finally, after the bottle was nearly empty and Paisley was barely able to function, he asked Adams why he wasn't joining him. Adams' response was, "I'll just wait until the police arrive."

I talked at length with one highly respected judge in Northern Ireland.[16] He commented to me about the paradox of the opposition to the Orange Order march on the Lower Ormeau Road, since the mixed perception is that it is either neutral or Unionist, but decidedly not Nationalist. However, it is probable that the pivotal event which gave rise to the organization of the Lower Ormeau Concerned Community had nothing to do with politics or religion of the residents. During the July 8, 1992, event, marching Orangemen made obscene gestures toward a betting parlor owned by Catholic Sean Graham.[17] It could be that this folly stretched the neutrality of the Lower Ormeau residents to the limit.

Even some Nationalists had no difficulty accepting Orange parades as a historical reality, but most nonetheless objected strenuously to participants' insistence that they be in primarily Nationalist areas. The result was a disruption to the lives of residents and their subjection to Loyalist and sectarian music and triumphant signs that they found offensive. Moreover, the costs of the necessarily increased security remained a sore subject.[18]

The aggravation came from both camps. *Sinn Féin* sent its politicians into Catholic areas to agitate those who lived there, inducing them to oppose parades routed in or near any predominately Catholic area. The reasons for this political strategy were two-fold: (i) to test the commitment of the British government's facial "parity of esteem" and (ii) to serve to provoke the Orangemen[19]—sort of a "taste-of-your-own-distasteful-medicine" approach. The good judge aptly compared this logic to animal instincts when he said, "Dogs and cats are not at their best when poked at with a stick." [20] The "sticks" were apparently used by both sides, and provocation only begat more provocation.

The "Queen" of Parade Difficulties: Drumcree

Southwest of Belfast lies the town of Portadown, generally regarded a solidly Unionist Protestant territory. "Union Jacks" (the flag of the United Kingdom) are visible in front of most houses in the major part of town, and the political-religious divide is evident even to the least discerning of eyes. A section on the outskirts of town is the Catholic section, but the remainder is heavily Unionist-Protestant. Portadown lies in County Armagh which borders the northeast of the Republic of Ireland. [Armagh Town is known as the "ecclesiastical capital" of the entire island, boasting two St. Patrick's Cathedrals at opposite ends of the tiny town, one Catholic, and the other Protestant (Church of Ireland).] Portadown's apparent docility is deceptive, for it is here that the most controversial of Orange parades takes place on each Sunday before July 12. The problems with the march on Belfast's Lower Ormeau Road pale in comparison.

Although the Orange Order is most often associated with the Presbyterian Church, the march in Portadown is directed from town to Drumcree Church, which is Church of Ireland. After attending the Sunday morning service, the Order marches back to downtown Portadown.

The church's high steeple can be seen from the Belfast-Dublin train, and the uninformed would think of Portadown as just another small place in Northern Ireland. However, July 12 is the date of a veritable host of Orange Order parades throughout Northern Ireland. Portadown is the actual "birthplace of Orangism," and the "touchstone of parade contention."[21] Because Protestants were massacred at Portadown in the 1641 rebellion, this demonstration is one of the Orange Order's most commemorative of marches. Moreover, it is in the general vicinity of the 1795 Battle of the Diamond, a victory for supporters of the crown of England.

Traditionally, marchers use the route along Garvaghy Road which they contend was chosen because it is the most direct and shortest way to reach Drumcree Church. The contention is caused by the concentration of Catholics in the area along Garvaghy and their opposition to this choice when an alternate route is available. Historian Kevin Haddick-Flynn, who has chronicled the highlights of the Drumcree problem since 1995, has sympathized with the security forces and their difficult position at Portadown, designating the RUC as the "piggy in the middle." [22] Referred to as "Drumcree I," 1994 marked the formation by *Sinn Féin* member Brendan McKenna of the Garvaghy Road Residents' Coalition.

Drumcree I (1995)

Some 6,500 Orangemen took a non-controversial route from Portadown Town to Drumcree Church, but returned via Garvaghy Road. RUC officers, garbed in riot gear, used Land Rovers to block the marchers' way. The RUC remained resolute in denying the demand of Harold Gracey, Worshipful Master of Portadown District Lodge of the Orange Order, to permit his marchers to proceed. The stand-off between the marchers and the RUC led to twenty-four hours of rioting and violent confrontations. More Orangemen arrived, shouting invectives to and throwing bottles at RUC on duty. In retaliation, the RUC used baton charges and plastic bullet rounds.

On July 10, Orange leaders proclaimed that the RUC's actions were a violation of their civil liberties, rather the police protection to which the marchers were entitled. On July 11, the Rev. Dr. Ian Paisley, not an Orange Order member himself, arrived to voice his emotional support for marchers. The following day, David Trimble shared the podium with Paisley in a rare unified front between the two. (Trimble is a member of the Orange Order.)

Catholic Cardinal Cahal Daly and Church of Ireland Archbishop Robin Eames tried to conciliate, achieving some degree of appeasement. The Orangemen accepted a compromise which would permit them to take the Garvaghy Road route in the future, provided they flew no more than one banner and did not speak, play music or sing.[23] (Surely, this is not the epitome of a parade!) Thus, the Order came out at Drumcree I as the "good guys."

Drumcree II (1996)

In the short time prior to the parade in 1996, RUC Chief Constable Hugh Annesley unsuccessfully endeavored to persuade the Order to reroute and to avoid the Garvaghy Road route per the previous year's compromise. When the Order refused, Annesley ordered a ban on the march in order to "preserve public order."[24]

This move engendered violence throughout the province. Loyalists threw rocks at Catholic residences in Belfast, businesses and homeowners reacted defensively by barricading their buildings, and the RUC's resources were nearly exhausted. A Catholic cab driver was murdered outside the divided town of Lurgan, south of Belfast in County Down. Five days later, Annesley succumbed and permitted the march, and the resulting Catholic retaliation was predictable. Approximately 2,500 Catholics were under a fifteen-hour curfew, and Catholics banged trash can lids and pans during the march, trying to drown the Loyalist music and drums accompanying the parade in violation of the agreement.[25]

The effect of the Chief Constable's well-intended moves, albeit inconsistent ones, was an unsurpassed loss of credibility of the RUC among Nationalists. Secretary of State Patrick Mayhew appointed a three-member Independent Review of

Parades on Garvaghy Road which met from August, 1996, until January, 1997. (The Secretary of State for Northern Ireland is a member of the Westminster Parliament and is appointed to this cabinet position by the Prime Minister.) Of its forty-three recommendations, the most significant and far-reaching was to establish a Parades Commission which would be charged with determining parades disputes, including any rerouting or banning. The procedure was for the Chief Constable of the RUC to appeal a Parades Commission ruling to the Secretary of State. The Parades Commission did not become a full-fledged statutory body until 1998. [26]

Mayhew's order also extended the notification period for parades to twenty-one days, the longest such legally required period since the original seventy-two-hour period was enacted in 1970. [27] Further, it banned all parades on Garvaghy Road from August 7 through August 31 of that year. [28] Annesley's reputation and effectiveness had been seriously undermined. More significantly, Drumcree II marked the first total parade ban, rather than a simple re-routing, since the six-month parade ban imposed by Northern Ireland Prime Minister James Chichester-Clark in July, 1970. [29]

Drumcree III (1997)

1997 was the first Drumcree march during which Sir Ronnie Flanagan served as Chief Constable of the RUC. This year's parade was suspenseful, since it was virtually unknown until shortly before the scheduled march whether the RUC would ban, or at the least, reroute. The parade was permitted, but about sixty Catholic families on Garvaghy Road were evacuated because of a Loyalist bomb threat. Just prior to dawn on July 6, the RUC moved all the evacuees back into their homes, using batons on Loyalist opposition when necessary.

Catholics were nonetheless still under a curfew, which meant that they could not attend church services. Behind one of the blockades, a priest dramatically celebrated mass. Sadly, this marked the first time since penal days that security forces had actually prevented Catholics from going to church.[30] Drumcree III was to be the last year to date that the Garvaghy Road route has been permitted.

Drumcree IV (1998)

This year's Marching Season was the first since the Parades Commission's establishment by statute.[31] Schedule I of the law created a Commission with a maximum of six members, appointed by the Prime Minister for a renewable three-year term, with one additional member to be appointed a Chair. A Code of Conduct for parade organizers was included[32] and procedural rules were established which required the Commission to announce its decision with regard to a particular parade at least five days before it was scheduled.[33] The statute set forth express

Guidelines for Commission decisions,[34] and the notification period prior to a parade was extended from the prior law's forty-eight hours to twenty-eight days.[35] Exempted were funeral marches,[36] and Salvation Army traditional marches planned along a customarily established route were also exempted in another statute adopted the same year.[37] The new Parades Commission law added another notice period of fourteen days for a planned protest, with criminal sanctions of up to six months in prison and/or a fine for violations.[38]

The July marches also closely followed the signing of the GFA (April 10) and the affirming referenda in both Northern Ireland and the Republic (May 22), so there was an overall sense among Northern Irelanders of truly wanting to put violence behind them and to progress forward with implementing the peace plan. Notably, however, each of the Loyalist orders publicly announced its refusal to recognize the legitimacy of the Parades Commission.[39] Catholic concerns were that the Chief Constable's right to appeal a decision by the Commission made him too powerful, but this office has never appealed such orders. The Parades Commission, then, has thus far had the effect the Parliament desired, to alleviate any pressure on the RUC.[40]

There are five statutory factors which the Commission is required to take into account in determining whether to reroute or ban a parade: (i) public disorder or damage which might result, (ii) likely disruption to life or community, (iii) the probable impact on community relationships, (iv) noncompliance of parade organizers with the statutory Code of Conduct, and (v) the desirability of permitting a procession on a customarily used route.[41]

Despite the new law, the Orangemen's obstinance in refusing to acknowledge any authority of the Commission presented a major roadblock. The Orange Order stood firm, and declined any requests to negotiate with the Garvaghy Road's Catholic residents. The Commission banned the march, and the RUC and British Army erected barricades to enforce the order, since marchers had publicly stated that they would ignore it.

Predictably, there was a redux of the standoff of Drumcree I (1995). Sectarian obscenities from shouting Protestants were coupled with their throwing smoke bombs, firing ammunition, and throwing rocks against security forces. The RUC response was to use plastic bullets which injured twenty persons. The general consensus within Northern Ireland was a favorable one for both the RUC and the British Army, and they were commended overall for their exercise of restraint.[42]

The tension mounted in spite of efforts by the police and army to contain any dissension which might lead to injuries or destruction or damages to property. The Rev. Paisley again made an appearance in support of marchers, lending them some degree of credibility among his staunch followers. He encouraged the Orangemen to continue their protests.[43] Approximately 50,000 additional Orange Order members were en route from Scotland and Liverpool to join in the standoff. Loyalist protests were organized throughout the province, and the resulting commercial stand-still was reminiscent of the workers' strike that had led to the demise of the short-lived Sunningdale power-sharing government. (See Chapter 5.)

Surely the greatest tragedy of the Drumcree difficulties in 1998 was the early morning July 12 death of three young Catholic brothers in Balleymoney, a quiet village in northern County Antrim. Militant Protestants who had been obsessed with the fomenting spirit of Loyalism set fire to their mother's house, presumably because she, a Catholic, was living with a Protestant. The deaths of the innocent Quinn children pained mothers all over the world. Subsequently, the Rev. William Bingham, chaplain for the Orange Order in County Armagh, was joined by David Trimble, Orange Order member and then-newly elected First Minister of the New Northern Ireland Assembly, in withdrawing their support for the marchers.[44] On Belfast's Lower Ormeau Road, Catholics held silent protests, holding black flags and signs reading "Shame on you" as marchers passed.

There were petrol bombs, shooting incidents, hijacking of cars, damage to property—Northern Ireland seemed to have reverted to her pre-GFA days. The RUC's subsequent investigation—significantly, an objective and sincere effort by the same body which Catholics had claimed was biased against them—pointed to the Ulster Volunteer Force (UVF) and Ulster Defense Association (UDA), both militant Loyalist groups, as the protagonists.[45]

Drumcree V (1999)

In view of the prior year's catastrophe, the Parades Commission again forbade the Garvaghy road route. As has become almost routine with the Drumcree march, there were the usual incidents of violence against opponents and attacks on the RUC. Not only the march, but now even the standoff, seemed to have become a tradition.

In general, protests over any Drumcree rerouting subsequent to the GFA have been credited to Unionist opposition to the agreement[46] and a review of the following year lends strength to that position.

Drumcree VI (2000)

Over 2,000 British soldiers arrived in Northern Ireland to stifle predicted troubles instigating in Portadown, bringing with them armored trucks, machinery for trench-digging, and razor wire for barricading. RUC officers were on standby as a pre-emptive measure. South African human rights lawyer Brian Curran was approved by the Parades Commission to mediate the anticipated revisit of the stand-offs of Drumcrees I, II and IV.[47]

Even before the Parades Commission issued its order on the Drumcree march, the Orange Order announced its plan to petition the European Courts on Human Rights in Strasbourg, France[48] to intervene and confirm the Order's right to march.

This court is the product of the 1950 European Convention on Human Rights[49] and the 1961 European Social Charter.[50] Its powers are, at best, limited. Although the Court's orders are supervised by the Council of Europe's Committee of Ministers, compliance is voluntary. Nonetheless, British legislation which was to incorporate into UK law the 1950 European Convention on Human Rights that this Court interprets and applies, was to become effective in the UK in October, 2000.[51] This 1950 Convention provides that "everyone has the right to freedom of peaceful assembly and to freedom of association with others."[52] The "peaceful" nature, of course, was clearly debatable with respect to the petitioning Orangemen.

The bitterness engendered in Drumcree escalated. On the heels of the Orange Order's adamant refusal to meet with Garvaghy residents and the South African mediator, the Parades Commission denied them access to Garvaghy Road for their planned July 9, march. This was (i) the first of four points of the Commission's order which also (ii) required the Order to enforce a moratorium which would require that they refrain from any protests or parades related to the decision, (iii) directed the Order to work with Currin, the South African lawyer-mediator, and the Garvaghy Road residents, and (iv) promised the Order in return a possible limited parade along Garvaghy Road within the following eight months.[53]

The night of July 4 was the third consecutive day of violence throughout Northern Ireland in response to the Commission's order. Protestors in Portadown set fire to an Army vehicle and threw missiles at police.[54] The "in-your-face" involvement at Drumcree of recently released Loyalist prisoners per terms of the GFA (see Chapter 6) made the already tense matters worse. Particularly disturbing was the participation of the most notorious of former Loyalist prisoners, Johnny "Mad Dog" Adair, who led a group of protestors at Drumcree the night of July 3, 2000. Northern Ireland Secretary of State Andrew Mackay described his feeling over Adair's activity as "horrified." Mackay bemoaned the necessity for the RUC to be a "thin green line between the rule of law and anarchy, and, speaking with typical British reserve, called the actions of so-called Loyalists...quite unacceptable." He described Adair and his minions as "thugs." [55] Adair's presumptuousness also drew the ire of RUC Chief Constable Ronnie Flanagan, whose verbal reproach followed Mackay's. The Chief warned that "(t)hey (organizations and individuals who had reaped the benefits of early release) should watch their behavior very closely." [56] He also voiced concern over the costs of containing the violence, adding that the RUC budget simply could not subsidize this added burden. Flanagan praised his officers and urged both communities to "work together to support the police service." [57]

The stubbornness of the Orange Order was clearly counter-productive. One member retorted that "Orange rights are continually eroded...All we do is give, and all the Nationalists do is take." [58] Even Unionist politicians were appalled at the Order's reactions. William Thompson, Member of Parliament responded that he "support(s) the Order...but when...they are supported by paramilitaries who attack police and hijack cars, it loses sympathy among the Unionist population." [59] Protestant clergy and bishops of several denominations in Northern Ireland expressed their displeasure with the Orange Order.[60] Perhaps the most chilling among these reactions was Church of Ireland Archbishop of Armagh Robin Eames' statement: "I see nothing of Jesus Christ in the nightly actions in Drumcree hill or on the roads and streets of Northern Ireland night by night... I do not consider violent protest...(as) appropriate before or after attendance of worship of Almighty God...(nor) the integrity of worship (to be)...enhanced by bitterness or attacks on the police before or after divine service." [61] Archbishop Eames reminded those responsible for such protests of the Biblical mandate to "render unto Caesar those things that Caesar's, and choose to turn the other cheek, rather than to smite." [62] As though in a time bubble, Portadown Master of the Orange Order Harold Gracey persisted in refusing "to condemn violence because Gerry Adams (Member of Legislative Assembly, *Sinn Féin*) never condemns it," adding that he "did not trust RUC Chief Constable Flanagan's statements of Loyalists attacking police officers." [63] Gracey's complete lack of understanding stoked the anger of both Nationalists and Unionists.

Drumcree was a true public relations nightmare for the Orange Order which left one with the impression of a body with no real leadership.[64] Even the former grand chaplain for the Orange Order of Ireland, the Rev. Warren Porter, condemned Orangeism as having "reached a new depth when Johnny Adair emerges as its patron." [65]

Some Personal Perspectives

I was at the Queen's University School of Law in Belfast during Drumcree VI, a project that would require also some time working at Trinity College and University College Dublin libraries on legal research, with interviews with principals in the peace process to be pre-scheduled in both Belfast and Dublin. My total stay was from July through most of August 2000, and I knew that the week of July 12 would necessarily be unproductive in Belfast. Most who have the option simply leave the city during this time, downtown (and many suburban) businesses, restaurants, and shops are not only closed, but boarded up in order to minimize damage from the inevitable rioting and looting, and the university itself is closed. Consequently, I could neither work in the university library nor schedule interviews. Cars are set afire (as are many shops), and windows of unboarded businesses are bashed. Somber advice to me had been not to remain in Belfast, so this was one of the weeks I chose to work in Dublin.

Mid-week prior to the planned march in Drumcree, police announced a bomb threat at Botanic train station, located about 100 yards from the Queen's housing where I was living. The ominous sight and sound of Army helicopters lasted throughout each of the nights of this week, and I could hear constant firings and explosives from nearby Sandy Row, a working class Protestant neighborhood known for its violent activity.

I took the Belfast-Dublin bus on Saturday, the day before Drumcree VI, avoiding the train because of threats from both Loyalists and Republicans to bomb railroad tracks on the route. The line waiting to board the bus reached all through the sizeable station and onto Great Victoria Street, but fortunately I had arrived early enough to be the very last person to be able to board the filled-to-capacity bus. More buses were called in to handle the crowds of passengers leaving Belfast. The usual two-hour forty-minute or so bus ride took four-and-a-half hours because of the increased traffic. Somewhat in jest, I asked an elderly Belfast woman sitting next to me how there could even be enough people left in the city to have a parade. She answered, "Those of us who have any sense at all leave." Fortunately, news reports on the Lower Ormeau Road march were uneventful. The reports on Drumcree and Gracey's defiant refusal to honor the Commission's order were, of course, much more repelling. Moreover, there was a fatality at an outbreak at an annual Orange Order bonfire in Larne, a small port city near Belfast on the Irish Sea.

Drumcree VII (2001)

The sudden resignation of David Trimble as First Minister on July 1, 2001[66] did not bode well for a peaceful Marching Season, nor indeed for the success of the GFA in general. The obstinance of the IRA in refusing to comply with its commitment to decommission only solidified as his announced July 1, date approached. This time, even the Nationalist *Irish News* pleaded with the IRA to disarm, reasoning that to do so would be a "sign of strength rather than weakness and would earn the gratitude of the Irish nation." [67]

In anticipation of Trimble's withdrawal, the streets of Belfast were reminiscent of pre-GFA, and even pre-1994, times. Rioters from both sides became virtual vigilantes, bombarding RUC and British soldiers with rocks, bricks, and gas bombs. In the Ardoyne area alone (a predominately Catholic section bordering the Falls and Shankill areas), more than 100 gasoline bombs and several homemade grenades injured thirty-nine officers. Sadly, some Protestants threw rocks at young Catholic schoolgirls leaving Ardoyne's Holy Cross Primary School, adjacent to one of the few Protestant streets in the section.[68] Drumcree VII loomed, and the picture was a bleak one.

The refusal of the Parades Commission to allow the Garvaghy Road route had by now become the general rule, rather than the exception such re-routings were originally intended to be. In 2001, more than 1,400 march participants gathered in protest at the blockade immediately following the Drumcree Church service on Sunday, July 8. The barbed wire and steel wall prohibiting access was approximately 16 feet high, and this time, some 1,600 additional British soldiers had arrived in Portadown, backed by NATO.

The estimated £6.5 million (over $9 million) for the necessary extra security was apparently money well spent, since the march itself was relatively peaceful. Two nights before the march, a convoy of thirty British Army trucks and tanks had indeed been attacked by stones thrown by some thirty Protestants in protest of their presence, but the march itself proceeded amazingly without incident, as RUC Chief Constable Flanagan had predicted. Trimble, together with Secretary of State John Reid, had called for a non-violent Drumcree, and the Rev. John Pickering's sermon at Drumcree Church reminded those in attendance that the barriers did not signify an end to the Orange Order. Rather, he reminded, that there should be a feeling "in our land...(of) hope and life for all of us." [69]

The residents of Portadown can take some consolation from the 2001 march, but the ominous entrance of additional troops, the blockade, and the public funds expended for security measures emphasizes the strife this annual event carries with it. Drumcree is a beast that seems determined to rear its ugly head annually, in spite of ample legislation to control the inevitable violence.

SOME COMPARISONS WITH RACIAL STRIFE AND DEMONSTRATIONS IN THE U.S.A.

It would be inaccurate and misleading to portray the United States as a country so plagued with demonstrations and the hostility they breed as is Northern Ireland. The relative size of the United States, the complexity of its population, and the absence of regular identification of virtually all the populace with one of two sides of a political-religious-cultural position all make a comparison difficult. Nonetheless, racial hatred has made its appearance in the parade/demonstration setting on American soil.

A Personal Experience

This is an issue on which I have some personal recollection from a legal perspective. In 1967, I practiced law as an associate with the Memphis, Tennessee firm of Burch, Porter and Johnson. The late Lucius E. Burch, Jr., the senior partner, assisted the Rev. Dr. Martin Luther King, Jr., in his efforts to obtain a marching permit. The purpose of the proposed march was to support the nearly all-black city garbage collection workers in their strike for higher wages and better benefits more in line with those of the general work forces. Mr. Burch was no stranger to legal controversy, and he was one of the most respected trial lawyers in the mid-South. He was a rare product of a patrician Nashville family (his father was dean of Vanderbilt Medical School, and the family had what is referred to in the South as "old" money), and he had compounded this substantial family wealth with his own earnings from years of a successful law practice. Nonetheless, he relished the opportunity to work *pro bono* for a cause in which he had a personal commitment.

As the firm's then "token-woman" (sexism was alive and well in the 1960's South), I usually was the first to arrive, and I had thus become the *de facto* maker of the coffee. (A good Southern lady always assumes such a domestic role as a second nature.)

While alone in the office one such morning a few days prior to the scheduled march through downtown Memphis, I answered the telephone. An angry female voice barked into the receiver, "That (expletive deleted) Lucius Burch will do anything for money. Tell him I hope he rots in hell for representing that n-----." She had hung up before I could explain that he was receiving no pay whatsoever for this work. So went life in an unenlightened, uninspired, and bigoted segment of the country in the 1960's....

Mr. Burch obtained the requisite permit, but the march was postponed because of an unexpected event—a snow storm. Such weather in Memphis, Tennessee in late March-early April was tantamount to a heat wave in the Austrian Alps in January. Nonetheless, Dr. King encouraged the workers to re-schedule the march for the following week, and he showed the sincerity of his support by remaining in Memphis, planning to march with them. The night before the second scheduled parade, he was shot and killed on the balcony of the Loraine Motel, where he was staying. This is an extreme example of the bitterness and hatred which can emerge in the United States from a demonstration in which race plays a role.

Constitutional Freedom of Speech

Although the First Amendment to the U.S. Constitution insures the right peaceably to assemble, it is another clause in the same constitutional section which is the basis for most claims of the right to demonstrate, *i.e.*, freedom of speech.[70] Interestingly, the right of peaceable assembly continues with the reason for such assembly, "to redress the government for grievances." In Northern Ireland, Unionists actually support their government, the United Kingdom. It is Nationalists who would be those who would engage in redress.

'Clear and Present Danger' and 'Fighting Words'

The Supreme Court has recognized action as "speech," provided it is expressive.[71] Nonetheless, there have been judicially created exceptions to speech that will not be afforded constitutional protection.[72] One of the earliest such exceptions is known as the "clear and present danger" doctrine which the Court adopted in *Schenck v. U.S.*, [73] a sedition case. Closely akin to the "clear and present danger" exception is the "fighting words" doctrine that removes from constitutional protection those words or expressive actions which would tend to arouse such anger in a reasonable person that he would respond with violence.

The "fighting words" principle was first used in *Chaplinsky v. N.H.* [74] It is difficult to distinguish between the two, since both are preventive in nature, much like the Parades Commission's preemptive banning or re-routing orders. Moreover, both are based upon the courts' belief that the freedom of speech which is limited is negatively counterbalanced by the harm which its exercise will incite. A fundamental distinction is that "clear and present danger" seemingly refers to the reaction of a group of people, a reaction that will likely have long-lasting harmful effects. The "fighting words" doctrine is generally used when the anticipated response to the message will come from a single person, or at least a small group of persons, and which will be spontaneous, reactionary, and immediate.

The "clear and present danger" doctrine was again applied in *Whitney v. California,* [75] in which the Court upheld California's Criminal Syndicalism Act that criminalized activity which advocated sabotage or other unlawful means of terrorism or voluntarily assembling in order to teach, inform, or advocate the illegal doctrines espoused. In *Whitney,* the convictions of members of a communist group were upheld after their public demonstration advocating communist principles. (Note that *Whitney* was overruled in 1969 by *Brandenburg v. Ohio,* [76] discussed below.)

As to the "fighting words" doctrine, the Court retreated in *Terminiello v. Chicago,* [77] a close (5-4) decision in 1949, actually a breach of the peace charge in which the First Amendment was the defense. The defendant had publicly criticized political and racial segments of society, referring to anyone who opposed his beliefs as "slimy scum," "snakes," "bedbugs," and other such unflattering—and offensive—terms. The difficulty with the *Terminiello* prosecution was the judge's overbroad charge to the jury of the meaning of breach of the peace. He had defined this crime as words that would "stir...the public to anger, invite dispute, (or) bring about a condition of unrest." Since the essence of the First Amendment is to protect language or expressive activity which invites dispute, had the definition been narrowed to exclude this phrase, it is likely that the conviction would have stood.

A somewhat erratic Court returned to the "fighting words" theory in *Feiner v. N.Y.* [78] In its 8-1 decision, the majority opinion viewed the defendant's soapbox appearance in a predominately black neighborhood in Syracuse, New York, as beyond the scope of constitutional protection. His speech was heard by seventy-five to eighty people, both black and white, a group sizeable enough to have impeded sidewalk passage for pedestrians so that they had to cross by going onto the street. (This had not been so in *Terminiello.*) The defendant had referred to the President of the United States as a "bum," to the American legion as a "Nazi Gestapo," and to the mayor of Syracuse as a "champagne-sipping bum...(who)...does not speak for the Negro people." Moreover, he urged blacks to "rise up in arms and fight for (equal rights)." Whether he intended his "stand up in arms" only metaphorically to indicate only that they persist and stay resolute is not clear. One bystander was heard to comment that if the police did not remove "that S.O.B.," he would do so himself. Most likely, in a similar situation in Northern Ireland in which a Nationalist urged fellow Catholics to "rise up in arms," the RUC would have taken immediate action to stifle his comments. In this sense, the *Feiner* opinion reflects the current security forces' probable duty in Northern Ireland. (Note, however, that the defendant in *Feiner* was supportive of blacks. This distinguishes these facts from those in later decisions where blacks are usually the objects of derision.)

In a 1969 decision, *Gregory v. Chicago*,[79] the Court addressed the situation in which public words had caused reaction unrest, even though this had not been the intention of the defendant. The opinion seemed to chastise the crowd for overreacting, making them essentially the guilty parties, rather than the defendant. Herein lies a pivotal legal proviso: would the Drumcree Catholics and the Lower Ormeau Road residents have been the "guilty" parties under the Gregory rationale?

Although not a racially charged expression, *Cohen v. California* [80] should be mentioned to illustrate the breadth of First Amendment protection in the United States. The defendant had worn a jacket with a profane anti-war message[81] in a Los Angeles courthouse in the presence of women and children. His conviction under the California disturbing-the-peace statute was overturned as an unconstitutional interference with his freedom of speech. Justice Harlan's majority opinion contained a conclusion that has often been quoted: "One man's vulgarity is another's lyric."

Gooding v. Wilson [82] concerned a Georgia breach of the peace law which the Court held invalid because of its overbroad language. Because of the facial unconstitutionality of the statute, the Court did not reach the merits, but the facts are significant in a comparison of racial hatred in the U.S. with the Protestant-Catholic animosity in Northern Ireland. During an anti-Vietnam rally (a war which unarguably did not bring out the best in many Americans) outside a draft office, the black defendant had shouted angrily to a policeman, "(you) white son-of-a-bitch, I'll kill you," surely not language which would inspire a mother of a young woman to invite him over for dinner. Transpose this language to a sectarian dispute with an RUC officer. Indubitably, the speaker would have been arrested and likely convicted, in spite of any sweeping words in the applicable statute. In the United States, the narrower the language, the more likely it is that a law that encroaches on constitutional rights will be upheld.

Collin v. Smith [83] was a case in which the Court denied certiorari. In such a refusal to rehear a case, particularly one with such controversial facts as in *Collin*, the message from the Court is generally assumed to have been a tacit affirmation of the federal appellate court's decision. This case involved a Nazi march which the court had permitted to take place on constitutional grounds. The law in question was a city ordinance of the city of Skokie, Illinois, the so-called "Racial Slur" provision. This law made it a misdemeanor to "public(ly) display...markings and clothing of symbolic significance" which would promote and incite racial or religious hatred. The group which had planned the demonstration was a Nazi organization, members of which would have worn Nazi uniforms and displayed swastikas for approximately one hour in front of the city hall. Significantly, Skokie had about 5,000 Jewish residents, many who were Holocaust survivors and for whom such visual reminders would inflict painful psychological memories and trauma. Traumatic consequences notwithstanding, the court held that "public expression of ideas may not be prohibited merely because the ideas are themselves offensive to some of their hearers."

Oddly, twenty-six years prior to *Collin* the Supreme Court had upheld an Illinois state statute that prohibited "group libel," defined as words that would prove offensive to identifiable groups, including those classified on the basis of race or religion. This 5-4 decision was *Beauharnais v. Illinois,*[84] a case which has not been expressly overruled. Nonetheless, it is questioned by many constitutional scholars as to whether it is still "good law," in view of later decisions. This holding approves a state's prevention of public social contempt of such an identifiable group of persons.

The Ku Klux Klan and Constitutional Freedom of Speech

Brandenburg v. Ohio, the case that overruled *Whitney,*[85] was a unanimous First Amendment victory in the spirit of *Collin.* Recall that the *Whitney* defendant had been convicted under an Ohio statute which prohibited any group meeting that taught or advocated any type of criminal syndication. A Ku Klux Klan leader, he had telephoned a Cincinnati television newsman to invite him to attend a KKK rally to be held on a farm not far from the city. The reporter accepted, and he filmed the activities. Twelve hooded people were at the rally, and some carried firearms. After gathering around a large wooden cross, they burned it. Even though the crude film made some of the speakers' words incomprehensible, some phrases denigrating both blacks and Jews were clear. A second film showed the defendant in KKK apparel, and his speech was in part: "We (the KKK) (are) not a revengeful organization, but if our President, our Congress, our Supreme Court continues to suppress the white, Caucasian race, it's possible that there might be some revenge taken. We are marching on Congress July the Fourth, 400,000 strong…(and later in)…St. Augustine, Florida…and Mississippi…. Personally, I believe the nigger should be returned to Africa, the Jew…to Israel." He also referred to Jews as "kikes."

In reversing the conviction and nullifying the Ohio statute as unconstitutional, the *per curiam* Court held that a simple abstract advocation of a resort to violence is not equivalent to actually readying a group to engage in violence. The distinction was between advocacy which was protected, and actual incitement to engage in unlawful activity which would not have been. Two concurring opinions would have expressly overruled the "clear and present danger" doctrine (Justices Black and Douglas, in separate opinions). Justice Douglas went somewhat farther, saying that in cases where the Court had applied the doctrine, "threats were often loud but always puny and made serious only by judges so wedded to the *status quo* that critical analysis made them nervous." Moreover, he classified the facts in *Brandenburg* as a "classic case where speech is brigaded with action." In his view, the speech and the act must be taken separately, and any prosecution should be launched only for the latter. He concluded that "government has no power to invade that sanctuary of belief and conscience."

If *Brandenburg* did not exalt freedom of speech sufficiently, *R.A.V. v City of St. Paul, Minnesota* [86] surely removed any doubt. This time, the Court was closely split (5-4). The majority struck down as unconstitutional a city ordinance which made criminal words which were insulting or which provoked violent acts "on the basis of race, color, creed, religion, or gender." Ruling that there simply are not any "categories of speech entirely invisible to the Constitution," the Court quite possibly issued an implied overruling of the "fighting words" exception created in *Chaplinsky*.

R.A.V. involved another KKK rally. The St. Paul city ordinance was among those generally referred to as "hate crime" laws which make criminal any activity specifically directed against a victim because of his belonging to an identifiable group (such as race or religion). Some forty states, including Wisconsin, had adopted such laws during the 1980's, but *R.A.V.* makes the future bleak for their constitutional validity. To compare with Northern Ireland, one might imagine members of a militant Orange Order as defendants who had used similar language about their Nationalist counterparts. A decision such as *R.A.V.,* which held them lawfully entitled to generate or foment physical violence, would probably be perceived as an official declaration that it is "open season" on Catholics.

An earlier lower court decision, *Knights of the KKK v. M.L.King, Jr. Worshippers*,[87] is a case on-target that involved an actual KKK march during a time that would prove offensive to non-participants. The Klan had filed an action in a Tennessee federal district court to compel local officials in the medium-sized town of Pulaski, Tennessee, to permit them to parade in the city streets on January 13, 1990. Their planned parade was to be a protest of the official designation of the birthday of Martin Luther King, Jr. as a federal holiday. A conflicting parade had been organized by the local Chamber of Commerce for the opposite purpose, *i.e.*, to serve as a observation of Dr. King's birthday.

A city ordinance permitted only one parade per day and gave preference to the group that first applied. Moreover, the ordinance forbade paraders to wear masks or disguises, an oblique reference to the usual regalia of the Klan. In this situation, the King celebratory parade organizers had submitted their application in August, 1989, and had already obtained the requisite permits for January 12, 13, 14, and 15, 1990, by the time the KKK objected and requested permission to continue with their plans for their own parade, a "Homecoming." Klan leaders claimed that their traditional Saturday-before-King's-birthday parade in Pulaski had been a custom of long-standing and this gave them the *de facto* right to march.

The federal judge held two provisions of the ordinance to be unconstitutional. One had provided for denial of a permit to "any individual or group based on anticipation of violence being instigated or riots incited…when, at the time of the (permit) application…there is a clear and present danger of imminent lawless action." The court cited *Hague v. C.I.O* [88] in holding this provision invalid because it could be used as an "instrument of arbitrary suppression of views on national affairs…." The Court also cited *Terminiello*, *Collin*, and *Brandenburg* as controlling. (*R.A.V.* post-dated the Tennessee dispute.) Similarly, the prohibition of masks and/ or disguises was also struck down, because of the strong symbolic message such attire connotes.

The victory for the KKK was a Pyrrhic one, however. The court enforced those provisions granting preference to the first applicant and limiting parades on the city streets to one per day (because of the size of the town, small relative to a city). Timing saved the Chamber of Commerce, but the court's message was unambiguous. Citing *Brandenburg*, the opinion reminded that the First Amendment does not allow proscription of expressive activity unless and until it is "directed to inciting or producing imminent lawless action and is likely to incite or produce such action."

A final KKK dispute probably will ultimately reach the U.S. Supreme Court. Because of the choice of counsel for the KKK (actually he was appointed by the American Civil Liberties Union, the ACLU), this situation was reported on national television. A Virginia statute expressly forbids any burning of a cross. As is typical of the Klan, a rally included such cross burning. Although the location was private property and the act was with the owner's consent, the event was seen by some by-standers who testified that they were disturbed by such activity. The defendant was a Klansman from Pennsylvania who had selected a rural southern town in conservative southwest Virginia (Carroll County) to hold his rally. After he was charged with having violated this state law, he contacted the Richmond, Virginia chapter of the ACLU for representation, and the task fell to David Baugh, a Richmond defense attorney of national reputation. (Baugh has since represented Mohamed Rashed Daoud al' Owhali, a defendant in the case involving the August 7, 1998, bombing of the American embassy in Kenya, resulting in the 213 deaths and thousands of injuries. The trial was set in New York state, but because New York had so recently resurrected the death penalty, there were no lawyers with capital murder representation experience as federal law requires for such charges. Baugh got the call, and he devoted an entire year to this work, away from his office in Richmond. He persuaded the jury to direct a sentence of life imprisonment rather than the death penalty which the government had sought.[89])

Why was the choice of counsel for the Klansman so newsworthy? It was because David Baugh is a black man, a member of one of the KKK's major hate-targeted groups. Nonetheless, he is an impassioned upholder of constitutional rights, and his list of despicable clients would probably reduce most mothers to tears. He told the author that he had expressly told the KKK defendant that he disliked everything about him, including what he had said and what he had done, but that he would work to the extent of his ability to uphold his right to express his beliefs, even in such a hate-filled manner. [Interestingly, the surname of the KKK-member defendant in the Virginia case is Black.] The Virginia Court of Appeals upheld the statute [90] but on appeal the Supreme Court of Virginia reversed, holding it unconstitutional on First Amendment grounds.[91] The Commonwealth of Virginia has petitioned the U.S. Supreme Court to grant certiorari. If the Court does hear the case, it would be difficult to predict a reversal, in view of *Brandenburg and R.A.V.*

Conclusion

Intolerance surely breeds hatred, and hatred breeds violence. There are some disturbing parallels between Northern Ireland's cultural-religious-political dissension and the racial divide in the U.S.A. It is perhaps the spirit of freedom for which the American states were created which elevates the law's relative permissiveness of activity, provided it is expressive in nature, even when it may result in rioting. Slavery and separation of the races was not initially an evident powder keg, so to speak.

Northern Ireland, on the other hand, has been from its inception a divided people, a by-product of the birth of the Free State of Ireland. It might be compared to young brothers, quite different in makeup, who do not play together well. One is eager to be taken to a movie, while the other more-active youngster prefers to be outside playing soccer. By parental order, they are confined to the indoors, where both are consequently miserable. Similarly, Northern Ireland as a region was in a congenital sense a combination of two distinctly disparate groups, neither of which is content with the *status quo* of sharing their single territory.

Probably much of the Orange Order activity would be routinely allowed under the American constitutional assurance of freedom of speech, and the rerouting and banning by the police and the Parades Commission would never meet constitutional muster. This only dramatizes the basic distinctions between the vast U.S.A. and the small province that is Northern Ireland. Most significantly, one must never forget the uniqueness of the history and background of the latter. Only in such light can both views—the American prevalence of constitutional rights, and the parade banning and re-routing possibilities in Northern Ireland—be understood as lawful.

Endnotes to Chapter 2

[1] BELFAST TELEGRAPH, July 3, 2000, explaining the Parades Commission's decision to reroute the 2000 Orange Order Parade in Portadown.

[2] A listing of these parades can be found in Kevin Haddick-Flynn, ORANGEISM: THE MAKING OF A TRADITION (Wolfhound Press Ltd., Dublin, Ireland, 1999), Appendix E.

[3] Neil Jarman, *Regulating Rights and Managing Public Order: Parade Disputes and the Peace Process*, 22 FORDHAM INTERNATIONAL LAW JOURNAL 1416 (1999).

[4] *Id.*

[5] Civil Authorities (Special Powers) Act (N.I.) 1922.

[6] Public Order Act 1936. *See* Jarman, *supra* note 3 at 1421.

[7] Public Order (N.I.) Act 1951.

[8] *See* Civil Rights Act of 1964, 42 U.S.C: §§2000 *et seq.*

[9] Jarman, *supra* note 3 at 1417.

[10] Haddick-Flynn, *supra* note 2 at 342.

[11] Hume was the leader of the more moderate of the two Nationalist parties, the Social Democratic and Labor Party (SDLP), during the peace negotiations. (The other Nationalist party, *Sinn Féin*, is considerably more extreme.) Hume and David Trimble, the first First Minister for the New Northern Ireland Assembly borne from the GFA, were awarded the prestigious Nobel Peace Prize for their work during the talks which led to the signing of the GFA. Trimble was the leader of the largest—and relatively moderate—of the Unionist parties, Ulster Unionist Party (UUP).

[12] Haddick-Flynn, *supra* note 2 at 342.

[13] Public Order (Amendment) Act (N.I.) 1970.

[14] Public Order (Amendment) Act (N.I.) 1971.

[15] Public Order (N.I.) Act 1987.

[16] Conversation, July 6, 2000, in Belfast. The judge requested that he remain anonymous.

[17] Haddick-Flynn, *supra* note 2 at 343.

[18] Jarman, *supra* note 3 at 1419.

[19] Haddick-Flynn, *supra* note 2 at 342.

[20] *Supra* note 16.

[21] Parades Commission Chair Tony Holland, quoted in the July 3, 2000, issue of BELFAST TELEGRAPH.

[22] Haddick-Flynn, *supra* note 2 at 343.

[23] *Id.* At 345.

[24] *Id.* At 346.

[25] *Id.* At 347.

[26] Public Prosecutions Etc. (N.I.) Act 1998, Ch. 2 (Eng.).

[27] *See* Public Order (Amendment) Act (N.I.) 1970, *supra* note 13.

[28] Jarman, *supra* note 2 at 1423.

[29] *Id.* At 1425.

[30] Haddick-Flynn, *supra* note 2 at 348.

[31] *See supra* note 26.

[32] *Id.* §3.

[33] *Id.* §4.

[34] *Id.* §5.

[35] *Id.* §6.

[36] *Id.* §6 (5)(a).

[37] Pub. Procession (N.I.) Act 1998 (Notice of Processions (Exceptions Order 1998).

[38] *Supra* note 26, §§ 7, 6(10), 7(9).

[39] Jarman, *supra* note 3 at 1432.

[40] *Id.* at 1433. Note that §9 of the law gives the RUC the right to appeal, a Commission order.

[41] Public Processions (N.I.) Act 1998. Ch. 2 (Eng.).

[42] Haddick-Flynn, *supra* note 2 at 351.

[43] A well-respected dean of a Church of Ireland parish in Belfast told me that, in his opinion, Paisley had been the single most influential person who had kept conflict alive in Northern Ireland, albeit unintentionally. Further, a notable judge in the province described the reverend-politician (one hardly knows which of Paisley's "hats" to list first) as "part of the problem, not part of the solution."

[44] Haddick-Flynn, *supra* note 2 at 351.

[45] *Id.* at 353.

[46] Jarman, *supra* note 3 at 1437.

[47] Liam Clarke, *Trimble plea for calm at Drumcree march*, THE SUNDAY TIMES, July 2, 2000, at 1.

[48] *Orange Order takes case to European court* THE SUNDAY TIMES, July 2, 2000, at 1.

[49] This treaty was signed by some forty nations (now forty-one, with Georgia, one of the former Union of Soviet Socialist Republics, being the most recent member).

[50] Twenty of the signatory nations to the EHRC are parties to this agreement.

[51] *Supra* note 48.

[52] Art. 11. Cf. With America's constitutional freedom of assembly, U.S. CONST. Amend. I.

[53] Full text statement from Tony Holland, Parades Commission Chair, THE IRISH NEWS, July 4, 2000, at 18. Chairman Holland warned Loyalists that the Grand Lodge's order to all members not to engage in any formal contact with the Commission, nor to permit any other members to do so, "just does not help their case."

[54] Ric Clark, *Parades can take place*, BELFAST NEWS-LETTER, July 5, 2000, at 1, col. 1-5.

[55] *Id.*

[56] Ross McKee, *Flanagan in warning to ex-prisoners*, BELFAST NEWS LETTER, July 5, 2000, at 4, col. 1-5.

[57] *Id.* Note the Chief's use of the word "service," rather than "force." This was no slip of the tongue, for he was intentionally using the term that would substitute for the word "force" in the new post-GFA law restructuring the RUC. Many of the changes are difficult for RUC members, and Flanagan himself told me of some personal pain with the projected name change from Royal Ulster Constabulary to Police Service of Northern Ireland, because of the RUC's history and tradition. His remark referring to the "service" characterizes Flanagan as a professional who accepts change and as one who seeks to appease, rather than to incite. (See Chapter 7 on police restructuring.)

[58] Monika Unsworth, *Portadown Loyalists are outraged as parade ban is upheld*, THE IRISH TIMES, July 8, 2000, at 6, col. 5.

[59] Darwin Templeton, *Orange concern at Drumcree violence*, BELFAST TELEGRAPH, July 6, 2000, at 1, col. 1-5.

[60] Ryan Harkness, *Archbishop call for restraint*, BELFAST NEWS LETTER, July 5, 2000, at 4, col. 2-4., quoting Archbishop of Armagh Dr. Robin Eames as "deplor(ing) and condemn(ing)" the violence and words or actions leading to violence, and Drumcree Church rector the Rev. John Pickering, as asking for the "utmost respect to be shown to church property."

See also Darwin Templeton, *supra* note 59, quoting Presbyterian Moderator Trevor Morrow as calling the protests all over Northern Ireland "essentially out of control" and asking the Orange Order to end its refusal to comply with the Parades Commission Order.

[61] *Archbishop warns on risks of protest*, THE IRISH TIMES, July 10, 2000, at 6, col. 5-8.

[62] *Church of Ireland cannot condone Drumcree events*, THE IRISH TIMES, July 11, 2000, at 14, col. 2-7.

[63] Paul Tanney, *Portadown district master refuses to condemn violence at Drumcree*, THE IRISH TIMES, July 8, 2000, at 6, col. 1-3.

[64] Gerry Moriarity, *Sequencing comes to the fore again on the eve of Drumcree*, THE IRISH TIMES, July 8, 2000, at 7, col. 1-5.

[65] Warren Porter, *Two voices calling us from brink of madness*, THE IRISH TIMES, July 8, 2000, at 7, col. 6.

[66] Trimble had given ample notice that he would step down on July 1, if the IRA had not fulfilled its already past-due GFA commitment to decommission (disarm).

[67] *Irish accord in peril*, RICHMOND TIMES-DISPATCH (NEW YORK TIMES News Service), June 23, 2001, at 1, col. 2-4.

[68] *Streets of Belfast awash in hate*, RICHMOND TIMES-DISPATCH (Associated Press), June 22, 2001, at A-4, col. 2-5.

[69] *Oranier-Parade verlief gewaltfrei*, (*Orange Parade goes peacefully*), SALZBURGER NACHRICHTEN (SALZBURG NEWS, Austria), July 9, 2001, at 6, col. 2-5.

[70] The so-called "four freedoms" in the First Amendment, the first of the 10 Bill of Rights adopted in 1791, are freedoms of speech, religion, press, and the right peaceably to assemble and to redress the government for grievances.

[71] *See, e.g.*, Texas v. Johnson, 109 S.Ct. 2533 (1989), where the Court held invalid a Texas statute which made it a criminal act to desecrate any of several listed revered objects, expressly including the state and national flags. The defendant had publicly burned the U.S. flag at a public demonstration in Dallas during the 1982 Republican convention during which President Reagan was re-nominated. He had rebuked the Reagan administration's war policy and had burned the flag to show his disgust for the federal government. A 5-4 Court held that such expressive activity was protected under the First Amendment's freedom of speech.

[72] *See, e.g.,* Roth v. U.S., 354 U.S. 476 (1976), in which the Supreme Court held pornography beyond the scope of constitutional protection.

[73] 249 U.S. 47 (1919).

[74] 315 U.S. 568 (1942).

[75] 274 U.S. 357 (1927).

[76] 395 U.S. 444 (1969).

[77] 337 U.S. 1 (1949).

[78] 340 U.S. 315 (1951).

[79] 394 U.S. 111 (1969).

[80] 403 U.S. 15 (1971).

[81] The jacket bore the words "F— the draft" in bold, large letters.

[82] 405 U.S. 518 (1972).

[83] 578 F.2d 1197 (7th Cir.), cert. denied, 439 U.S. 916 (1978).

[84] 343 U.S. 250 (1952).

[85] The citation for *Brandenburg* is in endnote 76, and *Whitney* is cited in endnote 75.

[86] 505 U.S. 377 (1992).

[87] 735 F.Supp. 745 (M.D. Tenn. 1990).

[88] 307 U.S. 496, 516 (1939).

[89] Alan Cooper, *Baugh: System met its challenge*, RICHMOND TIMES-DIS-PATCH.

[90] Record No. 1581-99-3 (December 19, 2000).

[91] 553 S.E.2d 738 (Va. 2001).

Chapter 3

Religion and Racism

"The trouble with Ireland (the island) is that we have too many Catholics and too many Protestants and not enough Christians."

Frank Carson, Irish comedian

Beloved Irish comedian Frank Carson's profundity reminds one that Christians, by doctrine, do not kill other Christians because they worship the same Christ in a different building and in a somewhat different manner. Nonetheless, since the plantation era and the Penal Laws, there has been a hostility between Catholics and Protestants in Ireland which has survived only in the divided province of Northern Ireland. This chapter will not re-hash the law-based early religious discrimination in Ireland already expounded upon in Chapter 1, but will rather begin with the religious objections to the 1920 partition and what this has portended for the province of Northern Ireland.

One can draw many analogies between Northern Ireland's division into two camps—Catholic and Protestant—and the ugliness of racism in the United States. Both stem from a lack of tolerance or appreciation of the inherent genetic or cultural differences between groups of people. From a more negative perspective, both have at times been solidified by the support of law.

The issue of religious differences in the U.S.A. has not been so divisive,[1] most likely because one of the funadamental reasons early Europeans left their homelands to seek a new home was to attain religious liberties. In its place has been a frequency of racially charged incidents which have produced in many ways the same problem as has the animosity arising out of religious differences in Northern Ireland.

Religious Division in Northern Ireland

Surely Daniel O'Connell's achievement of Catholic Emancipation in Ireland in 1829[2] was not expected to be a magic wand which would suddenly expunge all the years of anti-Catholic discrimination to which the law had lent a heavy helpful hand. The distrust of those who had demeaned and made unlawful the practice of their religion was embedded in the hearts and souls of most Catholics. History is simply not amenable to any such instant antidote.

The so-called Penal Laws were exactly as the name suggests—these statutes made their homeland a veritable prison for Catholics. Catholics were not legally permitted to own land. They had no right to vote. And they certainly had no right before O'Connell's miracle legislation to worship in their own churches. Most of Ireland's (Republic of Ireland and Northern Ireland alike) most glorious churches are Church of Ireland, rather than Catholic. 1829 was clearly past the age of Gothicism, so any Catholic church of that style is neo-Gothic. Perhaps in Dublin is this the most obvious, for the two large and most visited cathedrals are both Church of Ireland. The newer is St. Patrick's, the national cathedral, built in 1192, and the other, Christ Church, is the cathedral of Dublin, built in 1172. [For the American, perceiving something dated 1192 as "newer" is difficult indeed.] Christ Church has a lovely and intricate choral loft, Irish stone Gothic doorway, and sixty-eight foot high nave. Dean Jonathan Swift, author of *Gulliver's Travels, A Modest Proposal* (the actual title was "Modest Proposal for Preventing the Children of Poor People from Being a Burden to Their Parents"), and several other political satires in the late 17th-early 18th centuries, served as dean of St. Patrick's from 1713 until his death in 1745, and the grandeur of this magnificent edifice defies a verbal description. The two cathedrals are only a couple of blocks apart, visible as a part of Dublin's skyline and on every tourist book's list of "must-sees" in Dublin.

On the other hand, the Catholic St. Mary's Cathedral, or the Pro-Cathedral, is situated in a more down-graded section north of the River Liffey, down a smaller side street, away from most traffic. It is not surrounded by lovely grounds as is St. Patrick's, nor does it have the beautiful contiguous Gothic side-building (now *Dublinia*, museum of the history of Dublin) as has Christ Church. Moreover, the so-called Pro-Cathedral (which actually means "provisional," or temporary, cathedral, but rarely is indeed temporary) is not on the usual tourist route, and it is not a building particularly interesting from the exterior. The neo-classical interior somewhat compensates for the relatively drab outside, but it cannot compete with the detail and exquisite moldings of Christ Church and St. Patrick's. This was a product of the mindset of early 19th century Ireland, where Catholics might at last have been permitted by law to worship in their own churches, but they would not be as sweeping and impressive as the already established Churches of Ireland. The back-street drab location was the best that Dublin's Anglo-Irish rulers would permit. [3]

Ireland's nondenominational educational system was established under Edward Stanley in 1831,[4] veritably on the heels of O'Connell's legislative freedom for Catholics. The problem was that nondenominational schooling was a contradiction in terms to the Catholic hierarchy, to which education was regarded as a religious right. The trend in public education toward secularization made the Catholic Church cautious about a political change which might have implications for the education of Catholic children.[5] This was particularly so in the heavily Protestant North.

The first confirmation of these fears came via Ulster Unionist Sir Edward Carson's proposal to instigate a local body authorized by statute to assess an education tax in response to the rapid growth of school-age children in Belfast. [Author's note: Carson's statue rises in the foreground of Stormont, the imposing building where the first Northern Ireland Parliament was housed, as is the current New Northern Ireland Assembly. Having to pass this paragon to Unionism on their way into legislative sessions must have a significant effect on the rate of the adrenalin flow of *Sinn Féin* Assembly members.] Carson's plan blossomed into a full-fledged educational reform under the control of a department of education, an advisory committee, and county education committees.[6] The schools issue is the topic of a separate chapter (see Chapter 9), but this illustration of pre-partition Catholics' fears was to no small extent grounded in the effects to be wrought on public education.

Catholic Opposition to Partition

One priest in Down and Connor (now part of Northern Ireland), Bishop John Tohill, testified to a 1887 committee formed to inquire to claims of abuse of Catholics in Belfast that Catholics had been treated as "an inferior and conquered race."[7] Thirty years later during talk of the possibility of partition, the consensus among Catholic clergy was that partition would "insult...Irish nationality." [8]

Upon the assurance from Welshman David Lloyd George, United Kingdom Prime Minister, that any division would be a temporary one, a group of 130 priests voted at a Belfast conference on June 23, 1916 in favor of such a Unionist establishment.[9] The aura of deception led to the withdrawal of most support for the proposed division, but the seed of anti-partitionism had been planted, albeit on ground not fertile enough to prevent the passage of the law providing for the official division of Ireland.[10]

Partition gave twenty-six counties to the *Saorstát Éireann* (Free State of Ireland), permitting a dominion status of self-government.[11] The remaining six counties of the northeast, which were predominately Protestant, formed the province of Northern Ireland, which remained under direct control of the Westminster Parliament. The Catholic Church did not sit silently by on the sidelines when thousands of Catholic workers were terminated by the shipyards in Belfast in July, 1920. Bishop MacRory, Bishop Tohill's successor at the Diocese of Down and Connor, appealed to Boston's Bishop O'Connell for some aid to starving unemployed Catholics in Belfast, referring to Northern Ireland as being the left-over from a "mutilated" Ireland composed of "six amputated counties."[12] MacRory bitterly reproached the British Minister for his government's inadequate protection of Catholics in Northern Ireland during the Belfast riots. He reminded that the desire of four-fifths of the people of Ireland (*i.e.*, the twenty-six counties of the Free State and the minority in Northern Ireland of Catholics) had been ignored and supplanted by the wish of somewhat over three fifths of the less-populated northern six counties, resulting in a compulsion of the remaining 36% in the north (Catholics) to live under a British regime against their will.[13]

The effect of a treaty negotiated in 1921 [14] had been to make the later-Republic of Ireland (the twenty-six counties) much more autonomous than had the partition legislation of the prior year. The six counties remained as they were upon partition except for their having a separate Parliament, but Catholics were somewhat assuaged by the treaty's creation of a Boundary Commission to re-study the North-South border. One of the six Catholic Members of Parliament representing the province of Northern Ireland, Arthur Griffith, had unwisely given false assurances to Catholic bishops that (i) the treaty would contain sufficient safeguards on education, and (ii) Derry would be transferred to the Free State. On this basis, the bishops had supported the treaty,[15] a move they would later regret.

Michael Collins, no stranger to American moviegoers after the 1990's Liam Neeson-Julia Roberts film on the 1921 Civil War in Ireland, was another of the six Catholics representing Northern Ireland in Parliament. Collins had achieved the Free State status as his clear second choice to full independence, and many (including later Prime Minister of Ireland Eamon de Valera, another of the six Northern Ireland Catholic Parliamentary representatives) denounced him for having "sold out." [16] In an effort to restore some modicum of peace on the streets of Belfast, Collins' proposal to further the cause of Catholic rights was adopted.[17] This proposal created three committees, one each on (i) study of the policing issue, (ii) investigation of outrages, and (iii) oversight of governmental relief fund distribution. Reading the basis of the policing problems in 1922—under-representation of Catholics on the force and police mistreatment of Catholics—is an eerie repetition of the same complaints which later gave rise to the post-GFA Police Bill.

With regard to the Boundary Commission, a series of grievances was presented by Catholic clergy. One was Father Philip O'Doherty, who dramatically referred to Belfast as a "heathendom" where the politicians left Catholics with "no country," obsessed with a hate against all Catholics which would compel him (the politician), if possible, to "redden the soil of Ireland with the blood of its Catholic people." He further charged that this was a reprise of the penal codes which would, if allowed to continue, result in "the Mass...(being) forbidden, and the priest declared a felon." [18] Any hope which the Boundary Commission had instilled in Northern Catholics was doused when the head of governments in Ireland, Northern Ireland and Britain agreed that the boundary should remain as established in 1920.

Mary Harris, an Irish historian at the University of North London who specializes in the Catholic Church in Northern Ireland, assesses the politics of Northern Ireland by the end of the 1920's as having been "set firmly in a sectarian mold." [19] She notes a shift from the political front to the church for the efforts to attack the social ills which plagued Catholics. [20]

A Personal Perspective on Northern Ireland Clergy in General

Coming from a country literally founded on religious freedom principles, I am surely accustomed to a superfluity of denominations within Christianity. Somehow, I had expected the "three religions" in Northern Ireland to be Church of Ireland (counterpart to the Episcopal Church in the U.S.A.), Presbyterian Church (which I had figured would run a far second to the Church of Ireland), and Roman Catholic. It came as somewhat of a shock to learn that the Presbyterians substantially outnumbered the Church of Irelanders, and that among Protestant churches, Methodist churches are a fairly strong third. Even more surprisingly were the many, many evangelical sects, so many that Belfast, from the perspective of churches, resembles a typical section of the U.S.A.

The most pivotal two groups are, of course, (i) all Protestants and (ii) Catholics. The following represents my own deductions drawn from personal experiences, conversations and contacts while in Northern Ireland.

The Rev. Ian Paisley Sr.

The Rev. Ian Paisley is the leader of the most right wing of the Unionist parties, the Democratic Unionist Party (DUP) which he founded in 1971. He has served as North Antrim's representative to the Westminster Parliament since 1970, and has been elected to the European Parliament since 1979. His title includes the honorary doctorate (from Bob Jones University in Greenville, South Carolina; see discussion on U.S. law on racial discrimination later in this chapter), and his name is always—*always*—followed by the letters M.P., M.E.P., and now MLA (member of the New Northern Ireland Assembly, or Member of the Legislative Assembly). He is legendary for his hell-fire-and-damnation preaching and his hatred of anything Catholic. When Pope John Paul I died suddenly in 1978, Paisley publicly denounced Belfast City Hall for having lowered the British flag as a sign of mourning.

One anecdote tells of a fictional Catholic nun who ran out of gas while driving down a country road in County Antrim, Northern Ireland. She went into the nearest farmhouse for help, and the young farmer, who was the father of a two-year old, readily assured her that he would siphon enough gasoline from his truck to get her to a nearby town. However, he could find only a baby potty as a container for the gasoline. This did not disturb the grateful nun, who then began walking down the road carrying the potty filled with gasoline. As she was pouring the liquid into her empty tank, the Rev. Dr. Paisley happened to drive by in his spacious country car. Amazed at what he saw, he stopped, rolled down his window, and said to the good sister, "Lady, I wouldn't give a hoot for your religion, but I sure do admire you for your faith."

While at Queen's in Spring, 1998, I was determined to hear this man whom I had seen on American television for so many years. He is well-known for his so-called "silent collection," and as rumor goes, he has instructed the ushers at his Martyrs Memorial Free Presbyterian Church—always filled to the brim at the 11:30 am Sunday service—not to accept any coins. [It struck me that perhaps the Rev. Paisley has not read the New Testament parable of the widow with only two coins. When she was criticized by the pharisees for putting only two coins in the collection, Jesus rejoined them that she had given all she had and, thus, was to be praised rather than censured.[21]]

Another source told me of Paisley's inevitable vocal reprimand from the pulpit to any woman who appeared in his church either (i) not wearing a hat or (b) dressed in pants. [These accounts are not confirmed, but I heard each several times.] Although my practice is not to wear pants to church, neither is it to wear a hat. Thus, I opted instead of attending his church to hear one of the Rev. Paisley's Bible services each Friday at 12:30 pm in front of Belfast City Hall.

When I called City Hall to be certain that he would speak that day, the receptionist informed me that the city government had nothing to do with his appearances, since it was not on City Hall grounds, but rather on the public sidewalk. When I remarked to her that I really wanted to hear him before I returned to the U.S.A., she asked, "Where are you?" When I answered that I was at the law school at Queen's, a mile south of City Hall, she suggested, "Just open your window. I'm sure you'll hear him."

Indeed, the Rev. Dr. Paisley will never be accused of failing to project, or of needing a microphone. With his small bank of elderly street musicians and his omnipresent bodyguard, an ominous looking large young man garbed in a long black coat, Paisley boomed about the dangers of burning in hell, a fate from which he had convinced me in only twenty minutes that I had no hope of avoiding, nor did anybody whom I had ever met. He convinced me of the advisability of sticking with my more peaceful Church of Ireland Sunday morning atmosphere so as to avoid total depression.

Among my scheduled interviews during Summer, 2000, was one with Ian

Paisley, Jr., one of the elder Paisley's twin sons and the only one who has followed in his father's political footsteps. Also a MLA, the younger Paisley is presumably being groomed to take up the reins of the DUP leadership when his father retires or dies, whichever comes first. The DUP staunchly opposed the GFA, and its determined and inflexible anti-Agreement campaign had begun to gain momentum shortly before the May 22, 1998, vote. A young barrister in Belfast who was also my friend and colleague at Queen's University-Belfast told me of a DUP poster she spotted in heavily-Unionist North Belfast shortly before the referenda, which read: "Vote 'no' on the GFA and stop Popism, feminism, and sodomy." (My friend and I searched in vain to any such inference which might be drawn from the provisions of the GFA. However, at our post-election day chuckle, we did agree that surely if more of Northern Ireland's voting population had realized that the GFA endorsed these three principles, the outcome would have been different indeed.)

Mr. Paisley Jr. had confirmed months earlier his meeting with me for August 3, 2000. He had written that I should contact him when I arrived in Belfast on July 2 to confirm a time, which he preferred to be in the morning. I called, and asked that he return my call. Not having heard again about a definite time, I telephoned three times the week prior to the scheduled meeting. Each time I told his secretary (once) and assistant (twice) that I would suggest 10 am. He still did not return my call, so I called and left the message with his secretary that I would assume 10 am was convenient, if I did not hear further from him.

To reach the DUP office in southeast Belfast, one must take a bus into town and transfer to another bus, a somewhat time consuming task, since buses on the island of Ireland never seem to connect conveniently. Mr. Paisley was not in his office when I arrived promptly at 10 am, and his secretary told me that he was not even in Belfast that day. Moreover, she insisted that she was unable to reach him, and she seemed unconcerned, telling me only to call him the following week to see if he might meet with me another time.

My remaining time in Belfast was both short and full of appointments. Scheduling over twenty meetings within a month is a Domino-type process—should one cancel, it is nearly impossible to find an alternate time, since that would entail rescheduling another (and probably another because of the first rescheduled, etc., *ad infinitum*). This was the only time I was treated rudely during my nearly seven months work in Belfast. When I had asked if the Rev. Paisley Sr. might meet with me in his son's absence (his church is only a few doors away from the party headquarters), the office secretary told me was out of the city and would not return for two weeks.

This was untrue, for I passed the church on my way walking back to Queen's (I was too angry to take the buses). The sign out front announced that Dr. Paisley would preach that following Sunday (this was a Thursday) on the 54th anniversary of his ordination. It seemed quite quixotic that this rudeness and deception came from the son of and personnel who worked for the man who presented himself as a true man of God, demeaning all other denominations in the process.

This did not personally endear the Rev. Paisley to me, and it seemed to be a bigotry which might characterize one who considers himself religious, but who is indeed not spiritual. When Jesus was asked which of the Commandments were the greatest, He answered that firstly, one must love and serve God with his whole heart. Secondly, he is to love his neighbor as himself.[22] This may be an unfair conclusion, since I was unable to meet the Rev. Paisley himself, but somehow, my impression that day was that the Rev. Paisley and his colleagues perhaps had missed the second part of that scripture.

This solidified in my mind that the real issue had nothing to with religion and such, but, that, rather, politics and culture had been what had led the path into Troubles. (I should note that, after I insisted and refused to leave the office until she tried to contact someone with whom I might meet—rudeness begets rudeness—the secretary finally located Mark Robinson, another member of the Assembly. Robinson then advised her that he could meet with me at 12:30 pm, some two hours later, at DUP headquarters. This meeting did take place.)

Neither the secretary nor the assistant had offered me any help at all. This was my only meeting in Ireland or Northern Ireland where I was not greeted with friendliness and offered a cup of coffee or tea. Yet, there were religious pamphlets available for the taking. After the un-Christian treatment I had experienced, they seemed oddly out of place.

Church of Ireland

The Protestant Church of Ireland—Ireland's parallel to the Church of England and the Episcopal Church in the U.S.A. (*i.e.,* all belong to the Anglican Communion)—became the official state church in all of Ireland in 1671,[23] due to the British conquest. At that early date, approximately 300,000 of the population of the island was Protestant, and about 800,000 Catholic.[24] This official state status ended with the 1869 Church Disestablishment Act.

The 1937 Constitution not only assured freedom of religion,[25] but also provided for the absence of an established state church.[26] Nonetheless, there remains the name "Church of Ireland." This can indeed be somewhat confusing to the visitor to Ireland or Northern Ireland, since it understandably generates perceptions of an official state church. When one falsely believes that the Church of Ireland is indeed the state church, he is puzzled to be informed that the majority of the people in the Republic of Ireland nonetheless identify themselves as Catholic.[27]

The Church of England (which is the "mother church" of the Church of Ireland, both being parts of the Anglican communion, Protestant since Reformation) was first mentioned as far back as 314 A.D., when three British bishops attended the Council of Arles.[28] Interestingly, the Church of England recognized the pope as the head of the Church until the 16th century Reformation under Henry VIII.

This monarch was able to persuade Parliament to enact legislation making the king (or queen) the head of the church instead of the pope.[29] After partition, the Church of Ireland quite naturally remained the official church in Northern Ireland.[30]

My other two official visits with clerics proved not only informative, but also friendly and genuine. [Since the Rev. Paisley plays a dual role as both political figure and clergyman, I consider him a cleric, or, in this sense, at least a quasi-cleric. This is even though the purpose of my intended meeting with someone at DUP was for political, rather than religious or sectarian, information.] The first was with the Right Rev. James Moore, Bishop of Connor, the largest Church of Ireland diocese in Northern Ireland.

I had met Bishop Moore on one prior occasion when he came to my public lecture on U.S. law and the death penalty in March, 1998, while I was on the law faculty at Queen's University. He is an insightful and well-informed man, and I knew he would be able to give me a good perspective on the church's role and position in troubled Northern Ireland.

Bishop Moore has lived in the Republic of Ireland, but he has spent most of his professional life in Northern Ireland. Completely inapposite to the Rev. Paisley, he told me that he did not see his role as telling church people how to vote. He explained that his job is to "deal with their souls," not their political preferences! Yet he lauded the church for having encouraged persons from different denominations to talk together ecumenically. Because churches in Northern Ireland have automatically been identified with the division, placed on one side or the other, in his view such inter-church dialogue is imperative. With regard to the Rev. Paisley, the Bishop said simply that he "represents a large chunk of people" and that "they (Paisleyites) are (therefore) worth listening to." His main concern was the Paisley approach, which he termed "always on the attack, always negative—almost like an angry child." Nonetheless, he acknowledged that many good people see Paisley as "on their side," adding that he himself "fully appreciate(s) that feeling." His rejoinder revealed his own leanings, however, when he said—referring to Paisley's hard-line, anti-GFA stance—"but I think Trimble is right." (The bishop was speaking, of course, of Trimble's instrumental role in attaining approval of the GFA.)

The major thrust of Bishop Moore's communications with me indicated that he is a good man and a good Christian, one who does not distinguish Catholics and Protestants with regard to their relative "goodness." He frequently interjected levity into our meeting, and he told me that he was a "bit tired" from attending the recent weddings of two of his nephews. Both had married Catholic young women (a fact which the bishop found had no bearing whatsoever on their spiritual well-being), and one nephew had insisted that his uncle be permitted to participate in the marriage ceremony. Bishop Moore had been a part of the other nephew's ceremony, but that was in another parish and another town, and this one proved to be different. He laughed over his nephew's angry reaction when the priest told him that having his uncle be a part of the service would not be possible: "This is my Uncle Jimmy! And he's a *bishop!*" He surmised that this nephew had himself not been in church in a longer time than his uncle cared to know, so he had a chuckle over this sudden burst of dismay over sectarian decorum which his younger relative had deemed incorrect and narrow-minded.

Differences in Christian denominations bothered him "not a twit," he told me. He clearly is a man who realizes that we all are answerable to the same God, and— critical to the situation in Northern Ireland—that differences in groups of people must be recognized and accepted. When I asked his opinion on whether there would ever be a united Ireland, he responded that "in due course, there'll be an all-Ireland." His only proviso was an economic one. He compared the situation with the unification of East and West Germany, in which the West was financially able to sustain the newly annexed East and to survive the costs.

He added that he is "not so sure that the Celtic Tiger is strong enough (now) to absorb Northern Ireland." [31] ("Celtic Tiger" is a term referring to Ireland's burgeoning economy after years of relative poverty and unemployment.)

There is a Church of Ireland Board for Social Responsibility (Northern Ireland) established by the General Synod of the Church of Ireland (*i.e.*, the governing body of the Church of Ireland in its entirety). Members include both clergy and laity from all parts of the province. Since its purpose is to comment upon social issues and proposed legislation for Northern Ireland, its existence might at first seem to be somewhat at odds with Bishop Moore's position that the church's role is not a political one. However, this body is informative in nature, and its role is not that of taking a political stance. Rather, a church member might obtain some insight on current legal and political issues and ponder upon them individually, taking into consideration the doctrine and positions of the Church. [32]

The Catholic Church in Northern Ireland

The atrocities upon Catholics throughout history, the most diabolical having been carried out during the Cromwell era, are outlined in Chapter 1. Repetitious though it may not be, it is important to remember that although Catholics make up the vast majority of those claiming a religious affiliation in the Republic of Ireland (about 95%), they are a minority in Northern Ireland. However, they are growing in size in the province, and many Protestants joke that because of the rate of reproduction among Catholics and the church's official position on birth control, "they are gaining on us."

About twenty years ago, most figures listed 35% Catholics and 65% Protestants as the ratio. This imbalance is shifting, and the usual figure cited currently is nearly 45% to 55%. [33]

A few months prior to my scheduled arrival in Belfast in summer, 2000, I had contacted Clonard Monastery in the Falls area of Belfast to ask for a meeting with one of the priests. The new Rector, Father Brendan O'Rourke, surprised me by having responded by telephone from Northern Ireland. As a "newcomer" to Belfast (he had been there only since fall, 1999) and a native of County Wexford in the southeast of the Republic, he explained that a longer-serving member of the community (the term referring to the resident priests) would be much more informative for purposes of my research than would he. Father O'Rourke evidenced his newness to Northern Ireland when he added, "I must admit that each time I travel back home, I still breathe a sigh of relief when the bus passes from Newry and over into Dundalk." (Newry is a border town in Northern Ireland, and Dundalk is the first town in the Republic on the Belfast-Dublin route.)

Clonard Monastery is situated on Clonard Gardens, a cul-de-sac off West Belfast's Falls Road. The church—Church of the Most Holy Redeemer—is a massive French Gothic structure with a huge (22' diameter) rose window, and both the exterior and interior are impressive. The nave is 150' in length (1/2 size of a football field), and the area above the altar is laid with mosaics and a lamb's wool tapestry (fitting indeed for the island of Ireland!). Another usage of local resources is the altar, constructed of stone quarried in the famed Mountains of Mourne in County Down.[34] The surprisingly large brick monastery is attached, much as a parish house would be. The Redemptorists settled in Belfast in 1896, and the monastery was built in 1900. A relatively smaller church, called the "Tin Church," was the site for services until the dedication of the present church building in 1911.[35]

My meeting at the monastery with Father Peter Ward proved to be one of my most pleasant of mornings. Father Ward immediately reminded me of a smiling Barry Fitzgerald in the old American movie "Going My Way," absolutely exuding the same Irish cheer. I had arrived earlier than the time set for our meeting, and he was literally on his way to say mass in the church. He asked the receptionist to give me a cup of tea and offer me something to read while he was in the church. When he returned, his eyes twinkled and he said, "Tis ashamed I should be! I didn't even invite ye to mass. But then I didn't know if ye were a Fenian." ("Fenian" is another term, similar to "Taig," which is used affectionately among Catholics to each other. It comes from the Gaelic word *Fianna*, which means literally "Irish warrior.") I quite candidly told him that I was not Catholic, but that, because I work often in Europe and in places where a Protestant church akin to mine (Episcopal) is difficult to find, I frequently attend mass. When I added that I also take communion, he smiled and responded, "Good! God love you!"

This kind gentleman took me into the kitchen for another cup of tea (a cup of tea seems to be believed to cure all ills in Ireland and Northern Ireland) and introduced me to some of the other priests, a few who were apparently elderly. (He subsequently explained that "we're all getting old," but I have never seen such youthful spirits as I met that day.) Father Peter informed me that there currently were twenty-one resident priests at Clonard.

He responded to my query about the Redemptorists, the Order at Clonard, by explaining that they were established in Scala in Southern Italy in 1732. I asked my token dumb question: how does one select an order when he or she decides to become a priest or nun? Father Peter laughed, "It's whichever one grabs you first." He added that, for him, the Redemptorists had no real competition anyway, since he had grown up serving as an altar boy at Clonard.

Later he walked me down to the building where he attended primary school, now one of the branches of the unemployment office of the province. (Incidentally, all schools in the Falls area are Catholic.) Father Peter's eventual return to Belfast came after several detours. He studied for the priesthood in Limerick, in the west of the Republic, and he served for many years as a missionary in India. When the church returned him to Ireland, it was to a position in Dublin leading retreats such as those he had organized and conducted while in India.[36] Eventually, the church returned him to his childhood parish, where he is obviously very much loved and respected.

He took me into a house on the same little side street where the monastery is located, so that I could meet a couple of the parishioners, an adult son and his elderly mother. They told me that he keeps "a good check on us and always looks after us...a good, good man, he is." Walking down the Falls Road, everybody we passed greeted him by name, and I realized what a close community the Falls really is. Father Peter commended me for my "bravery," since I had "dared to take a bus" rather than the omnipresent-tour-book-recommendation not to do so, but rather to call a "black cab." (A black cab indicates that the driver is Catholic, and, thus, not reluctant to drive into the Falls.)

Indeed, I later decided to walk back the short distance into downtown Belfast and go into the Catholic Cathedral of St. Peter's on the way. I felt surprisingly safe, confirming what I had been told: that no one in Belfast will harm an American, since the targets are those obviously Catholic (*e.g.*, residents of the Falls) or Protestant (*e.g.*, residents of the Shankill). Indeed, as an American, I always felt safe in Belfast. I did learn, however, in which sections not to walk (albeit a precaution one should take in any other city, including my own city of Richmond, Virginia.) It would not be advisable, for example, to walk down the streets of North Belfast waving an Irish flag, nor through the Falls displaying a Union Jack.

Father Peter gave me a grand tour of the monastery, one which gave me much more insight into the Troubles than would have anything I might have read. Metaphorically, he was a walking book on recent Northern Ireland history. He took me into the room in the monastery where "it all got started—right here," he said. Father Al Reid of Clonard had convinced SDLP leader John Hume (later co-winner with David Trimble of the 1998 Nobel Peace Price for their work in the peace talks which led to the GFA) to meet with Gerry Adams, leader of *Sinn Féin*, in 1988.

SDLP and *Sinn Féin* are the two Nationalist Catholic parties, but *Sinn Féin* is the one with the connection to the Irish Republic Army (IRA) and thus the one considered the hard-liner on the Nationalist side. Hume and his party, on the other hand, had always taken a non-violent stance, and thereupon lay the major point upon which they disagreed. The only similarity was that both advocated a united Ireland. Father Reid had somehow convinced Hume of the importance of such a meeting, and the two began the first real peace talks among principals in this small room in Clonard where Father Peter took me.

However did this happen? Father Reid, my new friend explained, had been a friend of Albert Reynolds, then *Taoiseach* (Prime Minister) of the Republic of Ireland. Cardinal Daly had refused to talk with the IRA (paramilitary arm of *Sinn Féin*), but Reynolds convinced Father Reed to use his efforts. The good priest was successful, and he thereby became a part of history. Nonetheless, Hume himself came under great criticism because of his meeting with the *Sinn Féin* leader. According to Father Ward, there is a "diabolical hatred of *Sinn Féin* here" (*i.e.*, among many Northern Irelanders, both Unionists and Nationalists).

On a more somber note, he took me down the hall where a small altar had been erected, a memorial one. This, he told me, was the spot where Brother Michael Morgan, a twenty-eight-year-old Redemptorist brother was shot and killed on July 22, 1920, as he stood by the window and watched the riots visible in the nearby Shankill area. (Note that this was before partition, a date usually cited as the "beginning" of the Troubles.) A soldier had fired the three shots which killed the young priest, apparently under the assumption that he was a sniper. This story is particularly poignant, since the victim was a priest, a man of the cloth, one who epitomizes mercy and goodness. The anachronism was palpable, and it was apparent that this little altar is still an emotional place for Father Peter.

Elaborating upon some of the underlying hatred and bitterness, he reminded me that Catholics had really never been given their human rights, especially regarding equality in housing, job opportunities and the "one-man-one-vote" principle, the latter because of gerrymandering. This was not coming from an embittered politician, but from a kind and gentle priest, one from whom my senses assured me came the truth. He cited the Harland and Wolff enterprise and Stormont as "two great symbols of Protestantism." Note that "Protestantism" in this sense was meant to convey something negative only from a political perspective. It is impossible to think of Father Peter using the word "Protestantism" in the sense to convey a negative image from a religious, rather than a political, perspective.

Indeed, it is implausible that Father Peter would speak with any kind of antagonism over a branch of the church of Christ, and his statement about Harland and Wolff should be taken in context. To explain his comment, Harland and Wolff is the great shipping corporation which had built the doomed Titanic, and which significantly has served as a critical source of employment for Belfast. Father Peter's statement relates to the company's practices of discrimination against Catholics in hiring. Stormont is the building which housed the provisional Northern Ireland government until the United Kingdom re-assumed direct control in 1971, and in which the New Northern Ireland Assembly holds its sessions.

With respect to the earlier government, Father Peter quoted Lord Craigavon, Northern Ireland's first Prime Minister as having expressly referred to the Stormont government as "a Protestant government for a Protestant people."[37] There were clearly no subtleties in Craigavon's remark about protecting minority rights.

Sectarian Killings

When I arrived in Belfast in January 1998, I was shocked by the frequency of sectarian murders. It seemed that the news reported almost daily of someone killed or attacked because of his or her religion. This truism began to personalize for me the victims and their families, and the senselessness of it all was frustrating. I had been in Belfast less than a month when all the news in this one single week seemed to consist solely of sectarian attacks.

The first was the January 21, 1998, mortal shooting (five times) of Benedict Hughes, a Catholic father of three, while in his car outside his place of work. On the evening of that same day, a Catholic taxi driver was shot in the head while driving in Protestant North Belfast, but he was one of those more fortunate victims who survived. Also that same night, a Protestant man was critically wounded by two gunmen. All these attackers were sectarian paramilitaries.[38]

Two days later, Larry Brennan, a Catholic cab driver, was killed while driving his taxi down presumably "neutral" Ormeau Road in Belfast. The news photograph of his grieving elderly mother (who had lost a nephew to the Troubles some twenty-five years earlier) would break the heart of even the most caustic. That same day a Protestant shop owner, Jim Guiney, was also killed by paramilitaries in Belfast,[39] and the following day, Catholic Liam Conway was shot and killed while working on a digger vehicle in a Protestant section.[40]

Four days later, cab driver John McColgan, a Catholic father of three children, aged twelve, nine and three, was shot five times in the head by Loyalists who had flagged down his taxi. They left his body in the middle of a Belfast road. The priest at McColgan's funeral mass stated that he had been "guilty of being a Catholic," and expressly contrasted this hatred with the deceased's widow's pleas of "Christian charity...that there be no retaliation."[41] The news photographs of his oldest child, a boy, sobbing as he walked behind his father's casket, holding the hand of his little brother who was asking "Where's daddy?" lingers in my mind and in my heart.

McColgan's murder was highly publicized, but perhaps not as extensively as a double murder which was to occur in March of that winter, a little more than a month before the signing of the GFA. In the tiny village of Poyntzpass in County Armagh, two life-long friends—Presbyterian Philip Alan and Catholic Damian Trainor—were gunned down by Loyalist paramilitaries in the village's only pub, the Railway Bar. This was only a few weeks before Alan was to be married, Trainor to have been his best man.[42]

These were not just-another couple of the usual sectarian killings, since Poyntzpass was a quiet little market town which the Troubles had seemed miraculously to have been forgotten. The small Catholic and Protestant public schools even shared sports facilities and books, and everyone knew everyone else. They all were able to "get along," without any external evidence that they had even thought about their neighbors' respective religions. Essentially the entire town attended both funerals held on the same day, but two hours apart so that this would be possible. One commentator designated Poyntzpass a "model of community relations" in Northern Ireland.[43]

Yet, drawing a conclusion that it is "about" religion seems clearly in error. There is nothing spiritual or Christian about gunning down an innocent young father, or good friends because they worship the same Christ but belong to different denominations.

One more wonderful clergyman with whom I became good friends was the dean of the church I attended during my time in Belfast, the Church of St. Nicholas (Church of Ireland) in Belfast, Frederick Rusk.[44] St. Nicholas truly became "my" church, and Dean Rusk and his wife warmly welcomed me into the parish. I will not forget his homily on the Easter Sunday immediately following the signing of the GFA in 1998, during which he praised God for this hope of "peace for our island." He cautioned, however, that, although this was a significant movement towards a lasting peace, it was "just a chink"—and that there lies a long road ahead to a real solution of Northern Ireland's Troubles.[45] Dean Rusk's view was a prophetic one.

If these three representatives of the religious sector—two from the Church of Ireland (Dean Rusk and Bishop Moore), and one from the Catholic Church (Father Peter)—are typical and representative of clergy in Northern Ireland (and I believe that they are indeed), it would seem that religion is truly not the problem. I found myself wishing I could arrange for all three to meet together (Bishop Moore and Dean Rusk know each other well, but neither is acquainted with Father Peter), because I am convinced that they would enjoy a productive interface and would become fast friends. The two branches of Christianity, then, do not seem to be a difficulty. Indeed, they may eventually even provide a bridge toward a solution.

AMERICAN RACISM

Just as history has shown that Catholics in Northern Ireland have been relegated to a second class, the fate was historically similar for blacks in the U.S.A. Another striking similarity is that under the respective laws, equality is (now) required. Nonetheless, there remain charges of discrimination.

Most American lawyers and law professors would agree that *Dred Scott v. Sandford*[46] was the absolute nadir for American jurisprudence. Indeed, it has been called by some constitutional scholars "one of the great disasters in the history of the Supreme Court." [47] The case involved a pre-Civil War slave, Dred Scott, who claimed his freedom after having been taken by his former master to a free state.

A bit of American history is explanatory. The Missouri Compromise had proven to be but a temporary resolution to the increasingly divisive issue of slavery when it was adopted in 1820.[48] This law established a geographical line separating the more northern states from the southern ones, effectively permitting those south of the line to legalize the institution of slavery and prohibiting it in those states north of the line. Dred Scott was a slave who had been owned by a Missouri physician who took him to Illinois (a free state under both the state constitution and federal law, the Missouri Compromise) in 1834. They returned to Missouri (a slave state) in 1838. The physician-owner died, and his sister "inherited" Scott who was then sold to the defendant (Sandford). Scott's position was that his time in Illinois had freed him permanently.

The case was decided on a legally arcane jurisdictional question, but the significant historical parts of the decision are the references to any rights a black person might lawfully claim. In the 7-2 opinion, Justice Roger B. Taney wrote for the majority that slaves were neither "persons" nor "citizens" of the United States. To the contrary, they "were not intended to be included, under the word 'citizens' in the Constitution." Taney wrote further that at the time of the drafting and adoption of the U.S. Constitution (1787), blacks were "considered as a subordinate and inferior class of beings, who had been subjugated by the dominant race...(and remained) subject to their authority." Blacks were described as "unfit to associate with the white race, either in social or political relations...so far inferior, that they had no rights which the white man was bound to respect...[but were to be] treated as an ordinary article of merchandise and traffic...."

The Post-Civil War Constitutional Amendments

The end of the Civil War (1861-1865) brought an end to legalized slavery, and the U.S. Constitution was amended three times in succession to assure rights of former slaves. First, in 1865, slavery (*i.e.*, involuntary servitude) was abolished.[49] In 1868, slaves were acknowledged as "citizens" and given the privileges and immunities attendant to citizenship. Moreover, this amendment assured them—now regarded as "persons"—the right to equal protection of the laws.[50] Finally, in 1870, the black man was granted the right to vote.[51]

The U.S. Supreme Court, however, took a somewhat jaded view of what "equal protection" really meant. In 1896, the Court decided *Plessy v. Ferguson*,[52] holding that separate public transportation cars for the races did not violate the Fourteenth Amendment's Equal Protection Clause, since in the instant case they were equal in quality. (*Plessy* was the source of the famous "separate-but-equal" doctrine.) An interesting side note on the *Plessy* facts is that the plaintiff who unsuccessfully challenged the constitutionality of the Louisiana state statute requiring separate train cars for blacks and whites was himself only one-eighth black, and seven-eighths white. Indeed, he appeared in all respects to be a white man. Yet, state law defined him as black, and his mixed blood had marked him as one who might be set apart on racial grounds.

In *Brown v. Board of Education of Topeka* [53] the Court overruled the separate-but-equal doctrine, at least in the area of public schools. The unanimous *Brown* Court held that the separation of the races, regardless of any equality in tangible physical facilities, renders the respective educations unequal. Thus began a recognition at the highest judicial level that the law would not condone an across-the-board separation of the races. While *de facto—i.e.*, racial division as a matter of fact, as, for example, in residential patterns—might exist, the days of *de jure—i.e.,* division with the force of law—were in the past.

Restrictive Covenants in Home Ownership

What about racially separate residential areas protected by law? Typical in deeds had been a so-called "restrictive covenant" which forbade the subsequent transfer of the property to a black person. The purpose, of course, was to maintain the "lily-white" character of a neighborhood, hence retaining the value of its properties. In other words, it promoted the "salability" of the property.

It should be explained that so long as there is voluntary adherence to such a commitment in a non-governmental situs, no constitutional rights arise. This presumably would make it other than state action, and it thus would not violate the Equal Protection Clause. The U.S. Constitution protects individuals from the power of the federal and state governments, not from one in the private sector. The "public" element entered when such a restrictive covenant was challenged in a court of competent jurisdiction. Should the court—a public entity—then enforce the provision, the unconstitutional factor would be evident. A bare-quorum Supreme Court of six justices held in *Shelley v. Kraemer* [54] that enforcement of these racially restrictive covenants was unconstitutional.

World War II and Japanese-Americans

If *Dred Scott* marked a low-point for the Supreme Court, *Korematsu v. U.S.* [55] is arguably in second place. This World War II-era decision indicates the paranoia which an entire ethic group can incite. The Court in *Korematsu* affirmed a federal military regulation providing for the literal internment of anyone of Japanese origin (some of these persons were second generation Japanese who had been born in the U.S.A. and who thus were citizens) in designated areas on the American Pacific coast. The rationale was that there was a legitimate governmental purpose of protecting the country from possible espionage and subversion by people with Japanese sympathies.

This rings hollow indeed. These were people whose own choice had been to relocate to a new land, which they loved, and some were born here because of this choice by their parents. There had been no determination as to which, if any, might be guilty of espionage or treason, and no trials, nor even charges.

Anti-Miscegenation Laws

Another parallel with regard to religious discrimination in Northern Ireland and race discrimination in the U.S.A. is the reference to a so-called "mixed marriage." In Northern Ireland, this connotes a marriage between a Catholic and a Protestant. In the U.S.A., this automatically refers to a marital union of persons from different races. The similarity is the negative connotation generated by both. (Note, however, the all-Christian opinion of Church of Ireland Bishop Moore in Belfast, when referring to the marriages of his nephews to Catholic women.[56]) A critical difference is that in the U.S.A., mixed marriages once were forbidden by statute in some states.

Many American states had adopted statutes prohibiting interracial marriages (anti-miscegany laws), and Virginia was among them. The Virginia law made it a felony for a white person to marry anyone who was black, Asian, or American Indian.[57] Interestingly, one express exception was marriage to a "descendant of Pocahontas," apparently a "good" Indian, since she had married early settler John Rolfe and is generally regarded as a heroine in Virginia history.

In *Loving v. Virginia* the constitutionality of the Virginia statute was tested. Destined for the U.S. Supreme Court, the ultimate decision would determine the fate of the other sixteen states with anti-miscegany statutes in their law books. In *Loving*, a black woman had married a white man outside Virginia, but they returned to Virginia to live. They were subsequently arrested and convicted under the statute. The one-year prison sentence imposed was suspended, however, provided they left the state to live elsewhere. Any return to Virginia would be regarded as a violation of the terms of the suspension, and they would be imprisoned. The trial judge's statement was that "Almighty God created the races white, black, yellow, Malay and red, and He placed them on separate continents. And but for the interference with His arrangement there would be no cause for such marriages. The fact that He separated the races shows that He did not intend…(them) to mix." [Author's note: Perhaps this judge believed in the immorality of planes, since, had God intended for us to fly, He would have endowed us with wings.]

After having lived in the District of Columbia for a while, they decided to return to Virginia and consequently challenged the constitutionality of the statute. The Virginia Supreme Court of Appeals upheld the law,[58] reasoning that it applied equally to both races and served a legitimate state purpose, that is, "to preserve the racial integrity of its citizens" and "to prevent the corruption of blood...(and the creation of) a mongrel breed of citizens."

92

The U.S. Supreme Court reversed.[59] First, the purpose of the law was patently to preserve the purity of the Caucasian race and to maintain white supremacy, since all non-Caucasians could intermarry (*e.g.*, a black might lawfully marry an Indian, an Indian might marry an Oriental, etc.). Only Caucasians were forbidden to step out of their whiteness, so to speak, and marry a non-Caucasian, since that would (in the words of the Virginia Court) lead to the possible creation of a "mongrel breed." "Supremacy" by definition is the antithesis of "equality," and the Supreme Court held the statute unconstitutional.[60]

Racial Bigotry in the Churches

Although the theme of the portions of this book devoted to comparisons between the strife in Northern Ireland and the U.SA. is based on religion in the former and race in the latter, it is indeed possible that the two might overlap. Such was the situation in *Bob Jones University v. U.S.*

Bob Jones University is a private Baptist university in Greenville, South Carolina. (This is, incidentally, the university from which the Rev. Ian Paisley Sr. received the honorary doctorate which makes it possible for him to use the title "doctor." Moreover, the Rev. Bob Jones laid the cornerstone for Paisley's Martyrs Memorial Free Presbyterian Church in Belfast.)

On religious grounds, Jones' particular branch believes that God intended for the races to be kept separate and that interracial dating is a sin. To remove all temptation, applications were not accepted from black students. However, a federal appellate court had upheld an administrative decision terminating all Veterans Assistance to the university because of this discriminatory policy.[61]

In order to resume this funding, the university finally approved a rule that blacks were eligible for admission, but they would consider only black applicants who were married, and any interracial dating remained strictly forbidden. Constitutional expert Derrick Bell has termed this a policy "charitably defined as judiciously diluted white supremacy."[62]

Federal law[63] provides for a tax-exempt status for all religious and charitable institutions, but the exemption for Bob Jones University was revoked because of its racially discriminatory position and practice. The university challenged this revocation on constitutional grounds,[64] contending that this was an encroachment upon the university founders' and administrators' freedom of religion under the First Amendment.

The Court ruled 8-1 against the university. Using a balancing-of-interests approach, the Court held that the federal government's strong position against racial discrimination prevailed over any incidental effect on the institution's freedom of religion. The university was not prohibited from continuing to enforce the rule against interracial dating, but this would thereby result in sacrificing its privilege of remaining tax-free. Chief Justice Burger's opinion for the majority stated that the institution "must not be so at odds with the common community conscience as to undermine any public merit." [65]

Affirmative Action

Is opposition to racism indeed a "common community conscience" among Americans, as the former Chief Justice wrote in *Bob Jones*? If so, why do so many insist that there is a need for affirmative action and that it should be judicially enforced? That is, if the American conscience opposes racism, why is there a perceived need to take such drastic measures to see that its vestiges are removed?

The U.S. Supreme Court has not been consistent with regard to when affirmative action programs are lawful, particularly those granting preferential treatment to blacks.[66] Some have been approved,[67] and others have been struck down[68] (Note that there have been some such programs providing for preferences for women. For example, see *Santa Clara County v. Johnson*.[69])

This can be a major thorn in the side of qualified whites (especially men) who are passed over to make room for less qualified blacks, especially in the area of employment. Similarly, any advantageous treatment for Catholics, which lawmakers and/or law enforcers might read from the GFA and implementing legislation, has the potential to cause resulting friction among Protestants in Northern Ireland. (See Chapters 7 and 8.)

The University of Michigan (a state university, and thus subject to constitutional restrictions) has been the recent target of two lawsuits arising out of its diversity-directed affirmative action programs. The first is an undergraduate admissions policy that added points to minority applicants to the College of Literature, Science and the Arts. A federal district court for the Eastern District of Michigan upheld the policy, stating that diversity "constitutes a compelling governmental interest in the context of higher education justifying the use of races [as] one factor in the admissions process.[70]

The response of a different judge in the same federal district to the second challenge to the University of Michigan's diversity program in the law school was a classic 180-degree different position. Only because a different judge heard the case, the perspective on diversity was (no pun intended) diverse. Here, diversity, standing alone, was clearly rejected as a compelling state interest. [71]

The only apparent factual difference in the two Michigan decisions seems to be that the latter case involved admission to the university's law school, and the former, an undergraduate college. These distinctions are surely not substantial as to the reason for the disparity of outcomes.

The Supreme Court has scheduled oral arguments on this issue for April 1, 2003. The discussion will be the most significant one to date on the issue of affirmative action.[72]

An idea has germinated from the affirmative action principle is that of reparations. There has been a wave of demands for governmental payments of reparations to descendants of former slaves, much like the German government's commitment to make payments to former *Nazi* victims or their families. The difference is that many generations have passed since the American Civil War, and there are no surviving actual slaves. In Germany, there indeed remain some actual survivors of the *Nazionalsozialismus* horrors. There are other distinctions, since the concentration camp victims during World War II were tortured and murdered, whereas the American slave was a victim of involuntary servitude, but not usually subjected to such atrocities. Additionally, American slaves were intended to provide work, but the purpose underlying the *Nazionalsozialismus* philosophy was actually to extinguish a race their adherents deemed to be "inferior."

Interestingly, neither Irish Catholics nor Northern Ireland's Catholics have ever called for such monetary payments. Perhaps they view such thinking as does Leonard Pitts, an American syndicated editorialist who is a black man. Pitts wrote recently in response to a novel proposition of another American editorialist, Charles Krauthammer. Krauthammer suggested a trade-off: pay the reparations, and dispense with affirmative action. Recognizing that the American people owe a "special debt" to black Americans and that there is virtually nothing which compares with the sufferings of slavery, Krauthammer nonetheless reminds that "collective responsibility does not...mean collective guilt."

Contending that the affirmative action begun by former President Lyndon B. Johnson in the 1960s has served its purpose, he abhors the preferences afforded to one because of his skin color. The non-black is then charged with the obligation to pay in a personal way for a malign act or acts in which he had no part. Thus, Krauthammer suggests the payment of reparations and the end of affirmative action as a "way out of this cul-de-sac." [73]

Pitts' response was that, while intriguing, Krauthammer's proposal of a payment to $50,000 per family (along the same philosophy as in the German plan) would not end the problems he calls "systematic," *i.e.*, societal subjugation of blacks as a group. [74]

It is possible that the affirmative action laws for Catholics in Northern Ireland might indeed compound the problem. If there is an underlying hatred of Catholics, will such favoritism by the government make them an even greater object of hatred? Does affirmative action for American blacks have such an effect?

The War that Never Ends

To understand how the pain and suffering over the American slavery issue endure (although slavery officially ended with the 1865 Thirteenth Amendment), a few final examples are instructive. In early 2001, three former Confederate states experienced much contention over their continued use of the Confederate flag. In South Carolina, the issue arose over the traditional flying of the flag atop the dome of the state capitol. (The turmoil led to the moving of the flag to a nearby monument in fall 2000, but the NAACP staged a march on the birthday of Dr. Martin Luther King, Jr., in January, 2001, to protest its being flown on any state property.)

The state flags of both Mississippi and Georgia bear the Confederate flag. Mississippi voters were to be permitted to vote in April, 2001, as to whether or not to retain it, and the Georgia state legislature is entertaining bills on revising the flag so as to delete the Confederate emblem. The NAACP has used perhaps the most effective of tactics, urging a boycott of state tourism and businesses.[75]

Virginia, the Confederacy and Charges of Racism

Two other incidents involving Virginia are illustrative of how a facially neutral event can become a racial issue. Although not geographically in the Deep South, Virginia's capital city of Richmond was the capital of the Confederacy. Most of the Civil War battles which occurred in the South were on Virginia soil, and many of the more notable Confederate military leaders were Virginians. Thus, one has no doubt when in Virginia that he is in a state of the Old South. Moreover, with respect to the mentality of her residents, Richmond is arguably the most "Southern" of American cities.

Virginia's Confederate History Month

In the mid-1990s, then-Virginia Gov. George Allen (now U.S. Senator for Virginia) proclaimed April as an official month to honor Virginians who had fought for the Confederacy in the Civil War. After April, 2000, the state branch of the National Association for the Advancement of Colored People (NAACP) called for a boycott of all Virginia tourist attractions. Its position was that Confederate History Month is an insult to blacks and a glorification of a racist cause. Representatives of Confederate heritage organizations and descendants of those who fought for Virginia in the war (the author is one such person) countered that this was tantamount to converting a situation into a racist issue when it actually was a historical observance.

Virginia Gov. Jim Gilmore, Allen's successor, met several times with both sides to the controversy, and his compromise was to continue the month of April as one recognizing Virginia history, but to retitle the proclamation "In Remembrance of the Sacrifices and Honor of All Virginians Who Served in the Civil War." The NAACP praised the governor for having "done the right thing," [76] but other groups (in particular, the Virginia chapter of the Sons of the Confederacy) accused him of "cav(ing) in" to the NAACP and "cop(ping) out," thereby insulting Virginians and the history of the state.[77] [Author's note: While it is possible to find names of persons in any of the thirteen Confederate states who switched sides and fought for the union, the numbers are few. Thus, the governor's proclamation honoring

"All Virginians Who Served in the Civil War" is effectively one which would al-most exclusively honor those on the side of the Confederacy.]

The response to the governor's appeasement was the Sons' placement of a full-page proclamation in the Richmond newspaper. This paid advertisement re-counted the reasons for Virginia's secession prior to the Civil War, followed by a litany of battles fought on Virginia soil and a list of the more renowned names of Virginians who had fought for the Confederate cause.[78]

Richmond's Arthur Ashe Memorial

A second Virginia event surrounded the erection and placement of a memorial statue to former tennis great Arthur Ashe, a black man who died of blood transfu-sion-related AIDS in 1993. (He had suffered a heart attack at a young age, and this health problem haunted him throughout the remainder of his forty-nine years. The cause of his HIV-positive test was an earlier transfusion of contaminated blood, and the inevitable illness eventually took his life.) There were no voiced objections to such a memorial, since it is difficult to find a Virginian who does not take pride in claiming Ashe as our own. However, a segment of the black community in-sisted that any location other than Monument Avenue would be racist.

Monument Avenue is Richmond's signature street, her landmark. A beautiful tree-lined divided avenue which extends some seven miles leading into downtown Richmond, its name is derived from the five statues situated a few blocks from one another. Memorialized are the following Confederate figures: J.E.B. Stuart, sol-dier; Robert E. Lee, Commander of the Army of Northern Virginia and Commander-in-Chief of the Confederate forces; Thomas "Stonewall" Jackson, soldier, whom Lee called his "right arm"; Jefferson Davis, President of the Confederacy; and Matthew Maury, geographer who charted the seas for the Confederate Navy.

The street has long maintained this Civil War theme, and many famous Vir-ginians with no connection to the Civil War—including George Washington, Tho-mas Jefferson, James Madison, James Monroe, George Mason, Chief Justice John Marshall,[79] to name a few—have never been mentioned as meriting a statue on Monument Avenue. Interestingly, other famous statesmen and women never con-sidered for Monument Avenue include notable blacks, such as early American educator Booker T. Washington, dancer Bill "Bojangles" Robinson, singers Pearl Bailey and Ella Fitzgerald, and Maggie Walker, the first American woman to own a bank.

A majority of the population of the city of Richmond itself, in contrast to the surrounding counties (Virginia is the only state which politically separates cities from counties so that they do not overlap), is black, and the racial strife has been recurring and ugly. The summer of 1997 was among the worst in this regard.

Any statement that this street was the wrong location for the Ashe memorial statue was only incendiary. Other recommendations were the front of the large convention building bearing Ashe's name (the Arthur Ashe Center), or one which Ashe's widow herself preferred, the Maymont Park public tennis courts. When Ashe's talent first became evident, he was not permitted to play on the public tennis courts in Richmond because of his race. Consequently, his father sent him to St. Louis to live with an uncle to develop his extraordinary athletic abilities, since his home city made this impossible. In his wife's opinion, her husband's own choice would not have been for the situs of his memorial to be a street adorned with generals and other principals in a war which had been fought at least in part to defend the institution of slavery.

The controversy raged throughout the summer, but black activists won the battle. Ashe's statue stands as the most westerly one on Monument Avenue (logically, the only suitable spot remaining, but the least attractive, since it the closest to an interstate exchange). He is the only 20th century Virginian, in addition to the only one with no connection whatsoever to the Civil War, whose memorial statue is on Monument Avenue.

A Few Comparative Remarks

These events exemplify a situation much like the Orange Order parades in Northern Ireland. (See Chapter 2.) One might compare Northern Ireland's marching Unionists to America's Confederate historians, since they both view symbols and commemorations as reflective of a culture and a significant part of the history of the region. (One difference is that the South lost the Civil War, but Northern Ireland is still a part of the United Kingdom.)

Northern Irish Catholics might identify with American blacks, for whom such marches and/or symbols revisit painful memories. Indeed, the civil rights efforts of Northern Ireland Catholics was encouraged by the American black civil rights movement. Rational arguments become non-existent, and emotions rule the day. These are situations where there are no easy answers, probably because both opposing positions are understandable. It cannot be denied, however, that the bedrock of the ensuing violence and disregard for human life in both religiously-torn Northern Ireland and those parts of the U.S.A. which are still racially divided is simple hatred.[80]

Conclusion

It would be idealistic to anticipate that anti-Catholicism will be erased from the face of Northern Ireland in the near future. It would be equally unreasonable to think that racism will not exist in the U.S.A. any time soon.

The law may mandate equality, but any amount of legislation and any number of court orders cannot achieve a metamorphosis which will change what has been bred in part by culture. It should not be forgotten that not all group differences in people produce hatred, but there is sufficient enough mean-spiritedness on both sides on each side of the Atlantic to continue to feed these problems of intolerance. At any rate, even if malice is absent, ill intent is not a prerequisite for the infliction of pain.

Reality is that dealing with innate prejudices is not a suitable role for the legal system, and it should not be expected to provide a panacea.

Endnotes to Chapter 3

[1] Religion has nonetheless spawned its share of lawsuits in the litigious U.S.A., particularly in the employment setting. *See, e.g.*, Carol Daugherty Rasnic, *Rendering Unto the Boss and Rendering unto God: Freedom of Religion in the U.S. Workplace after City of Bourne and Some Comparisons with Austrian Law*, 4 HUMAN RIGHTS LAW REVIEW (published by Nottingham, England, School of Law), pp. 3-22 (April, 1999).

However, the sheer diversity of religious beliefs has achieved an atmosphere of acceptance and toleration relative to Northern Ireland. Conflicts generally arise only when a religious practice creates a conflict with another's rights. *See, e.g.*, TWA v. Hardison, 432 U.S. 63 (1977), in which the U.S. Supreme Court held that a company was not obligated to violate a collective bargaining agreement and ignore seniority rights by giving one worker his choice of scheduling in order that he might have Saturdays off work for religious reasons.

Here, an employee had objected to his employer's requirement that all workers attend a weekly Bible session in the workplace. As an atheist, he found this offensive, and the Court agreed. The owners had unsuccessfully contended that they understood their religious duty to be to share the Gospel, and to prohibit them from doing so infringes upon their constitutional right to freedom of religion.

[2] Roman Catholic Relief Act 1829 (10 Geo. 4).

[3] IRELAND: EYEWITNESS TRAVEL GUIDES, at 87 (Dorling Kindersley Publishing, Inc., London, England, 1995).

[4] Mary Harris, *The Catholic church, minority rights, and the founding of the Northern Irish state*, NORTHERN IRELAND AND THE POLITICS OF RECONCILIATION 62 (Dermot Keogh and Michael H. Haltze, eds., Woodrow Wilson Press and Cambridge University Press, Cambridge, England, 1994).

[5] *Id.* at 62-62.

[6] *Id.* at 63, *citing* Seamus O'Buachalla, EDUCATION POLICIES IN TWENTIETH CENTURY IRELAND 53 (Dufour Editions, Inc., Dublin, 1988).

[7] *Id.* at 64, *quoting from* Report of the Belfast Riots Commissioners, Minutes of Evidence and Appendices 1887 (C.4925), 507.

[8] *Id, quoting* Bishop Patrick McKenna, DERRY JOURNAL, June 9, 1916.

[9] *Id.*

[10] Government of Ireland Act 1920.

[11] According to Brendan O'Leary, Professor of Political Science at London School of Economics, "free state" was then-British Prime Minister David Lloyd George's term, used to emphasize Irish independence. The Irish language seemed to have no translation for the term "republic," and the nearest Lloyd George could contrive was *Saorstát Éireann* ("Free State of Ireland"). As Professor O'Leary put it, this was simply a "proposal to get him [Lloyd George] and the Irish delegation off a conceptual hook." He adds that there is no technical distinction between a "dominion," which was then the status of Canada and Australia, and "free state." (Communication from Professor O'Leary, December 13, 2001.)

[12] Harris, *supra* note 4, *quoting from* IRISH CATHOLIC DICTIONARY (Dublin, 1922), at 508.

[13] IRISH INDEPENDENT, March 28, 1921.

[14] Ango-Irish Treaty 1921.

[15] Harris, *supra* note 4 at 69.

[16] Michael Collins was killed in his home County of Cork on August 22, 1922, shortly after the agreement to partition and to establish the Free State of Ireland. Although the murderers were not apprehended, one common theory is that they were from his own camp of activists. The rationale is that this was retaliation against Collins for "copping out" and not fighting until complete freedom from the United Kingdom was achieved and Ireland was a republic. One who had bitterly accused Collins of such was Eamon DeValera, later President of the Republic of Ireland and primary drafter of the Irish Constitution of 1937.

[17] Craig-Collins Pact, March 30, 1922.

[18] Harris, *supra* note 4 at 76, *quoting* Father O'Doherty as reported in the IRISH INDEPENDENT, November 3, 1923.

[19] *Id.* at 83.

[20] *Id.* at note 81, citing the IRISH CATHOLIC DICTIONARY (Dublin, 1938) at 10, as confirming that 1/5 of all those at the 1937 conference of St. Vincent de Paul, a Catholic association devoted to relief for the poor, were in the diocese of Down and Connor, *i.e.,* Belfast.

[21] Luke 21:1-4.

[22] Matthew 22:36-40 relates Jesus' response to the question of which were the two greatest commandments: to love the Lord Thy God, and to love thy neighbor as thyself. This same directive is reflected in St. Paul's letter to the Ephesians 4:32: "Be ye kind one to another, tenderhearted, forgiving one another, even as God for Christ's sake hath forgiven you."

[23] Paul Johnson, IRELAND: A CONCISE HISTORY FROM THE TWELFTH CENTURY TO THE PRESENT DAY) at 58 (Academy Publishers Chicago, 1984).

[24] *Id.*

[25] *Bunreacht na hÉirann* 1937 (Constitution of Ireland), Article 44 sec.2 (1)

[26] *Id.,* Article 44 sec 2 (2). This provision states that the "state guarantees not to endow any state religion."

[27] *Ireland,* 40 THE WORLD BOOK ENCYCLOPEDIA at 332b (1978).

[28] *Church of England,* 3 THE WORLD BOOK ENCYCLOPEDIA at 422 (1978).

[29] 1534 Act of Supremacy.

[30] For a detailed history of the Church of Ireland, *see* W.A.Phillips (ed.), HISTORY OF THE CHURCH OF IRELAND (3 volumes) (London, 1933-34).

[31] Interview with the Right Reverend James E. Moore, Bishop of Connor (Church of Ireland), August 7, 2000, Church of Ireland House, Belfast.

[32] The Church of Ireland Board for Social Responsibility (Northern Ireland) lists as its source for contact the Church of Ireland House, 61-67 Donegall Street, Belfast BT 1-2QH, telephone (from U.S.A.) (011) (44) (28) 23 38 85, fax 32 17 56.

[33] Surprisingly, the Alliance Party's figures are approximately 44% Protestant, 45% Catholic, and 11% "other," (Interview with Stephen Farry, Alliance Party Policy Advisor, August 1, 2001, Alliance Party Headquarters, Belfast.) This would mean that Catholics would now hold a narrow majority, rather than the reported minority.

[34] Patrick O'Donnell, CLONARD CHURCH AND MONASTERY 1896-2000 at 25, (Church and Monastery, Belfast, 2000).

[35] *Id.* At 6, 9, 24.

[36] Father Peter has written two books, and the pattern of his professional life is sprinkled in parts of both. *See* Peter Ward, THE GOD OF WELCOMES (The Columba Press, Blackrock, County Dublin, 1996) and Peter Ward, SILENCED BY PRAYER (The Columba Press, Blackrock, County Dublin, 1999)

[37] Interview with the Reverend Peter Ward, C.Ss.R., July 5, 2000, Clonard Monastery, Belfast.

[38] Gordon Adair, *Slaughter*, BELFAST NEWS LETTER, January 22, 1998, at 1, col. 3-5.

[39] Dick Walsh, *Politicians must work together to stop the killing*, THE IRISH TIMES, January 24, 1998, at 14, col. 1.

[40] Theresa Judge, *Catholic man killed as UFF ends campaign*, THE IRISH TIMES, January 24, 1998, at 6, col. 1-2.

[41] Gary Kelly, *Day of tears as children weep for lost dad*, BELFAST NEWS LETTER, January 28, 1998, at 7, col. 3-7.

[42] *Day of tears as families mourn sons*, BELFAST NEWS LETTER, March 5, 1998, at 5, col. 1-6.

[43] *Village of Grief*, BELFAST NEWS LETTER, March 5, 1998, at 1, col. 1-5.

[44] Dean Rusk has since retired, and he and Mrs. Rusk now live in Lurgan, the County Down town where they were both born and reared. Incidentally, Lurgan has been the situs of more than its fair share of sectarian violence, including the murder of Catholic human rights lawyer Rosemary Nelson. The Nelson killing is reported in more detail in Chapter 1.

[45] Remarks of the Very Reverend Frederick Rusk, Easter morning service, April 12, 1998, Church of St. Nicholas (C. of I.), Belfast.

[46] 60 U.S. (19 How.) 393 (1857).

[47] Geoffrey R. Stone, Louis M. Seidman, Cass R. Sundstein, Mark V. Tushnet, CONSTITUTIONAL LAW 478 (Little Brown and Co., 2d ed., 1991).

[48] Act of March 6, 1820, 3 Stat. 545.

[49] U.S. CONST. Amend. XIII (1865).

[50] *Id.* Amend. XIV (1868).

[51] *Id.* Amend. XV. (1870).

[52] 163 U.S. 537 (1896).

[53] 347 U.S. 483 (1954).

[54] 334 U.S. 1 (1948). The Court was nonetheless unanimous, and the decision was 6-0.

[55] 323 U.S. 214, 65 S.Ct.193 (1944).

[56] *See supra* note 29 and accompanying text.

[57] VA. CODE ANN. Sec. 20-58.

[58] 206 Va. 924, 147 S.E.2d 78.

[59] 388 U.S.1 (1967).

[60] The actual holding, however, was based on the Due Process Clause of the Fourteenth Amendment, rather than the Equal Protection Clause.

[61] Bob Jones University v. Johnson, 529 F.2d 514 (4th Cir. 1975).

[62] Derrick Bell, RACE, RACISM, AND AMERICAN LAW 92 (Little, Brown & Company, New York City, New York, Third ed. 1992).

[63] Internal Revenue Code §§501(c)(3), 170(c).

[64] The U.S. Constitution assures freedom of religion. UNITED STATES CONST. Amend. I (1791).

[65] 461 U.S. 574 (1983).

[66] *See, e.g.*, Carol Daugherty Rasnic, *The Supreme Court and Affirmative Action: an Evolving Standard or Compounded Confusion?* 14 EMPLOYEE RELATIONS LAW JOURNAL 175-190 (autumn, 1988).

[67] *See, e.g.,* Weber v. Kaiser Aluminum/United Steelworkers, 443 U.S. 193 (1979), and U.S. v. Paradise, 107 S.Ct. 1053 (1987).

[68] *See, e.g.,* Firefighters Local Union No. 1784 (City of Memphis, Tennessee) v. Stotts, 467 U.S. 561 (1984) and Wygant v. Board of Education, 476 U.S. 267 (1986).

[69] 480 U.S. 616, 107 S.Ct. 1442 (1987), in which the Court approved an affirmative action move to promote a woman in lieu of a better qualified male applicant.

[70] Gratz v. Bollinger, 122 F.Supp.2d 811 (E.D. Mich. 2000).

[71] Grutter v. Bollinger, No. 97-CV-75928-DT 2001 WL 293196 (E.D. Mich., March 27, 2001).

[72] The appellate court decision is Grutter v. Bollinger, 288 F. 3d 732 (6th Cir. 2002). As expected, the Supreme Court granted centiorari. 123 S. Ct. 617 (2002).

[73] Charles Krauthammer, *Here's the Deal: Go with Reparations, Stop Affirmative Action,* RICHMOND TIMES-DISPATCH (Washington Post Writers Group), April 8, 2001, at F-7, col. 1-5.

[74] Leonard Pitts, *Case for Reparations Forgets Discrimination,* RICHMOND TIMES-DISPATCH (Tribune Media Services), April 24, 2001, at A-13, col. 4-5.

[75] Larry Copeland, *3 states wrapped up in flag battle,* USA TODAY, January 8, 2001, at 3A, col. 2-5. Note that the NAACP had already successfully staged a boycott which led to South Carolina's removal of the Confederate flag from atop its state capitol building in Columbia.

[76] Michael Hardy, *NAACP extends praise,* RICHMOND TIMES-DISPATCH, March 22, 2001, at B-1, col. 5.

[77] A. Barton Hinkle, *A Common Mainspring Winds Both Sides,* RICHMOND TIMES-DISPATCH, April 10, 2001, at A-11, col. 1-3.

[78] RICHMOND TIMES-DISPATCH, April 9, 2001, at B-5.

[79] John Marshall is perhaps the most famous of American chief justices, having authored Marbury v. Madison, 5 U.S. 137 (1803). This decision was the first articulation of the separation-of-powers doctrine, holding that the Supreme Court was constitutionally empowered to declare an act of Congress unconstitutional.

[80] Susan McKay, an acclaimed non-fiction writer who was born and reared in Londonderry/Derry, has similarly compared the animosities in these two settings. *See* Susan McKay, NORTHERN PROTESTANTS: AN UNSETTLED PEOPLE at 336-337 (The Blackstaff Press, Belfast, Ireland, 2000).

Part II

The Good Friday Agreement

Chapter 4

Chapter 4

Summary of the Good Friday Agreement: Constitutional Amendments, the Three "Strands," Negotiations, the Agreement and the Referenda

"I do not believe that it is possible to negotiate a better agreement from the point of view of anybody."

John Bruton, former Taoiseach of Ireland[1]

"Over the whole scene [GFA] hangs the dark cloud of Sinn Féin/IRA—as strong, as armed, as unreconciled to peace as in the past, and perhaps even freer than ever. No, these are not good days for the Union."

Ian Paisley Jr.[2]

On April 10, 1998, after nearly two years of negotiations, Northern Ireland's major political parties and the governments of the United Kingdom and the Republic of Ireland reached agreement on a proposal for achieving peace in Northern Ireland. This was a phenomenal accomplishment, one which came as a surprise not only to those on the island of Ireland, but also to most others throughout the world who had followed the progress—or lack thereof—in this effort.

This is a document which did not emerge overnight, but one which came after nearly two years of intense and, at times, heated talks among representatives of the affected parties and governments. The actual inception had been the Anglo-Irish

Agreement in 1985, continuing with the 1993 Downing Street Declaration. This chapter is a meager effort of an American lawyer who had the good fortune to be on Irish and Northern Ireland soil during only the culmination of these efforts to retell what transpired.

Parts of the Good Friday Agreement (the GFA) are dealt with in separate chapters. [Chapter 5 describes the Northern Ireland Assembly (the legislature); Chapter 6, the dual process of decommissioning and release of political prisoners; Chapter 7, the issue of reforming the Northern Ireland police force, the Royal Ulster Constabulary (RUC); and Chapter 8, the human rights and equality provisions.] This chapter treats the document in a summary fashion, elaborating only upon the necessary constitutional changes in the Republic of Ireland, the negotiations and the participants, the Agreement, and the two referenda. These were exciting days indeed for an American to be on the island of Ireland.

Some Personal Reflections: The Week Before the Settlement

The date was Good Friday. It was spring vacation at Queen's University, so my husband, Jack, and I were traveling in the Republic. That day we took the train from an unseasonably cold Galway to an equally chilling Kilkenny. It had actually snowed in Galway, in the midwest of Ireland on the Atlantic coast, an event which is about as rare as watching the Cubs play in the World Series. The fierce winds seemed to coincide with the general mood, since the possibility of a settlement for Northern Ireland between the two negotiating political camps appeared to be diminishing with each news report.

Former U.S. Senator from Maine George Mitchell had been appointed to chair the talks, and he had set a personal deadline of midnight the previous day, April 9, 1998. His stated reason was timeliness. Anglo-Irish tradition sets aside at least a month for campaigning before a legislature could be elected (the New Northern Ireland Assembly, in this case). This meant that at least a month would be necessary for referenda in Ireland and Northern Ireland over the question of whether the people accepted the settlement that was to be the GFA. If so, another month would be devoted to campaigning prior to an election of Assembly members. Since both governments were eager to have all this behind them when the marching season began in July, the April 9, date seemed reasonable.[3] However, one of the participants of the talks ventured a more reasonable guess at Mitchell's reasons for the deadline: he had promised his wife that he would be home by Easter.[4]

Mitchell surely had good cause for his frustration and desire to bring the protracted talks to a conclusion. He had actually begun his work in Northern Ireland back in 1995, a task to establish a trade conference that he was assured would take only about six months.[5]

The entire week before the settlement had been replete with bad news regarding any consensus by the deadline. On Tuesday, April 7, the UUP had rejected the portion of Mitchell's draft regarding the creation of a cross border body between the Republic and Northern Ireland (known as Strand Two of the Agreement). Mitchell's draft had been pursuant to lengthy negotiations with both governments, and the refusal of the UUP to accept it had come as a harsh blow. Late that evening Bertie Ahern, Ireland's *Taoiseach*, decided to renegotiate these provisions on which the Irish negotiators had so tediously labored and deliberated. Sadly, this was the evening before the funeral for Ahern's mother, the reason for his sudden return to Dublin. (Most of the talks took place at Stormont in Belfast, although there were intermittent sessions in London and in Dublin Castle. These culminating talks in April, 1998, were back in Stormont, which was symbolic. It is in the imposing series of buildings in East Belfast in which the first Parliament of Northern Ireland had been housed where the problems with this draft arose.)

News had indeed been topsy-turvy. Unionists would reject a portion of a draft, and Nationalists would be dissatisfied with a revision of a part which had been acceptable to Unionists. Keeping up with "who's on first" (with apologies to Bud Abbott and Lou Costello for the comparison) was tricky at best.

My husband Jack and I had listened to the news in Galway that Good Friday morning. Again, one side had agreed to accept the latest revision, and the other had not. This was a reversal from the respective positions on Thursday evening.

After a cold train ride, we arrived at a B & B in Kilkenny early Friday afternoon, and I left immediately to attend Good Friday services at a nearby church. Upon my return, Jack told me, "They've switched again." At that point, it was *Sinn Féin* Nationalists who were balking at the most recent draft. The reality of a settlement seemed not only remote, but indeed impossible. It was then that I personally conceded that there would in fact be no agreement.

We braved the elements to leave for dinner. To my husband's chagrin, Kilkenny's many pubs were closed by law. (Jack had not believed my statement that federal law prohibits the sale of alcoholic beverages on Good Friday. Interestingly, this is the only day throughout the year –not Christmas, or even Easter – for such mandatory closures.) We finally located one—the White Oak Pub and Restaurant—where food—but no alcohol—was served.

The pub/restaurant had two television screens, one in the pub section with the omnipresent football game (soccer, to the American for whom football means a veritably lethal sport), and the other, in the front of the restaurant, set on the news channel.

I was facing the television in the front which was visible but not audible from where we were seated. Suddenly, Senator Mitchell appeared on the screen. His strained, tense and weary demeanor and expression during the past few months had been disturbing. The peace talks had apparently taken an emotional and physical toll on the senator. The man I saw on the television screen, however, was clearly a different George Mitchell. He was absolutely beaming. I recall saying to Jack, "Something has happened. George Mitchell is actually smiling!"

I hurried up to the front of the restaurant to hear the news that all the parties had reached a settlement. I was nearly apoplectic!

Surprisingly, my mood seemed to be the exception. Others in the pub —and on the train to Dublin and then on to Belfast the next day—appeared absolutely nonplussed, even apathetic. The men in the pub that evening continued reading their newspapers or racing forms without missing the proverbial beat, obviously unaffected by this news which was, to me, so startling and profound.

The reasonable deduction was that to the average citizen who had witnessed decades of strife in Northern Ireland, these were simply idealistic decisions made by lofty politicians who still had the burden of proving that such an agreement was meritorious. Our cab driver in Belfast the next evening stated in a very matter-of-fact manner, "We'll see, we'll see. This fightin's been happenin', seems like forever. This ain't gonna make it stop."

These nay-sayers were not about to burst this American's optimistic bubble! Nonetheless, having been in Northern Ireland for nearly four months by then, I fully understood this pessimistic, but admittedly realistic, perception among the Irish and Northern Irelanders. That Easter Sunday morning, the rector at my Church of Ireland articulated this candor perhaps best when he said, "Finally we have a chance for peace in our land. But it is only a chink...only a chink. We have so much yet to do, and I pray that we'll up to doing it." [6]

The Good Friday Agreement

The Agreement actually contained two separate documents.[7] The shorter one is the British-Irish Agreement,[8] in which both sovereign governments commit themselves to take the necessary domestic legislative and constitutional measures to implement the GFA. Only the representatives of the two governments signed this agreement, *Taoiseach* Bertie Ahern for the Republic of Ireland and Prime Minister Tony Blair for the United Kingdom.

The second one—the part which was the product of much compromise after prolonged contentious negotiations—is considerably lengthier and more detailed. This is the so-called Good Friday Agreement (GFA)[9] that was submitted to voters in both the Republic of Ireland and Northern Ireland for approval on May 22, 1998.

Constitutional Issues

There would be only one question on the referendum ballot for voters in Northern Ireland. They would simply approve or disapprove of the GFA.

For those in the Republic of Ireland, an additional question was necessary. Substantial revisions of the 1937 Constitution of Ireland were a fundamental part of what led to Unionists' acceptance of the final draft. This second question on the ballot in Ireland dealt not with the present, but rather with the future concerning the possibility of a united Ireland.

Technical Changes Assuring Jurisdiction

First, there had to be certainty that the proposed constitutional changes would themselves be constitutionally correct. [*Author's note: A word of warning to the non-lawyer is appropriate here*: This section is legally technical and may indeed have the same effect on the layperson as would Sominex.]

A procedural, but significant, problem arose with the constitutionality of the method in which the GFA proposed that the Constitution of Ireland be amended. This issue points to a distinction between the two constitutions of 20th century Ireland.

The 1922 document was conjoined with 1920 partition. This Constitution provided for amendment by statute (solely by act of the legislature). Conversely, the 1937 Constitution required a process with two sequential steps: (i) submission to the *Dáil* and approval by the *Oireachtas* (the entire legislative body, consisting of the *Dáil Éireann* and *Seanad Éireann)* and (ii) subsequent approval by a majority of voters in a referendum.[10] This was a clear change from the legislative amendment method of the 1922 Constitution.[11] Importantly, Article 46 of the 1937 Constitution also expressly stated that any provision of the Constitution might be amended.[12]

The GFA, however, provided for amendment by only the step-two referendum circumventing the necessity for approval by the *Oireachtas.*[13] This was in effect a one-time change from the usual manner of amending the Constitution as established in Article 46.

Never estimate the innovative logic of an imaginative and clever lawyer. Two barristers challenged the constitutionality of this aberration as being itself unconstitutional. This argument viewed the constitutional provision in Article 46 that all provisions were subject to amendment as excepting by implication Article 46 itself. In *Riordan v. Taoiseach,* the High Court (the appellate court in the Irish judicial system from which appeal is to the Supreme Court of Ireland, the highest court) held the GFA method to meet constitutional muster,[14] and the Supreme Court affirmed.[15] This paved the way for the GFA to be implemented.[16] (Note: If the reader who is a layperson is not sufficiently confused, perhaps he or she might consider applying to law school, since these are arguments that only a constitutional purist could love.)

The Proposed Substantive Amendments

First, it would be necessary to augment Article 29 of the 1937 Constitution of Ireland, the section addressing Ireland's relationship and affairs with other nations. The relevant provisions are:

Article 29

1. Ireland affirms its devotion to the ideal of peace and friendly co-operation amongst nations founded on international justice and morality.

2. Ireland affirms its adherence to the principle of the pacific settlement of international disputes by international arbitration or judicial determination.

3. For the purpose of the exercise of any executive function of the State in or in connection with its external relations, the Government may to such extent and subject to such conditions, if any, as may be determined by law, avail of or adopt any organ, instrument, or method of procedure used or adopted for the like purpose by the members of any group or league of nations with which the State is or becomes associated for the purpose of international co-operation in matters of common concern.

4. Every international agreement to which the State becomes a party shall be laid before *Dáil Éireann* [the primary house of the Irish legislature].

5. No international agreement shall be part of the domestic law of the State save as may be determined by the *Oireachtas* [the combined two houses of the Irish legislature].[17]

Obviously, it was critical that the government of Ireland would be constitutionally empowered to accept and carry through its obligations under the GFA. These obligations would include the creation of the Irish component of the to-be-established cross-border body (Strand Two of the GFA) and the Council of the Isles (Strand Three).

A bit of legal history in 20th century Ireland (the island) will clarify the need for amending Article 29. The 1920 Act of Ireland which had partitioned the island created a Council of Ireland. This body, comprised of representatives from the Irish *Dáil* and the Northern Ireland Parliament, was to have a consultative role in the adoption of any domestic laws by one which would affect the other, or which would have an effect upon the island as a whole. When the British government suspended the Northern Ireland Parliament in 1972 as a result of the Troubles and resumed direct control over the province, the Council met its demise.

After this brief hiatus, the Council was again resuscitated, but not for long. In 1974, there was an attempt to renew some self-government in Northern Ireland in the form of the power-sharing effort known as Sunningdale (for the situs in England of the talks leading to this short-lived government). This agreement included the intent to revive the old 1920 Council of Ireland.

This body whose members would be members of the Irish *Dáil* and the Northern Ireland Assembly created by Sunningdale became non-existent when the trial government (the Sunningdale assembly lasted less than one-half year, from January until June, 1974) itself folded, and Westminster again assumed control over the province.

The idea of reviving some type of cooperative body between Northern Ireland and the Republic was only dormant, not dead. The 1985 Anglo-Irish Agreement,[18] the brainchild of British Prime Minister Margaret Thatcher and Irish *Taoiseach* Garret Fitzgerald, created anew the old Council established in the 1920 statute. This was actually a treaty passed by the two governments of the United Kingdom and Ireland, however, without approval of the people of Northern Ireland. Therefore, there were bitter objections. Ian Paisley referred to the Anglo-Irish Agreement as an intrusion upon the "integrity of the Union between Great Britain and Northern Ireland," one achieved "over the heads of the people" and a "formal interference in our [Northern Ireland's] affairs."[19] This document had given the Irish government the right to be consulted in Westminster's policy on Northern Ireland, much as had the Council of Ireland of 1920 and 1974.[20] Quite naturally, Unionists were unified in opposing the Anglo-Irish Agreement.

The next joint British-Irish agreement came in 1993 with the Downing Street Declaration between Prime Minister John Major and *Taoiseach* Albert Reynolds.[21] This agreement referred to an intra-island cooperative council in a more formal fashion.[22]

On Good Friday, 1998, an all-island council was set in concrete, provided the GFA was approved in both referenda. The first of the agreements adopted the British-Irish Agreement between the two governments (Ireland and the United Kingdom), would repeal and take the place of the 1985 Anglo-Irish Agreement.[23] Strand Two of the GFA would then establish a new North/South body.[24] In order that this entity would have legal status, it was necessary that the government of Ireland be authorized to establish such a body under Article 29 of the 1937 Constitution.

The primary substantive constitutional changes of the GFA concerned the Irish government's claim to sovereignty over the island of Ireland.[25] The significance of the wording of these amendments is discussed below, but whether any input from the new Northern Ireland government into the affairs of Ireland is itself constitutionally valid became the initial question. This may seem a reversal, since the argument had generally been Unionists' position that the Republic of Ireland was not justified in interfering in Northern Ireland's affairs. This time, the argument was that the Irish Constitution forbade such interference *from* the North.

The similar institution set up by the 1985 Anglo-Irish Agreement had been legally opposed in a case which would seemingly have established a precedent for the legality of the North/South body contemplated by the GFA. The McGimpsey brothers were Northern Ireland Unionists. They went to the Irish courts to file a back-door challenge to the constitutionality of the all-Ireland institution, alleging that it violated the Irish constitutional territorial claim to the entire island in Articles 2 and 3. Clearly, Unionists did not support this claim, but the plaintiffs' intent was to use it as a vehicle for trouncing the council which had been created by treaty, without input from the voters in Northern Ireland. So by arguing that the 1985 Agreement facially violated the Irish Constitution as an infringement upon the sovereignty of the Republic of Ireland, their desired result would be the nullification of a treaty which they found odious. Thus, both sides supported the position that the territorial claim was a legal right.

The High Court held the Anglo-Irish Agreement constitutional. Pending the McGimpseys' appeal to the Supreme Court of Ireland, that Court decided *McGlinchey v. Ireland and the Attorney General*.[26] The *McGlinchey* Court addressed the meaning of the Irish constitutional claim to territorial ownership of the entire island espoused in Articles 2 and 3 and held this claim to be a valid one, but one which was *political*, rather than *legal*.

The Court in *McGlinchey* had applied the reasoning of its holding in a 1977 decision, *Article 26 and the Criminal Law (Jurisdiction) Bill 1975*.[27] [Author's note: An Article 26 case is a request by the President that the Court determine the constitutionality of a bill before he or she signs it into law.[28]] This 1977 case had involved the constitutionality of the opinion had classified the claim to sovereignty as one "*not* in the *legal* but in the *political* order."

Relying largely on the *Criminal Law (Jurisdiction) Bill* decision of 1977 and its decision in *McGlinchey,* the Supreme Court of Ireland affirmed the High Court's holding in *McGimpsey* that the 1985 Anglo-Irish Agreement was constitutional. As in *Criminal Law (Jurisdiction) Bill* and *McGlinchey*, the Court in *McGimpsey* viewed the Articles 2 and 3 claim to territorial sovereignty as indeed valid, but in a *political,* rather than a *legal,* sense.[29]

Whether an issue is "political" or "legal" is an arcane constitutional question, but a look at U.S. law is helpful. Because of the American separation-of-powers doctrine between the legislature (Congress), the executive (president), and the judiciary (courts), one branch cannot constitutionally intrude on the powers of another. Terming an issue "political" means essentially that it lies in the domain of the legislature and is thus not appropriate for a court to decide. The seminal American case on the "political doctrine" issue is *Baker v. Carr.* [30]

Oddly, the Irish Supreme Court had earlier expressly held the Irish constitution in its entirely to be both a political and a legal document. Notably, the Court's opinion in the *1977 Criminal (Jurisdiction) Bill* case quoted its decision in *Russell v. Fanning* [31] which called the reunification of the two Irelands—the "national territory"—a "constitutional imperative." [32] The view of the *McGimpsey* Court appears inapposite.

However, the rationale in *McGimpsey* was fundamentally different, since the

Court recognized that any change in Northern Ireland's political status must be compatible with another provision of the Irish Constitution—Article 29, quoted above. This section affirms the adoption by the government of Ireland of the rule of peaceful settlement of international disputes.[33] Chief Justice Finlay, however, again quoted the "constitutional imperative" language in the *Russell* decision that the declaration of the extent of the national territory cited in Article 2 was indeed a claim of a *legal* right. The circular rationale of the *McGimpsey* Court's holding concluded by referring the the express language of the Constitution [34] that the *Dáil* is prohibited from enacting any law of "greater extent than the laws of *Saorstát Éireann*," but reminded of the qualifier, "pending the integration of the national territory." The "greater extent" language was apparently viewed in this situation as geographical extent. The *Sáorstat Éireann*—Free State—had no ability to enact laws which applied to Northern Ireland, but the "pending" language in the 1937 Constitution inferred that this limitation on the powers of the *Dáil* was temporary. Thus, the *McGimpsey* Court seemed to rationalize and to say that the *Dáil's* power is merely put on jurisdictional hold.

This book is not a treatise on the Irish Constitution, but any explanation of the GFA must include a summary of these constitutional intricacies. For those interested in this particular issue involving the GFA, the article by O'Donnel [35] is a "good read," as the Irish would say. Other informative and detailed sources of Irish constitutional law are by Kelly, Hogan, and Whyte [36] and David Gwynn Morgan. [37] Finally, a good scholarly article by James Casey on amending the Irish constitution is in a volume of articles on the Constitution in general, published in 1988.[38]

[Author's note: The non-lawyer reader might now awake and resume reading.]

Substantive Changes to the Irish Constitution: Articles 2 and 3

The first constitution was the 1922 version, the offspring of the 1920 Westminster statute on partition[39] and the subsequent failed civil war in Ireland (1921-1922). This was the Constitution of the *Sáorstat Éireann*, the Free State of Ireland. This quasi-independent status permitted the 26 counties of the south of the island and Donegal in the northwest to govern themselves, with their own legislature or parliament (the *Dáil*) and Prime Minister (*Taoiseach*). Nonetheless, the allegiance of the Free State remained with the crown of Great Britain. One of those who had been disappointed by the Free State status rather than total independence was Eamon DeValera who had been the first President of Ireland and who would later serve as *Taoiseach*.

The 1937 Constitution was DeValera's bold and almost defiant document. Approved by referendum, it declared Ireland a virtual republic a presumptive statement that "Ireland" referred to the entire island which it termed a "nation." [40] It is important to remember that the remaining six counties became the province of

Northern Ireland which had its own Parliament, but remained a part of the United Kingdom where British laws were applicable. However, since the island included Northern Ireland, this constitutional claim of the Free State obviously encompassed the entire thirty-two counties. Moreover, the Free State of Ireland was not completely independent from the United Kingdom, but had the status of a dominion (as did Canada, Australia, New Zealand, and South Africa).

Interestingly, the Irish courts do not have the same luxury as American courts in interpreting the framers' intent. In the U.S.A., judges might look to documents such as Alexander Hamilton's *The Federalist Papers* and other supplementary materials written during the 18th century constitutional debates.

To the contrary, the 1937 Irish Constitution of Ireland was the product of secret meetings, and the debates in the *Dáil* were replete with partisan bickering rather than by any genuine effort to determine what the drafters meant by the language they had used.[41] Moreover, although lawyers authored the 1922 Constitution, the 1937 version was the product of laymen. One difference from the earlier 1922 Constitution is that the 1937 Constitution has been regarded as relatively "rigid," and not so malleable or open to judicial construction.[42]

Americans refer to James Madison as the Father of the Constitution, and the Irish may well confer that title upon Eamon DeValera, politician *par excellence*. Some commentary on DeValera the person is instructive.

DeValera

Often called the "Tall Fellow" to distinguish him from Michael Collins (Minister of Defense and Finance of the new *Sáorstat Éireann*) who was known as the "Big Fellow,"[43] DeValera was born in New York to an Irish mother and a Spanish father. His father died when he was only two years of age, and he came to Ireland with his mother to live with her family in County Limerick. "Dev," as he is generally called, was among those imprisoned, but not executed, in the 1916 Easter Rising.

It has been presumed that his American birth had saved him, from the death penalty since the British did not relish invoking the wrath of the U.S.A.[44] His Constitution has proven to be a source of an ongoing debate as to whether it is "legal" or pure political philosophy. DeValera himself was not a lawyer.

How did the GFA propose to alter the "territorial claim" language in Articles 2 and 3? One must look at the 1937 Constitution's versions and the GFA proposed amended versions.

Article 2
1937 Constitution

The national territory consists of the whole island of Ireland, its islands and the territorial seas.

GFA

It is the entitlement and birthright of every person born in the island of Ireland which includes its islands and seas, to be part of the Irish nation. That is also the entitlement of all persons otherwise qualified in accordance with law to be citizens of Ireland. Furthermore, the Irish nation cherishes its special affinity with people of Irish ancestry living abroad who share its cultural identity and heritage.

Article 3

1937 Constitution

Pending the reintegration of the national territory, and without prejudice to the right of the Parliament and Government established by this Constitution to exercise jurisdiction over the whole of that territory, the laws enacted by that Parliament shall have the like area and extent of application as the laws of the *Saorstát Éireann* and the like extra-territorial effect.

GFA

1. It is the firm will of the Irish nation, in harmony and friendship, to unite all the people who share the territory of the island of Ireland, in all the diversity of their identities and traditions, recognising that a united Ireland shall be brought about only by peaceful means with the consent of a majority of the people, democratically expressed, in both jurisdictions in the island. Until then, the laws enacted by the Parliament established by this Constitution shall have the area and extent of application as the laws enacted by the Parliament that existed immediately before the coming into operation of this Constitution.

2. Institutions with executive powers and functions that are shared between those jurisdictions may be established by their respective responsive authorities for stated purposes and may exercise powers and functions in respect of all or any part of the island.

[Author's note: The author did not misspell "recognising." The text is as the original. The British have strange ways indeed to the American eye of spelling such words as "labor" ("labour"), "organize" ("organise"), and the like.]

What do these changes mean, other than that the revisions are visibly longer than the 1937 articles? A change in the constitutional territorial claim was a linchpin if Unionists were to accept the Strand Two cross-border institution and the emergence of another power-sharing government.

What did the changes accomplish? To some Unionists, it was a great deal. This is particularly so with respect to Trimble's UUP. He has referred to the post-Downing Street Declaration Frameworks document of 1995 as being "obviously unacceptable"[45] because of its provisions calling for more extensive all-island co-operation and its failure to resolve the territorial sovereignty claim in the Irish Constitution.

The purpose of the Frameworks document had been to settle constitutional confusion emanating from the *Russell, Criminal Law (Jurisdiction) Bill*, and *McGlinchey* decisions and their progeny. Trimble has distinguished the GFA amendments for two reasons: (i) the revised Article 3 is aspirational, rather than absolute; and (ii) any change in the status of Northern Ireland will require referenda in both the Republic and Northern Ireland.[46] This would eliminate any possibility of outside interference in the affairs of the province. Anti-GFA opponents, such as Paisley, would, of course, deem the Republic itself to be an "outsider."

Thus, the Trimble camp viewed the changes to Articles 2 and 3 as having compensated for many parts of the GFA which were not so palatable to Unionists, such as the RUC reform, d'Hondt system assurance of Nationalists (particularly *Sinn Féin*) in the Assembly, and release of prisoners. Trimble emphasized that the language of the GFA acknowledged the fact that the present wish of the majority of the people of Northern Ireland is to remain a part of the United Kingdom.[47]

Additionally, David Byrne, then Attorney General of Ireland, explained the amendments as a modernization of Articles 2 and 3 in relation to the jurisdiction of the Republic, the "nature of the nation, and the aspiration of Ireland for unity."[48] Byrne pointed out that the replacement of the language in Article 2 which stated that "the whole island of Ireland, its islands and the territorial sea" was a "generous and inclusive definition of the Irish nation as all of those born in Ireland...[as] for the first time mak[ing it] clear that it is the entitlement and birthright of every person born on he island...to be part of the Irish nation."[49] [Author's note: This must have been a thrilling revelation to the Rev. Dr. Paisley to know that he, too, can be "part of the Irish nation."]

Byrne viewed this language actually as improved from the viewpoint of Nationalists, since it was the first "explicit acceptance by the British government of the right of the people in Northern Ireland to hold Irish citizenship."[50] Notably, the 1937 Constitution permitted statutory law further to define who is eligible for citizenship,[51] and a 1956 statute permitted persons born in Northern Ireland to become citizens also of Ireland.[52]

Byrne has pointed out that the primary difference between citizenship rights for those born in the Republic of Ireland (for whom citizenship is automatic) and those born in Northern Ireland and whose parents were not citizens is that the latter must take positive steps to attain Irish citizenship. One first must be an adult, or a minor whose parents speak on his behalf, and declare himself to be a citizen of the Republic of Ireland. In such cases, this person shall be deemed to have been a citizen since birth.[53] Interestingly, the current President of Ireland, Mary McAleese, was born and reared in the Ardoyne section of Belfast, but she is such a professed-as-an-adult citizen of Ireland. Her seven-year term in this office began in 1997.

Another perspective on the constitutional changes to Articles 2 and 3 comes from Dr. Martin Mansergh, Special Assistant to *Taoiseach* Bertie Ahern, and one who played a major role in the negotiations. The changes in Article 2, he has written, are a reformulation in terms of the people of the island, rather than the land itself. Moreover, a "one nation theory" had endured, but on a basis which would occur only voluntarily and according to the will of the people of both Irelands. He added that all persons who resided on the island of Ireland, whether in the Republic or in Northern Ireland, were deemed to "share the territory," such that the constitutional changes conferred an "Irishness" of sorts on people in the prov-ince.[54]

Finally, the changes were lauded by Professor Brendan O'Leary as an "open-ended mechanism for Northern Ireland to expand its autonomy from the rest of the United Kingdom, albeit with the consent of the Secretary of State and the approval of Westminster." Professor O'Leary notes in particular that neither the Scottish Parliament nor the Welsh Assembly, both also recently devolved, has this possibil-ity. In his words, the province of Northern Ireland can "gain maximum autonomy while remaining within the Union provided that there is agreement within the North-ern Ireland Assembly." [55] Thus, even though the United Kingdom relationship is yet intact, the proverbial door is open for a change in that status. It is difficult to perceive this as a benefit to any group other than Nationalists.

Of course, anything that is a boon for Nationalists is bitter medicine for Union-ists. Therefore, for those Unionists outside the UUP-interpretation of the constitu-tional changes, the version as amended has been of no benefit whatsoever. Clearly, this camp views them as a poor tradeoff indeed for their concessions, particularly on the power-sharing Assembly and the release of prisoners.

Professor Dennis Kennedy of Queen's University is among those who view these changes as cosmetic, at best. Professor Kennedy does not affiliate himself with either Nationalists or Unionists. He voted for the GFA, but "against my better judgment," [56] and he has assessed the constitutional changes caustically.

Kennedy has described these alterations as removing "only the explicit [terri-torial] claim, leaving an implied one and much of the nationalist myth on which it is based." [57] (Professor Kennedy also does not adhere to the belief that there is a "distinct Irishness," which he termed "utterly nonsense." [58] Significantly, Prof. Kennedy was born in the Republic of Ireland, but he attended Queen's University Belfast and did his graduate study at Trinity College Dublin. Thus, he has lived on both sides of the border.)

Sinn Féin Assembly member Mitchel McLaughlin said that "we [the Nationalist negotiators] created space which Unionists could accept for the inevitable"—a united Ireland.[59] Thus, there is ample support for the position that the constitutional changes were either of no effect, or even positive changes for Nationalists. This is despite the fact that this was a *quid pro quo* for Unionist acceptance of the RUC reform, admission of *Sinn Féin* to a new Assembly, and release of political prisoners.

The position of the Rev. Dr. Paisley was anticipated. He has written that he "suspect(s) that the Irish Government could not believe their fortune that the Ulster Unionists, instead of rejecting the Anglo-Irish process, so fully embraced it and through this Agreement has embellished it." [60] He views the change as leaving Northern Ireland without its "British status…roll[ing] the two—status and change—…into one, indicating that the status has and will continue to change." [61] This author would take issue only with his past tense conclusion –the status has *already* changed. Nonetheless, the implication of the amended language seems to be that, presumably, *it will* indeed change.

This American observer perceived the GFA in general as a godsend to Nationalists. The overwhelming support of voters in the Republic (overwhelming Catholic and true believers in the reunification of the two Irelands) and Nationalists in Northern Ireland and the somewhat less enthusiastic—however, a majority—of Unionists in Northern Ireland approved the GFA would appear to confirm this judgment.

The jury out is on the extent of the significance of the constitutional amendments.

Strand One: The New Northern Ireland Assembly

This 108-member body is representative of inclusiveness in the extreme, one that Bill Maher would never, ever classify as "politically incorrect." The GFA and subsequent supplementary legislation expressly state that both Nationalists and Unionists must be included as members of the Assembly.[62] Its cross-community basis of decision-making essentially means that any measure passed must be approved by a majority of each of the two sectors. This is an official protection of rights of the minority (now Nationalist) in a manner which many politicians and scholars view as extreme. To be sure, it can surely decelerate the law-making process.

The d'Hondt method of electing legislators and the careful balancing of Assembly members' votes so as to assure protection of both Nationalists and Unionists has been the target of harsh criticism. There is a built-in assurance that there will be a proportional number of minority (Nationalist) Assembly members, and the requirement that each side—Unionists and Nationalists—must approve a bill in order for it to be adopted into law solidifies this power sharing.

Perhaps the most vocal and impassioned critic was the Rev. Dr. Paisley. His characterization of the Assembly as an "undemocratic institution" which gives Nationalists parties an absolute veto over any debated proposed legislation[63] is accurate indeed. The flip side is also true: if Unionists were to become the minority, they would be afforded the same protection.

The moderate—and unaffiliated with regard to declaring themselves as Nationalist or Unionist[64]—Alliance Party has also objected to the election and voting systems as being undemocratic. Alliance voiced a preference for a "genuine liberal democracy" election process by which neither side would be assured a percentage of representation. Such a democracy would disregard ethnicity, culture, and/or religion and would treat the individual, rather than groups, as the "cornerstone of society." [65]

In this author's opinion, this required-by-law designation of each party's Assembly members as "Nationalist," "Unionist" or "neither" perpetuates the cleavage which has made Northern Ireland the divided society which it is. Nonetheless, it is the product of much compromise, and this entrenched power-sharing *modus operandi* was one of the provisions that were a *sine qua non* of the GFA, a document that is indeed the embodiment of give-and-take. Even the Alliance Party concedes that the problems that are unique to Northern Ireland simply make intercultural assimilation a prerequisite for an ideal democracy.[66] And characterizing the situation in Northern Ireland as not an ideal one is a stark understatement.

Strand Two: The Cross-Border Council

Strand Two, the provision which provided for an all-island body comprised of representatives from both Northern Ireland and the Republic, proved to be one of the most contentious provisions, one which nearly derailed the negotiations during the final few days. David Trimble and his UUP rejected Chairman Mitchell's draft early in the week before Easter because of the section on the North-South institution.

According to Trimble, the main concern of Unionists was the possibility of a body with supranational oversight, one which would empower Ireland as a virtual co-pilot in the governance of Northern Ireland.[67] Any such cross-border institution which would be acceptable to Unionists, then, could not be an independently empowered institution, but one which would be accountable to both the Irish *Dáil* and the Northern Ireland Assembly.

A body resembling the 1974 (Sunningdale) Ministerial Council would be abhorrent to Unionists, since it had been imposed upon the people of the province without a referendum or consultation with any of the political parties. In Trimble's view, this had further alienated Loyalist groups, and the counterproductive result was an escalation of violence.[68] Thus, a repeat of such an institution which could wield power over the proposed Northern Ireland legislature would have to be avoided if Unionists were to come back on board.

Both Chairman Mitchell and Trimble's UUP expressed serious concerns about the length of the draft provision. As Trimble put it, the "pudding had been over egged." [69] Not only did renegotiations result in a paring down of the cumbersome and overburdened wording, but there were also significant substantive changes. As revised, the agreement provided that the Northern Ireland Assembly and the Republic of Ireland would determine which areas are appropriate for referral to the cross-border council.

Of notable importance to Unionists was the addition of language providing that all GFA-created institutions—the Assembly (Strand One), the North/South Ministerial Council, commonly known as the cross-border council (Strand Two), and the British-Irish Council, commonly known as the Council of the Isles (Strand Three)—would commence to exist simultaneously. [70] This would assuage any Unionist fears that the input from the Republic in an institution which might be a reality before Assembly elections, could possibly subsume the new Assembly.

The final draft provided that members of the North-South Ministerial Council would be members of the respective executive bodies of the Republic and Northern Ireland. (For the American reader, it is important to remember that those on the "executive" are plural in number, not an elected president whose election is independent from the election of members of the legislature, *i.e.*, the Congress, as is the case in the U.S.A. In a parliamentary system, the executive is comprised of elected legislators. For example, both Prime Minister Tony Blair and *Taoiseach* Bertie Ahern are elected members of their respective parliaments.)

From Northern Ireland, this body would include the First Minister (Unionist, as the majority sector) and Deputy First Minister (Nationalist, as the minority) and other "relevant members." From the Republic of Ireland, members would be the *Taoiseach* and the same other "relevant members" of the *Oireachtas* (parliament). (One might wonder whether the use of this term would infer to those not selected that they are "irrelevant.")

The Council is to meet at least twice annually. Its duties are to consult and to co-operate on matters "of mutual interest" and to decide by agreement "common policies" on those areas on which there is not only this "mutual interest," but also an "all-island benefit." [71]

The transitional Northern Ireland administration and the Irish government (with consultation with the British government) would, by October 31, 1998, earmark twelve areas suitable for such co-operation. [72]

Note that an annex to Strand Two lists several areas which this list may include: agriculture, education, transport, environment, waterways, social security and welfare, tourism, European Union programs, inland fisheries, aquaculture and marine matters, health, urban and rural development. (For the American lawyer, this listing might be compared to a Uniform Act or Model Act prepared by the American Law Institute in an area where consistency among the states is desirable. Since the detailed and tedious work has already been prepared in such cases, the state legislatures would be expected to adopt such legislation more quickly, needing only to iron out any minor provisions. Similarly, this selection of twelve possible areas of co-operation was in a practical sense a "done deed " already accomplished within the GFA.) This would be prior to the actual transfer of power to the devolved government of Northern Ireland. At its first meeting, the North-South Ministerial Council would then agree upon no fewer than six areas of co-operation.[73] Since members of this body are answerable to their own legislature (the *Oireachtas* and the Northern Ireland Assembly),[74] a supranational power which had been so distasteful to Unionists was avoided.

Professor Brendan O'Leary, Chair of the Department of Political Science at London School of Economics, has pointed out an interlocking effect of Strand One (Assembly) and Strand Two (Council of the Isles). After the approval of the GFA via referenda in both Ireland and Northern Ireland, no Unionist majority could unilaterally present a roadblock to any action by the Council. Strand One would require a majority also of Nationalists to prevent any Council decision from being implemented.[75]

Any institution which is praised by Nationalists would necessarily be objectionable to many Unionists. The Rev. Dr. Paisley has deplored this body not only because it provides for power for the minority (Nationalist) in Northern Ireland, but also because the balance of power island-wide is so overwhelmingly Nationalist. The first two Northern Ireland members are balanced (the Unionist First Minister and the Nationalist Deputy First Minister). Even if one were to assume that a third member is Unionist, the addition of the three members from the Republic of Ireland which would presumably favor a united Ireland would condemn Unionists to a 4-2 minority status.[76]

Dr. Martin Mansergh, Special Assistant to the *Taoiseach*, has expressed another fear of anti-GFA Unionists, that the Council of the Isles might be a precursor to a united Ireland. In instances where cultural identities are at issue, those opposed to a reunification might be swallowed by an all-Ireland mentality, with a "single island economy" as well as an "all-island political entity." [77]

On the other hand, Professor O'Leary assesses the potential for Northern Ireland benefits from the cross-border co-operative body as quite good indeed. In his opinion, the so-called Celtic Tiger—a reference to Ireland's booming economy during the past two decades—surely will spill over into the province as a result of these combined efforts. Additionally, he sees the potential for attracting more substantial funding from the European Union for agriculture and tourism as enhanced when requests are from the island as an entity.[78]

Strand Three: The "Council of the Isles"

This second confederation is comprised of the two sovereign governments of the United Kingdom (including the newly devolved governments of Scotland, Wales, and Northern Ireland) and the Republic of Ireland. Reaching agreement on this body was a relative "piece of cake," so to speak.

Although this may facially appear to balance Unionists' fears of absorption into oblivion by the North/South Council, this inter-island body is generally regarded by experts to be the considerably weaker and less significant of the two.[79] The British-Irish Council (BIC)—or Council of the Isles—is essentially a consultative, rather than a policy-making, body.

Unionists had advocated the supremacy of the Council of the Isles over that of the North/South (cross-border) body, but there is in fact no relationship between the two. First, the GFA mandates the establishment of the North/South Ministerial Council, since it is linked to the Northern Ireland Assembly.[80] That is, one can neither exist nor function without the other. On the other hand, although the GFA language referring to the Council of the Isles is expressly mandatory,[81] the document is silent with respect to any such linkage between this institution and the Northern Ireland Assembly. The inference is that it might in reality be a voluntarily established body, indeed, even an optional one.

Moreover, the government of the Republic of Ireland may be hesitant to participate seriously in any discussions carried out by this institution because of the "out-numbered" factor. Its British counterparts are many: England, Scotland, Wales, Northern Ireland, the islands of Jersey and Guernsey, and the Isle of Man.[82] Consequently, relative to the North/South Council, the Council of the Isles is relatively watered-down and impotent.

Other Relevant Provisions of the GFA

The revamping of the Royal Ulster Constabulary (the RUC, Northern Ireland's police force), decommissioning of paramilitaries, release of so-called political prisoners, and the human rights provisions each are discussed more elaborately in separate chapters. The connecting trend is that each of these represents a trade-off of sorts, a concession by one sector or the other in exchange for another provision deemed favorable. The cross-community nature of the GFA projects from every page.

Some Remarks on the Negotiations

The Senator Mitchell factor

George Mitchell's entry into the effort to arrive at a modicum of peace in Northern Ireland actually began on January 9, 1995, just a week after his departure from the United States Senate. A simple diplomatic mission to organize a trade conference to be held in Washington, D.C. in spring of 1995 marked his initiation into this work. His task on this conference, which would include businesses in

Northern Ireland, was his debut into the quagmire of the Troubles. This duty led to his participation in a follow-up to the conference which continued until late that year.[83]

The reader should recall that he had been assured that his work would take no more than six months, an assurance which should serve as a red-light for any serious baseball fan, as is Mitchell. (Mention of his name as a possible Commissioner of Major League Baseball had recurred since he had announced that he would not run for re-election to the Senate in March, 1994.) The good senator's familiarity with baseball lore should have reminded him that the designated hitter rule (used in the American League, but not the National League, in major league baseball) was introduced back in 1973 only on an experimental and temporary basis. In *déjà vu* fashion, the British government's "emergency" and "temporary" statutes were also effective in Northern Ireland in the early 1970's. The designated hitter rule and the "emergency" statutes are still both alive and well. Apparently, "temporary" is synonymous with "permanent" only in baseball and in Northern Ireland politics.

The second chapter in Mitchell's involvement in Northern Ireland came immediately upon the heels of the first. In response to the desire of the Republic of Ireland to make the Troubles in its neighbor to the North an issue of international dimensions, the British government agreed to establish a three-member commission of members not affiliated with the island to study and make recommendations on the complex problem of paramilitary disarmament (decommissioning).

The Irish government chose Harry Holkieri, former prime minister of Finland, and the British government selected General John de Chastelain, chief of the Canadian Defense Forces. As the largest super-power, the U.S.A. was asked by the two governments to intervene directly and to appoint the third member. President Bill Clinton chose Mitchell for this task, one which the British government predicted would last only "about two months."[84]

Although Mitchell's principles of democracy and non-violence were accepted, British Prime Minister John Major rejected the Commission's proposals because of the lingering dispute over whether disarmament of paramilitaries—"decommissioning," as the British and Irish termed it—must occur concurrently with any peace negotiations. Major finally proposed a start to decommissioning as an alternate,[85] and the peace process had begun.

Mitchell was then asked to chair the talks. With his decision to accept this task, his "two-month stay" in Northern Ireland was prolonged. Indeed, the chairing of the peace talks—already some one and one-half years after his first work in Northern Ireland—was to take only about six months. The British emissary advised him, "you should be home by Christmas [1996]."[86]

The talks, which actually began on June 10, 1996, continued until Good Friday—April 10—1998, a long "six months" indeed. Anyone who might doubt Mitchell's commitment should keep in mind that during the period beginning when he first answered President Clinton's first call to work on the trade commission in Northern Ireland, he had remarried (December 10, 1994); his wife had suffered a miscarriage (September, 1996); his brother had died (July, 1997); and his son Andrew was born (October 16, 1997).[87] Moreover, he returned to the province after the Assembly had been in action in order to mediate the inevitable difficulties which had arisen in the power-sharing environment. Mitchell's resolve and determination to achieve peace in Northern Ireland are admirable and extraordinary by anyone's standards.

For Senator Mitchell, the process was much like the legendary cat with nine lives. During his work, the talks survived a *Sinn Féin* cease-fire on August 30, 1994, followed by a similar abandonment of violence by Loyalist paramilitaries on October 6, 1994; a retraction by *Sinn Féin* of its agreement to forego violence on February 9, 1996, because of the failure of the parties in the negotiations to admit them to the talks; and a resumption of the cease-fire when *Sinn Féin* was admitted to the talks in July, 1997. A negative result of this recognition of the legitimacy of *Sinn Féin*, the political party connected to the IRA, was the permanent walk-out from the negotiations of Paisley's DUP.[88]

With the departure of the DUP and UKUP party representatives (both parties which ultimately were publicly opposed to the eventual settlement document), the group which finally participated in drafting the GFA had dwindled to sixteen in number.

The Final Week

After Chairman Mitchell's imposed deadline of midnight Thursday, April 9, 1998, even those areas which had been assumed to be relatively non-controversial again emerged. Strand Three—the Council of the Isles—presented little if any difficulty, as did (surprisingly) the police reform issue. (The reconstruction of the RUC later did become a major controversy, however, after the publication of the Patten Commission Report. Chapter 7 details the progress on this issue.) The provisions which generated the contention that so protracted the negotiations were Strand One (the composure and voting methods of the Northern Ireland Assembly) and Strand Two (the North/South Council).

On April 6, 1998, David Trimble's UUP rejected the two governments' presented draft on Strand Two. Negotiating anew the North/South Council at this point would truly be a house of cards. Moreover, it would naturally be objectionable to Irish *Taoiseach* Bertie Ahern, who had worked long and hard in arriving at an agreement with the British government on this section. The trickiness had been finding a wording which presumably would be acceptable to Unionists, but which would at the same time produce a cross-border body sufficiently authoritative to appease Nationalists.

A re-opening of discussions on this fragile subject would likely revisit other sensitive issues, primarily the release of prisoners and decommissioning. Some of these provisions had involved much haggling. Agreeing to re-enter the Strand Two talks would likely have a Pandora's Box effect of renewing consideration of other issues on which settlement had been reached after arduous talks.

For example, the fragile and emotional subjects of early release of prisoners and decommissioning of paramilitaries in particular would trigger a domino-like process. Both sides had made many concessions in the form of trade-offs on these provisions to arrive at language favorable to them, and the precariousness of revisiting Strand Two in order to please Unionists could unravel settlement on other issues which had involved tense negotiations and considerable give-and-take.

Ahern's plight was compounded by a personal tragedy. His mother had died suddenly, and he was back in Dublin to plan her funeral. When news reached him that Trimble had not agreed to the draft of the two governments, Ahern was downcast. On the evening before the requiem mass for his deceased mother, he decided to renegotiate Strand Two. Mitchell called this a "big decision by a big man," one which "made possible everything that followed." [89] After the funeral, a weary Ahern returned to Belfast to meet again with Tony Blair. Their attentions were once again focused on how to modify Strand Two enough to make it acceptable to Unionists, but not so much so as to damage Nationalists' approval.

According to Chairman Mitchell, no section was sacrosanct. Decommissioning was as controversial as it had been throughout the negotiations,[90] as was the release-of-prisoners issue so closely connected to decommissioning. Unionists insisted on the latter, and Nationalists, the former.

Mitchell has noted the apostasy of David Trimble, who had been one of those so bitterly opposed to the 1974 Sunningdale government because of what he viewed as excessive concessions to Nationalists, and, by inference, Republicans, via Sunningdale's power-sharing government. In 1998, Trimble desperately attempted to accommodate the most extreme of Nationalist parties, *Sinn Féin*, in order to achieve a cross-community government with similarities to the 1974 agreement he had deplored. Mitchell saw Trimble's change of course as complying with the yearning of the people in Northern Ireland who were simply tired of the constant fear and violence.[91] If concessions had to be made, they were two-way concessions,

According to Chairman Mitchell's memoirs, the Assembly issue (Strand One) had been intertwined with the cross-border one (Strand Two) as late as afternoon on Good Friday, shortly before agreement was reached. Unionists longed for a revived devolved government, and Nationalists wanted a cross-border body. Mitchell has written of "nearing the finish line" and "driving to a conclusion," even after the Thursday deadline had passed. He had announced late Wednesday evening that they would keep at it until they finished, either with an agreement or with the realization that they were in effect a "hung jury." [92]

The cumbersome language of the Strand Two draft rejected by Unionists had been pared down considerably. The majority of those still in the talks (Paisley's DUP had walked out when *Sinn Féin* was permitted to participate) settled on the method of Assembly voting which would assure protection of the minority sector and on a cross-border body which satisfied Unionists.

Just before 5 pm on April 10, 1998, an exhausted, but ecstatic, group of negotiators announced to the press and to the people that the peace agreement—the so-called Good Friday Agreement—had been executed.

The Preliminaries

The all-inclusive nature of the process was evident from the inception. Before the talks that officially began on June 10, 1996, a Forum where issues could be debated was established. This body was a 120-person group drawn from the province's ten strongest political parties. (To the American accustomed to a two-party system, this multiplicity of parties rings strange. To be sure, the several-party system can be counterproductive because of the difficulty of obtaining a majority, rather than simply a plurality.) The composition of this Forum was as follows:

(U) Ulster Unionist Party (UUP): 30 members
(U) Democratic Unionist Party (DUP): 24 members
(N) Social Democratic and Labour Party (SDLP): 21 members
(R) *Sinn Féin*: 17 members
(NA) Alliance: 7 members
(U) United Kingdom Unionist Party (UKUP): 3 members
(L) Progressive Unionist Party (PUP): 2 members
(L) Ulster Democratic Party (UDP): 2 members
(NA) Northern Ireland Women's Coalition: 2 members
(U) Labour: 2 members [93]

Legend:
"U"=   Unionist
"N"=   Nationalist
"R"=   Republican (Nationalist party attached to paramilitaries; note that
         Sinn Féin is attached to the Irish Republican Army [IRA])
"L"=   Loyalist (Unionist party attached to a paramilitary; note that PUP is
         attached to UVF (Ulster Volunteer Force), and UDP, to UDA
         [Ulster Defence Association)
(If these repeated acronyms are confusing, refer to the appendix on who is who.)
"NA"=not applicable (*i.e.*, neither Unionist nor Nationalist)

From this group, each party represented in the Forum would elect two negotiators, for a total of twenty. Those who were chosen to participate in the talks were David Trimble and John Taylor (UUP); Ian Paisley and Peter Robinson (DUP); John Hume and Seamus Mallon (SDLP); Gerry Adams and Martin McGuinness (*Sinn Féin*); John Alderdice and Seamus Close (Alliance); David Ervine and Billy Hutchinson (PUP); Monica McWilliams (a Catholic) and Pearl Sager (a Protestant) (Women's Coalition); Gary McMichael and David Adams (UDP); Robert McCartney and Cedric Wilson (UKUP); and Malachi Curran and Hugh Casey (Labour).

In order to be regarded as an agreement, a document would require the approval not only of the Northern Ireland negotiators, but also of both the governments, British and Irish. Moreover, no party would be permitted to participate in the talks without making a firm commitment to the "Mitchell Principles," democracy and non-violence.[94]

Because of the IRA's revocation of its cease-fire announced in August 1994, *Sinn Féin's* Gerry Adams and Martin McGuinness were not among the initial participants. This decision to cease all violent activities had been based on the promises that negotiations would be forthcoming. The 1994 cease-fire by *Sinn Féin* had induced the largest of the major Loyalist paramilitaries, the LVF, to follow suit.

The IRA, however, resumed its attacks in February 1996, because the anticipated negotiations had not yet begun. This resumption came in the form of the bombing of Canary Wharf in London, an attack which killed two, injured more than 100, and caused substantial property damage.

Furthermore, the DUP and UKUP delegates had already left the delegations twice in the first month of the talks (once because of their opposition to Mitchell as Chair). Delegates from both the parties permanently departed in September 1997, because of the decision of other negotiators that *Sinn Féin* would be permitted to participate within six weeks after a cease-fire.[95]

A Few Words on Some of the Principals

Who were these participants in the negotiations, and what were their backgrounds and their personalities? I was fortunate to be able to meet a few, and I have read much about some of the others. A brief commentary upon a few of the most well-known should provide for the reader some humanization to the talks.

Secretary of State Marjorie "Mo" Mowlam

No book on the Troubles would be complete without some words on Secretary of State for Northern Ireland throughout the talks, Marjorie "Mo" Mowlam. A cancer survivor, Ms. Mowlam wore turbans to cover her head while undergoing chemotherapy, but she seemed never to miss a beat.

The role of the office of the Secretary of State was to develop some framework for the negotiations and—post-GFA—to negotiate with parties to implement the supplementing legislation after the Agreement.[96] Alliance Party Policy Advisor Stephen Farry viewed Mowlam as actually peripheral to the peace negotiations, however, since "Downing Street office 'ran' the United Kingdom's side." [97] (Downing Street is the residence of the British Prime Minister.) Nonetheless, her commitment to the process was well-publicized.

During the first week of January, 1998, she made the controversial move of visiting Loyalist prisoners in the dreaded Long Kesh Prison, commonly referred to simply as "the Maze" for the name of the village on the outskirts of Belfast where it is located. The timing was an issue, since less than a month earlier, prisoners belonging to INLA (one of the most violent of Republican terrorist organizations) killed Billy ("the Rat") Wright, leader of the LVF Loyalist paramilitary group. The "tit-for-tat" response following Wright's murder was a series of killings of Catholics by the LVF.

Ms. Mowlam felt that a dialogue with these LVF prisoners would be constructive. Even if this were not the result, she saw no harm in trying. Fate dealt her a trump card, for by making this move she virtually kept the peace process alive, albeit on life support. The Secretary's gamble was fruitful, since these LVF inmates were receptive and open in discussing with her their concerns. She was thereby able to get the talks back on track, and she was mightily lauded for her courage.[98]

Ms. Mowlam was reportedly not at all pleased when Prime Minister Tony Blair replaced her in October, 1999, with Peter Mandelson, a man whose pre-Parliament background had been in journalism and public relations communications. She had longed to see the process through personally.

Jackie Johnson, Political Advisor for the Office of the Secretary of State, quoted her as having said, "It takes a long time to get Northern Ireland out of your system." Johnston also described her style of management as more "hands-on" than was Mandelson's.[99] (Mandelson himself left this post in the midst of embryonic investigations about charges of wrongdoing. His successor was John Reid, a Member of Westminster Parliament from Scotland.)

The general consensus, as I perceived it, was that most felt that Ms. Mowlam had been treated unfairly when Blair removed her from the Secretary's position.

Dr. Martin Mansergh

Dr. Martin Mansergh has been the Special Advisor to a veritable herd of Irish *Taoiseachs* of competing parties (including Charles Haughey [1989-February, 1992, *Fianna Fáil*, the party founded by De Valera in 1926 when he left *Sinn Féin*], Albert Reynolds [February, 1992-December, 1994, *Fianna Fáil*] and Bertie Ahern, [June, 1997-present, *Fianna Fáil*]. He explained that *Taoiseach* John Bruton [December, 1994-June, 1997, *Fine Gael*, the party which had formed the first government for the Free State of Ireland] had kept his distance from the issue of Northern Ireland.

A major participant in the negotiations for the Irish government, Dr. Mansergh described his duties as Special Advisor as a "mixture between a policy advisor and a political advisor."

He explained to me the air of dislike among the various representatives which had caused such a delay in getting the talks underway. He described the participants as having consistently "spoke(n) *at* each other, not *to* each other,"[100] Trimble and Gerry Adams refused throughout the talks to address each other directly.

My scheduled meeting with Dr. Mansergh (pronounced "Man-sir," with the accent on the first syllable) was in his office in the lovely mid-18th century Government Buildings complex, which includes Leinster House, the situs for the Parliament (and thus, the *Taoiseach* and his staff). A tall and stately man, he is an obvious intellectual with a desk covered with papers. Sporting his signature dark horn-rimmed glasses and a tweed suit, he greeted me with a warm welcome. Despite his friendliness, he was quite formal, particularly when compared with the general informality of the typical Irishman.

I had heard much about this kind gentleman, and he readily spoke to me about his background. I was not surprised to learn that he was "Anglo-Irish" (see Chapter 4 for the history of the island), a pedigree strain indeed.

Stephen Farry of the Alliance Party described Mansergh as the "Henry Kissinger of southern Irish politics," [101] and Women's Coalition co-founder Monica McWilliams referred to him as "the one who did the work for the Irish government" in the negotiations.[102]

Dr. Mansergh viewed the most difficult issues in the negotiations as Strand II on the cross-border institutions; police reform in Northern Ireland; and constitutional change in Ireland. He appeared to be genuinely dedicated to peace in Northern Ireland, despite its being a part of the United Kingdom rather than the Republic of Ireland.

The Rev. Dr. Ian Paisley, Sr.

Veritable tomes have been written about the Rev. Dr. Paisley, including a considerable amount in Chapter 2 of this book. Founder of the DUP in 1971, and ordained to the ministry at age twenty in 1946, Paisley has been both a preacher and a politician par excellence. In the former role, he has been most vocal in his denunciation of the Catholic Church, which he views as un-Christian. In his revealing and provocative book on Paisley, *Persecuting Zeal*, Methodist minister Dennis Cooke has described the good reverend's sermons as decidedly anti-Catholic, and his characterization of Pope John Paul II as the "anti-Christ, the man of sin in the church."[103] One beloved (and unidentified herein) Church of Ireland clergyman told me that "Paisley hates the Catholics, but we [Church of Ireland] are a close second on his hate list."

Paisley, the son of a Baptist minister, was born in County Armagh in 1926. Following some dissension in his County Armagh church, the family moved to Ballymena in County Antrim when young Paisley was only two years of age. His political activities seemed to be a natural and cohesive evolvement with his religious zeal. He is a staunch Unionist.

His demonstrations, counter-demonstrations, rallies and marches probably have served to increase his flock of admirers, and he has never wavered from his deep commitment to Unionism. His conviction for the crime of illegal assembly in 1966 came from his factious demonstrations opposing "Romanization" (*i.e.*, the Catholic church's appeal for ecumenism which had gained some degree of interest in Northern Ireland). His refusal to pay a fine resulted in a prison sentence. Whereas such activities surely brought notoriety to the Rev. Dr. Paisley, he is also praised by his followers as being the "true voice of Ulster."[104]

As the ultimate politician, Paisley was first elected to the Westminster Parliament in 1970, and to the European Parliament in 1979. He is perhaps the most adamant and vocal opponent of the GFA in general.

John Hume (SDLP)

John Hume has been a classic advocate of peaceful protest, and he might be referred to as Northern Ireland Catholics' counterpart to American blacks' Dr. Martin Luther King, Jr. Elected to the European Parliament in 1979 and to the Westminster Parliament in 1983, Hume could attest to what it was like to grow up in the poor Catholic Bogside of Derry/Londonderry, where he was born in 1937.

His early plans to become a priest were altered because of his fear that he would be without a vocation in majority Protestant Northern Ireland. He studied at Patrick's College (in Maynooth, in the Republic) and returned to his pre-university alma mater, St. Columb's College in Derry to teach history. (In Ireland and Northern Ireland, the word "college" is also often used in reference to its counterpart, an American high school.)

Hume's entry into politics was via a sort of by-pass, for his passion was developing the inadequate community and housing provisions in Derry. His involvement with the civil rights movement in the late 1960's probably was a major factor in his election to the Northern Ireland Parliament in 1969. The following year, he founded the Social Democratic and Labour Party (SDLP) which espoused the peaceful reunification of the two Irelands. Hume was elected to the European Parliament in 1979, and to Westminster Parliament for his district of Foyle (the river at Derry/Londonderry City) in 1983.

His perseverance led to his 1988 talks with Gerry Adams, whose party's (*Sinn Féin*) goal was the same as the SDLP's, but who deemed this to be achievable only by violence. Hume and David Trimble were co-recipients of the Nobel Peace

Price in late 1998 because of their work on the GFA.

Despite the Nobel award, most participants have minimized Hume's actual contributions to the negotiations. Alliance Party's Stephen Farry has lauded Hume's immense popularity in the province, calling him an "amazing public persona." Nonetheless, Farry's opinion is that Hume is simply not politically realistic and that he is more of a figurehead. According to Farry, most of the SDLP participation was by Seamus Mallon, later to become Deputy First Minister of the Northern Ireland Assembly. Monica McWilliams, co-founder of Women's Coalition, concurred with Farry's statement that Mallon played the greater negotiating role for SDLP. [105]

However, Farry did commend Hume for his pre-negotiation work, particularly his having commenced the talks with Adams, but he assessed these activities as having been a "legitimization" of *Sinn Féin*. The trend, according to Farry, is a gradual "taking over" of SDLP by *Sinn Féin* on the Nationalist side. Coincidentally, he noted the creeping-toward-majority status among Unionist parties of the most extreme of Unionist parties, Paisley's DUP, over the Unionist party currently holding the most support, Trimble's UUP. [106]

Gerry Adams

Gerry Adams' background is one where violence was an everyday way of life. Born in 1948 in West Belfast, his father was an IRA member, and many of his mother's family were active in the Republican movement. [107] Adams, too, joined the IRA at a young age.

He was imprisoned without trial (see Chapter 7 for discussion of Diplock trials) in March, 1972, for his paramilitary activities, but was released after a few months in order to join some Republican colleagues in discussing with government officials a cessation of paramilitary activities. He resumed serving his term in July, 1973, and he was released in 1977, only to return to prison for seven months in 1978 for similar activities. [108]

Adams was granted a visa through the intervention of President Bill Clinton in 1994, and to say that his trip to the U.S.A. was controversial (both in many of the American states and in much of Northern Ireland) is indeed an understatement. Although George Mitchell credits Clinton's act as leading to the IRA's 1994 cease-fire, [109] many differ with this conclusion, since it was not until three years later that Adams (on behalf of *Sinn Féin*) was admitted to the negotiating table.

Perhaps what I saw was misleading, but the television coverage of Hume and Trimble's Nobel Peace Prize announcement showed a pensive, and perhaps disappointed, Gerry Adams. One had the feeling that he felt that he had actually traveled much further politically in delivering what was necessary to reach a settlement than had Hume, who was already committed to a peace agreement long before the process had begun.

Nonetheless, stories abound about Adams (who has written three books and is quite articulate) that portray him as a witty and good-humored man. This author views the GFA in general as much more favorable to Nationalists than to Unionists, so I fully understand Adams' genuine delight over the final document.

I was not able to meet with Adams, but I found *Sinn Féin* to be sincerely receptive and willing to permit me to interview the parties' principals. Among these interviewees was Mitchel McLaughlin.

I was in Derry for an interview on July 28, and I would be there for only one night. Adjacent to the B & B where I stayed was *Ogmios*, an Irish language bookstore, and shortly before my meeting, I was perusing the books (as though I had the foggiest idea as to what the words meant). While there, I talked with some of the sales clerks and teachers. They seemed genuinely concerned over my remark that to date, I had not been able to talk with a *Sinn Féin* Assembly member. Gerry Adams lives in Belfast, but his co-negotiator (and a former IRA leader), Martin McGuinness, lives in Derry. Gerry O'Hara, also owner and manager of the language center and a member of Derry's City Council, then called McGuinness. He was unable to meet with me because he was in the midst of several days of nonstop partying – his daughter's wedding was set for the following day. (These "mandatory" parties are never disturbing to an Irishman.)

O'Hara's next call was to McLaughlin, who was so accommodating that he immediately arranged to weave me into his schedule, rather than vice-versa. He was convivial and responsive to my questions, and he appeared pleased that an American was so interested in the future of Northern Ireland.

David Trimble (UUP)

The accessibility of the Assembly members amazed me. First Minister David Trimble's office not only immediately responded positively to my written request for an interview well in advance of my arrival in Belfast, but his personnel also offered to provide me with confidential (everything in Northern Ireland seems to be confidential) telephone and fax numbers and addresses, together with names of their secretaries, of leaders of each political party represented in the new Assembly. Scheduling a meeting with Trimble was something I had anticipated as being impossible because of his office and stature. To the contrary, he was not only responsive and willing to meet with me, but he volunteered invaluable help with these other contacts.

Indeed, no one whom I contacted seemed to "put me off," with one exception. This was the President of the Republic of Ireland, Mary McAleese, one with whom I had believed a meeting to be assured, since she had been on the faculty of Queen's and was acquainted with most on the Faculty of Law. By then these people were not only my colleagues, but also my friends, so it seemed certain that she would agree to a meeting in the spirit of collegiality.

I sent several letters to Ms. McAleese's office, the first several failing to elicit a response. Finally, she summarily declined to grant any such meeting because of her political position. It is possible that she would have offered little of relevancy, but I had thought that her dual citizenship, her personal experience of growing up Catholic in the Ardoyne section of Belfast (the section where Holy Cross School is located, the site requiring additional security during fall, 2001 and early 2002, because of Loyalist violence) would have lent a unique perspective. Her having declined to meet briefly with me regarding this research project was a surprise and, fortunately for me, an aberration.

Although Dr. Mansergh probably ran a close second, Trimble may well have been the most formal of all those with whom I had scheduled meetings. This is surely not to imply that either was discourteous, or even distant. To the contrary, both were the penultimate gentlemen. Their personalities are simply not geared toward the informal, "down-home" approach (as we would say in the South) which I experienced with most others.

Being a reticent man, Trimble was not an easy person to interview. For example, his response to my question as to what he regarded as the most contentious and difficult issue of the negotiations was a simple "many." I had the impression that if one were to ask Mr. Trimble if he could explain Einstein's theory of relativity, his response would be a concise "yes." I knew right away that this was a man whom it would be difficult to pin down.

The closest to enthusiastic he became that day was when I talked to him about legal nuances from the stance of the law. He fully concurred with my assessment that early release of prisoners should be regarded as a violation of equality laws, since the so-called political prisoners (*i.e.*, paramilitaries) were being granted preferential treatment over other convicted criminals. He reacted to this statement by leaning forward in his chair, and responding (relatively) excitedly, "I agree! I have argued that myself."

He also saw some parallel between the "yes" or "no" vote alternative on the GFA with the upcoming choices in the American (now famed) November 2000 presidential election, since many on both sides of the Atlantic felt the choice was simply the worse of the two – *i.e.*, not a great many seemed fully to endorse either. Trimble's response was, "There is an element of truth in that. As with so many things in life, the 'good' is at times the enemy of the 'bad.' "[110]

Trimble obviously "thinks like a lawyer," because that is what he is. His law degree is from the School of Law at Queen's, and he has served on the faculty there. His burden as negotiator for UUP (a party which has surely had its fair share of internal dissension) and as First Minister has been, and remains, an immense one. His gracious wife, Daphne, was in his office when I met with her husband, and she—herself a solicitor (lawyer)—told me that when he had been elected to Westminster Parliament and had become a full-time politician, she had quit work to be his aide and confidante. It was assuring to know that this man has a spouse who understands the demands made upon this leader of the largest party in Northern Ireland and who thus is the First Minister of the Assembly.

One of the more prominent and respected members of the faculty of the School of Law at Queen's had the highest of praise for her former fellow faculty member. Many are indifferent about Trimble the person, but he truly seemed to have no avid enemies outside the political arena. Whatever their political preferences, virtually everyone in Northern Ireland seems to concede that he has shown an impressive level of fortitude thus far in facing the political baggage which comes with the territory of this position.

David Ervine

My very first meeting was with David Ervine, PUP member of the Assembly. Ervine is the flip side of Gerry Adams, in that he served with the largest Loyalist, rather than Republican, paramilitary, the Ulster Volunteer Force (UVF). Also like Adams, Ervine served a substantial amount of time in the legendary Maze prison. The crime for which he was convicted was carrying a bomb in his vehicle. He was arrested when stopped by security forces when he was only in his early twenties. Ervine's imprisonment was from 1975-1980, and he later became a prominent member of the PUP.

This was a man who ultimately made a 180-degree turn. Following the lead of the IRA, he (as a Loyalist) called for a like cease-fire in 1994. This seemed to be a total conversion. In a 1999 BBC documentary, the commentator asked Ervine if he had been prepared to kill, as a paramilitary. The immediate response was, "without question...totally. My decision was made by me and me alone."

He had long been on the IRA's death list, a fact that motivated him to move his place of residence several times. Moreover, he has received similar death threats from rival Loyalist organizations.

Not only was Ervine elected to the new Assembly, but he also currently serves on the Belfast City Council. His direction is to separate religion from politics (a lofty goal, one which would greatly benefit Northern Ireland). Along this line, he has appealed to his PUP community to engage in non-sectarian Unionism, "free from the Pope, the Queen, and King Billy (William of Orange)."[111]

Ervine was born and reared in East Belfast. He is a tall, balding, mustached man, a pipe-smoker who appeared to me to be contemplative and open-minded. His comparison of Paisley to Israel's former Prime Minister Benjamin Netanyahu and Gerry Adams to Palestine's Yasser Arafat because of their respective extremisms struck me as especially profound.

His constant referrals to pivotal historical events in the politics of Northern Ireland led me—then ignorant of his prior paramilitary activity—to say, "You talk like a historian. Is your background in history?" (I was referring to his educational background.) His response was, "My background isn't in anything. I did not attend university."

Later I mentioned this remark to the law school secretaries at Queens, and one of them commented. Meave corrected my quote from Ervine. She said bluntly, "That's not exactly right. He *does* have a background, but it's in *prison*," a statement which was followed by guffaws from the other secretaries (who are indeed my good, good friends). This proved retroactively embarrassing to me until I recalled his manner of responding. Ervine is indeed a polite man, and I doubt that my question had been at all offensive.

He spoke of George Mitchell as a "good friend," and he differed with my suggestion that perhaps Mitchell should have been one of the Nobel winners. Ervine explained that "Mitchell could not himself have achieved peace—he could only facilitate the process, and he did a magnificent job." He added that the actual achieving of the agreement was the result of the concessions and determinations of Hume and Trimble, whom he said had been "rightfully selected." His major disappointments with the GFA were the absence of taxing powers for the Assembly and the compulsory party coalitions.[112] (This is discussed in greater depth in Chapter 5 on the Assembly.)

David Ervine was the only politician other than Monica McWilliams who seemed never to be maligned. Virtually everyone extolled this man's virtues, including other members of the Assembly, clergy (on both sides), and the proverbial man-on-the-street, whether Unionist or Nationalist.

Monica McWilliams

A description of a somewhat awe-inspiring visit to Stormont is instructive. This majestic building in East Belfast which was built 1928-32 for more than $1.5 million pound sterling (over $2 million) for the purpose of housing the new Parliament of the recently partitioned Northern Ireland. Stormont is actually the affluent area in which it is located, but in this context it refers to the series of buildings. The main building is a grandiose and imposing edifice with contiguous parks and a prodigious one-mile road and walking entry.

In order to enter the grounds, either by foot or by vehicle, a visitor must state to the guard his or her purpose (which may be to jog, walk his dog, or walk through the verdant parkland). If his visit is for a scheduled meeting, he must register at the building entrance and acquire a security clearance badge. This is after the receptionist has telephoned the person with whom he is to meet. Both at the gate and at the door, the visitor is required to present identification.

The visitor is then directed into a sumptuous palatial foyer where he awaits a representative of his scheduled appointment. This representative, who is usually a secretary or an aide, then escorts him to that person's office. (Once, I was escorted by an assistant to the assistant of the office-holder!) The process is formal and, from necessity, security-conscious. Even if one has two consecutive meetings scheduled, it is necessary that the visitor return to the foyer (he might have registered both meetings, indicating a time) and await the next representative.

Immediately following my meeting with Trimble, his assistant re-escorted me to the entrance where I would wait until someone from Monica McWilliams' office came to retrieve me for the meeting with her. I was eager to meet this Catholic woman from County Derry, since I had heard much about her, all positive.

The three core principles of the Women's Coalition which she co-founded in April of 1996, are inclusion, human rights and equality. No Unionists-Nationalist arguments here! She and Kate Fearon, Political Advisor to the party's MLAs, have written that the group has "women from both Nationalist and Republican traditions, in the main, but not exclusively, Catholic, and from Unionist and Loyalist communities, in the main, but not exclusively, Protestant."[113]

Sitting on the marble bench in this lovely entrance room to await someone from Monica McWilliams' office, I noticed an attractive and energetic woman striding down the circular steps (Members of the Legislative Assembly – MLAs – are on the second floor) who very much resembled the photographs I had seen of Ms. McWilliams, except that this lady had a much shorter haircut. She cheerily greeted by name everyone she passed and seemed to know all the guards, security officers, and other personnel. Could this be Ms. McWilliams' secretary?

When this same perky lady spotted me on the bench—I was gazing at the grandeur of the room, in true country-girl fashion—she came over to greet me with an extended hand and the words, "You must be Professor Rasnic! I'm Monica McWilliams." Surprised, I said, "You caught me off guard, Ms. McWilliams—I expected your secretary!" She instantly responded, "Carol, my name is Monica. And your appointment is with *me*, not my secretary." I had just met a kindred spirit.

En route up the stairs, she grinned and told me, "You know, Carol, this place is not 'ours' (women MLAs) – we're just 'borrowing' it!" Many times during our meeting in her office, she was interrupted by the ringing telephone, always a disturbing message from or about one of her clients in her profession as a social worker. (She graduated from Queens University with Masters and Ph.D.'s in Urban Studies.)

In her talk with me, she interjected a few horror stories about spousal and child abuse, commenting that she suspected there may even be some MLAs who were guilty of such. This was one of the many abuses of human rights and inequalities which her Women's Coalition Party is determined to alleviate, and her frustration over such atrocities was patent. Monica said to me that "people who've lived—and have had loved ones to die—in Northern Ireland's awfulness are the ones most committed to peace."

While she talked excitedly about the negotiations and the GFA ("hey— I was the only woman to sign the document!"), she spoke of her party's representatives' success in persuading others to include a sixty-member Civic Forum with business

chosen from three communities: business, trade unions, and voluntary participants.[114] Established to complement, not oppose, the Assembly's work, the Forum
will, in the words of Fearon and McWilliams, "seek to promote reconciliation and
to dedicate itself to ensuring that the voices of those most disadvantaged and
marginalized are heard."[115] Monica told me, "we protested all night over this issue. When it became 'crisis time,' Trimble let it go unamended." Recalling this
stage in the talks, she absolutely beamed.

The Women's Coalition members faced some ominous opposition over even
being able to participate in the negotiations,[116] but their encouragement came from
PUP, UDP, and even *Sinn Féin*. Monica spoke with both affection and respect of
fellow MLAs Gerry Adams and, particularly, David Ervine. Referring by inference to members of other parties in the negotiations, she told me that, "we were
called 'naïve,' but we were determined. [Our position was from a stance of] 'when,'
not 'if,' there's an agreement."

I then asked her a question to which I have never received a satisfactory answer, perhaps because those whom I ask are similarly bemused: how can Ian
Paisley serve as an MLA, an elected member of an Assembly which he deplores
and detests? I have also queried as to why *Sinn Féin* occupies posh and sumptuous
offices in Westminster Parliament, although those elected still refuse to attend sessions.[117]

With regard to Paisley, Monica's answer was simply that he rationalizes his
participation because he has "always wanted a devolved Northern Ireland." A
strong woman who does not hesitate to speak her mind, she added that Paisley's
walking out of the negotiations was the "best thing that happened for the GFA." A
witty (and, at times, acerbic, because of her fortitude and doggedness) woman, she
impulsively added that he was currently suing her for defamation for allegedly
having "intimidated" them in the Assembly.[118] (I am not aware of the outcome of
this lawsuit.)

Monica McWilliams and her message will not fade softly into the night. She
has a most impressive manner of communicating, an engaging personality, and a
"never-say-die" attitude, all which assure that Women's Coalition will continue to
be much in the news from Northern Ireland for a long time to come.

The Referenda and Assembly Elections

I had become so enthusiastic about the peace process by the time of the referenda that I very nearly felt that I should somehow be entitled to vote as an adopted
Northern Irelander.

Approval in the overwhelmingly Catholic Republic of Ireland was almost a
foregone conclusion. In Northern Ireland, the situation was much more precarious. Paisley's group had launched an invective campaign, imploring voters to
defeat the GFA, one which began almost in the wake of the GFA. He was a regular

on BBC television, casting venom on the evils of this "reprehensible deal" and a "crime against their own[Unionists']."[119]

Published in the *Belfast News Letter* on April 17 by the Silent Majority, a group which purported to be non-sectarian and unaffiliated with any political party, was a two-page manifesto published entitled "20 reasons why it's suicidal to vote yes."[120] These included denunciations of a "puppet Assembly," the "economic ruination of Unionist areas," "Unionists—the permanent minority," the "pan-Nationalist Mafia," and the "perversion of justice." At lease one denouncement seemed particularly accurate, that the proposed government was "sectarian entrenched." (This is a position with which it is difficult to take issue because of the d'Hondt method discussed in Chapter 5 and the affirmative action measures in the proposed policing reform.)

Requisite to adoption of the GFA was approval by a majority in *each* voting region, Northern Ireland and the Republic. Approval in the Republic was predicted, albeit by a skeptical electorate. One Dublin hotel assistant manager stated to me that he planned to vote "yes," but that "I don't think it will make much difference. It [the Troubles] has just gone on too long, and I can't see any change because of a 'yes' vote." [121]

A simple majority would suffice in the Republic. However, with regard to Northern Ireland, it would have been regarded realistically as a defeat if the "yes" vote was less than 60%. This is puzzling to an American, to whom a much lower victory can be considered a mandate.

The reason is the political alignment in the province. The general consensus was that the vote among Northern Ireland Nationalists would be over 95%. (This should explain the perception that the GFA overall was quite favorable to Nationalists.) However, approximately 60% of the electorate was in the Unionist camp.

Fewer than 60% total vote would assume that, coupled with the substantial approval by the Nationalist sector, only a *minority* of Unionists had voted "yes." Even 65% would be considered a virtual draw and, thus, a defeat for Trimble, who had worked assiduously campaigning for approval. This meant that at least a 70% "yes" vote in Northern Ireland would be required in order for Trimble to claim real victory.[122] Such a margin of victory was not anticipated in light of increasing support for Paisley's anti-GFA advocates.

Some Personal Recollections

My cousin Mary Molly was visiting me in Belfast at the time of the May 22, 1998, dual referenda. Two nights prior to the vote, we were in Belfast's famed Crown Liquor Saloon (the only pub on the National Trust, situated directly across the street from the Europa Hotel which has the dubious distinction of reputedly being the "most bombed hotel in the world"). The Crown is aptly named, for it is one of Belfast's crown jewels, a detailed Victorian treasure with stained-glass windows and sumptuous woodwork.

We sat with a couple in their twenties in one of the ornate church-pew-like enclosed booths constructed of deep mahogany. He was a Unionist, and his girlfriend, a Nationalist. Both told us they would "probably" vote "yes," but their apathy was evident.

The next day, Molly and I—in true American fashion ("if it's Friday, it must be Scotland")—took a long (6 a.m., beginning with cab to bus station, bus to ferry, another bus to ferry docks, and final return to Belfast about 10 p.m.) day trip. We went via ferry to Scotland, taking a bus only as far up as the exquisite town of Ayr, home of poet Robert Burns. Europeans marvel at this American way of travel, to compress as much as possible in a single day, rather than spend "quality time" in one place.

Scores of young voting-age people were on the ferry en route to Glasgow for a rock concert. They laughed when I asked why they were not staying at home long enough to vote, and one young man said, "yeah – I guess my children will sometime ask me, 'hey, Da, where wuz you on the day of the referendum?' Then I'll have to say, 'I was juking it in Glasgow!'"

Back in my apartment in Belfast later that night, we asked my landlady Jean about the result. Surprised, she responded, "Well, we won't know until late tomorrow afternoon." This was another incredulity for Americans, we who were accustomed to knowing the results of a national election by projections and concession speeches even before all the polls have closed! In Northern Ireland, security dictates that ballots from the entire province be placed in sealed or locked containers and taken by armored trucks to King's Hall in South Belfast, about one and one-half miles south of where I lived. They would be hand-counted the following day.

On Saturday, the waiting was making me nervous. While I went to Queen's Physical Education Centre that afternoon to swim, Mary Molly slept. In the locker room after my swim, I asked a university student simply, "Do they know the results yet?" It was obvious from her quizzical look that she had no idea of my point of reference, so I explained that I was asking about the referendum outcome. She answered with a shrug and an apathetic, "I don't know, and I don't really care. *I didn't vote.*"

It was at the reception desk that the student workers (they and the lifeguards had become my fast friends) told me that it had been "yes" by a substantial margin. I literally raced to the nearest newsstand to purchase a late edition newspaper. A five-inch bold heading, "It's yes," graced the entire top of the *Belfast Telegraph*.[123] I was so happy for the people of Northern Ireland, and I told the very young clerk so. Her nonplussed reply was, "I guess it's okay. *I didn't vote.*"

Was *everybody* so nonchalant? Back in my apartment, Jean (who had planned to vote "no;" I do not know how she actually cast her ballot) was unassumedly reading her newspaper, but she knew me well enough to have anticipated my enthusiasm. She laughed and said, "Get Mary Molly and take her somewhere." The two of us took the bus downtown and went to White's Tavern, Belfast's oldest (1630), where a terrific group known as the Smugglers regularly played Irish pub music and ballads.

In White's, the mood was euphoric. It was teeming, and the crowd was singing, "Whiskey in the Jar," "I Wish I was Back in Derry," "The Fields of Athenry," "Danny Boy," and yelling, "Give peace a chance!" (or, as this is pronounced in Northern Ireland, "Give pace a chawnce"). Those who were old enough to have lived through the worst of the Troubles were joyous. It seemed to be the younger ones who viewed the peace agreement simply as life-as-usual. Those with enough maturity to have had a memory of the worst were joyous.

I am reminded of a story which David Ervine had told me that might indicate one possible reason for this demographic disparity. He spoke of a young girl who had voiced of her opinion that the GFA would make no difference, summing up to him that "there will never be peace in Northern Ireland." David understood her perspective by explaining that she had been *only eleven years of age* at the time of the first paramilitary cease-fires. She could not compare "what *was*" with the relative calm of the present. He mused, "those who know what peace is are those 'closest to the war.'"[124]

The numbers were compelling. In Ireland, the vote had been 94.4% (1,442,583) for the GFA and the proposed constitutional changes, and only slightly over 5% (85,174) against. Significantly, the unexpected more-than-70% approval in Northern Ireland had actually been the outcome. 71.12% (676,966) had voted "yes," and only 28.88% (274,879) had voted "no."[125]

One need not be a Rhodes Scholar or a Solomon to know that Senator Mitchell, Bertie Ahern, Tony Blair, John Hume, Gerry Adams, David Trimble, David Ervine and Monica McWilliams were celebrating that evening. It was also a truism that Ian Paisley (along with the other "no" advocates) was dejected indeed, if not angry.

Postscript

Elections to the Northern Ireland Assembly followed on June 25, 1998. The party line-up of the 108-member body was:

> UUP (largest Unionist party): 28
> SDLP (largest Nationalist party): 24
> DUP: 20

Sinn Féin: 18
UKUP: 5
Northern Ireland Unionist Party and United Unionist Assembly Party: 3
Alliance Party: 6
PUP: 2
Women's Coalition: 2

[Gary McMichaels' UDP did not garner a sufficient number of votes for representation.]

The newly devolved government was ready to "let the games begin."

Endnotes to Chapter 4

[1] John Bruton, *Why Decommissioning is a Real Issue*, 22 FORDHAM INTERNATIONAL LAW JOURNAL 1200 (1999).

[2] Ian Paisley Jr., *Peace Deal?*, Joint Statement by (part of) Ulster Unionist Party and Democratic Unionist Party at 44 (1998), quoted in THE DAILY TELEGRAPH.

[3] George Mitchell, MAKING PEACE 144 (Alfred Knoph, New York City, New York, 1999)

[4] This participant was Monica McWilliams, co-founder of the Women's Coalition Party. Interview with Ms. McWilliams, July 21, 2000, in her office at Stormont, Belfast.

[5] Mitchell, *supra* note 3, at 26.

[6] The Very Rev. Frederick J. Rusk, Dean of Connor and Rector, Church of St. Nicholas, Belfast, Easter morning service, April 12, 1998.

[7] The independence, but correlation, of these two parts is lucidly explained in David Byrne, *The Irish View of the Northern Ireland Peace Agreement*, 22 FORDHAM INTERNATIONAL LAW JOURNAL 1206, 1207 (1999).

[8] Agreement Reached between the Government of the United Kingdom of Great Britain and Northern Ireland and the Government of Ireland, April 10, 1998, hereinafter British-Irish Agreement.

[9] Agreement Reached in the Multi-Party Negotiations, April 10, 1998, hereinafter Good Friday Agreement (or GFA).

[10] Art. 46.2, Art 47.2, *Bunreacht Na hÉireann* (Constitution of Ireland) of 1937.

[11] *Id.,* Art 5, now removed by express provision in the newer Constitution, which had provided for the same method of amendment by statute as had been in effect in the 1922 Constitution of *Saorstát Éireann* (Free State of Ireland). However, this section was applicable only for the first three years of the new Constitution. In 1941, the current two-step process became effective.

[12] *Id.,* Art. 46.1, 46.2.

[13] GFA, Constitutional Issues, Annex B.3.

[14] Unreported case, May 20, 1998.

[15] Unreported, Barrington, J., November 19, 1998.

[16] *See* discussion of *Riordan* in Donal O'Donnell, *Constitutional Background to and Aspects of the Good Friday Agreement – a Republic of Ireland Perspective,* THE [IRISH] BAR REVIEW 174 (Jan./Feb. 1999).

[17] Art. 29.1 1; 4.2; 5.1; and 5.6 *Bunreacht Na hÉireann* (Constitution of Ireland) of 1937.

[18] Agreement Between the Government of the United Kingdom of Great Britain and Northern Ireland and the Government of Ireland, November 15, 1985, U.K. – Ir., Cmnd. 9657 *reprinted* in Tom Hadden and Kevin Boyle, THE ANGLO-IRISH AGREEMENT 15-48 (1989).

[19] Ian Paisley, *'Peace' Agreement – or Last 'Piece' in a 'Sellout' Agreement,* 22 FORDHAM INTERNATIONAL LAW JOURNAL 1273, 1277 (1999).

[20] *Supra* note 18, Art 1.

[21] The Joint Declaration by An *Taoiseach*, Mr. Albert Reynolds, T.D., and the British Prime Minister, The Right Hon. John Major, M.P., December 15, 1993, U.K.-Ir. Cm. 2442, hereinafter the Downing Street Declaration.

[22] *Id.* The Downing Street Declaration provoked a significant split within the Unionist group in Northern Ireland. While the UUP apparently was now content with the plan for *some* consultation between Northern Ireland and the Republic of Ireland, the DUP regarded such an idea as a legitimization of the continuing violence committed by the (Nationalist) Republicans. *See* Paisley, *supra* note 19, at 1278.

[23] Art. 3, Constitution of Ireland of 1937, *supra* note 8.

[24] GFA, Strand Two, North/South Ministerial Office.

[25] Arts. 2 and 3, Constitution of Ireland or 1937, *supra* note 8.

[26] [1990] IR 220.

[27] [1977] IR 129.

[28] Art. 26 para. 1, Constitution of Ireland, *supra* note 8.

[29] [1990] Unreported, Finlay, C.J., Walsh, Griffin, Hederman and McCarthy, JJ.

[30] 369 U.S. 186 (1962). This is the well-known "one-man-one-vote" decision. Although Justice White's opinion for the majority enunciated the "political question" doctrine—that political issues inappropriate for judicial review—the Court in *Baker* viewed this issue as one of law which the Court was competent to determine.

[31] [1988] IR 505.

[32] *See also* Attorney General v. Paperlink [1984] ILRM 348, for similar language.

[33] Art. 29, paras. 1 and 2, Constitution of Ireland of 1937, *supra* note 8.

[34]*Id.,* Art. 3.

[35] *Supra* note 16.

[36] J.M. Kelly, Gerard Hogan and Gerry Whyte, THE IRISH CONSTITUTION (Buttersworths, Dublin, Ireland, 3d ed., 1994).

[37] David Gwynn Morgan, CONSTITUTIONAL LAW OF IRELAND (The Round Press, 2d ed., 1990).

[38] James Casey, *Changing the Constitution: Amendment and Judicial Review,* Thomas Davis Lecture Series, DE VALERA'S CONSTITUTION AND OURS 152-162 (Gill & McMillan, Dublin, Ireland, Brian Farrell, ed., 1988).

[39] Act of Ireland 1920.

[40] Arts. 1 and 2, Constitution of Ireland of 1937, *supra* note 8.

[41] Kelly, Hogan and Whyte, *supra* note 36, at cxvi.

[42] Casey, *supra* note 38, at 152, 153. Note that despite the tighter language, the Supreme Court of Ireland has held that the Constitution is to be "liberally construed," Sullivan v. Robinson [1954] IR 151, and is to be "read not as dealing with words but rather with the substance of liberty," Melling v. Ó Mathghumhna [1962] IR 1.

[43] Paul Johnson, IRELAND: A CONCISE HISTORY FROM THE 12th CENTURY TO THE PRESENT DAY 183 (Academy Chicago Publishers, Chicago, Illinois, 1984).

[44] Séamas MacAnnaidh, IRISH HISTORY 252 (Parragon Publishers, 1999).

[45] David Trimble, *The Belfast Agreement*, 22 FORDHAM INTERNATIONAL LAW JOURNAL 1145, 1147 (1999).

[46]*Id*. At 1153.

[47]*Id*., n. 7, referring to GFA, Constitutional Issues, para. 1(iii).

[48] David Byrne, *The Irish View of the Northern Ireland Peace Agreement: the Interaction of Law and Politics*, 22 FORDHAM INTERNATIONAL LAW JOURNAL 1206, 1215 (1999).

[49] *Id.* at 1217.

[50] *Id.*

[51] Art. 9(1) (2), Constitution of Ireland of 1937, *supra* note 8.

[52]Irish Nationality and Citizenship Act of 1956, No. 26 (1956), para. 7(1).

[53] Byrne, *supra* note 48, at n. 31, citing Irish Nationality and Citizenship Act of 1956 para. 7(1). Byrne further suggests that the 1956 statute be amended in accordance with the changes eddected by the GFA.

[54] Martin Mansergh, *Some Fundament Ideological and Constitutional Issues in the Northern Ireland Peace Process* 33, paper delivered at a conference on Constitution – making, conflict and transition in Divided Societies, Villa Serbelloni, Bellagio, Italy, February 15,1999.

[55] Brendan O'Leary, *The Nature of the Agreement*, 2 FORDHAM INTERNATIONAL LAW JOURNAL 1628, 1647 (1999).

[56]Interview with the Professor Dennis Kennedy, July 19, 2000, in his office at Queen's University, Belfast.

[57] Dennis Kennedy, *Dash for Settlement: Temporary Accommodation of Lasting Settlement?*, 22 FORDHAM INTERNATIONAL LAW JOURNAL 1440, 1461 (1999).

[58] *Supra* note 56.

[59] Interview with Mitchel McLaughlin, MLA (*Sinn Féin*), July 26,2000, in his constituency office, Derry/ Londonderry.

[60] Paisley, *supra* note 19, at 1296.

[61] *Id.*

[62] *See* GFA, Strand One section, and 1998 Northern Ireland Act section 33. Each of the 18 constituencies (which are earmarked as Unionist or Nationalist) has sex members. [The Assembly is explained in more detail in Chapter 5.]

[63] Paisley, *supra* note 19, at 1273, 1289 (1999).

[64] *See*, however, the shift of the requisite number of Alliance Assembly members as "Unionist" in Fall 2001, in order to secure the re-election of Trimble as First Minister. The events of October and November 2001, are chronicled in Chapter 5.

[65] Stephen Farry and Sean Neeson, *Beyond the 'Band Aid' Approach: and Alliance Party Perspective upon the Belfast Agreement*, 22 FORDHAM INTERNATIONAL LAW JOURNAL 1221, 126 (1999).

[66] *Id.*

[67] Trimble, *supra* note 45, at 1154.

[68] *Id,* at 1145.

[69] Mitchell, *supra* note 3, at 166.

[70] Trimble, *supra* note 45, at 1155. *See* GFA Strand Two section 7 which provides for the inauguration of members of bodies created by the three Strands in the GFA "[a]s soon as is practically possible after elections to the Northern Ireland Assembly…" *See also* GFA, Validation, Implementation and Review, section 3.

[71] GFA Strand Two sections 1,2,3(i) and 5.

[72] *Id.* Section 8. This end-of-October date allowed ample time for the referenda, the election of Assembly members, and preliminary transitional necessities.

[73] *Id.* section 9

[74] *Id.* section 6.

[75] O'Leary, *supra* note 55, at 1644.

[76] Paisley, *supra* note 19, at 1291.

[77] Mansergh, *supra* note 54, at 37.

[78] O'Leary, *supra* note 55, at 1645.

[79] *Id.*, Farry and Neeson, *supra* note 64, at 1238, and Paisley, *supra* note 19, at 1292.

[80] GFA, Strand Two section 1.

[81] GFA, Strand Three reads, "A British-Irish Council *will* be established..." (Emphasis supplied.)

[82] *See* O'Leary, *supra* note 55, at 1645, 1646, for this position.

[83] Mitchell, *supra* note 3, at 9, 11, and 20-21.

[84] *Id.* at 26.

[85] *Id.* at 40-41.

[86] *Id.* at 45.

[87] *Id.* These personal highs and lows are chronicled throughout Mitchell's memoirs of his work in Northern Ireland. *See supra* note 3.

[88] Gerry Adams, *To Cherish a Just and Lasting Peace*, 22 FORDHAM INTERNATIONAL LAW JOURNAL 1179, 1184 (1999), and Ian Paisley, *supra* note 19, at 1281.

[89] Mitchell, *supra* note 3, at 171.

[90] *Id.* at 172.

[91] *Id.* at 174.

[92] *Id.* at 176, 177, 173.

[93] *Id.* at 43-44.

[94] *Id.* at 53, 71, 95.

[95] Chairman Mitchell's telling of these events are found in his memoirs of the talks. *See supra* note 3, at 40-41, 53-57, and 60-63.

[96] Interview with Jackie Johnston, Political Affairs, Office of the Secretary of State for Northern Ireland, July 21, 2000, at Castle Buildings, Stormont, Belfast.

[97] Interview with Stephen Farry, Policy Advisor for Alliance Party, August 1, 2000, Alliance Party Headquarters, Belfast.

[98] *See, e.g.,* Alf McCreary, *Peace deserves another chance,* BELFAST NEWS LETTER, January 14, 1998, at 13. McCreary wrote of his admiration for the Secretary who "stay(ed) on the high wire," ignoring criticism from politicians who themselves had failed to keep the talks on track.

[99] *Supra* note 96.

[100] Interview with Dr. Martin Mansergh, Special Advisor to the *Taoiseach*, July 10, 2000, Parliament Building, Dublin.

[101] Farry and Neeson, *supra* note 64, at 97.

[102] Interview with Monica McWilliams, *supra* note 4.

[103] Dennis Cooke, PERSECUTING ZEAL 219, 63 (Brandon Books, Dingle, County Kerry, Ireland, 1996).

[104] Martin Wallace, FAMOUS IRISH LIVES 101, 105 (Appletree Press, Belfast, Ireland, 1999).

[105] *Supra* note 102.

[106] Interview with Stephen Farry, August 1, 2000, SDLP Headquarters, Belfast.

[107] *Gerry Adams,* WORLD BOOK ENCYCLOPEDIA YEARBOOK 38 (1996).

[108] Mitchell, *supra* note 3 at 112.

[109] *Id.* at 113.

[110] Interview with David Ervine, July 21, 2000, in his office at Stormont, Belfast.

[111] BBC Profiles, March 16, 1999, David Ervine: *Leaving the past behind.* CBBC's webpage, *http://news.He.co.uk/hi/english/uk/northern_ireland.*

[112] Interview with David Ervine, July 3, 2000, in his office at Stormont, Belfast.

[113] *Supra* note 102.

[114] GFA, Strand Two, Relations with other institutions para, 34.

[115] Kate Fearon and Monica McWilliams, *The Good Friday Agreement: a Triumph of Substance over Style,* 22 FORDHAM INTERNATIONAL LAW JOURNAL 1250, 1257 (1999).

[116] Mitchell, *supra* note 3, at 44. Mitchell wrote that the women participants were insulted in the pre-talk forum and not taken seriously, adding that "I [he] would not permit such conduct in the negotiations."

[117] *Sinn Féin members take British offices,* RICHMOND TIMES-DISPATCH (The Associated Press), January 22, 2000, at A-7, col. 2-6.

[118] *Supra* note 4.

[119] Paisley, *supra* note 19, at 1318, 1924.

[120] *20 Reasons why it's Suicidal to Vote Yes,* BELFAST NEW-LETTER, April 17, 1998, at 10-11 (entire pages).

[121] Conversation with manager of Othello Hotel, Dublin, May 18, 1998.

[122] THE TIMES (Dublin edition), May 22, 1998, at 12, col. 4-6.

[123] *It's yes,* BELFAST TELEGRAPH, May 11, 1998, at 12, col. 4-6.

[124] *Supra* note 112.

[125] My thanks to Colin Harvey of Queen's University School of Law and Criminology for these figures. *See* Colin Harvey, *Legality, Legitimacy, and Democratic Renewal: the New Northern Ireland Assembly in Context*, 22 FORDHAM INTERNATIONAL LAW JOURNAL 1389, at n. 3 (1999).

Chapter 5

The New Northern Ireland Assembly

"If the Assembly operates through 2000, it will be indestructible."

David Ervine, Progressive Unionist Party and
Elected member of the nNIA[1]

David Ervine is clearly one of the most ardent supporters of the GFA, truly dedicated to making the legislative process of the region of Northern Ireland functional and successful. This good man is no Pollyanna, but neither he nor anyone else involved in the process should have been expected to envision the events which were to transpire during the remainder of 2000, and throughout 2001-2002.

A crucial component of the success of the principles underlying the GFA is the new Northern Ireland Assembly (hereinafter "NIA"). Strand I of the GFA provided for a legislative body for Northern Ireland, a body which was to adopt statutes for the region on "devolved," or "transferred," matters. In lay terms, these are subject areas upon which the UK Parliament (Westminster) would yield its sovereignty and empower the regional legislature to govern.[2] "Devolved," or "transferred," matters, then, are hands-off for Westminster Parliament.

This chapter will begin with a summary of the history of Northern Ireland legislatures since partition in 1920. Secondly, some comparisons will be drawn between the NIA and the two other recently devolved governments in the United Kingdom, Scotland and Wales. Finally, the somewhat complex structure of the NIA is explained.

Precursors to the NIA

Northern Ireland Parliament, June 7, 1921-March 30, 1972

The statute ordering partition in 1920[3] defined the border between the twenty-six counties of the new *Saorstát Éireann* (Free State of Ireland) and the six counties to the north. To give the reader some perspective as to relative sizes, the now Republic constitutes 5/6 of the island, leaving only 1/6 for what would become Northern Ireland. This official division of the island became effective when signed by the designated representatives of the United Kingdom and the area to comprise the Free State.[4]

Fifty years later, the opinion of at least one historian was that the land division—*i.e.*, between the twenty-six counties and the six—represented a far greater separation than does the sea division—between the island of Ireland and the island of Great Britain.[5] This same scholar—one with obvious Nationalist leanings—assessed the six counties as a "Celtic banana republic,"[6] a region with "ultimate loyalty to Ulster and secondary loyalty to the crown."[7] How would this new tiny post-partition region be governed?

The Westminster statute provided for a so-called "Parliament" for Northern Ireland, and this designation is indeed accurate, at least according to its form. A true parliamentary government is one which fuses the legislative and executive powers without separate elections for the head of government (prime minister) and legislature, as in the American system. The leadership—*i.e.*, elected members—of the party holding a majority on the legislature form the executive, *i.e.*, the cabinet. The most widely used form of government in the world, the parliamentary form is structured so as to prevent any prolonged disagreement between the legislative and executive parties. It does this by permitting the legislators to give or withhold confidence in the executive. A "no-confidence" vote would dissolve the legislature, and new elections would be held.[8] To the American accustomed not only to voting separately for members of Congress and for President (or Governor, at the state level), but also to the American strict separation-of-powers principle, this may be a difficult concept to grasp. Indeed, many Americans prefer a President of one party and a majority in the Congress of the other party, as a curb toward essentially vesting either with an uncontrolled power to govern. In the parliamentary system, on the other hand, the executive is actually drawn from elected legislators in the majority party, so there is an innate identity between the two.

Other than form, however, the designation of the Northern Ireland legislative body as a "parliament" is somewhat of a misnomer. This term is generally used for an independent country, rather than for a fledgling[9] region governed by another independent state. Some confusion has emanated also with regard to the term "free state," the status of Ireland after partition and before full independence. According to Brendan O'Leary, Professor of Political Science at London School of

Economics, any difference between the two terms is largely semantic, with little, if any, fundamental distinctions. He views the term "parliament" as somewhat more prestigious. Additionally, he explained that, unlike an assembly, a parliament enacts legislation and typically has taxing powers. Professor O'Leary describes the Northern Ireland Assembly as a "hybrid" of sorts, since it passes laws, but does not have the power to tax.[10]

The partition statute barred the Northern Ireland Parliament—generally referred to as "Stormont," the area where its grandiose building is located and the name given the building itself—from encroaching upon most significant areas. These included enacting any laws which would affect the crown, peace, war, armed forces, treaties with foreign nations, treason, naturalization, trade outside Northern Ireland, radio, air navigations, minting of coins, lighthouses, weights and measures, copyrights and patents, post offices, and banks. This exhaustive listing which excluded from Stormont's powers most truly significant areas, having mentioned just about everything other than the proverbial partridge in a pear tree. This was ultimately summarized in the statute simply by reference to the Westminster Parliament as the "supreme law of the land."[11]

So what powers were left for this "Parliament," this Stormont? The statute expressly permitted the regional parliament to govern with regard to the region's courts and administration of justice, police, agriculture, and housing. However, this authorization at times rang hollow indeed, since the same law vested Westminster with the authority to override this legislation.[12] One political scientist described British imperialism at the time as a "love for its Ulster concubine [which] only appeared when its Leinster [Dublin government] left it."[13]

Comparing the region with the southern states in the USA which seceded to trigger the start of the Civil War (1861-1865), a theoretical question might arise as to how Northern Ireland could have seceded from the U.K. This would have been difficult, if not impossible, since the entire military (and ultimate) police power was Westminster itself.

What, then, of the minority (*i.e.*, Catholics) in Northern Ireland? Would minority rights be protected as in the "American way"? This question is a rhetorical one in light of the statement of Lord Craigavon, first Prime Minister of North Ireland, in the first Stormont's opening session on June 7, 1921: "This is a Protestant Parliament, and I am an Orangeman."[14]

Perhaps Northern Ireland was from its inception a setting where an onset of horrible incidents of violence was just waiting to be sparked. The violence which led to suspension of the Parliament in 1972[15] was not something which suddenly erupted fifty years after the creation of the province, but it had been "born with the baby," so to speak. In 1922, 232 were killed and approximately 1,000 wounded in political riots in Northern Ireland.[16]

The series of events of 1969-1972 chronicled in Chapter 1 led to the resumption of Westminster control and the immediate suspension of the Northern Ireland

Parliament.[17] "Suspension" clearly connotes something that is temporary, and, indeed, the statute affecting it was entitled "Temporary Provisions Act." These so-called "temporary" measures were still in effect when the GFA was signed some twenty-six years later.

Sunningdale: January 1-May 28, 1974

In December 1973, a four-day conference aimed toward restoring some modicum of limited self-government for Northern Ireland was held in Sunningdale, England. Any football fan who understands the saying that a win was "nasty" will appreciate the comparison. The achievement of the agreement at Sunningdale was "nasty" indeed, one probably doomed from the start.

This was the first attempt to establish a so-called "power-sharing" government for the province, one which in retrospect obviously pre-dated its time. The subsequent statutory approval by Westminster created a seventy-eight-member Northern Ireland Assembly,[18] a significantly larger body which had been the old sixty-member Stormont Parliament prior to its dissolution. This was simultaneously revolutionary and idealistic, a "power-sharing" body comprised of two cross-purposed segments. The assurance of representatives of the minority position required more legislators than in Stormont, but all were not willing participants.

The first attempt to revive the law-making body in Northern Ireland used the same terminology as did the later GFA. The Stormont legislature was a "parliament," and Sunningdale, an "assembly." Jackie Johnston of the Office of the Secretary of State for Northern Ireland explains the assembly-parliament nomenclature distinction as being between one of consensus and administrative-based (assembly) versus contentious and political-based (parliament).[19]

The Sunningdale effort was an abysmal failure. The statute had provided for elections based on constituencies which necessarily included Catholic Nationalists, both on the Assembly and on its executive body, a "power-sharing" body which seemed to be a wonderful compromise in theory. It was, however, completely unworkable in practice, as is obvious from its early demise.

Sunningdale was a strange creature. Unionists hated it, and *Sinn Féin* Nationalists were so suspicious about its underlying concept that they boycotted sessions. The Rev. Dr. Ian Paisley Sr., one of those Unionists elected to the Assembly, led a group of other Unionists in refusing to vacate their seats to those SDLP Nationalists chosen for the executive. Mild civil disobedience is not the Rev. Paisley's style, and he was the leader of a noisy and boisterous protest. It took eight policemen to remove the large man from the Assembly chambers, and the session was completely disrupted.[20] Unionists in general were enraged at the expectation that they participate in any governing process with Nationalist Catholics, a group which at least Paisley believed to be composed primarily, if not entirely, of terrorists.

Belfast ship workers, a strong element of the city's working class, went on strike to protest any such power sharing, and on May 28, Unionist members of the Assembly resigned. The government thus collapsed, and Westminster resumed direct rule by default.

Sunningdale seemed to be vivid proof that there could be no working consensus between the two camps. Nonetheless, the two governments of the Republic of Ireland and the United Kingdom were determined to exhaust all efforts to attain some degree of peace in the province. The sense prevailed that if peace were ever to be a possibility, there must be an agreement for a bottom-line compromise of sorts, at least in form.

1985: The Anglo-Irish Agreement

There were no moves to resurrect Sunningdale, but the U.K. and the Republic of Ireland had not given up on the province of Northern Ireland. The next substantive move towards peace was the Anglo-Irish Agreement, executed at Hillborough Castle on November 15, 1985. (Just outside Belfast, Hillsborough Castle was the residence of the Governor of Northern Ireland during the days of Stormont. There may have been some symbolic significance in this choice of a situs so identifiable with the fifty-year devolved government.) This thirteen-article treaty negotiated and agreed upon by Gearoid MacGerrailt on behalf of *Taoiseach* (Prime Minister) Charles Haughey for the Republic of Ireland and Prime Minister Margaret Thatcher for the United Kingdom was in many ways a "Reader's-Digest-condensed" version of the GFA which was later to replace it. This is reflected particularly in the agreement's adoption of the same principle of governmental collaboration between Northern Ireland and the Republic which makes up Strand II of the GFA.

An Intergovernmental Conference was established for the purposes of meeting regularly to discuss consensus on (i) political matters; (ii) security and related matters; (iii) legal matters, including the administration of justice; and (iv) a general promotion of cross-border cooperation.[21] The Irish government agreed, however, not to forward to this Conference its views on any proposal involving possible devolution of Northern Ireland.[22] The exception permitted presenting its views on the "modalities of bringing about a devolution in Northern Ireland, in so far as they relate to the interests of the minority community."[23] This meant that the Anglo-Irish Agreement confirmed the legitimacy of Northern Ireland's minority, the Nationalist Catholic segment which identified with the Republic rather than with the U.K. It was this exception which permitted the Republic and its representatives to participate in the talks leading to the GFA.

The two governments agreed to work together to (i) accommodate rights and identities of the "two traditions" in Northern Ireland, and to (ii) achieve peace, stability and prosperity throughout the island by promoting "reconciliation, respect for human rights, (and) co-operation against terrorism" and by developing "economic, social and cultural co-operation." [24] The Anglo-Irish Agreement even went so far as to confirm the support of both governments if the Dublin and Westminster parliaments decided in the future to establish an Anglo-Irish parliamentary body similar to the Council of the Isles of the GFA (Strand III). [25]

The section of the Agreement which dealt with the administration of justice provided for extradition and extra-territorial jurisdiction between Northern Ireland and the Republic in some instances. Expressly included was the plan for the eventual creation of "mixed courts in both jurisdictions for the trials of certain offences." [26] Northern Ireland had long enforced the use of the controversial so-called "Diplock courts" (bench trials without a jury) for politically related charges of terrorism. Significantly, the Anglo-Irish Agreement did not address this process, one which continues. (Diplock trials are summarily described in Chapter 7 on the policing issue. [27])

Was the Anglo-Irish Agreement simply verbose "feel-good" stuff which expressed lofty ideals, but which contained little, if any, substance? One might give the classical rhetorical response of "yes" and "no." If nothing else, what it achieved was the first formalization of any participatory role of the Irish government in Dublin with regard to Northern Ireland affairs. The Agreement established Dublin's right to be consulted by Westminster on any proposals and/or decisions related to the province.

Northern Ireland's Unionist parties strongly opposed the 1985 Agreement. Professor Dennis Kennedy of Queen's University has explained the positive nature of the treaty from the Nationalist perspective, since those aspiring to a united Ireland have always advocated some type of joint authority over Northern Ireland to be exercised by the Dublin and Westminster governments. [28] For the first time, the Dublin government had this consultative status.

1993: Joint Declaration

The principals—but not the *principles*—had changed, and the plot had thickened somewhat since the 1985 agreement. The 1993 agreement— generally referred to as the Downing Street Declaration—was the product of negotiations between two different heads of government: Albert Reynolds was now *Taoiseach* of Ireland, and John Major, Prime Minister of the U.K. This document contained the first express statement from the Westminster government that it had "no selfish, strategic, or economic interest" in Northern Ireland, but rather that its primary goal was to facilitate an ultimate "peace, stability and reconciliation" for all people on the entire island of Ireland. [29] This message might be interpreted as the U.K.'s position that it would prefer to wash its political hands of the province, but that it nonetheless has not only a vested interest in, but a lawful commitment to, the attainment of peace.

This document also made it clear that whether the "two Irelands" are ultimately united, or whether Northern Ireland remains a part of the U.K. is "for the people of Ireland, North and South, to achieve by agreement without outside impediment." "Outside" here obviously refers to the U.K. government itself, since it was not listed as a country or province whose people are to decide this issue. The Downing Street Declaration also pulls no devious punches as to the only reason the province remains with the U.K. The majority in Northern Ireland are still Unionists, as the declaration acknowledged in the provision which stated that "Irish unity will be achieved only (if) those who favour this outcome persuad(e) those who do not...." [30]

Then-Secretary of State for Northern Ireland Sir Patrick Mayhew minced no words in his speech preceding the declaration. Obviously directing his words to the IRA, Mayhew said that the terrorist group's problem was not with the British, but rather with people of Northern Ireland who do not believe that violence is productive. He made a logical argument that a continuation of violence made no strides whatsoever towards uniting Ireland, since only a cessation of violence could lead to putting this issue "on the table" so that the relevant principals might discuss it.[31] Mayhew made it clear that a necessary precursor of peace in Northern Ireland must be a bipartisan discussion and dialogue.

Some Devolution Comparisons:
Scotland, Wales, and Northern Ireland

The familiar adage that the "sun never sets on the British Commonwealth" is unequivocally a reference to history. If devolved governments portend ultimate independence (which many believe may be the eventual case, at least with Scotland), even the United Kingdom is being chipped away. Northern Ireland's impending devolution became a reality when the May, 1998 vote in both the province and the Republic approved the referenda on the GFA by substantial majorities. The referendum in Scotland had been on September 11, 1997, and the vote in Wales, on September 18, 1997. The electorates approved all three, but the situations differed.

First, experts have emphasized that none is a federalism with the devolved areas being "states" as in the American model. The individual American states have broad autonomy in regulating many areas, and profound differences among them are evident.[32] Nonetheless, Colin Harvey of the Queen's University School of Law points out that, although a classification as a "quasi-federal" structure would be "strictly legally inaccurate," Westminster will still have considerable difficulty if it attempts to claim any authority over devolved, or transferred, matters in any of the three devolved regions.[33]

Scotland has always seemed to be its own "breed of dog," so to speak. It has always had its own separate legal system, and there are concrete differences between this system and those in other parts of the U.K. One vivid example is the

Scottish criminal courts' use of findings of "guilty," "not guilty" or "not proven." This latter additional possibility does not infer innocence, but rather, likely guilt of the defendant. This finding really means that the jury (or judge, as the case may be) in fact believes him to be guilty, but is unable to reach such a verdict because of (usually) some procedural error. Moreover, Scottish evidentiary rules liberally permit introduction of hearsay evidence if a witness is unavailable, and evidence obtained without a warrant in criminal cases is not excluded.[34]

The statutory reference to Scotland is a "nation," while Wales is a "region." [35] The devolvement legislation for Northern Ireland refers to the province simply as "Northern Ireland." The word "nation" has been defined as referring to a "social group that shares a common ideology, common institutions and customs, and a sense of homogeneity," with an emphasis not on territorial borders, but rather on a "sociocultured perception of the group." [36] It connotes a greater cohesiveness than does the word "region." Concededly, it would stretch the imagination even of the most creative of thinkers to view Northern Ireland as an area with "homogeneity." It could well be that the legislators' refusal to classify the province expressly was an appeasement measure, since "region" would have pleased Unionists, and "nation" would have absolutely elated Nationalists.

Perhaps the statutory reference to a Scottish "parliament" [37] and an "assembly" for both Northern Ireland and Wales[38] was indeed intended by the Westminster Parliament to indicate a subtle distinction. As noted by Professor O'Leary, the Scottish Parliament has taxing powers,[39] whereas the other two do not. When asked what he would choose to alter if he had the unilateral power to change any provision in the GFA or its implementing legislation, David Ervine of Northern Ireland's PUP political party (Unionist) responded that he would vest the nNIA with the same taxing powers as has the Scottish legislature. This illustrates Ervine's opinion that the primary problems the nNIA will face are financial, rather than substantive.[40]

Scotland

Scotland had been united with England and Wales since the United Kingdom of Great Britain was formed in 1707. There have always been rumblings of Scottish independence, and the Scots always point out that they are "Scottish," rather than "British." [41] In an earlier referendum on devolution held March 1, 1997, 32.9% voted "yes," and 30.8%, "no." Because of the failure of 36.3% of the electorate even to vote, this close outcome was not regarded as a majority. In contrast, the 1997 vote showed a 60% turnout (still not a resounding majority), with 74.3% voting "yes," on the devolvement issues, and only 25% voting "no." (The second question on the ballot was passed, but by a lower margin. On whether to have taxing powers, 63.5% voted "yes," and 36.5%, "no.")[42]

The Scottish Parliament numbers 129, representing eight regions, with each legislator serving a four-year term.[43] There is a three-member executive[44] composed of the First Minister (appointed by the queen from among the elected Ministers,[45] the Lord Advocate (criminal prosecutor), and the Solicitor General (state attorney for civil matters). The First Minister then appoints committee chairs from among the Ministers to make up the cabinet (*i.e.,* the executive).[46] The first elections for the devolved Scottish government were on May 6, 1999.

Wales

In Wales, there have been sporadic efforts to devolve, some as early as the beginning of the 20th century. The most recent prior to the 1999 devolution was in 1978.[47] With only a 58% turnout for the March 1, 1979 referendum, the "no" vote won by a whopping 4-1 margin.[48]

The Welsh populace's apathy over the devolution issue was apparent by the mere 51% turnout for the 1997 referendum. (Compared with Wales, the Scottish electorate seems impressively patriotic.) The vote, although affirming devolution, was a squeaker: 50.3% "yes," and 49.7% "no." And this was only the choice of a little over one-half the electorate!

The Westminster statute for Wales is modelled somewhat after the 1979 statute which was repealed after the voters' failure then to approve devolvement. The Welsh Assembly—the *Cynulliad Cenedlaethol Cymru*—has sixty representatives, forty elected by a plurality (in British terms, this is referred to as "first past the post"—*i.e.,* no majority is required), and twenty by an "additional member" system from the province's five precincts (*i.e.,* at large). The head of government's title is First Secretary, rather than First Minister, as in Scotland and Northern Ireland, and he is elected by the Assembly. He then appoints "Assembly Secretaries" (*i.e.,* members of the cabinet) which then name committees.[49] The "Executive Committee," then, is made up of the First Secretary and the Assembly Secretaries. This fusion of the legislature and the executive is alien to American politics, but it is characteristic of a parliamentary system, whether it is designated a "parliament" or an "assembly."

One interesting provision in the subsequent legislation which distinguishes it from the other two-devolvement statutes is the Wales law's reference to the Welsh language. "Equal treatment" for English and Welsh—which is widely spoken in North Wales—is assured.[50] Interestingly, since adoption of a 1949 statute, the Welsh courts had permitted either language if one would "disadvantage others" since 1942.[51]

This came after a rocky road with an interesting history. The formal repudiation by Westminster of the Welsh language began in 1846 with a document titled *The Treason of the Blue Books* (known among the Welsh as the "Treacheries of the Blue Books"). Three English barristers, assisted by eight others (seven were English), were appointed by the British crown to investigate the language situation in

163

Wales. The conclusion was that too much use of the Welsh language in the courts was working to the detriment of the English language. William Williams, Member of Parliament, referred to Welsh as the "language of slavery." [52] Westminster enacted the report into statutory form, and the law barred the language in all court proceedings. A little over a quarter of a century later, the Welsh lauded the 1870 Wales Education Act for making education mandatory for all Welsh children, but decided the downside was not worth the benefits: the law also banned all use of the Welsh language in schools.

The 1942 statute permitting the use of Welsh in courts had been a breakthrough. In 1967, it was subsumed by the Welsh Courts Language Act which permitted use of the language in court without the proviso that a litigant or witness would otherwise be at a disadvantage. Finally, the 1993 Welsh Language Act authorized a bilingual court system, at the discretion of the court. [53] This history likely explains the automatic inclusion of the reference to the Welsh language in the devolvement statute. [Author's note: Anyone who travels through the small village in northwest Wales named *Llanfairwllgwyngllgogerychwytndrobwillllantsiliogoch* will appreciate those who have mastered this tongue. Fortunately for those who live there, this village is generally called simply *"Llanfairpwllgwngyll,"* still a tongue twister for an American. The translation of the longer official name is "Mary's Church by the white hazel pool near the fierce whirlpool with the Church of Tysilis by the Red Cave." And most Americans think the *German* language is extreme about combining several words to make a single one!]

Numbers of Representatives on the Three Legislatures

The respective strengths of representations merit a comparative comment. The parliament of the devolved government of Scotland, with a population of about 5.3 million (9.1% of the United Kingdom) has 129 representatives. Wales' Assembly, representing about 2.8 million (4.8% of the population of the United Kingdom), has sixty members. In contrast, Northern Ireland, with an approximate population of only 1.2 million (3.2% of the U.K.), has a 108-member NIA. [54] For the rationale for this imbalance, read on.

Strand I of the GFA: The New Northern Ireland Assembly

The Northern Ireland Assembly is a revisitation of what Sunningdale had hoped to be, a true power-sharing body in the fullest sense of the term. Political scientists know this principle as "consociationalism," a structure drafted by Dutch political scientist Arend Lijphant. Such a body has four characteristics: (i) a cross-community executive which shares power; (ii) proportionality by rules in both governmental and public sectors; (iii) community-level self-government; and (iv) veto rights for minorities. [55] Brendan O'Leary, Professor of Political Science at London

School of Economics, adds an element to the Dutchman's general framework which he sees in the NIA, an external dimension. Usually the "communities" mentioned in the first characteristic are formed because of ethnic and religious similarities. O'Leary sees in Northern Ireland also a national element coming from both the U.K. and the Republic, a protection of the minority, currently Nationalists, but which may indeed later be Unionists.[56] This is because of the increasing population in the Nationalist segment.

O'Leary is a man of high respectability, a frequent commentator on BBC, and his words are indeed worth contemplating. He articulates what the NIA embodies vividly and accurately as a "novel model of double protection...[a] bargain derived from mutually conflicting hopes about its likely long-run outcome, but [one] that may not destabilize it."[57] This "double-protection" to which O'Leary refers is the protection of the minority. He clearly sees the strong possibility that the majority of Unionists of today may indeed be the minority in Northern Ireland in a perhaps not-too-distant tomorrow. This may have been the saving grace of the GFA for Unionists, for the concessions they made in accepting the agreement were perhaps prophylactic in nature, insurance for what may come down the road. For Nationalists, the GFA gave the long waited for foot-in-the-policy-making door.

The seemingly large 108-member body was necessary to accommodate the inclusion of both sides of the political fence, *i.e.,* both Unionists and Nationalists. Scotland and Wales did not have this two-sided fissure, this long-standing animosity and lack of toleration by each for the other. I once asked Professor O'Leary why, in addition to these diametrically opposite groups of people, there had been such a resort to violence in Northern Ireland, in particular violence against those who support the British crown which has simply not been the case in Scotland or Wales. He reflected only briefly, and one could sense that he had already thought about this phenomenon. He responded, "I think it is because the British have always permitted the Welsh to be 'Welsh,' and the Scots to be 'Scottish.' They have never let the Irish be 'Irish.' "[58] Indeed, the GFA now permits Nationalists to be "Irish."

The first necessary legislation subsequent to April 10, 1998 signing of the GFA was the cursory statute authorizing an election of Ministers (*i.e.*, legislators) per its provisions.[59] This is a lock-step process, and the statute may have been short-lived (such as had been the preparatory statute for Wales in 1979), had the elections the following month had a different result. This election empowerment statute was adopted by the U.K. Parliament on April 22, 1998, and the queen signed it into law on May 7, 1998. Both referenda approved the GFA by sizeable margins on May 22, and the elections for Ministers were held June 25, 1998.

Who Gets (How Many) Seats

The system is one which only a statistician can appreciate. The referenda had been structured so as to indicate whether the voter was Nationalist or Unionist. (Author's note: I often wondered if anyone falsified this, as is often the case in American exit polls at voting precincts.) Thus were allocated, according to percentages in each sector, Nationalists and Unionists in the population, superimposed upon the "yes"-"no" votes in that sector, the number of seats each side would be assured. This meant that there would be members of the NIA from both sides.

The British have a special term for such a body elected before it has been vested with powers by statute: a "shadow" body. This means that it will be transformed into a true entity with law-making powers only after the necessary statute has been adopted. Until then, it is, metaphorically, only a "shadow." This comprehensive bill passed the Westminster Parliament on November 19, 1998, and it was immediately signed into law by the queen.[60]

The method of voting also differs from the norm. Since each of the eighteen constituencies is allotted five Assembly members (the remaining number are at large and selected from the total number of points), the voter lists five names. They are, however, listed in order of his preference, so each candidate scores a proportional number of "points." In an American election, of course, the voter is permitted to vote for one candidate per position.

Professor O'Leary's chart, in Table 1, explains the allocation of seats according to this process.

Table One: The Shares of Blocs in the 1998 Assembly
*(*Percentages do not add up to 100 because of rounding)* [61]

Bloc	Seats Won	First Preference Vote (%)	Seats Won (%)
Nationalists	42	39.8	38.8
"Yes" Unionists	30	25.0	27.7
"No" Unionists	28	25.5	25.9
Others	8	9.4	7.4
Total(s)	108	*100	*100

Borrowing again from Professor O'Leary's expertise, his chart indicating the seats won by each party within the two respective groups, is reproduced in Table 2, below.

Table Two: Party Performances in a 1998 Assembly Election
(*Percentages do not add up to 100 because of rounding) [62]

Party	Seats	First Preference Vote (%)	Seats Won (%)
SDLP	24	22.0	22.2
Sinn Féin	18	17.7	16.6
Other Nationalists	—	0.1	—
UUP	28	21.0	25.9
PUP	2	2.5	1.8
UDP	—	1.2	—
Other "Yes" Unionists	—	0.3	—
DUP	20	18.0	18.5
UKUP	5	4.5	4.6
Other "No" Unionists	3	3.0	2.8
Alliance	6	6.4	5.5
Women's Coalition	2	1.7	1.9
Others	—	1.3	—

Two items to note from Table 2: (a) the "no" votes were also assured seats on the NIA, a body which they had not wanted; and (b) the first two blocks separated by one line are both sectors' "yes" votes, Nationalists (first) and Unionists (second) (since a greater percentage of Nationalists approved the GFA than was the percentage of Unionists, voting "yes," O'Leary has listed these parties first); the second two blocks separated by a line are both sectors' "no" votes."

The chart clearly shows that the party with the most seats is the Ulster Unionist Party. David Trimble, as party leader, was practically the automatic First Minister, since the Assembly later would elect the person to serve in that office. Irrespective of the percentages on the Assembly, the office of deputy First Minister would automatically fall to the minority side, *i.e.*, Nationalists. As the largest Nationalist party, the Socialist Democratic Labour Party (SDLP) would have this post. By Assembly election, that party's candidate (party leader Seamus Mallon) became the deputy First Minister. (This process is known as the "d'Hondt" method, commented upon in more detail in the section describing voting on bills. Here it should be sufficiently confusing to include a provision of the legislation which provides for the appointment of Ministers.[63]

The formula used is:

$$\frac{S}{1+M}$$

where S is equal to the number of Assembly seats held by members of the party on the first Assembly meeting following the election, and M is equal to the number of Ministerial offices (if any) held by members of the party. (One gets the occasional sense that he is reading an algebra textbook, rather than a statute.)

"Devolved" Versus "Excepted" or "Reserved" Matters

What has Westminster empowered this legislative body to do? All possible areas of legislation were separated into three major groupings, "excepted," "reserved," and "transferred."

Basically, "excepted" and "reserved" matters are identical with regard to what the NIA *cannot* do. There are twenty-two-items falling under "excepted" matters[64], and some sixteen items under "reserved" matters.[65] A primary distinction between these two groups is that "excepted" matters in general are, as envisioned by the GFA and adopted in the subsequent legislation, areas in which jurisdiction is in either the Strand II cross-border (the Republic of Ireland and Northern Ireland) and/or the Strand III ("Council of the Isles," *i.e.*, the island of Ireland and the island of Great Britain) bodies. These include such areas as international relations, extradition, Human Rights Convention issues and European Communities law, defence and national security, coinage, banks, and taxes.

"Reserved" matters, on the other hand, are to be decided only by Westminster.

Thus, the U.K. ceded certain powers except for those it "reserved." (Examples are Northern Ireland functions which relate to the Crown, and probably more importantly, the police in Northern Ireland and the Emergency Powers Act. These included the establishment of the so-called Diplock courts to hear and decide charges of political terrorism without a jury.)

Rather than list specifically which matters are "devolved" or "transferred" to the NIA and the judicial and administrative bodies in Northern Ireland, these are referred to as a type of "left over." That is, what is neither reserved not excepted is transferred.[66] These areas are generally reflected in the titles of the Ministerial posts (*i.e.,* the executive body), such as Health, Education (separated into two departments, one each for secondary and higher education), Health Care, Environment, Social Development, Regional Development, Cultural Arts and Leisure, Agriculture, and Finance and Personnel (including trade and enterprises). These ministerial posts are rotated on a Nationalist/Unionist basis. Note that the Deputy Minister for each must be from the opposite side.

The statute provided for no more than ten such Ministers,[67] and the NIA decided upon this maximum number. Because of the weights of votes in the first Assembly election, Unionists were entitled to five Ministers (*i.e.,* three for UUP, the larger of the two main Unionist parties, and two for DUP), and Nationalists, to five (similarly, three for SDLP, the larger of the two parties, and *Sinn Féin*, two). At a glance, this seems to add up to "something to offend everybody."

Voting on Bills

If understanding the consociational theory and the method of determining the allotment of Nationalist/Unionists and "yes"/"no" seats to be on the NIA required that one be a statistician the d'Hondt rules require that one have a higher degree in some arcane area of mathematics. Indeed, it was devised by a Belgian mathematician, Viktor d'Hondt. (The drafters of the GFA seemed to have a penchant for the Dutch and the Belgians.) These rules applied to the allocation of Assembly seats according to the Nationalist/Unionist "yes"/"no" votes and to the selection of Ministers.

Because of the sheer power vested in a Minister and the Deputy, an example might clarify for the American reader the effect of this dichotomy. Suppose that, in the 2000 presidential elections Democrat Al Gore had been elected President, with Republican Dick Cheney named as his Vice President, to achieve "cross-community" fairness. Or, as is the case, Republican George W. Bush was elected President. Assume, however, that Democrat Joe Liebermann were named his Vice President. The two would rarely, if ever, come to any consensus.

William Orbinson, a young barrister in Belfast, laughingly said to me after the referenda that he had made the statement that, if the GFA passed, he would vote for "any candidate who could clearly explain to me the d'Hondt system" [68]

Unarguably, most people in Northern Ireland have no understanding of this method.

The method of voting also insures cross-community participation across the board. This was the principle which applied to the selection of First and Second Ministers, and the Ministers who would serve on the executive. The GFA and the statute broadened the d'Hondt concept with the idea of having "parallel cross-community voting." This principle has three requirements: (a) Assembly members must designate whether they are Nationalist or Unionist; (b) the general rule for passage of a bill is that majority rule will suffice (see the exception explained in the following text); and (c) the d'Hondt system is applied.[69]

The simple majority vote is something which will be unknown to Assembly procedures, at least on items of major significance, and the rule will swallow the exception in (b), above. If as few as thirty of the 108 MLAs classify an issue as "controversial" (glance above at the number of Assembly members on each side, Nationalist and Unionist, to realize how easily this can occur), the cross-community support requirement kicks in.

The first alternative is referred to as "parallel consent." This would require a majority of each side, Nationalist and Unionist, for approval.[70] Such a vote would be at least twenty-two Nationalists' votes and twenty-nine Unionists' votes for adoption, in addition to an overall majority. (This majority would be sixty-five, if all 108 members were present and voting.) The alternative to this majority/majority process is what is known as the "weighted majority." This option requires 40% of each side (*i.e.*, seventeen Nationalists votes, and twenty-four Unionists votes), and 60% of all present and voting.[71]

The statute requires the first method to be used, and if the number present is fewer than the entire body and a result cannot be reached, the second alternative is used. Thus, one can see the real meaning of "power sharing," or "cross-community support," an absolute requirement for the enactment of legislation under this d'Hondt system and its offshoots.

What if there is no "support" across the two communities? Can this possibly work, or is this process a built-in deadlock?

For a consociational agreement such as the GFA to survive, there must be regular, systematic, and continuous oversight by the primary government(s) involved. In the case of Northern Ireland, these are, of course, the U.K. and the Republic of Ireland. Professor O'Leary adds to this the necessity that there be an informal recognition on both sides that they may benefit more in the long term if they neither insist upon short-term benefits—benefits to be gained by taking advantage of the other side's difficulties—nor "over-hype" their own difficulties."[72]

Stephen Farry, Chief Policy Advisor for the Alliance Party, distinguishes between the two possible methods of governing in a divided society, "consociationalism" and "integrationalism," the latter being a true cooperative model which still permits the overall majority to rule. The idea of compulsory identification as "Nationalist" or "Unionist" by all Assembly members is troubling indeed to his party (which is neutral on the issue of a united Ireland versus a continued affiliation of Northern Ireland with the U.K.).

This is a forced coalition rather than a voluntary one, as is the case in most continental European countries. For example, the current ruling party in Austria, the *Österreichisches Volks Partei (ÖVP)*—Austrian Peoples' Party—is not a majority party, holding only about 22% support. Unlike the United States' two-party system, most European countries have several political parties, so a majority is difficult, if not (in practicality) impossible. Thus, two parties may agree to join forces—*i.e.*, to coalesce, as has the *ÖVP* with the *Frei Partei Österreich (FPÖ)*— Free Party of Austria, with about 20%. This resulted in their combined greater power than the actual largest party, the *Sozial Partei Österriech (SPÖ)* – Social Party of Austria, with about 30%.

In Northern Ireland, there is an *automatic* statutory coalition of all Unionist parties, and another of all (*i.e.*, both) Nationalist parties, even if a party may actually prefer to "go it alone." Farry describes his party's stance on this provision of the GFA as one which prefers a "genuine liberal democracy" as the ideal, one which presumes the individual (to be) "the cornerstone of the society."[73] Speaking both personally and on behalf of Alliance, he sees the current process as leading to group identity at the expense of the individual.[74] Each person is already identified and entrenched in one camp or the other, a paradigm which this perpetuates.

Importantly, Professor O'Leary sees a plus-for-Nationalists in the GFA in addition to those already mentioned, one which shows another distinction between the Northern Ireland devolvement statute and those for its Scottish and Welsh neighbors across the Irish Sea. In his opinion, the 1998 Northern Ireland Act, has "created an open-ended mechanism for Northern Ireland to expand its autonomy from the rest of the UK."[75] The inference is that by using the word "autonomy," Professor O'Leary means an ultimately united Ireland is one quite fairly drawn. Northern Ireland, standing alone, could not be economically autonomous.

This view, needless to say, is not one shared by the Unionists who approved the GFA.

A View From the "Pro" Side on the
GFA "Cross Community Support" Principle"

One obvious plus is that for the first time since the dissolution of Stormont in 1972, the province has its own law-making body. Secondly, the primary participants in the process did not view the GFA in general as an absolute solution, so they anticipated difficulties. Provided they are minor ones, the drafters believed that they would not derail the entire process. Thus, there is the overall recognition that the legislative body and process for which the Agreement provides are only "starters" with rough edges which must be ironed out, so to speak, as the workings of the Assembly proceed. This should prevent over-optimism as to what the Assembly might accomplish. John Hume called the GFA a "framework for a healing process," not the "solution." [76]

The virtual overwhelming public endorsement of the entire Agreement—95% in the Republic of Ireland, and over 71% in Northern Ireland (with majorities from both Nationalist and Unionist sectors)—is indicative of the peoples' desire for the governing body to work. The PUP's David Ervine, clearly among those who insist the NIA can be effective, warns against letting the extremists on either side be the horse that directs the legislative cart. Referring to these extremists, Ervine compared Ian Paisley to Benjamin Netanyahu (at the time Prime Minister of Israel), and Gerry Adams to the Palestine Liberation Organization's Yasser Arafat. In the summer of 2000, Ervine stated that he believed strongly that there would be a "growing acquiescence to the GFA" and its governing body, and cautioned against viewing the Agreement from a strictly legal and simplistic perspective. [77]

I had the good fortune of meeting and getting to know the Right Reverend James Moore, Bishop of Connor, the largest Church of Ireland diocese in Northern Ireland. A gentle and well-read man, Bishop Moore would indeed make a "believer" of anyone who thinks that a cleric cannot be politically logical-thinking and astute. While acknowledging that the Assembly is a product of the peace process and that the process is fragile, the good bishop nonetheless lauded the NIA as a concept which he calls a "wonderful (one)...that can have devolved government in a part (Northern Ireland) of a country (U.K.) completely based upon cooperation and collaboration between two different groups." He pointed that such a process could not work as a governing body of an independent entity, but seemed to see some glimmer of hope that the Assembly could function. [78] (Note that virtually everyone in Northern Ireland refers not to "peace," but to the "peace *process*." This is a tacit concession that there is, as of yet, indeed no real peace, and a simultaneous expression of hope that peace will evolve out of the process. This is somewhat reminiscent of an alcoholic's reference to himself as "recovering," rather than "recovered," recognizing that he must continue to be vigilant of his problem and that his effort in conquering it is never really accomplished.)

One of the most positive principal figures with regard to the efficacy of the NIA is Monica McWilliams, founder of the Women's Coalition. Similarly to the Alliance Party, the Women's Coalition does not focus on the united Ireland versus remaining-part-of-U.K. issue, but rather on the attainment of lasting peace based on non-discrimination and supported by a thriving economy. Educated at Queen's University with degrees in urban studies, she—like David Ervine—does not approach the GFA and the Assembly from a strict legalistic viewpoint. Ms. McWilliams has kept her exuberance over the fact that such polar groups actually came to an agreement, and she clearly does not appear to focus on negatives. For her, the Assembly, conjoined to the GFA, will "work" because it simply *must*, in light of the alternative of resuming a submission to everyday violence. [79]

A summary view of the positives are inductive, rather than deductive—based on theory rather than law and fact, and hopeful rather than historical. It will take these people and others like them, resolutely committed both to creating a well-oiled process and to achieving a resulting peace, in order for the Assembly to function effectively.

The Negative Stance:
The GFA's "Cross Community Support" Principle is Unworkable

Unfortunately, the not-so-good prospects for the Assembly seem more objective than are the subjective ones on the positive side. An honestly critical view of such a mandatory coupling of two sides which agree on very little, if anything, is not a recipe for success.

The primary objections are directed toward the d'Hondt process. Queen's University's Prof. Dennis Kennedy assesses this concept as "crazy." He emphasizes that the only way the GFA will actually succeed is for the Assembly's ten-member Executive to agree. Since the GFA and the legislation require that this body proceed by consensus, and in practice it is split 5-5 between Unionists and Nationalists, it is virtually a dead-end. The result is what he referred to as an "apartheid solution." [80]

Professor Kennedy is one of the founders of the Cadogan group which proceeds on the recognized European custom of acquiescing to fixed geographical borders. From this base, the goal should be to assure that peoples within those borders are accommodated and that their civil rights are protected. In his view, both the 1993 Downing Street Resolution and the GFA have simply "encourage[d] [both] hopes and fears of Irish unification," further dividing the two communities.[81] This comes from a learned man who told me that he had voted "yes" on the GFA, albeit reluctantly, as he assessed it as the better of two choices.

The Alliance Party's Stephen Farry, too, would change from the d'Hondt provision's form of mandatory power sharing. Farry says that, had they had the opportunity at the time of the GFA talks, Unionists would have "jump[ed] at" reversing what was developing and instead reviving the 1974 Sunningdale agreement. This had been the government which Unionists themselves had essentially demolished because of its relatively innocuous power-sharing concept.

Sinn Féin, though titularly part of the short-lived Sunningdale Assembly, had actually abstained from any participation. As the much more extreme of the two Nationalist parties, *Sinn Féin* had representatives on the Sunningdale Assembly only because John Hume of the SDLP, the more moderate of the two, had worked so hard to reinstitute devolution. Hume apparently thought that this all-inclusion plan embodied by Sunningdale was the only path to this end. Under the GFA, however, *Sinn Féin* constitutes a significant segment of the NIA, a block that can put a fateful veto on any legislation proposed by Unionists.

In Farry's opinion, John Hume (whom he nonetheless praised—"to be fair to the man"—for having been instrumental in commencing SDLP talks with *Sinn Féin's* Gerry Adams) has created a long-term problem for his party by making *Sinn Féin* "legitimate." Farry predicts that *Sinn Féin*, rather than SDLP, will soon be the greater of the two Nationalist parties. He sees Hume as detached from reality, a man with great popularity throughout the province and an "amazing public persona," but one who still speaks in "streams of platitudes." With regard to concessions Unionists made by agreeing to the GFA's proposed cross-community Assembly, Farry pointed out yet another benefit for Unionists in the Sunningdale Agreement which is not in the GFA. At least Sunningdale did not have the mandated "Nationalist" or "Unionist" declaration for legislators as does the GFA, a factor which even deepens the polarization of the two groups.[82]

Farry's thoughts struck me as among the most reasoned I had heard. A likeable young man with an omnipresent smile, he was clearly not angry or bitter over provisions in the GFA with which he and his party took issue. He simply bemoaned the fact that the NIA reflects the "ethnic competition" which is still politics-as-usual in Northern Ireland, and he would have put the political process sequentially before the peace process. While the author offers this thought neither as a criticism nor endorsement for either, Farry's approach does appear to be one by which the participants would have thought with their heads, rather than their hearts.[83]

Yet another difficulty—different from the d'Hondt issue, but tangentially similar—was pointed out by one prominent judge in Northern Ireland with whom I spoke. Citing a statutory stepchild of the d'Hondt principle, the judge finds the NIA "inherently unstable" because of its "cabinet [executive]-without-responsibility" characteristic. Since the First Minister (David Trimble, UUP) and then Deputy First Minister (Seamus Mallon, SDLP) have identical authorities, they veritably cancel each other's power. This trickles down into the remainder of the Ministers on the Executive, except that the Minister (rather than the Deputy) is in control of decisions within the confines of the particular committee.

The same judge referred to an example, one on which he did not voice an opinion on the advisability of the Minister's decision, but which he offered simply to explain his point. *Sinn Féin's* Barbaire de Brun, Minister for Health, unilaterally decided to close a maternity ward in a large Belfast hospital. Other Ministers (on both sides) were opposed, but since she has total authority over her domain, it could not be a topic for discussion.[84] Contrary to the general spirit of the NIA, it is indeed a challenge to find any "cross-community power sharing" in such an executive model.

No discussion of the faults of the GFA's provisions setting up the NIA would be complete without some reference to those who were "naysayers" from the onset. Among these, surely the Rev. Dr. Ian Paisley was the most vocal—and most vitriolic.

Generally, one can ultimately think of something positive to say about nearly anything, even though at times this may be difficult. For example, it is often said of the Italian dictator Mussolini that at least he got the Italians trains running on time. However, Paisley found nothing—absolutely nothing—of any merit whatsoever in the GFA. His objections, however, were to the document in its entirety and, to be sure, its spirit. He did not confine his opposition to simple intricacies about how the Assembly might function, but rather he objected to the institution itself. (More detail regarding his input and his activities during the negotiations are in Chapter 4 on the talks, the signing, and the content of the GFA.)

How Has It "Played" Thus Far?

The Assembly was suspended in February, 2000, and very nearly suffered the same fate in March, 2001. During mid-to-late 2001, the NIA barely survived yet a third crisis. However, the issues which made the lawmaking body such a precarious creature have not been the cross-community-d'Hondt voting and executive make-up requirements. Rather, the destructive issues have been with regard to the interpretation of the GFA itself, specifically with respect to decommissioning by paramilitary groups.

David Trimble publicly announced in early May, 2001[85] that he would resign as First Minister on July 1 if the IRA had not begun to disarm by that date. This Republican paramilitary had promised a year before Trimble's announcement that it would work with the Commission on Decommissioning to place its stockpiled weapons "completely and verifiably beyond use," and Trimble had then taken the politically tenuous step of persuading his fellow UUP Assembly members to place their faith in this commitment.

Although the IRA had indeed cooperated with the Commission by permitting inspections of weaponry, its unwillingness actually to surrender arms had induced the First Minister to take the stance he did in spring, 2001.[86] This proved not to have been merely a politician's ploy, for Trimble indeed stepped down on July 1, as promised. International newspapers indicated disgust with both sides. For example, an editorial in Vienna's *Der Standard* called this a test of manliness by political "musclemen" just to see which side would fold first.[87] The looming Portadown Orange Order parade (described in Chapter 2) came, then, under a government without a rudder, an ominous sign.

Politically, the British government did not dissolve the Assembly, but rather used its constitutional power to suspend it for six weeks—until August 12—in hopes that the IRA would commence disarming and that it would then be back-to-the-business of legislating for the Assembly. During the days following the July 12 parades, the Protestant section of North Belfast was subjected to riots which resulted in serious injuries to some 113 police officers.[88]

The response of *Sinn Féin* and the IRA was to demand the same demilitarisation of Loyalist paramilitaries. The general assumption in the province was that, if no conciliation of this issue had taken place by August 12 (the end of the six-week suspension period), there would be either (i) permanent resumption of direct control of Northern Ireland by Westminster Parliament, or (ii) new elections for Assembly members. The fear among Unionists was that the latter might tip the majority to Nationalists.[89] By the first week of August, the impasse continued.

Meanwhile, the Commission on Decommissioning approved an IRA offer to permit further inspection of its weapons by this international neutral body and to comply with any Commission decision as to what remained to be done to put all arms completely beyond use. Trimble and his Unionists rejected this offer because there was no accompanying explicit time schedule for total disarmament.

The Commission had lauded this move by the Republican paramilitary, and the Irish *Taoiseach* called it a "historical breakthrough" of "enormous significance." However, Trimble's UUP insisted on the IRA's designation of a definite date by which all weapons would be surrendered to authorities.[90] On a CNN International news program August 7, *Sinn Féin's* Michael McGuinness adamantly criticized Trimble for having disregarded a plan that the Commission had found sufficient, adding that "I hope he reflects on this…[He has made a] grievous misjudgement." *Sinn Féin's* position was that the Commission's acceptance of the offer from the IRA should be controlling.

The following day, *Sinn Féin* party leader, Gerry Adams appeared on CNN International and stated that Trimble had made a mistake of "historical enormity…but [that] there is still time." Trimble's rejoinder was that a timetable for disarmament was an absolute necessity before Unionists would agree, and that the mere promise to put weapons "beyond use" was inadequate.[91] CNN's conclusion was that "this troubled province remains in a state of crisis."

Many (at least this writer) were surprised at the virtual eleventh hour decision of Secretary of State John Reid to suspend the Assembly for yet another six-week period. British Prime Minister Tony Blair's opinion was that "[w]hen we have come so far…people would agree with both governments [the U.K. and Ireland] that we should allow the parties more time to try and bridge the remaining gaps."[92]

McGuinness was livid. Speaking for *Sinn Féin*, he accused Reid of "bowing to Unionist pressure."[93] Reid's statement to CNN on August 23 was that "we have a commitment to make the [Good Friday] Agreement work." CNN's analysis was that Northern Ireland remained "as divided as ever." Two days later, the IRA withdrew its earlier offer to put weapons beyond use.[94] The dissension was now back to square one.

Oddly, Blair was then vacationing in Austria, as he had been since prior to the Commission's proposal to accept the IRA's offer. Moreover, Trimble then left for a three-week vacation (also in Austria),[95] so that he would be out of the country for one-half of the six-week period granted to attempt to reach a settlement. The priorities of these two principals were decidedly in question.

Not surprisingly, the second six-week period expired without any consensus,

Reid's decision was to grant yet another six-week suspension after the second such suspension had ended. Still defiant on the issue of decommissioning, all UUP members of the Assembly's executive resigned on October 18, 2001. (Note that this did not mean that they had resigned as elected Assembly members. Should they have done so, a new general election—or, as the British say, a "fresh" election—would have been required.) Apparently, this provided the impetus for the IRA's announcement on October 23 that it had begun disarming. Secretary Reid now could rest peacefully, since this move would presumably put the Assembly back on track before this suspension was to end on November 3.

However, to borrow from the familiar (dubious) profundity of former New York Yankees' catcher Yogi Berra, "it ain't over 'til it's over." Trimble's re-election as First Minister was anticipated to be a grand slam, since he was assured of a strong majority of Nationalist support, and, surely the required majority of his fellow UUP party members. The GFA had been overwhelmingly endorsed by Nationalists, and Trimble—despite his abrupt resignation on July 1—was generally acknowledged to have been the catalyst that had gained enough acceptance of *Sinn Féin* to have resulted in their participation in the power sharing government.

As expected, the Nationalist vote in the Assembly was unanimous for Trimble. Also as expected, the UUP rival party Unionist but anti-GFA party, Paisley's DUP, voted unanimously against his re-election as First Minister. Unexpectedly, however, was the vote within his own party.

Two strong-willed UUP mavericks—Pauline Armitage and Peter Weir—voted against their own party leader. The quixotic result was that, although Trimble had the overall support of more than 70% of the entire Assembly, the close (but negative) vote in the UUP meant that he was barely short among the Unionists. The combined Unionist vote was 30-29 against Trimble[96] and the power-sharing structure required approval by both sectors.

BBC described Weir as a thirty-two-year-old unmarried North County Down (Bangor) barrister who had been a solid opponent of the GFA from its inception. Ms. Armitage, from East Londonderry/Derry, had been a member of UUP since 1969. A former manager of an infants' retail clothing store, she also had been a soldier in the Ulster Defence Regiment. The UUP vouched that it would "punish [these two] rebels."[97]

Committed GFA-supporters' determined reaction was to find a resolution to salvage the process. It is important to keep in mind that those elected to the Assembly must declare their designation as "Nationalist," Unionist" or "neither" upon taking office.[98] The "neithers" included the Alliance Party's five members.

Solely to preserve the Assembly and, with it the peace process, three members of the Alliance Party were permitted to switch their designation so as to declare them (temporarily only) "Unionists." This would give Trimble the majority among "Unionists" which he needed for victory. Alliance Party leader David Ford confirmed the continued neutrality of his party on the Unionist/Nationalist issue, but insisted that "[I]f there is any message which should go out, it is that the Alliance Party is working to save the Agreement." [99]

So, what is wrong with this political picture from an American perspective? First, the accepted rules of the game were changed in mid-stream. Alliance Party members were given this one-shot authority to designate other than they had originally done solely so that Trimble might be re-elected. This mold-the-rules-to-fit-the-desired-outcome would be anathema to politics in the U.S.A. Secondly, a party member in the American political system is free to vote according to his own volition without fear of any formal reprisal or sanction from his peers. David Trimble has proven himself to be the Rasputin of Northern Ireland, emerging once again from what appeared to be a sure demise and snatching the legendary "victory from the jaws of defeat." In typical Northern Ireland fashion, there was a veritable physical clash among Assembly members following the return of Trimble and company to power.[100]

Meanwhile, the inevitable legal action has been filed, challenging the legitimacy of the switch in affiliation by Alliance. BBC reported November 8, 2001, that Ian Paisley had led the DUP to fight the procedure and the re-election of Trimble in court. Paisley's petition disputed the lawfulness of Secretary of State John Reid's November 19, 2001 decision to review (and, ultimately, to change) some of the Assembly's established voting procedures, and Reid's determination that no new Assembly elections would take place prior to 2003. One must stay tuned for further developments in the continuing saga of the Northern Ireland Assembly.

Most recently, the Assembly was suspended for the third time on October 13, 2002 and remains so at this writing. The issue was the same: the absence of total disarmament by the IRA. The United Kingdom government again assumed direct control over the province, dashing the hopes which had emerged through the dark days of late 2001.[101]

One must stay tuned for further developments in the continuing saga of the Northern Ireland Assembly.

Conclusion

The Northern Ireland Assembly is the cornerstone of devolved government in the province, but its operability has been sporadic and intermittent. The cross-community spirit permeating the GFA presupposed an end to acts of terrorism. It is this spirit upon which the GFA provisions establishing the Assembly were based, a possibly flawed premise which sadly appears to be its unavoidable weakness.

The recurring barrier to the peace process is paramilitaries' refusal to decommission, or—in American parlance—disarm. As long as this refusal persists, there can be no successful implementation of the GFA. Continued possession of these weapons stokes the fires and fears of resumption of the violence the GFA that has become associated with Northern Ireland.

Ironically, it was violence which led to the demise of the 50-year-old Northern Ireland Parliament in 1972, and this is the same activity the parties to the GFA pledged to cease. This issue continues to be the root cause of the inability of the Assembly to function as the drafters of the GFA ad envisioned, and without the Assembly, there is no self-governance.

A solution has thus far been elusive. The decommissioning problem—the remaining thorn in maintaining a devolved government in Northern Ireland—is a bargaining card which the UUP apparently will not surrender.

Endnotes to Chapter 5

[1] Interview with David Ervine, July 3, 2000, Stormont, Belfast.

[2] There is a similar, but not identical, American constitutional provision with regard to the federal-states division of powers. The 10th Amendment (1791) to the U.S. Constitution vests the states with power to govern all matters which the Constitution has not expressly reserved for the federal government, nor denied to the states. One apparent difference from the U.S. constitutional provision of the Northern Ireland devolvement legislation is that the U.K. statute lists which matters are not transferred to the New Northern Ireland Assembly. The U.S. Constitution's language is concise but broader in this section, using the more general reservation clause. *See notes 61 and 62* and accompanying text for which matters are not devolved to the NIA.

[3] Government of Ireland Act 1920.

[4] Anglo-Irish Treaty 1921.

[5] M.W. Hislinga, THE IRISH BORDER AS A CULURAL DIVIDE at 11 (Van Gorcum and Comp. N.V., the Netherlands, 1971).

[6] *Id.* At 63.

[7] *Id.* At 57.

[8] Jack C. Plano and Roy Olton, THE INTERNATIONAL RELATIONS DICTIONARY at 453-454 (ABC-CLIO, Santa Barbara, California, 3d ed. 1982).

[9] Time and again one hears in Northern Ireland references to the province as a "statelet." I heard this term used both by the Rev. Peter Ward at Clonard Monastery, Belfast, July 5, 2000, and Judge John Martin, Chief Judge of Social Security and Child Commissioner of Northern Ireland, Belfast, July 6, 2000.

[10] E-mail communication from Professor Brendan O'Leary, Dec. 13, 2001.

[11] Art. 75 Government of Ireland Act 1920.

[12] *Id.* Articles 6 and 75.

[13] C. Desmond Greaves, THE IRISH CRISIS at 26 (Lawrence and Wishart, London, 1972).

[14] *Id*. At 74.

[15] March 30, 1972, Temporary Provisions (N.I.) Act which reinstated direct rule over Northern Ireland by the Parliament at Westminster.

[16] Sydney Elliott and W.D. Flackes, NORTHERN IRELAND: A POLITICAL DIRECTORY 1968-1999, (The Blackstone Press, Belfast, 1999).

[17] The actual catalyst was "Bloody Sunday," the massacre by the British military of 14 Catholics in Londonderry/Derry in January 1972. *See* Chapter 1 for a description of this event and its consequences.

[18] §1(1) Northern Ireland Assembly Act 1973.

[19] Interview with Jackie Johnston, July 21, 2000, Office of Secretary of State for Northern Ireland, Stormont Castle, Belfast.

[20] Elliott and Flackes, *supra* note 15 at 386.

[21] Art. 2(a) Agreement Between the Government of the United Kingdom of Great Britain and Northern Ireland and the Government of the Republic of Ireland, November 15, 1986, U.K.-Ir. Cmnd. 9657.

[22] *Id*. Art. 2(b).

[23] *Id*. Art. 4©.

[24] *Id*. Art. 4(a).

[25] *Id*. Art. 12.

[26] *Id.* Art. 8.

[27] Perhaps the most thoroughly researched and well-written work on Diplock Trials is by two of my friends and colleagues on the law faculty at Queen's University, Sean Doran and John Jackson, JUDGE WITHOUT JURY: DIPLOCK TRIALS IN THE ADVERSARY SYSTEM (Oxford University Press, Oxford, England, 1995). This book is complete, yet concise, in its coverage of the law, and it is extremely readable both for the jurist and the layman.

[28] Dennis Kennedy, *Dash for Agreement: Temporary Accommodation or Lasting Settlement?* 22 FORDHAM INTERNATIONAL LAW JOURNAL 1440, 1447 (1999).

[29] Joint Delaration December 15, 1993, p. 7, para. 4.

[30] *Id.* Para. 7.

[31] Kennedy, *supra* note 27, at 1449, referring to Sir Patrick Mayhew's December 1992, speech in Coleraine, County Antrim, in the far north of the province.

[32] One stark example was shown in the November 2000 U.S. presidential election. Most Americans were unaware of the variances among the states of the voting methods and even the times absentee ballots must be postmarked and/or deposited with the particular electoral office.

[33] Colin Harvey, *Legality, Legitimacy, and Democratic Renewal: the New Assembly in Context*, 22 FORDHAM INTERNATIONAL LAW JOURNAL 1389, 1392 (1999).

[34] Jeffrey Ghannam, *Perilous Journey*, AMERICAN BAR ASSOCIATION JOURNAL at 18-19 (August 2000).

[35] Harvey, *supra* note 32 at 1394.

[36] Plano and Olton, *supra* note 8 at 33.

[37] Scotland Act 1998 (c. 46) (November 19, 1998), Part I.

[38] Government of Wales Act 1998 (c. 38) (July 31, 1998), Part 1, *para* 2.

[39] *Id.* Pt. IV para. 73-80. The Scottish Parliament can vary the basic income tax rate established by Westminster by 3%, higher or lower.

[40] *Supra* note 1.

[41] Many even resent being called "British," although Scotland is geographically on the island of Great Britain. I recall making a remark to one of the exchange students from the University of Aberdeen at the law school at Universität Regensburg (Germany) during summer, 1991, about "your queen." She promptly retorted, "She's not *my* queen!" Accurately, of course, she is queen not only for England, but also for Scotland, Wales, and Northern Ireland.

[42] CURRENT LAW STATUTES 1998, at 46-5 (Sweet and Maxwell, Dublin, Ireland, annotations by C.M.G. Himsworth, University of Edinburgh).

[43] Scotland Act 1998, Schedule 1, §§2(1), 2(3), and 2(2), respectively.

[44] *Id.* §44.

[45] *Id.* §45.

[46] *Id.* §47.

[47] Wales Act 1978 (c. 52).

[48] CURRENT LAW STATUTES 1998, at 38-6 (Sweet and Maxwell, annotations by Prof. David Foulkes). This resulted in a repeal of the devolution statute by Order in Council (S.I. 1979 No. 933).

[49] Government of Wales Act 1998 (c. 38), July 31, 1998, §§53(1),(2).

[50] *Id.* §47.

[51] 1942 Welsh Courts Act.

[52] J. Graham Jones, HISTORY OF WALES 122-123 (University of Wales Press, Swansea, 1990).

[53] Heine Gruffud, THE REAL WALES 52, 70 (New South Wales Press, Sydney, Australia, 1998).

[54] Statistics are from 1995. *See* Harry Drost, WHAT'S WHAT AND WHO'S WHO IN EUROPE at 27 (Cassell, London, 1995).

[55] Brendan O'Leary, *The Nature of the Agreement*, 22 FORDHAM INTERNATIONAL LAW JOURNAL 1628, 1630 (1999).

[56] *Id.* at 1649.

[57] *Id.* at 1631.

[58] Question-and-answer session following Prof. O'Leary's address to Fulbright Scholars, Westminster, London, January 28, 1998. Note that this pre-dated the GFA.

[59] Northern Ireland (Elections) Act 1998.

[60] Northern Ireland Act 1998 (c. 47).

[61] O'Leary, *supra* note 53 at 1665, Table One.

[62] *Id.*, Table Two.

[63] Northern Ireland Act 1998 Part III, §18(5).

[64] *Id.* §4(1), Schedule 2.

[65] *Id.* §4(1), Schedule 3.

[66] *Id.* Section $41.

[67] *Id.* Part III §17(1).

[68] Conversation with William Orbinson, May 30, 1998, Hillsborough, Northern Ireland.

[69] O'Leary, *supra* note 53 at 1661-1663.

[70] Northern Ireland Act 1998, Part IV §42.

[71] *Id.* Part I §5(a),(b).

[72] O'Leary, *supra* note 53 at 1659-1660.

[73] Stephen Farry, *Beyond the 'Band-Aid' Approach: an Alliance Party Perspective upon the Belfast Agreement,* 22 FORDHAM INTERNATIONAL LAW JOURNAL 1221, 1227-1229, and 1237.

[74] *Id.* at 1226, 1239.

[75] O'Leary, *supra* note 55 at 1647.

[76] John Hume, *Ireland—the Healing Process,* 22 FORDHAM INTERNATIONAL LAW JOURNAL 1171, 1176 (1999). (Emphasis added.) Note that Mr. Hume's Nationalist viewpoint is evident from his use of the word "Ireland," rather than "Northern Ireland."

[77] *Supra* note 1.

[78] Interview with the Rt. Rev. James Moore, August 7, 2000, Church of Ireland Diocesan Offices, Belfast.

[79] These conclusions are based uon the author's interview with Monica McWillliams, July 21, 2000, in her office at Stormont, Belfast.

[80] Interview with Professor Dennis Kennedy, July 19, 2000, in his office at Queen's University, Belfast.

[81] Kennedy, *supra* note 28, at 1452.

[82] Conversation with Stephen Farry, Alliance Party Policy Analyst, August 1, 2000, Alliance Party Headquarters, Belfast.

[83] Oddly, this same "process-rather-than-product" preference was also espoused by Alex Attwood, MLA for the SDLP, Hume's own party. (Interview with Alex Attwood, July 31, 2000, SDLP Party Headquarters, Belfast.) As a lawyer, the author can identify with this conclusion, a logical one from the perspective of the jurist. Attwood is a solicitor. (Note: In the Irish and British legal systems, a lawyer is either a solicitor or a barrister. Rather than being competitive, they serve in different roles. A solicitor prepares documents, gives advice, and makes references to a barrister, when needed. The barrister's sole function is to appear in court, which the solicitor may not do. Howver, a solicitor must refer a case to a barrister before he can make any contact with the client, so they have working relationships.) Farry, a political scientist, also would instinctively be more of a stickler for rules and procedure than would the Monica McWilliamses and/or the David Ervines from the social-sciences mode.

[84] I interviewed this judge in August, 2000. Indicative of the nature of the problem in Northern Ireland is his request to remain anonymous.

[85] Trimble: *Disarm or 'I will resign,'* RICHMOND TIMES-DISPATCH (The Associated Press), at A-5, May 9, 2001.

[86] *IRA lag on arms alleged,* RICHMOND TIMES-DISPATCH, at A-5, June 1, 2001.

[87] Martin Alioth, *Nordirische Ritual* (Ritual in Northern Ireland), *DER STANDARD* (Vienna), at 24, col. 1, July 2, 2001.

[88] *Belfast: Nacht der Gewalt* (Belfast: Night of Force), *SALBURGER NACHTRICHTEN* (Salzburg, Austria), at 9 col. 1-4, July 14, 2001.

[89] *Nordirlands 'letzte Chance'* (Northern Ireland's 'last chance'), *id.*, at col. 2-5, and *Die Zeit laüft – zugunsten der Friedensgegner* (Time is passing – peace opponents cannot agree), *RHEINISCHE POST* (Düsseldoef), at 4, col. 2-5, August 6, 2001.

[90] *Fester Zeitplan für die Entwaffnung fehlt* (Definite timetable for disarmament is lacking) *KÖLNER STADT-ANZEIGER* (Cologne, Germany), at 5, col. 1-2, August 7, 2001, and *Trimble unzufrieden* (Trimble isn't satisfied), *DIE TAGESZEITUNG* (Frankfurt), at 2, col. 2-4, August 8, 2001.

[91] Rosie Cowan, *Reid wins six weeks of breathing space*, THE GUARDIAN, at 6, col. 1-8, August 11, 2001.

[92] Rosie Cowan, *Stormont assembly put on ice*, THE GUARDIAN, at 1, col. 1-3, August 11, 2001.

[93] *Id.*

[94] Marianne Quoirin, *Für die IRA ist der Krieg noch nicht zur Ende* (The war isn't over yet for the IRA), *KÖLNER STADT-ANZEIGER* (Cologne, Germany), AT 7, COL. 3-6, august 15, 2001.

[95] *IRA zieht Angebot zur Entwaffung wieder zurück* (IRA revokes offer to disarm), *FRANKFURTER ALLGEMEINE* (Frankfurt, Germany), at 1, col. 2-4, August 15, 2001.

[96] *Trimble re-election bid fails,* RICHMOND TIMES-DISPATCH (The Associated Press), at A-4, col. 4, November 3, 2001.

[97] *Id.*

[98] *See supra* note 69 and accompanying text.

[99] *Neutrals to join Protestant block*, RICHMOND TIMES-DISPATCH, at A-4, col. 4-5, November 4, 2001.

[100] *Trimble promises stability,* RICHMOND TIMES-DISPATCH (The Associated Press), at A-4, col. 2-4, November 7, 2001.

[101] *Direct rule reinstated*, BELFAST TELEGRAPH, at 1, October 14, 2001.

Chapter 6

Release of Prisoners and Decommissioning: The Troublesome "Siamese Twin" Issues

"[T]here's been no more nauseating sight than the release of our paramilitary 'soldiers.'"

Gail Walker [1]

The Belfast Telegraph called the GFA's promised release of so-called political prisoners the "most unpalatable aspect" [2] of the GFA for the people of Northern Ireland. Lending credence to this conclusion is the seriousness with which this question was dealt during the negotiations. Throughout each phase—the talks, the GFA, the referenda, and the Assembly elections—the prisoner release issue remained the most significant one. [3] However, the most critical issue on the last day of the talks was the one regarding decommissioning—or disarmament, in American parlance—by all paramilitary groups. [4]

The general consensus is that these two provisions of the GFA and the supplementing legislation were joined at the bargaining chip, so to speak. *Quid pro quos*, neither would have survived, or even emerged, without the other. This is so, even though neither document expressly links the two so as to make one conditional upon, or contemporaneous with, the other. [5] Indeed, Mitchell McLaughlin, one of the most visible of *Sinn Féin* MLAs (Members of the Legislative Assembly), has said that a "major sticking point" for his party was to link prisoner releases to decommissioning, [6] irrespective of what is stated in the GFA and the statute. On the other hand, for the UUP, the largest Unionist party, the release provision was the most difficult of all concessions. In the end, these proved to be mutual concessions by both sides in return for something positive.

Release of those prisoners convicted of politically motivated crimes—provided they were qualified for release under the statute—is a *fait accompli*. The last of the "eligible" inmates were freed on July 28, 2000. In contrast, the decommissioning issue has proved to be the obstacle for the Northern Ireland government—it refuses to go away. Implementation of this provision has been the trigger each time the fledgling government has been on the verge of collapse.

What indeed is a "paramilitary" group, and why should those convicted of terrorism be given preferential treatment over other convicts? And why cannot the surrendering of arms by these groups be accomplished without further dissension? These are complicated and volatile questions, ones which arouse the passions of even the most uninvolved of Northern Irelanders.

THE PRISONER RELEASE ISSUE

The language in the GFA expressly assured that "political prisoners" would be released.[7] The provisos—*i.e.*, qualifying conditions—would be in the implementing legislation. In order to qualify, the statute required simply that one had been convicted of a "terrorist offence" prior to April 10, 1998 (the date of the signing of the GFA), have served at least two years of a longer sentence, and be a member of a paramilitary which is currently engaged in a genuine cease-fire.[8] For those who had been given life sentences, there was an added condition: he must not, in the opinion of the presiding judge, pose a "danger to the public."[9] Interestingly, the necessity that one be in a paramilitary group in order to be eligible for early release lends some legitimacy to these groups whose sole method is violence.

There were both objective and subjective objections to this provision in general. Pure legalists opposed such an "unprecedented interference with the criminal justice process."[10] The rejoinders were both historical and political. First, such early releases for prisoners have been historically prominent in the area of international conflicts.[11] Moreover, they had been the norm even in Ireland's quest for independence in the post-1916 Easter Rising days,[12] and in the aftermath of the 1919-1921 Irish Civil War. The political rationale was that neither Republicans nor Loyalists would have ceased the violence which was erupting even during the peace talks unless the release-of-prisoners issues was seriously on the bargaining table.[13]

For those who suffered the enduring pain of having lost someone whom they loved because of the brutality of the murderous paramilitaries, there truly is no meaningful response. And it is difficult to find anyone in Northern Ireland who did not personally know someone who had been a victim. This is something I learned on my first day in Northern Ireland.

Several of my landlady's neighbors came by to meet "the American (me)," and one couple, Danny and Kiera, were particularly delightful. After they left, my wonderful landlady, Jean, told me that they had five children, adding immediately, "Well, it really was six, but one was killed in the Troubles." Her explanation left me chilled.

It should be explained that this was a haven for me, a place that really became "home" in the truest sense. I loved Jean and her friendly neighbors, and I loved living in this quiet and lovely residential area. This was one of the sections of Belfast generally referred to as "neutral"—*i.e.*, both Catholics and Protestants lived there, and nobody really cared about their neighbors' religious or political preference. However, where hatred reigns, tragedy does not recognize zones. In the onset of the Troubles—in the early '70's—Sammy and Greta's oldest son and a friend had sat on the back row at the 11 a.m. Sunday mass at St. Bridget's Catholic Church so that they could slip out early for a quick smoke. St. Bridget's is located in the same general area where Jean and Sammy and Greta live, quite close to Queen's University. It is a large church with an adjacent school, and both are modern buildings that accommodate a sizeable and growing congregation. There was no evidence of any poverty in this area, and no shabby or run-down residences. The church is situated on a major street, Malone Road, with a British Army base only a few blocks south. Indeed, the soldiers would wave to me each day from their lookout-tower post as I walked down Malone to my work at Queen's.

As soon as the two nineteen-year-olds were outside the church, a Loyalist group (nobody knows which, since they were never apprehended) gunned down both, killing them instantly. These two young men were students at Queen's, veritable boys yet, who came from loving, Christian families and who had all the aspirations characteristic of the young . They were not "involved" and probably never would have been. I later asked my seminar in discrimination law at Queen's if any of them had personal acquaintances who had been killed in the violence of Northern Ireland, or if they knew anyone who had had lost a family member. There were ten students (a couple who were from the Republic), and each one answered affirmatively. Indeed, the majority cited two or more such experiences. Thus, the term "paramilitary" invokes a sad memory for virtually everyone in Northern Ireland.

An estimated 50-70% (figures vary) of those incarcerated in Northern Ireland at the time of the signing of the GFA had been convicted of politically motivated crimes and were connected in some fashion with one of the several paramilitaries.[14] Of Northern Ireland's approximately 1.6 million people, some 25,000-30,000 were serving terms for such convictions. In Belfast alone, there were 10,000 such prisoners, since the larger prisons (in particular, the gloomy Long Kesh prison in the Belfast suburb of Maze and thus usually referred to simply as "the Maze") were located there. When approached with the question of why these people should be granted early releases with the stroke of a pen, David Ervine, MLA for the Unionist party PUP, acknowledged that this had been difficult, but added that it was necessary to reaching a consensus. Referring to the fact that concessions had to be made and neither side would be 100% satisfied with any agreement which could have come from the peace process, Ervine—who is a former member of the UVF (Loyalist paramilitary) and one who has served time in prison —said poignantly, "We proceeded to the beauty parlor and came out with warts on our noses." [15] The inference is that one may have gorgeous hair, but that this metaphorical ugly wart remains. The metaphorical "wart" for many was the prisoner-release section.

Paramilitaries

Oddly, U.S. newspapers seem to focus so solely on the Irish Republican Army (IRA) that many Americans are unaware that there are paramilitary groups on both sides. Moreover, each side has several such groups. The word "paramilitary" is enigmatic, since these are self-formed bodies that use terrorism to attain their political goals. They are indeed not, in the strict sense of the word, members of the "military," nomenclature generally reserved for official governmental security enforcement bodies.

Charles Townshend, Professor of Modern History at the University of Kent, has written that this descriptive word gives these terrorist groups a degree of legitimacy, referring to academics' use of words in the context of Northern Ireland such as "paramilitaries" and "parapolitical" activity. His rhetorical question relating to these coined phrases is that if we can have "parapolitics," does this mean that we can have "parawar"?[16] Townshend's parody is an apparent objection to viewing these groups as anything within the legal framework. They should be seen, rather, for what they are in reality—persons acting unlawfully and contrary to the achievement of real peace.

Republican "paramilitaries"

To be sure, the IRA is the "granddaddy" of these groups of terrorists, although at its inception it neither deserved nor received its later-earned negative reputation. It did in fact begin as a military unit, formed in resistance to continued British rule over Ireland. Originally named the Irish Volunteers (later, the IRA), this citizen's army was founded in the late 1700's. Interestingly, it was comprised at first almost entirely of Protestants who favored Irish independence.[17] Now the paramilitary wing of *Sinn Féin*, its prominence reached a peak during the 1916 Easter Rising in Dublin and the 1919-1921 Irish Civil War. The IRA's Minister of Finance and Commander in Chief of the Provisional Government was at the time a young Michael Collins, a name most Americans will recognize from the late 1990's film starring Ballymena (County Antrim)-born actor Liam Neeson and titled simply "Michael Collins." Collins was assassinated during the war (probably by his own forces who tagged him a traitor for having settled for Home Rule for Ireland rather than complete independence from Britain).[18]

The "official" outbreak of the Troubles in 1969 led to a revival of IRA activity in the so-called "Provisional IRA" (sometimes referred to as "Provos"), connoting the (hoped-for) temporary nature of the reason for its re-emergence. It was actually a defensive, rather than offensive, group, whose purpose was to protect West Belfast Catholics from any recurrence of events such as the August 15-16, 1969, burnings and lootings against Catholic homes and establishments.[19]

Gerry Adams, *Sinn Féin* party leader, was an active IRA member, and Martin McGuinness, Minister of Education for the new Assembly, had earlier led the large IRA unit in Derry/Londonderry. McGuinness' IRA affiliation had been an "open secret" until late spring, 2001, when he testified before the British tribunal investigating the January 30, 1972 event in Derry known as "Bloody Sunday." [20] (*See* Chapter 1 for an account of this tragedy.)

Other Republican paramilitary groups are probably lesser known, except for the relatively recent "Real IRA." This group consists of former IRAs who believe that the 1994 cease-fire and the non-violence promoted by the GFA were "cop-outs," so to speak. They maintain that violence is the only way that an ultimately united Ireland will result, and they are usually responsible for the resumption of sporadic bombings (such as the August, 2, 2001, bombing of a West London nightclub). Indeed, *Sinn Féin* leader Gerry Adams immediately thereafter publicly condemned such actions by the Real IRA.

In addition to the (i) Provos (IRA) and the (ii) Real IRA are the (iii) Irish National Liberation Army (INLA, also known as the "IRPS," derived from an incorrect sequential listing of the initials of its political wing, the Irish Revolutionary Socialist Party), and the (iv) Officials (which split from the IRA in 1970 because of the Officials' much-doubted non-militant claim; also referred to as the "stickies" because of their wearing of an Easter lily by use of adhesive tape, to commemorate the 1916 Easter Rising).[21]

Loyalist "Paramilitaries"

On the Unionist side, the Ulster Defense Regiment (UDR) is in fact a lawful body, actually a regiment created by the British Army in 1970. Nonetheless, it should be mentioned in the context of paramilitaries. While it is in reality not considered a paramilitary, in 1985, former Irish *Taoiseach* Garret Fitzgerald termed it "dangerous" and a "force ...[whose] loyalty does not lie with the British Crown," one which "Catholics must...fear."[22]

Bona fide Loyalist paramilitaries include the (i) Ulster Defense Association (UDA, the largest Loyalist paramilitary group[23]), (ii) the Ulster Volunteer Force (UVF, the paramilitary wing of the Populist Unionist Party, or PUP; current MLA David Ervine served time in prison for his activities with this terrorist group), (iii) the Ulster Defense Association (UDA), (iv) the Ulster Freedom Fighters (UFF), (v) the Loyalist Volunteer Force (LVF, which boasted as among its members Billy Wright, murdered in the Maze prison in December, 1997, presumably by Republican inmates), (vi) the Red Hand Commandos, and (vii) the Protestant Action Force.

Some Remarks on Paramilitaries in General

Despite the visibility and household-name status of the IRA, an early-Troubles statistic is telling. By the end of 1984, Republican paramilitaries had killed 496 Protestant civilians. On the other hand, Loyalist paramilitaries had killed 569 Catholic civilians. A look at the number of security force members killed during this time by the respective groups, however, is the opposite: 705 such killings by Republicans, and a relatively unimpressive 90 by Loyalists.[24] Perhaps this imbalance is indicative of the general distrust among Republicans of the predominately Protestant RUC.

John Conroy, an American journalist who lived in Catholic West Belfast for a considerable time during the early days of the Troubles, noted also the difference in the *modus operandi* between the two factions' paramilitaries. While Republicans routinely killed policemen in the presence of their wives and young children, Loyalists tended to use more torture of their Catholic victims short of outright murder. A couple of October, 1982, examples Conroy cites are terrifying. One report is of Loyalists tying one Catholic man to the chair in which he was sitting and sawing off his hand with a hacksaw. A few days later, they pulled a Catholic's teeth. This victim, however, did lose his life, because this was followed by their slitting his throat and chopping his body into pieces with an axe. The mutilation was so thorough that he could only be identified by the wristwatch on one of his dismembered hands.[25]

Such events have been commonplace in the paramilitary context. The people who committed such atrocities reaped the benefit of the GFA's early release mandate.

Legislative and Judicial Responses to Paramilitary Terrorism

Much pre-GFA legislation had been adopted by the Westminster Parliament aimed toward controlling the violence and making certain that those responsible were dealt with accordingly by the justice system. The efficacy of these efforts is debatable when one considers the total number of Troubles-related casualties during the thirty-year period beginning with 1969. The actual end-of-1998 numbers were 3,289 dead and 42,216 wounded.[26] These tallies did not include corollary deaths related to sectarianism such as suicides, highway mortalities, and prisoners' hunger strikes. Nor did they include those killed in the Republic, Great Britain and the continent of Europe. Moreover, there have been still more sectarian killings since the signing of the GFA. John Hume sadly reminded that, even though Belfast has one of the highest rates of church attendance in urban Europe, it was necessary to build thirteen walls in the city in order to separate one set of Christians from another.[27]

The most sweeping Westminster legislation was the 1972 statute which suspended the fifty-year old Northern Ireland Parliament. This law abolished the powers of the Governor of the region and transferred powers to a Secretary of State for Northern Ireland.[28] The one who held this new post would be a cabinet member (and thus, a member of the Westminster Parliament) appointed by the Prime Minister. Regarding the judicial system, the powers of the then-Attorney General for Northern Ireland were immediately transferred to the Attorney General for England and Wales.[29] The status of the province would remain the same, *i.e.*, part of the United Kingdom of England, Wales, Scotland and Northern Ireland.[30]

On December 5, 1974 (following the demise of the aborted effort in Sunningdale, described in Chapter 5), The Prevention of Terrorism Act which was already effective in England was extended to Northern Ireland. This concept, one which is clearly alien to American jurisprudence since it permits a terrorist to be held up to seven days without having been charged,[31] illustrates the gravity of the situation. Conditions in Northern Ireland were unique, and traditionally accepted rules of justice simply were regarded as inapplicable here.

The Realities of Releasing Political Prisoners: Was this Provision Lawful?

From a legal viewpoint, it is doubtful that such a blanket early release program would meet constitutional muster in the U.S.A. because of the obvious denial of equal protection.[32] For example, suppose that Sean, a paramilitary, is serving fifty years for two sectarian murders. Pat entered prison approximately the same time as did Sean, and he, too, is serving fifty years. His crimes were murdering two in the course of robbing a grocery. Sean, as a "political prisoner," is released under the terms of the GFA, but Pat is not. Is this fair to Pat? Is this equality of justice?

I raised this point with First Minister David Trimble, a former barrister and member of the law faculty at Queen's. Trimble responded that, as a lawyer, he had been similarly concerned, and he seemed a bit puzzled that all the imprisoned (hypothetical) Pats had not posed a legal challenge. In Trimble's opinion, the European Court for Human Rights (ECHR, in Strasbourg, France) would be a suitable forum. This court is the creature of the 1950 European Charter on Human Rights,[33] and its jurisdiction is limited to issues involving this convention and a later one, the European Social Charter.[34] Although decisions of the ECHR are "supervised" by its Committee of Ministers, there is no real enforcement leverage. However, the Westminster Parliament's adoption of the European Charter on Human Rights as domestic legislation was effective in October 2000,[35] so any human and social rights insured by that convention would be applicable in Northern Ireland and enforceable by domestic courts.

An ancillary issue on the same theme arose the summer of 2000 in the Republic. Four IRA members who had killed Irish *Garda* (police) detective Jerry McCabe in County Limerick, 1996 claimed eligibility for the GFA's parole provision. *Taoiseach* Bertie Ahern refused to permit their release, insisting that they did not "qualify." His position, of course, was buttressed by pleas from McCabe's family and former colleagues of the *Gardai*, but the question of whether or not the murder had been sectarian had concededly been arguable, since it was actually a raid of the police office. However, the IRA had later admitted responsibility. (The word "claim" is generally used for accepting such responsibility, a term which indicates pride in such acts of violence.)

Another Republican terrorist whose impending release was troubling from a legal standpoint was Dessie O'Hare. O'Hare had served twelve years of a forty-year sentence for his conviction on charges of kidnapping and mutilating Dublin dentist John O'Grady. O'Hare had a despicable record, having been linked to some thirty killings for both the IRA and the INLA.

His actual conviction, however, had not been sectarian-related, since the murder had been self-motivated rather than political in nature. The ultimate decision that he nonetheless qualified for the GFA release was based on the fact that he had rejoined the INLA while in prison, and this group was currently on cease-fire. Ahern was forced into a public relations corner, obligated to permit the releases not only of McCabe's killers but also of O'Hare.[36] There would be no arbitrary selections of those who would remain imprisoned, provided only that they meet the legislative conditions to qualify.

Regardless of any potential challenges to the early release commitment under equality law, all those eligible were released in the summer of 2000. The only exceptions were those few still serving out the requisite two years.

Post-Release Treatment of Former Prisoners

For a province as small as is Northern Ireland—roughly the same size of the American state of Connecticut—the region has a relatively ample number of prisons. Before the GFA's prison release scheme was implemented in summer, 2000, Northern Ireland had four prisons. The largest was the legendary Long Kesh in suburban Belfast. The "Maze" is the institution's unofficial title, this usual reference denoting the name of the village where it is located. It was the high-security prison in which most of the now-released terrorists were housed. When the last man walked out of the Maze by the grace of the GFA's early release provisions, this large foreboding building was empty, thus becoming obsolete. The remaining three are Maghaberry, located in Lisburn (just south of Belfast), a high-security center for long-termers; McGilligan, between Coleraine and Derry (in the north-west of the province), for short-to-medium term detainees; and the Young Offenders Center in Belfast, for those under the age of twenty-one.

One Belfast office has become a fairy godmother of sorts for prisoners, both current and released. The Northern Ireland Association for the Care and Resettlement of Offenders (NIACRO) is a non-governmental organization (NGO), established in 1971 for the purpose of assisting released prisoners in securing gainful employment. Despite its NGO status, NIACRO receives approximately 75 % of its funding from the government. Operating on an annual budge of British pound sterling 2.7 million (approximately U.S. $4 million), the association maintains a full-time staff of sixty-five, in addition to about twenty-five part-time workers.

According to NIACRO director Dave Wall, high-risk offenders—such as those convicted of sex crimes—are required to report to his office upon release. Additionally, anyone sentenced to life in prison who has been granted an early release is obligated to report. For others, the contact is voluntary. NIACRO also works with prisoners' families to facilitate their re-entry into society.

Interestingly, Northern Ireland does not have a parole system similar to the American concept, but refers to one who has been released prior to the expiration of his sentence as "out on license." The distinction is that a "license" is an official permission to serve only a part of his sentence. On the other hand, a "parole" in the American sense is granted only after a prisoner has applied for and has been granted a hearing before a governmental board which then determines whether or not his so-called "good behavior" during imprisonment merits an early release.

NIACRO directly contacts businesses to act as a liaison for former prisoners in need of jobs and attempts to persuade these employers to alter their recruitment practices. Wall explained that this role as agent for released prisoners involves convincing businesses that these folks are to be neither feared nor avoided. Only in post-GFA Northern Ireland is there a sufficient enough segment of the population which has reaped the benefits of the early release provision to give credibility to Wall's argument. He tells businesses, "if you exclude former prisoners, you're excluding a large portion of the labor pool." [37] Wall seems custom-made for this task: he has a degree in psychology and masters degrees in both criminology and occupational development.

In addition to its employment-agency type work for former prisoners, NIACRO also provides benefits to still-detained convicts. Perhaps the most significant of these benefits is the opportunity to earn a university degree.

During my stay in Belfast in summer, 2000, I lived in university housing located in a courtyard-type setting just around the corner from the law school at Queen's. This small complex connected Botanic Avenue on the East with University Road on the West, and at the corner of University was a small two-story building, the Open University. Not until I spoke with Dave Wall did I understand the function of this institution. It operates a distance-learning college-level program strictly via correspondence. Most of the students are current or former prisoners for whom this education is subsidized by prisons' government allocation. To complement this public aid, NIACRO has instituted an education trust fund to pay costs of Open University post-graduate work for these inmates and released prisoners. These are benefits available only to those who have been convicted of crimes, and as such seems a sort of affirmative action which some might view as rewarding them for their illegal activity. Law-abiding citizens are not so rewarded. One is reminded of George Orwell's writing—slightly paraphrased here—that "some of us are 'more equal' than others." [38]

Personalizing the Early Paroles

The release of a total of eighty-six paramilitary convicts was completed in July, 2000, and the Belfast newspapers had plenty of fodder for front-page news. *The Belfast Telegraph* called this provision the most difficult one in the GFA. [39] The following provides some detail on a few of the more publicized cases.

LOYALISTS

Perhaps the most well known of Loyalists to have gleaned the benefits of the GFA were Johnny "Mad Dog" Adair and Michael Stone. Adair was the first person to have been convicted in 1995 of actually directing sectarian terrorism, and Stone is the so-called "cemetery murderer." Both were members of the UFF.

Johnny Adair

Johnny Adair was one of the first to be released. He had served five and one-half years of a sixteen-year sentence, and he immediately acted in defiance of the mercy afforded him by the terms of the GFA by participating in the Portadown Orange Order standoff preceding the July 12, 2000 Loyalist marches. (*See* Chapter 2 for elaboration on the parades issue.) One of the conditions of release was that the ex-prisoners engage in no more violent activity, and applause for Adair in Portadown as hooded members of the UVF arrived at the parade scene hit the nerve of many, including shadow Secretary of State Andrew McKay. (A "shadow" in this sense is one appointed to a cabinet post by the minority party in the ruling government, in this case the Conservatives ["Tories"]. If an election were to shift power from the majority labor government, the "shadow" secretaries would assume their respective cabinet positions.) McKay was particularly critical of then-Secretary of State Peter Mandelson, who rebuked Adair's actions but insisted that re-imprisonment for him could only follow actual engagement in terrorism. [40]

Later during that summer, Adair's UFF (affiliated with Ulster Democratic Party, UDP) became embroiled in an internecine series of attacks with Loyalist paramilitary UVF. Even PUP's Billy Hutchinson (PUP, or Populist Unionist Party, is linked to UVF) admitted that this intra-paramilitary battle was "out of control and on a roll." [41] During these fights, Adair was returned to jail for having violated the no-violence condition. This came by order of Mandelson after he had been briefed by the RUC on Adair's activities. This Loyalist vs. Loyalist feud had already resulted in two killings, as well as the need to evacuate several residents of the Shankill, the site of the attacks.[42] Most disturbing was the ominous feeling that sectarian violence was not something of which one would be "cured," so to speak, making the release provision appear to be a sham.

Unquestionably, Adair evokes fear. He is a short (5'3"), stocky man with a shaved head and tattooed arms. The number of Nationalist Catholics whose murders he had directed is estimated at roughly thirty. When asked once if a Catholic had ever ridden in his car, he gruffly answered, "Only a dead one." [43]

Ironically, young Loyalists place him on a pedestal. Andy Wilson, a Shankill resident in his teens, openly expressed his admiration for Adair. The implication was that he aspired to be a paramilitary like his hero and to do his part to perpetuate the fighting. [44]

The result of this late-summer 2000 "family feuding" between Loyalist paramilitaries was the arrival onto the streets of Belfast of more British troops. The general sense was that Northern Ireland was now right back to the legendary "square-one," right back in the Troubles, if in fact they had ever been in remission. By this time, the Human Rights Bureau in Belfast reported sixty-four terrorist killings in the twenty-seven months since the signing of the GFA.[45]

Michael Stone

Michael Stone's release on July 23, 2000 came after he had served only sixteen months of a life sentence plus nearly 700 years. His convictions numbered three, all for murders stemming from his appalling 1988 random gunning into a crowd of mourners at the gravesite of three IRA members. At the burial at Milltown Cemetery in West Belfast, Stone had actually co-mingled at the cemetery with those who had attended the joint funeral, pretending to be among the mourners. Once at the graves, however, he tossed hand grenades and opened fire into the crowd. He later stated that he was pleased with the results except for some disappointment over his failure to hit his two major targets. *Sinn Féin* leaders Gerry Adams and Martin McGuinness were among those grieving the dead, but they had escaped his attack.

Oddly, Stone's official statement upon his release was that he "regretted" the murders, but he refused to apologize. His rationale? He was a volunteer in a "war," and wars have casualties.[46] Regretful, but not "sorry"....

His hero status among Loyalists may be unparalleled. Songs have been written in his honor, and autograph seekers overwhelmed him as he left the gates of

Long Kesh Prison (the "Maze"). The bomber jacket he had worn to the cemetery on the day of the murders was the object of a successful raffle at a Shankill pub, locks of his hair were sold for up to twenty pound sterling each (approximately $30 U.S.) in local Loyalist bars, and a female group dubbed the "Stonettes" sent him naked photos of themselves. Stone has become the idol of the Shankill, rivaled only by Adair.[47]

For survivors of those he had killed, his release was torteous. Alice Murray, whose 26-year-old son John had been one of Stone's victims, called Stone "evil" and a "coward," saying that his release was "more difficult than [I] had ever anticipated." She added, "I don't know how any of us [the Murray family] are going to get through it…" and "May God look down on the people who are suffering like us…." Nonetheless, she insisted that she still "whole-heartedly endorses" the GFA.[48] Every mother who read Mrs. Murray's words grieved with her.

Norman Coopey

Another released Loyalist was Norman Coopey. His life sentence for the mutilation and killing of sixteen-year James Morgan came to a halt after he had served only a little more than two years. At age twenty-eight, Coopey—who had murdered young Morgan only because he was a Catholic—likely has a long life ahead of him.

The facts of Coopey's act are especially gruesome. James had been hitchhiking home from his County Down Catholic school when Coopey and an accomplice saw him. They bludgeoned him with a hammer, doused him with gasoline, and set fire to his body. They left his remains in a pit filled with decomposing animals only a few miles from his home. Several days later, authorities found the body which was identified by his dental records.[49] James' older brother, Joseph, now a twenty-one-year old Queen's University student, bitterly responded to Coopey's release by saying that he (Coopey) is "probably laughing at it." James' parents keep a photograph of their son and the mass card from his funeral in the living room of their Castewellan home.[50]

Torrence Knight

One more among the Loyalists who was released merits mention. Torrens Knight was convicted of killing seven in the Rising Sun Bar in Greystone, County Derry/Londonderry. (There were actually eight victims. A 76-year-old man died from his injuries a few days after Knight's attack.) The night of the murders was a Halloween evening, and he had yelled, "Trick or treat!" when he entered the bar, just before he opened fire. At his trial, Knight turned and laughed at relatives of those he had murdered, and several of the newspapers ran this photograph. He has been described by some of those who have met him as "chilling."[51]

REPUBLICANS

It is not possible to chronicle all of the more despicable among those early released Republicans. Those described in the following text are mentioned primarily because of the enormities of their crimes.

The "Shankill Bombers"

In October, 1993, two IRA men killed ten people with a five-pound home-made bomb. Although they had fitted the bomb with a timer so as to give them eleven seconds (presumably ample time to escape) after they had triggered it, one of them was nonetheless among those killed. Posing as fish delivery men, Sean Kelly and Thomas Begley had planned to place the bomb atop a refrigerator in Frizell's Fish Shop in the heavily Protestant Shankill area of Belfast. (This shop had been chosen for a reason: Ulster Defense Association headquarters were located above Frizell's.) The premature explosion blew Begley into pieces, instantly killed nine others, and severely injured Kelly.

During his trial, Kelly defiantly told the judge, "I refuse to recognize this Diplock court. This system is corrupt." His GFA release came after he had served only eight years of a life term.[52]

Canary Wharf Bombing

IRA member James McCardle's release came when he was thirty-one years old, after having served only three years and three months of a life sentence for the murder of two men. The significance of this 1996 bomb attack was its timing. This incident officially ended the IRA's then two-year cease-fire. The only issue surrounding McCardle's release was when, not if, it would occur. Would he be credited with time spent in an English prison, or would he "lose" this time and await a deferral date of March, 2001?

McCardle's good fortune exceeded that of his victims. He left prison in July 2000. His particularly early release was praised by *Sinn Féin* MLA Gerry Kelly as being "only right" and in accordance with the GFA.[53]

Bernard McGinn is a citizen of the Republic of Ireland. From County Monaghan on the border, he joined the IRA at age fifteen. In addition to the crimes for which he was convicted—a series of sectarian murders—he also admitted making a bomb which had killed three in a 1992 London attack, and being involved in the 1996 Canary Wharf bombing. He had served two years of three lifetime sentences plus 435 years when he was released. According to an oblivious McGinn, making a bomb was just "a day's work."

Martin Mines is also a member of the IRA. One of four involved in a 1997 attack, his conviction for murder and possession of arms netted him a fifty-year sentence. When he entered prison in March, 1999, he laughingly waved at supporters and shouted, "See you in eighteen months!" Mines was scoffing at the length of his sentence by impliedly referring to the GFA's early release assurance.

Michael Caragher was convicted of the 1997 killing of British trooper Stephen Restorick at an Army checkpoint in Northern Ireland. The characteristic of Restorick's murder which makes it stand out among many is that he was the last British soldier to have lost his life (to date) in the Troubles. Caragher was believed to have killed at least seven security force members in southern County Armagh, and he is proud of his affiliation with what has generally been regarded as the most feared IRA unit in the entire province. He served three years of his 105-year sentence.[54]

The Westminster Parliament's effort to console the families of the released paramilitaries' victims was miniscule, considered by many even to be tantamount to an insult. The British government has established a fund to compensate each family of one killed in the Troubles up to 10,000-pound sterling (approximately $15,000 U.S.).[55]

DECOMMISSIONING:
THE ACHILLES HEEL OF THE PEACE PROCESS

The promise of paramilitaries to decommission[56]—*i.e.*, to achieve the total disarmament of all paramilitary organizations—is generally acknowledged to have been the trade-off for the prisoner release provision. Those who participated in the negotiations agree that these two commitments were conjoined,[57] even if neither the GFA nor the implementing legislation specifically states such a linkage.[58]

What about the provision which mandates total decommissioning within the two-year period following the approval by referenda (May 22, 1998), a date long past?[59] One neutral barrister in Dublin does not read the GFA as absolutely requiring the paramilitaries' surrender of arms during this expressly stated term. His reason relates to whether the terms of the agreement signed by all parties, as contrasted with the other agreement signed by the two governments, is legally enforceable. His opinion on the words stating a time frame is that they may have been approximate, or suggestive. His explanation—in classic legal terms—was his interpretation of the decommissioning language. Because this document was not drafted by lawyers but by politicians who did not have the power to bind the governments, his view was that to construe it as an absolutely legally binding document would be an attempt to render a "legal reading of a laymen's text." He reminded that the Belfast Agreement actually contained two parts: (i) the GFA which he termed as political, rather than legal, in nature; and (ii) the Multi-Party Agreement which has legal status.[60] However, David Byrne (the former Attorney General of Ireland) has described both of the parts of the Belfast Agreement as two legally enforceable and independent agreements."[61] (Byrne is now Ireland's Commissioner to the European Union.) Thus, good legal minds can rationally differ on this point.

For Republicans, the so-called linkage is more complicated. They insist that decommissioning is to follow not only the release of prisoners—a GFA promise which has been fulfilled—but also withdrawal of British troops from the province and substantial police reform.[62] Unionists had actually insisted on decommissioning before the talks began, and it was their adherence to this position which had triggered the cessation of the 1994-agreed upon cease fire by IRA (which, sadly, resumed its violent tactics in 1996—the cessation of the cease fire).[63] Since decommissioning still remains the issue which may yet be the death knell for Northern Ireland's devolved government, it obviously has not occurred. The resumed cease-fire, however, was the product of putting the prisoner release provision on the bargaining table. In fact it is generally acknowledged that the GFA would never have happened without the early release commitment.[64]

Former Irish *Taoiseach* (Prime Minister) John Bruton has written that he "do[es] not believe that it is possible to negotiate a better agreement from the point of view of anybody." [65] He continued, however, by saying that, although in a coalition all parties are—at least theoretically—on an "even playing field," a party linked to a paramilitary group has an "extra lever": the threat of violence.[66] Neither Bruton nor his successor, current *Taoiseach* Bertie Ahern, believe the PUP's (Unionist) assertion that it is not affiliated with the paramilitary UVF, or *Sinn Féin*'s insistence that it is separate from the IRA. Bruton reminds also that in 1997, both PUP and *Sinn Féin* made an "absolute commitment" to see that these two groups have disarmed and that the GFA "reaffirmed these commitments." [67] Keep in mind, however, that Bruton is a politician. Some, but not all, legalists do not view the GFA standing alone as a completely legally binding document.[68]

The new government has already been suspended three times, and very nearly a fourth. Each such occasion was caused by the dissension generated by the decommissing issue.

The First Suspension of the Northern Ireland Devolved Government: February, 2000

Before his replacement as Secretary of State for Northern Ireland, Peter Mandelson suspended the Assembly in February, 2000, only two months after the new power-sharing government had been officially formed. The root cause of this suspension was the IRA's refusal to give any meaningful commitment on disarmament.

This impasse was broken in May of that year, when the IRA's public statement was that it would render its arsenal of arms "completely and verifiably beyond use." [69] This probably was responsive to the joint British-Irish statement just one day earlier that they would extend until June 2001 the original May 22, 2000 date established by the GFA for total disarmament. This promise from the IRA was that it would disclose its tons of stockpiled weapons to the de Chastelain Independent International Commission on Decommissioning (the IICD, a body whose name is a classic alliteration). This would be by way of divulging to the Commission's international arms inspectors the whereabouts of weapons they would then inspect, artillery which had been smuggled from Libya and buried in unknown places in the Republic.

The Near-Suspension of March 2001

The political pot resumed a full boil in March, 2001, when Unionists insisted that mere inspections by the de Chastelain Commission (which had indeed taken place) were not tantamount to surrendering of arms. Thus, the question amounted to an interpretation of what the intent was underlying the GFA's label of "decommissioning." Must the IRA simply permit open inspections of all arms? Or must its members actually surrender all weapons to the inspecting authorities?

During this month of March, 2001, while in Dublin and Galway for a couple of lectures, I took the train to Belfast to visit with colleagues. The air was tense indeed. Each newspaper seemed to present a different slant, but finally the major principals reported that they had made "considerable progress" (whatever that means in the context of Northern Ireland). Mandelson's replacement as Secretary of State (after a bit of a scandal over non-related affairs), Scotsman John Reid, presented a firm front. Until the IRA made "substantive" moves on decommissioning, the British government would not act on the policing and demilitarization issues.[70] Nonetheless, an interim deal was reached to prevent Westminster's resumption of control over Northern Ireland. The Dublin and London governments issued a joint statement confirming their commitment to continuing the power-sharing government, expressing "optimism" that these problems could be resolved "over the coming months."[71] Strictly speaking, "coming months" could be translated into years, but this temporary non-decision at least kept the government on a respirator.

One of the Nationalist-leaning newspapers printed the IRA's anticipated response to the British government's decision to defer any suspension. Its self-commendation referred to its "unprecedented series of substantial and historic initiatives to enhance the peace process," such as maintaining a seven-year cease fire and permitting regular monitoring by the International Commission of its arms, despite the "abuse of the peace process by those who persist with the aim of defeating the IRA and Irish Republicanism, and the obvious failure of the British government to honour its obligations"[72]—translate "British government" to read "Trimble's UUP." However, even Trimble himself—who had earlier characterized the IRA's promise to "re-engage" with the International Commission "simply a pre-emptive strike attempting to shift the blame for (its) failure on others"—mellowed. He (at least publicly) changed his opinion, calling it "specific progress."[73]

(Note the use of the word "failure" by both sides in referring to the other's genuine moves toward implementing the GFA.) The sense was that a wait-and-see period until after the British elections in May, 2001 would be appropriate.

The British government promised in return to deal seriously with a "range of issues," including, most importantly, withdrawal of British troops from the province and finally reforming the RUC (Royal Ulster Constabulary, the police force in Northern Ireland). The reply from the IRA was its indisputable expectation that these issues would be finalized by the same June, 2001 date the two governments had given the IRA for completion of disarmament. Significantly, the same IRA statement insisted that by having opened all weapons to inspection by the de Chastelain Commission it had fulfilled its GFA obligations, but that the British government had not.[74] Unionists took the opposite position, of course, stating that their release of prisoners the prior summer had been the fulfilment of the counterpart to the IRA's duty to disarm and that it was they, rather than Nationalists, who had met their commitments. John Lynch, Professor of Irish Studies at Queen's University, phrased this dichotomy bluntly but articulately when he said to me that "the GFA was drafted carefully, so that one can read from it what he wants."[75]

The Second Suspension: August 10, 2001

The next move was Trimble's surprise announcement. On May 8, 2001, he issued a statement that unless disarmament had actually begun by July 1, 2001 he would resign as First Minister, effective immediately.[76] He submitted a post-dated (July 1, 2001) letter of resignation to Alliance Party's Lord Alderdice, speaker of the Assembly, which Trimble explained he would withdraw if his ultimatum were met.

Trimble had traveled a bumpy political road since the events of 1998. His own party—UUP—had been bitterly divided since before the referenda in May 1998, and it had been he who had convinced a majority of Unionists to accept the promises of the GFA. Since the new government's inception, he had literally had to survive many serious challenges to his policies from within. On May 28, 2001, the UUP ruling membership voted 53%-47% to continue to support Trimble and his pro-GFA stance. The numerical vote was 454-403, not exactly a landslide victory.[77] His primary intra-party opponents (writhing at the bit to become party leader in lieu of Trimble) are the classic politician, John Taylor (who regularly changes his positions after raising the proverbial wet finger in the air to feel the sense of those in the electorate) and a young, bright Jeffrey Donaldson.

If bets were on that Trimble was simply playing roulette with the regional government, they were wrong. On July 1, 2001, his resignation became effective,[78] and the six weeks' statutory clock began to run until new elections must be held.[79] In the quite recent regional elections in Northern Ireland, the extreme parties on both sides—*Sinn Féin* for Nationalists, and DUP for Unionists—had made impressive and substantial gains. This did not bode well for the moderate SDLP and UUP, so predictions were that new elections would mean a shift of leadership, and thus control, in the two polar sides. The only alternate avenue for the British government would be to suspend once again the province's devolved government.

Meanwhile, the IRA accepted a proposal by Ireland's Ahern and Britain's Blair which they presented after a marathon session. Significantly, it had also been endorsed by the de Chastelain Commission. *Sinn Féin* leader Gerry Adams called the IRA's move "very, very strong proof that it is committed to a continuation of the peace process." Trimble's UUP did not agree, calling it a "meaningful step in the right direction," but still insisting upon a timetable on total surrender of all weapons.[80] Again, the problem centered on the essential meaning of "decommissioning"—total disarmament, or simply assurance that weapons were beyond use, as determined by the neutral Independent Commission. (I was reminded of my conversation with Trimble when we discussed briefly the differences—if any— in the word "parliament" [for Scotland's devolved legislature] and "assembly" [for those in Northern Ireland and Wales]. A pensive man of few words, he replied simply, "It takes us back to 'Alice in Wonderland'...words mean what one intends." [81] But – which one is "one"? Perhaps a resurrection of Lewis Carroll, author of that wonderful book, might lend some insight.)

Sinn Féin's response was a vitriolic rebuke of Trimble. Martin McGuinness, *Sinn Féin* MLA, Minister of Education of Northern Ireland, and former IRA leader from Derry, bitterly termed this a "grievous misjudgment" by Trimble, and he reminded that both sides are bound to abide by the directions of the International Commission. *Sinn Féin* party leader Gerry Adams called Trimble's rejection a mistake of a "historical enormity." [82] Trimble was firm about not accepting any offer which did not include a timetable for total disarmament, and any settlement before the looming six-week deadline after his resignation on August 12 seemed improbable.[83]

On August 10, Secretary of State for Northern Ireland John Reid suspended the devolved government. *Sinn Féin*'s reaction was venomous, calling it a "bow to Unionist pressure." [84] This proved, however, to be a suspension of only twenty-four hours duration, one which was literally meaningless in the practical sense because the Assembly was on a summer recess.

The immediate reaction of the Westminster Parliament to Reid's action was to lift the suspension and to grant another six weeks for the parties to settle the issue.[85] This decision predictably invoked the ire of *Sinn Féin*ers who were eager for a new election. (Subsequent events are outlined in Chapter 5.)

Indeed, within the week, the IRA withdrew its original offer to put its weapons beyond use an offer which, it is important to remember, had been both accepted and praised by the de Chastelain Commission. Oddly, Trimble had left the day before the short-lived suspension of government, having gone to Austria for a three-week family vacation. This was puzzling, since it meant that he would be away for one-half the six-week extension period (which would end on September 21). If there were no resolution by then, new elections would be called.[86]

There was in fact no election but October 13, 2002, the British government again resumed control of Northern Ireland because there had been no progress toward disarmament. (The events affecting the Northern Ireland Assembly are described in Chapter 5. That same chapter also details the arcane legal twists subsequent to September 21, 2001.)

Endnotes to Chapter 6

[1] Gail Walker, *The evil that men do lives after them*, THE BELFAST TELEGRAPH, July 31, 2000, at 10, col. 3-6.

[2] Viewpoint (editorial), *Mixed Feelings as Maze jail is shut*, THE BELFAST TELE-GRAPH, July 22, 2000, at 9, col. 1-2.

[3] *See* Kieran McEvoy, *Prisoners, the Agreement, and the Political Character of the Conflict in Northern Ireland*, 22 FORDHAM INTERNATIONAL LAW JOUR-NAL 1549, 1556 (1999).

[4] Interview with Monica McWilliams, MLA and founder of the Women's Coalition, July 21, 2000, in her office at Stormont, Belfast. Ms. McWilliams named the power-sharing provisions for the Assembly as the second most critical last-minute issue.

[5] McEvoy, *supra* note 3 at 1565-1566.

[6] Interview with Mitchel McLaughlin, July 26, 2000, *Sinn Féin* Constituency Office, Londonderry/Derry.

[7] "Prisoners," GFA p. 25.

[8] Northern Ireland (Sentences) Act 1998 ch. 35 (Eng.) §2.

[9] *Id.* §3.

[10] McEvoy, *supra* note 3 at 1542.

[11] *Id.* at notes 9 and 10, referring to comparisons with conflicts in South Africa and Israel.

[12] It should not be forgotten, however, that the 1916 Easter Rising ended with Britain's immediate execution of the 14 leaders at Dublin's Kilmainham Jail. The government had apparently believed that the triviality of trials—and, indeed, de-mocracy—were worth neither its time nor effort, clear evidence that the fate of the participants had been summarily determined at the onset.

[13] McEvoy, *supra* note 3 at 1542, 1548.

[14] *Id.* at 1539.

[15] Interview with David Ervine, July 3, 2000, in his office at Stormont, Belfast.

[16] Charles Townshend, *The Supreme law: public safety and state security in Northern Ireland*, at 84, 98, NORTHERN IRELAND AND THE POLITICS OF RECONCILIATION (Dermot Keogh and Michael H. Haltze, eds.) (Woodrow Wilson Center Press and Cambridge University Press, Cambridge, England, 1994).

[17] Paul Johnson, IRELAND: A CONCISE HISTORY FROM THE TWELFTH CENTURY TO THE PRESENT DAY, at 73 (Academy Chicago, 1984).

[18] *Id.* at 182.

[19] *See* John Conroy, BELFAST DIARY, at 28-35 (Beacon Press, Boston, 1987), for a recount of this destruction. Conroy notes at 35 that some 1,820 families in Northern Ireland were forced to leave their homes during July, August, and September, 1969, because of the lootings and burnings. 82.7% were Catholics.

[20] Laura King, *Sinn Féin leader plans to testify about IRA past*, RICHMOND (Virginia) TIMES-DISPATCH (The Associated Press), May 1, 2001, at A-4, col. 4-5.

[21] Conroy, *supra* note 19 at 49.

[22] *Id.* at 48.

[23] McEvoy, *supra* note 3 at 1549.

[24] Conroy, *supra* note 19, at 49.

[25] *Id.* at 49-50.

[26] Sydney Elliott and W.D. Flackes, A POLITICAL DIRECTORY 1968-1999, at 638 (The Blackstaff Press, Belfast, 1999).

[27] John Hume, *Ireland—the Healing Process*, 22 FORDHAM INTERNATIONAL LAW JOURNAL 1171 (1999).

[28] Northern Ireland (Temporary Provisions) Act 1972, §1(2).

[29] *Id.* §1(2).

[30] *Id.* §2.

[31] *See, e.g.*, Mallory v. U.S., 354 U.S. 449, 77 S.Ct. 1356 (1957), in which the U.S. Supreme Court reversed a rape conviction because the defendant had not been properly arraigned prior to his confession (which had been admitted into evidence). He had been neither charged nor arraigned until the morning after his early afternoon arrest. In the interim, he had been questioned extensively without the benefit of counsel and subjected to a lie detector test.

The Court applied Rule 5(1)(a) of the Federal Rules of Criminal Procedure (1946) which requires that the arresting officer take the suspect to a commissioner or other officer authorized to charge and arraign him "without unnecessary delay."

[32] U.S. CONST. amend. XIV assures that the states will not deny to any person the equal protection of the laws.

[33] Council of Europe Convention for the Protection of Human Rights and Fundamental Freedoms (ECHR) (1950).

[34] European Social Charter (1961).

[35] *See especially* section 3(1) Human Rights Act 1998, effective October 2, 2000.

[36] Kevin Rafter and Liam Clarke, *Advisers told Ahern to free IRA men*, THE SUNDAY TIMES (London), August 6, 2000, at 1-1, col. 1-3.

[37] Telephone conversation with Dave Wall, August 10, 2000, Belfast.

[38] In ANIMAL FARM, Orwell used animals as similes to explain his perceptions of humans. His actual statement was, "Some animals are more equal than others."

[39] Viewpoint (editorial), *A painful week for the victims*, BELFAST TELEGRAPH, July 24, 2000, at 10, col. 1-2.

[40] *Mandelson in Adair row*, BELFAST TELEGRAPH, July 7, 2000, at 5, col. 1-7.

[41] David McKittrick, *Mad Dog at heart of convulsions in loyalist Belfast*, THE INDEPENDENT (London), August 21, 2000, at 4, col. 1-7.

[42] Dominic Cunningham, *Adair back in jail as loyalist crackdown ordered*, IRISH INDEPENDENT, August 23, 2000, at 1, col. 1-2.

[43] Kathy Donaghy, *Tattooes, muscles, murders mark the badge of hatred*, IRISH INDEPENDENT, August 23, 2000, at 9, col. 1.

[44] Kim Singupta, *Under an orange sky, it seems like the Troubles all over again,* IRISH INDEPENDENT, August 23, 2000, at 9, col. 2-5.

[45] Dominic Cunningham, *Adair in jail takes fear off street—Mandelson,* IRISH INDEPENDENT, August 23, 2000, at 9, col. 2-5.

[46] Martin Breen, *Mass murderer who is a local 'hero',* BELFAST TELEGRAPH, July 24, 2000, at 6, col. 1-8.

[47] *Id.*

[48] Sinéad McCavana, *A mother's anguish at release of son's killer,* BELFAST TELEGRAPH, July 24, 2000, at 6, col. 1-3.

[49] Suzanne Breen, *Short walk to freedom for the last of Maze inmates,* THE IRISH TIMES, July 27, 2000, at 8, co. 1-7.

[50] Anne Madden, *Family's distress at killer's release,* THE IRISH NEWS, July 26, 2000, at 4, col. 2-5.

[51] Suzanne Breen, *supra* note 49.

[52] *Id.*

[53] Paul Tanney, *Decision to release bomber criticized,* THE IRISH TIMES, July 27, 2000, at 8, col. 1-7.

[54] Suzanne Breen, *supra* note 49.

[55] Rachel Donnelly, *Northern Ireland families to receive compensation,* THE IRISH TIMES, July 27, 2000, at 8, col. 3-7.

[56] "Decommissioning," p. 20, GFA.

Incidentally, Prof. Dennis Kennedy of Queen's University and an expert on European Political Affairs, has written that the use of the word "decommission" was a concession to paramilitaries, one which gave them an appearance of some legitimacy. *See* Dennis Kennedy, *Dash for Agreement: Temporary Accommodation or Lasting Settlement?* 22 FORDHAM INTERNATIONAL LAW JOURNAL 1440, 1455 (1999).

[57] Interview with Mitchel McLaughlin, July 6, 2000, *Sinn Féin* Constituency Of-

fice, Londonderry/Derry.

[58] *See supra* note 5 and accompanying text.

[59] "Decommissioning," p. 20, GFA, paragraph 3.

[60] I spoke with this young barrister in his office in Dublin on August 16, 2000. Although he conditioned the interview on my not identifying him as my source, he has followed the process closely, and he has studied the document with much discernment.

[61] David Byrne, *An Irish View of the Northern Ireland Peace Agreement: the Interaction of Law and Politics*, 22 FORDHAM INTERNATIONAL LAW JOURNAL 1206 (1999).

[62] McEvoy, *supra* note 3 at 1556.

[63] *Id*. at 1564.

[64] *Id*. at 1541.

[65] John Bruton, *Why Decommissioning is a Real Issue*, 22 FORDHAM INTERNATIONAL LAW JOURNAL 1200 (1999).

[66] *Id*. at 1203-1204.

[67] *Id*. at 1201.

[68] *See supra* notes 60 and 61 and accompanying text.

[69] *IRA breaks weapons deadlock*, RICHMOND TIMES-DISPATCH, May 7, 2000, at A-1.

[70] Monika Unsworth, *No concessions on policing unless IRA moves—Reid*, THE IRISH TIMES, March 10, 2001, at 8, col. 1-2.

[71] *The Agreement Survives*, THE IRISH TIMES (editorial), March 10, 2001, at 17, col. 1.

[72] *IRA still 'on board,'* THE IRISH TIMES, March 9, 2001, at 8, col. 1-2.

[73] Marc Brennock, *Optimism after talks for North Process to Continue*, THE IRISH

TIMES, March 9, 2001, at 1, col. 2-3.

[74] *Nationalist parties betraying the spirit of GFA*, letter to editor of THE IRISH NEWS, March 16, 2001, at 7, col. 1-4, from Cathal McGlade of Belfast. McGlade, in the true spirit of both major Unionist parties, wrote that "their (*Sinn Féin's*) policy is taking as much as possible and giving as little as possible in return." He described *Sinn Féiners* as "crude, unsophisticated men in the political game...[who operate]... on a primitive level of shooting and bombing anybody and everybody who differ[s] from their point of view," and who "have made no move whatsoever towards abolishing their weaponry."

[75] Interview with Dr. John Lynch, July 31, 2001, Queen's University, Belfast.

[76] *Trimble: Disarm or 'I will resign,'* RICHMOND (Virginia) TIMES-DISPATCH The Associated Press), May 9, 2001, at A-4.

[77] Martin Peter, *Neue Chance für Nordirland-Frieden Regionalregierung wieder im Amt* (*New Chance for Northern Ireland's Peace Process and Provincial Government*), DIE PRESSE (Vienna), May 29, 2001, at 5, col. 1-3, and *Nordirlands Friedensprozeß erhält zweite Chance* (*Northern Ireland's Peace Process has a Second Chance*), DER KURIER (Vienna), May 28, 2001, at 4, col. 3-5.

[78] *Schwere Rückschlag für den Nordirland-Friedensprozeß*, (*Substantial Setback for the Northern Ireland Peace Process*), DER KURIER (Vienna), July 2, 2000, at 6, col. 1-2.

[79] Northern Ireland Act 1998 §32(3).

[80] *Fester Zeitplan für die Entwaffung fehlt* (*No Definite Time Plan for Disarmament*), KÖLNER-STADT-ANZEIGER (Cologne), August 7, 2001, at 5, col. 1-2.

[81] Interview with David Trimble, July 21, 2000, in his office at Stormont, Belfast.

[82] CNN-Europe (television broadcast), August 7, and CNN-Europe, August 8, 2001.

[83] Euronews (television broadcast), August 9, 2001.

[84] Rosie Cowan, *Stormont assembly put on ice*, THE GUARDIAN (London), August 11, 2001, at 1, col. 1-3.

[85] Rosie Cowan, *Reid wins six weeks of breathing space*, THE GUARDIAN (London), August 11, 2001, at 6, col. 1-6.

[86] Marianne Quorin, *Für die IRA ist der Krieg noch nicht zu Ende* (*For the IRA the War has not Ended*), KÖLNER-STADT-ANZEIGER (Cologne), August 15, 2001, at 7, col. 3-6, and *IRA zieht Angebot zur Entwaffnung wieder zurück* (*IRA takes back its offer on Weapons Release*), FRANKFURTER ALLGEMEINE (Frankfurt), August 15, 2001, at 1, col. 2-4.

Chapter 7

The Policing Issue: The GFA's Goal to Demilitarize Northern Ireland

"...[u]nless policing becomes more representative, accountable, and respectful of human rights, the continuation of negative contact between the police and the policed will create tension and conflict and ultimately threaten the peace."

Linda Moore, Human Rights Commission[1]

"For thirty years now, the RUC has quite simply been the arbiter between anarchy and order."

RUC Chief Constable Sir Ronnie Flanagan[2]

Since its inception beginning with the 1922 partition, the Royal Ulster Constabulary (RUC) has been the target of charges of discrimination against Catholics. Nationalist Catholics have long claimed that the security forces—both the RUC and the British Army since its entry into Northern Ireland at the onset of the Troubles—have routinely treated them unfavorably. These allegations of discrimination relate to RUC hiring policies, as well as to selective police brutality.

Indeed, those who believe statistics to be convincing in the process of deductive reasoning cite supporting evidence for such allegations. Before GFA implementing legislation, the composition of the RUC was heavily Protestant. Approximately 88% were Protestant, while only 8% were Catholic.[3] Externally, the victims of lethal force on the part of the police force have been overwhelmingly Catholic. During the period beginning April 19, 1969 until January 27, 1994, security agents of the state killed 350 persons. Only thirty-nine of these (11%) were Protestant, while 304 (85%) were Catholic.[4] This imbalance makes Catholics in general reluctant to apply for positions with the RUC because of their fear of internal retaliation, leading to a "Catch-22" situation where a remedy for the paucity of Catholic officers is difficult at best.

There is, however, another side to the story. A substantial number of police officers themselves have made the ultimate sacrifice in the line of duty. Since the Troubles began in 1969, 302 RUC officers have lost their lives defending the safety of the province.[5] These men and women are at constant risk because they have accepted the duty of protecting communities throughout the province from the security threats and terrorism which, sadly, have become a part of everyday life for so many.

Although the police reform issue has usually been viewed as a third component, together with the release-of-prisoners and decommissioning issues, this is likely only because it has been the last of the major and most controversial provisions of the GFA which was yet to be implemented. Prisoner releases were accomplished in summer 2000, albeit with much pain and difficulty. (See Chapter 6.) Only decommissioning and policing remain as roadblocks to major progress in achieving the goals of the GFA, and both continue to be volatile and divisive.

The substance of the many charges of anti-Catholicism among the police and British army ranks are essentially human rights issues and are treated with particularity in Chapter 8 on that topic. This chapter will address the history of policing in Northern Ireland, the evolving body of relevant law—both statutory and judicial—and the effect of the GFA on the structure of the entity known as the Royal Ulster Constabulary.

The polarity of the problems in Northern Ireland makes compromise on policing difficult at best, and impossible at worst. The principals have proceeded with caution and deliberation in an area in which legally enforced concessions are inevitable.

As with most peace-making issues in the province, police reform evokes emotionalism and bitterness. Also as with most of the problems in Northern Ireland, the difficulties with policing require one to consider the region's history in order to discern the reasons for the disparity between the two sides on this question. However, as seems to be characteristic of all the divisive issues in Northern Ireland, understanding the reasons may not point to a resolution.

The Royal Ulster Constabulary (RUC)

The forerunner of the Royal Ulster Constabulary (RUC) actually pre-dated partition by exactly 100 years. Westminster Parliament established a county constabulary system in Ireland in 1822.[6] This structure evolved into an all-Ireland police force in 1836.

The British government's efforts to achieve impartiality of security officers were draconian. All policemen were required to live in special barracks, and the law forbade them from voting and belonging to any political or religious group other than The Society of Freemasons.[7]

Because of the constant danger of Nationalist insurrection, the Constabulary's primary duty was to maintain state security. Thus, its members were armed, since their role was that of a quasi-military force.[8] This was a departure from convention: policemen in Great Britain did not carry weapons. After the Constabulary's suppression of the 1867 Fenian Uprising, its title became the Royal Irish Constabulary (RIC). As the very first royal police force, the RIC provided a model for other police forces around the globe.[9]

One result of partition was to disband the 11,000-member RIC as an all-Ireland security force and to incorporate its officers in the six counties that became the province of Northern Ireland into the Royal Ulster Constabulary (RUC) in June, 1922. New recruits joined this northern portion of the former RIC to form its 3,000-member successor. The old RIC in the remaining twenty-six counties which formed (post-partition) the *Sarostát Éireann* (Free State of Ireland) became *An Garda Siochana*. The former island-wide political violence was largely confined thereafter to the new six-county province. The RUC, then, had a dual security role: to control crime in general, and to take care of the armed subversive activity of the Irish Republican Army (IRA). As of 1999, 296 RUC officers and reservists had been killed and more than 7,000 injured as a result of the province's security situation.[10]

The Current RUC

Charges of Anti-Catholicism: The Negative Side

When the GFA was approved, there were 13,000 RUC officers (regular force of 8,500, fulltime reserve of 2,900, and part-time reserve of 1,300).[11] Those who have charged the police force with anti-Nationalist/Catholic discrimination point to the imbalance among the ranks as evidence: remember that 88.1% are Protestant, while only 8% are Catholic.[12] (The remaining 3.9% are listed as "other.")

The animosity of Catholics toward the RUC is never more evident than in the Falls area of West Belfast. Large posters with the message "Disband the RUC" were plastered on sides of building near St. Peter's (Catholic) Cathedral in summer 2000, and murals throughout this section of the city had negative images of the police force.

Several highly publicized instances of brutality have been the primary incitement of Nationalists' disdain for the RCU and the British Army. In addition to events such as "Bloody Sunday"—January 30, 1972 (Army killing of 14 Catholic demonstrators in Derry/Londonderry) and the ultimate acquittal of British soldier Lee Clegg in his trial for the murder of a young Catholic "joy-rider"—there are veritable horror stories of other legally permissible forced confessions of those suspected of having committed political crimes. (The Bloody Sunday and Clegg incidents are reported in detail in Chapter 1).

In June, 1978, Amnesty International published a report containing interviews of Nationalist suspects and prisoners as to how RUC members had treated them. They mentioned beatings and kicking; bending wrists backward; forced standing or running in place for hours at a time; pulling out of chest hairs; lifting by one's moustache; pouring cola into a prisoner's ears; holding prisoners' heads under water; kicking and squeezing testicles; covering one's head with items such as plastic bags, hoods, or soiled underwear; forcing a prisoner to eat mucus from a policeman's nose; burning a prisoner's hand on radiator piping; and forcing a prisoner to stand with his underwear tied to his knees while he endured insulting comments about his genitals. Some of the women interviewed told of having been threatened with rape. Three of those interviewed admitted having attempted suicide while imprisoned or detained, and four had to be placed under psychiatric care upon release. Several had suffered organic brain damage.[13]

Objections to Titles and Symbols

Other oft-cited indications of the RUC's aversion to Nationalists are its name, symbols, and official indicia. The word "royal" is generally offensive to those who aspire to a united Ireland, since it designates the crown. The SDLP has called this word "overtly British."[14] This is a puzzling stance, since the police force is an arm of the state, an agency of an official province of the United Kingdom. Not only is the Royal Ulster Constabulary "royal," but there is also the Royal Mail. The refusal of then–Northern Ireland Assembly Second Minister Seamus Mallon of the Nationalist SDLP political party to acknowledge this reality is characteristic of most Nationalist-Catholics. Mallon repeatedly referred to the province as "the North of Ireland," inferring that the province of Northern Ireland actually is the geographically northern segment of the Republic of Ireland.

The crown is indeed at the top of the RUC symbol, its official insignia. Countering (or complementing) the crown, however, is the harp which comprises the lower oval portion of the symbol, a portion that is at least twice the size of the crown. This musical instrument is the symbol of the Republic of Ireland, appearing on official government documents. Enhancing the Irish elements evidenced by the harp is a half-circle of Irish shamrocks . Thus, it would appear that it would be Unionists who might object to the symbol, since it includes two Irish symbols and only one British one. This is in spite of the province's political affiliation with the UK, rather than the Republic of Ireland.

Moreover, the terms "Ulster" and "constabulary" are irritants to Nationalists, and there are logical reasons. Ulster is one of four official geographical regions the island of Ireland. (The other three are Leinster in the Mid- and Southeast; Munster in the Southwest; and Connaught in the Mid-West.) If anything, the use of this term should appease Nationalists. The geographic region of Ulster contains not only the six counties comprising the province of Northern Ireland, but also three counties in the Republic (Cavan, Donegal, and Monaghan). However, even if one were to assume that the term "Ulster" technically refers solely to the six counties and is synonymous with "Northern Ireland," the subordination of Northern Ireland within the United Kingdom clarifies the designation of the police force as being responsible for that designated part.

"Constabulary" connotes an armed police force, one with military characteristics.[15] Perhaps the perception that it is anti-Catholic is derived from the greater percentage of Nationalist Catholics killed in conflicts with police in Northern Ireland. Additionally, the term is almost universally identified with Britain.

The charge of police brutality against Catholics is a substantive one that factually justifies that community's animosity toward the RUC. However, the complaints that the symbol itself reflects any bias seems, at least to this writer, to be totally without merit.

The RUC as Upholder of State Security: A Positive Spin

There is indeed ample evidence of police bias against the Nationalist community, and this clearly merits substantial restructuring. However, the dedication of the officers who are in harm's way in their role as insurers of security within the province must be viewed alongside the RUC's negative aspects. To give a bit of perspective as to the dangers confronting these officers, one need look only to the numbers of reported offenses against the state—*i.e.*, political crimes related to the Troubles—with which they routinely deal. Interestingly, the GFA did not diminish these incidents. In 1998-99, there were 459 reports of such incidents against police personnel, a slight increase over the previous year's 457.[16]

The severity of the hazards officers face is demonstrably evident. One example, the RUC's vehicles, is indeed shocking to the initiate to Northern Ireland. Large khaki-colored oversized jeeps, they are totally bulletproofed and virtually windowless, with only slits for what normally would be a broad windshield, just large enough to provide minimum visibility for the driver. Both the British Army and the RUC maintain lookout towers strategically placed at geographic intervals where past violence has been the most concentrated.

From the usually confirmed beginning of the Troubles in 1969 through June 30, 2000, 302 RUC officers had been killed because of the security situation.[17] Chief Constable Sir Ronnie Flanagan has publicly stated his position that the GFA would not have been accomplished absent the "dedication, commitment, professionalism and sacrifice for others" which the RUC has demonstrated throughout the Troubles.[18]

Personal Reflections

An organization is often gauged by the quality of its leaders. I was privileged to have had the opportunity to meet with Sir Ronnie Flanagan in summer 2000, and my impression of this man's zeal and devotion to public service in general and to members of his police force in particular was both memorable and positive.

My communications with his office had lasted several months prior to my arrival in Belfast. There were the understandable clearance measures, including the requirement that I divulge even some information on my deceased parents. All exchange of data had been precise and to the point, and I anticipated a formality atypical of Ireland or Northern Ireland and more akin to a military setting. These expectations could not have been more wrong.

The RUC Headquarters are located in a lovely section of East Belfast just off Newtownards Road, the main street which leads to Stormont. The headquarters building itself is imposing and tasteful, laden with ivy and quite the reverse of the usual gray-official-state-building structure I had envisioned. I had taken the local bus to the nearest stop on Newtownards and walked onto Knock Road, the street where the Headquarters are situated, passing several churches—Methodist, Church of Ireland, and Presbyterian, solidly Protestant. The homes indicated the area to be relatively affluent.

The cheery guard at the security gate welcomed me warmly, such that I began to have the feeling of going to a reception rather than to the headquarters of a police department. Christine Marks, one of the young employees in the office now designated Change Management (to reflect the then–impending post-GFA modifications of the RUC) and who had been my liaison, proved both friendly and helpful. Christine provided me with several indispensable documents during my stay in Belfast, including the Chief Constable's annual report, the RUC response to both the Patten Report and the subsequent statute (discussed later in this chapter), and other sundry information on the RUC. She gave me a tour of the building, speaking with obvious pride about both the organization and her colleagues. We went into the RUC Museum, a small part of the building which houses exhibits of badges, uniforms, official documents, and other historical memorabilia. The curator appeared surprised, but genuinely delighted, to have an American visitor.

Sir Ronnie proved to be the antithesis of the heel-clicking epitome of a soldier I had expected. Dressed in "civilian clothing" rather than an RUC uniform, he welcomed me with a broad smile and a handshake, thanking me profusely for "taking the time to visit us." These folks were honestly making me feel as though I were doing them a favor, instead of vice-versa! His manner was completely unaffected, and he was the classic gentleman.

The omnipresent offer of a cup of tea or coffee—one of the consistent gestures which endears folks in Northern Ireland and Ireland so to Americans—was followed by a most open, frank and informative meeting. Sir Ronnie responded matter-of-factly but completely to each of my questions, and his elaborations were insightful indeed. He spoke of his thirty-year career with the RUC, and his pride in the organization was palpable. My unequivocal sense of his loyalty to and his passion for his work was somehow encouraging with respect to the future of the security situation in this province which had become for me a second home.

Sir Ronnie clarified much about the controversy surrounding the annual Orange Order march in Drumcree. (The parades issue is discussed in Chapter 2.) He walked over to a giant map on his wall, an outline of the area on the outskirts of Portadown, pointing out to me the locations of Drumcree Church (Church of Ireland and the destination of the marchers) and Garvaghy Road (the predominately Catholic residential area). Contiguous to this current map was an earlier one, and both were marked in green (to connote the Catholic residential section) and orange (the Protestant residential part). It was obvious that the "green" area had expanded over recent years and that the contested route was along a road which had become an entirely Catholic area. Rather than criticize any obstinacy or unreasonableness on the part of either group, he expounded upon the sincerity of the logic of both positions. Almost excitedly, he remarked, "Look at how this area has *changed*— it's now completely *green!*" He countered by confirming that the Order had the legal right to march, provided that no violence resulted. It seemed clear that this "man in charge" not only understood, but also appreciated, the emotions of both sides. The "no-win" character of this event was much more apparent to me than it had been prior to this meeting. Sir Ronnie's demeanor was professional and resolute, and he expressly accepted the responsibility for safeguarding both marchers and residents.

Without hesitating, Sir Ronnie responded to my query about his personal stance on the proposed change of name of the RUC to Police Service of Northern Ireland and the inevitable demise of the symbol. He admitted to some nostalgia and sadness over these changes, but added that he understood the reasons and the emotion they evoke for Catholics. Nonetheless, he pointed out the patently compromising nature of the symbol, with the British crown and the Irish harp and shamrocks. Despite his insistence of understanding the complaints of Nationalist Catholics to the symbol, he queried, "What in the world could be more Irish than that?!" If there was any anti-Catholic bias on the part of this public servant, he surely concealed it on that day. My unequivocal impression was that he assumed his role humbly and that he was capable, dedicated and sincere.

His staff exhibited an uninhibited admiration and respect for Sir Ronnie, and it was apparent that this was reciprocated. I was totally convinced of his devotion to his police officers and his staff, and of his commitment to maintaining security in Northern Ireland. While the evidence of RUC discrimination is well documented, my unconditional belief is that this man's leadership qualities have enabled him to manage these instances with professionalism and responsibility and that he would continue to do so. No organization is immune from those who would demean (and work contrary to) its purposes and duties, but a strong and determined leader at the helm can indeed minimize and reduce such instances. Sir Ronnie struck me as a man from the "Harry Truman" mold, one who truly meant it when he stated that day the equivalent of "the buck stops here." Although he had publicly stated that he expected to be replaced once the changes in the new statute have been implemented, at least this observer was of the opinion that this would be an unnecessary loss for Northern Ireland policing.

Christine had informed Sir Ronnie that I had scheduled some meetings at Stormont shortly after our meeting concluded, and he insisted that Ken, one of the constables, drive me. I had planned to take the bus, but Sir Ronnie would "not hear of it," since I would "have to walk all the way to Newtownards Road [only about 200 yards] and then wait who-knows-how-long for the bus." Ken, too, was every inch the gentleman which somehow came by then as no surprise. When the Chief Constable and his staff invited me to return for another visit, their sincerity and their spirit of welcome were not in doubt.[19]

Diplock Trials

Closely interrelated to the police controversy is that of pre-GFA procedures in the administration of justice. A perusal of the so-called "Diplock trial" process is imperative for one's understanding the uniqueness of the situation in Northern Ireland and its effects on policing and administering justice. This anomaly within Anglo-American jurisprudence sheds some light on the necessarily intense manner policing and rendering justice have been affected by the Troubles.

By the early 1970's, the U.K. government seemed to have acknowledged the probable lengthy life of the crisis in Northern Ireland. A special commission headed by Lord Diplock was established to make recommendations on how the justice system might best respond to the continuing political violence.

The report recommended non-jury trials for those persons charged with crimes related to the Troubles.[20] My friends and colleagues John Jackson and Sean Doran of Queen's University School of Law assessed the jury to be the "[most] potent symbol of the common law tradition."[21] Indeed, renowned British legal scholar W.L. Twining characterized the jury trial as the "paradigm of all [criminal] trials."[22]

How, then, could the Diplock Commission and the lawmakers advise removing the right to trial by jury in a criminal trial, a true paragon of British-American jurisprudence? The explanation was that the elimination of the usual trial-by-jury was determined to be necessary to deal effectively with the mounting sectarian violence. The underlying rationale was that those on the "other side"—*i.e.*, Protestants if a Catholic were charged, and vice-versa—would fear retaliation if the verdict were to go the "wrong way." Additionally, unlike an impartial and objective-minded judge, jurors would be subjected to pressures and even threats during trial.

The Diplock process is an anomaly for the American lawyer. The U.S. Constitution assures the right to trial by jury in both criminal[23] and civil[24] cases, and it is particularly bewildering to him or her that this fundamental right can be abrogated in the criminal setting. Ironically, the 1973 law[25] implementing the Diplock recommendations was one of the several statutes enacted for Northern Ireland which was designated "emergency" or "temporary." Yet they have not been repealed in the nearly thirty years since they were adopted—an enduring "emergency" and lengthy "temporary" situation indeed.

The very first such "temporary" law actually dates back to 1938.[26] (It is the predecessor to the Diplock statute) and two supplementing additional "temporary" measures enacted in 1984 and 1989.[27] The latter two were not limited to Northern Ireland, but applicable throughout the United Kingdom.

All criminal charges in Northern Ireland proceed in a fashion similar to the American system until they have reached the stage of actual prosecution. The first person to act in this part of the process is the Director of Public Prosecutions (DPP), an office created in 1972 as a safeguard against unjustified prosecutions. If the charge falls within a statutory schedule of offenses, it is "scheduled" to be tried in a Diplock court without a jury.[28] The file is then forwarded to the British Attorney General (in the parliamentary system, an elected member of the U.K. Parliament) who determines whether the charge "is indeed appropriate for a non-jury trial, as a terrorist-related offense."[29] He either "deschedules" the case (if he has concluded that there is no evidence of terrorism) or approves it for a non-jury (Diplock) trial. The general rule has been that the Attorney General requires "hard evidence" of terrorist-related activity in order to approve the non-jury procedure.[30]

What about the accurateness of the assumption that Diplock trial judges are objective? Questioning this position, Professors Jackson and Doran believe that statistics confirm the "hardening" of judges such as to result in their growing innate bias against acquittals. Notable is the decrease of Diplock acquittals from 53% in 1984 to only 29% 1993. In comparison, the acquittal rates for other criminal cases tried by jury in Northern Ireland during this same period were 49% and 48%, respectively.[31] This high conviction rate has disturbed many lawyers, especially in light of several highly publicized pre-GFA releases of those convicted as terrorists but later proven innocent.[32]

The Diplock process is significant from the policing perspective primarily because of the changes effected in the pre-charge phase. First, both the British soldier on duty in Northern Ireland and the RUC officer are empowered to arrest without a warrant, provided he has a reasonable expectation that the suspect has committed a crime. In fact, the arresting soldier need not give to the suspect the reason for the arrest, although a policeman must specify the charges upon making the arrest.[33]

In contrast to American constitutional law, British law in general has abrogated the criminal suspect's right to remain silent, a rule sacrosanct in the U.S.A.[34] During trial, the court or jury is expressly permitted to draw a negative inference from a defendant's failure to testify as to any fact which might be relevant to his defense, in sharp contrast is the rule in the U.S.A. The Warren Supreme Court held in *Miranda v. Arizona*[35] that the Fifth Amendment protection against self-incrimination applies to any interrogation which might possibly result in taking the questioned person into custody. *Miranda* requires that he be fully informed of his constitutional rights to remain silent (and of his right to counsel). A 1988 British statute did require the judge at least to warn the defendant that his silence might lead to the inference that he is guilty as charged,[36] but a 1994 amendment excuses this judicial warning as long as the judge is "satisfied" that the defendant is actually aware of these consequences.[37] This "satisfaction" standard is a subjective one, since there are no statutory guidelines whatsoever. Significant for policing is the applicability of this rule from the arrest stage through trial.[38] The arresting officer is under no obligation to "read the rights" to one being charged as fully as in the American sense, but he must caution the suspect accordingly before any police might interview the suspect: "You do not have to say anything, but I must caution you that if you do not mention when questioned something which you later rely on in court, it might harm your defense. If you say anything, it may be given in evidence." [39]

Another patent dissimilarity to American criminal procedure is the relaxed rule in Northern Ireland on the admissibility of confessions. The common law rule—still inflexible in American jurisprudence—is that a confession is admissible only if it had been voluntarily made. In the violent atmosphere of the province, the Diplock Commission deemed that retaining this practice would impede the orderly course of justice. Thus, in Diplock proceedings, the presumption is that a confession is admissible unless the defendant produces compelling evidence that his interrogator(s) had deliberately used force. "Force" is rather loosely construed, since the statute allows a "moderate degree of physical maltreatment"[40] of the suspect in order to obtain a confession. Thus, mere involuntariness would not automatically exclude a confession as evidence.

Nonetheless, one Northern Ireland court held that the judge has the discretion to exclude a confession if he decides that it would be "appropriate...in order to avoid unfairness to the accused or otherwise in the interests of justice."[41] Anachronistically, the statute makes it clear that any violence on the part of the interrogators will be deemed to be "unfair."[42] Apparently, there is a difference (albeit a narrow one) between the "moderate degree of physical maltreatment," which is permitted, and the "violence," which is not.

R. v. McAlister[43] illustrates this dichotomy in the rules for Diplock trials as to whether or not a confession was voluntarily given. In *McAlister*, the presiding judge held a confession to be inadmissible solely because the constable who had questioned the defendant had *erroneously* believed that the situation would be scheduled for a Diplock trial. This suspect had been subjected to intense and prolonged questioning before he finally succumbed and confessed. The judge found that his confession had been against his will, and thus excluded it. The inference is that the physical abuse he had endured would not have rendered his confession inadmissible had the facts supported a charge of terrorist-related crime.

This procedure manifested a discretionary power in law enforcement officials which might in fact have instigated some brutality during questioning. If the law permits some abuse of suspects, those executing the law should not be expected to bear all the blame for faults in the process. Fortunately, this rule has been modified so that if the accused presents direct evidence showing that he had been subjected to torture, inhumane or degrading treatment, violence or threat of violence in order to induce him to make a statement, the burden will shift to the prosecutor to disprove this evidence. If the accused's evidence is not disproved, the confession will be excluded.[44] Thus, this perverted version of "tough love" has been modified to a more humane practice. The GFA did not address Diplock trials, and the process continues.

The GFA, Patten, and the Police Bill

Policing and the administration of justice have always been at the essence of the conflict in Northern Ireland. There have been frequent and recurring charges of RUC collusion with Loyalist paramilitaries and harassment of Nationalist Catholics. Moreover, the "shoot-to-kill" policy which was rooted in the Special Powers Act[45] has compounded this sense of anti-Catholic bias.[46] Among the most vocal criticisms of the RUC had been over-militarization, an inadequate system of accountability, and an ineffective structure to handle complaints against the police. A further negative inference was drawn from the fact that by the time of the GFA, the RUC and British Army troops together had killed some 360 persons in their counter-terrorist activities, but none had been convicted of any criminal wrong-doing.[47]

The GFA on Policing

The provision in the GFA addressing Policing and Justice is notable for its brevity: only three pages of this twenty-nine-page document deal with both issues in a package fashion.[48] The GFA altruistically called for a "new beginning to policing in Northern Ireland with a police service capable of attracting support from the community as a whole."[49] Notable is the use of the term "service" rather than "force" or "constabulary," an overt reference to the intent to de-militarize. Protection of human rights and professional integrity are listed as the abiding principles.[50] Accordingly, the participants in the peace negotiations directed that an independent commission be established for the express purpose of studying and making appropriate recommendations for implementing legislation to achieve these goals. The deadline on these recommendations was September, 1999.[51]

The Independent Commission on Policing for Northern Ireland (The Patten Commission)

The eight-member Commission was established on June 3, 1998.[52] Appointed to chair the Commission was Chris Patten, then-chair of the British Conservative (Tory) Party and member of the Westminster Parliament, and former governor of Hong Kong. (Patten's post-Commission position is European Commissioner for External Affairs.) Significantly he has publicly stated that he "was born, brought up, remain, and will die a Catholic." [53] This was presumably not coincidental, but rather it was a political move to avert criticism that the Commission itself had an anti-Nationalist bias.

The Patten Commission held fifteen months of meetings with numerous interest groups totaling some 10,000 persons, including 1,000 speakers. They deliberated upon more than 2,500 submitted written comments.[54] Their timely filed report was a plenary and exhaustive 128-page document containing 175 recommendations.

Even prior to commencing work, the Committee received submissions from political parties. The SDLP asked for a transition to "normal policing" and (predictably) an affirmative action hiring goal to give preferential treatment to Catholics. This moderate Nationalist party also asked for a total demolishment of the RUC, replacing the Chief Constable with an internationally recruited Police Commissioner.[55] Perhaps the most drastic request was for the complete disarmament of police officers.[56]

The Women's Coalition's submission was more muted. The call was for a broader reflection in all police personnel of society as a whole, referring specifically to gender, political or religious belief, class and community background, ethnicity, and sexual orientation.[57] This party also deemed it "desirable" to have a "routinely unarmed" police force.[58] Interestingly, the Women's Coalition retained the word "force" rather than "service," the term the SDLP had used, the latter usually regarded as being less military in nature and as serving the needs of the people.

Patten was the second such commission established by the British government to review policing in Northern Ireland, the first having been the Hunt Commission which began its sessions in October, 1969. Marked differences between the two final reports are evident. The sheer breadth of Patten's 175 recommendations dwarfs the forty-seven recommendations in Hunt.[59] Probably of considerable significance are the respective tempers of the times.[60] Hunt came during the height of the escalation of sectarian violence. On the other hand, the Patten Commission meetings took place shortly after the GFA, a time of relative peace. Since the 1994 paramilitary cease-fires, life in Northern Ireland had become somewhat calmer, and the post-GFA days might even be described as euphoric.

The final Patten Report was published in September, 1999. Although the overall reception was positive, there were serious reservations from expected sources. The most contentious provisions seemed to be five:

(1) change of name to Police Service of Northern Ireland (recommendation 150);

(2) change of badge and symbols, so as to remove any indicia of allegiance either to the United Kingdom (*e.g.*, the crown) or to Ireland (*e.g.*, the harp and the shamrocks) and the no-flying-of-British-flag (the so-called Union Jack) from police stations (recommendations 150,151 and 152);

(3) replacement of the existing Police Authority with a nineteen-member Policing Board (ten members from the New Northern Ireland Assembly by the d'Hondt method described in Chapter 5, and nine from the community at large, to reflect both segments of society) (recommendations 8 and 17); this proposed Board would be empowered with more oversight regarding complaints lodged against the police (including a Police Ombudsman) relative to the mere supervisory role of the Police Authority;

(4) reduction of size of the police service from its then-current 13,000 to 7,500 (recommendation 105), eliminating the presence of British Army troops "as quickly as the security situation will allow" (recommendation 58), and a move toward an unarmed police service (recommendation 65); and

(5) a 50% quota in hiring and recruiting so that the police personnel ultimately will reflect an even membership from the two sections (recommendation 121).

The beginning of the report set the tone of the human rights commitments of the GFA,[61] expressly referring not only to that document, but also to Westminster Parliament's subsequent incorporation of the European Convention on Human Rights[62] into domestic law in 1998.[63] The report explicitly mentions pre-trial procedures (Chapter 7 on Human Rights elaborates upon this), bail decisions on persons held in custody, right to privacy, and potential civil liability of police officers in situations where safeguarding the public is paramount. Patten expressly acknowledged that the Commission was appointed "in the atmosphere of hope and generosity of support that attended the Referendum vote on the Agreement [GFA]."[64]

Responses to Patten

RUC

Most of the RUC's responses to each of the Patten recommendations were qualified or conditional agreements. However, some were "agreements in principle," with explanations of the police force's reservations which were close to outright objections. An exhaustive and thorough response, the 85-page document listed and directly assessed each of the 175 recommendations, most with lengthy explanatory commentary.

The forward from Chief Constable Flanagan acknowledged the "milestone" the document was for policing in Northern Ireland and for the society of the region which Patten represented. His following statement however, was an expression of disappointment that "only fleeting mention was made" of the loss of the lives of many RUC officers and the serious injuries of "tens of thousands" of others sustained in their efforts to achieve security for the province. The Chief Constable pointed to these sacrifices collectively as an "outstanding cornerstone upon which any policing arrangements could be built." [65] This statement may have been a political one, but it nonetheless augmented Unionist admiration for the Chief, who had stated a fact with which few on either side could credibly disagree. Having met him, I personally regarded it as sincerely rather than politically motivated.

It was clear that the RUC reply had been submitted only after detailed analyses of each of the 75 recommendations. Few were referenced simply as "agreed." Rather, most—even those where agreement was indicated—were accompanied by commentary, many signifying that the recommendation was redundant, since it merely restated current RUC policy. (For example, recommendation 33 was that every police beat manager strive for a consultative forum in his area. In fact, the RUC response pointed to 144 such groups which already existed.) Many others indicated agreement in principle, but with serious reservations as to practicality in view of the security situation. For example, recommendation 105 proposed that the force be reduced in the next ten-year period from its current 13,000 to 7,500, and recommendation 65 proposed a move toward an unarmed police force. Others pointed out the impracticality of much in Patten, citing costs as a factor. This seemed to infer a bit of naïveté on the part of the members of the Commission, an idealistic "wish list" where no existing funding was available. (For example, recommendation 93 called for a review of the RUC's information technology system, 123 called for the provision of child care facilities for police personnel, and 131 called for a new purpose-built police college.) On others, the RUC response seemed to "call the hand" of the Patten Commission, in particular on recommendation 69, which decried any continued use of the plastic baton round (PBR). The reply simply reminded that this defense mechanism was routinely used throughout the U.K.

The two areas in which the RUC response voiced the strongest objections were the quota-hiring proposal of recommendations 120-121 and the name and symbol changes in recommendations 150 and 151. With regard to the former, the reply rather curtly stated that such a rule would first require substantial amendments to current fair employment statutes. The proposed name, badge and symbol changes evoked the strongest invective, calling the change of title of the RUC to the Police Service of Northern Ireland "the most emotive in the entire report." These responses took the form of outright rebuttals, objecting to the Commission's wholesale decision without obtaining any "empirical evidence" of what the people of Northern Ireland preferred, a passionate reminder that "(t)he police service does not belong to police officers....[but to] all the people." The opinion expressed in the response was that such changes had the "potential to alienate a substantial section of the Northern Ireland community" and would cause great "hurt and distress."[66] Moreover, recommendation 152's proposed prohibition of flying the Union Jack at police buildings was subject to question by the RUC as an inexplicable distinction between police stations and other public buildings.

SDLP

The SDLP quickly replied to the report with a 67-page document which largely lauded the strides toward Nationalist equality. As expected, this party had little disagreement with a document generally evaluated as being sympathetic to Nationalists. However, one provision to which the SDLP took issue was recommendation 125. Intended as a measure innocuous to Nationalists—perhaps even beneficial—this proposal states that "young people" should not be disqualified from police service because of convictions of "relatively minor criminal offenses." The evident intent of the Commission was to provide a sort of absolution for one who had engaged in criminal activity at a relatively tender age. However, by implication it was feared that this recommendation would summarily disqualify one older than a "young person" (presumably under age 18) for such "minor offenses," and could also have the effect of automatically disqualifying the young if they had been convicted of more serious offenses.[67] Apparently, this party viewed eligibility for police service much in the same light as it viewed (and advocated) release of those convicted and imprisoned for political crimes.

Predictably, SDLP applauded the 50-50% quota proposal for hiring. Indeed, the party challenged objectors to this provision to explain precisely how such a law would violate either European law or the European Convention on Human Rights.[68] (It is difficult to ascertain any differences in the effects of the quota proposal [recommendation 121] and the one suggested by SDLP.) Despite this affirmative action recommendation, the SDLP response expressed disappointment in the "slow pace of change" in this regard.[69]

Predictably, this party strongly supported the proposed change of name and symbols and prohibited flying of the British flag at police stations.[70] In fact, the only real addendum SDLP would attach to the recommendations would be an express incorporation of the human rights and equality laws into the implementation of this measure.[71] (This calls to mind the so-called "reverse-discrimination" cases in the U.S.A. pursuant to enforcement of affirmative action programs.[72] The obvious argument is that granting preferential treatment to one because of his race—or, in case of Northern Ireland, his religion or political preference—is the essence of inequality.)

Additionally, the SDLP welcomed the authority recommended to be vested in a new Police Board and Police Ombudsman (recommendations 8-43), but would have made life yet more difficult for an officer charged with crime or misconduct. This party preferred a lower standard of proof for a guilty finding, "balance of probabilities." [73] (Note to the American reader: The burden of proof in a criminal case in the U.S.A is "beyond a reasonable doubt," which is the strictest upon the party bringing the charge, *i.e.*, the state or federal government. A much lower burden is imposed on the plaintiff in a civil action, "by a preponderance of the evidence." The latter equates to the SDLP's proposal for a finding of an officer's guilt in what is, in many situations, tantamount to a criminal charge.)

Alliance Party

It is important to keep in mind that the Alliance Party designates itself as "other"—*i.e.*, neither Nationalist nor Unionist. Thus, its opinion, while reflective and measured, is generally not antagonistic nor overly critical. The work, commitment and sacrifices of the RUC during the Troubles were lavishly praised in Alliance's response to Patten. In a sense, this served as a mild reprimand to the Commission for having failed adequately to acknowledge this depth of service. In the same paragraph, Alliance recognized that some members of the force had indeed acted unlawfully and caused pain to others. [74]

This middle-ground party essentially found fault with two areas of the recommendations. First, its reply voiced strong disapproval of the proposed quota hiring system, deeming such a measure to be an unequivocal violation of the Fair Employment Act which forbids such discrimination. [75] Second, the party opposed the d'Hondt system (see Chapter 5 for explanation of d'Hondt) which virtually assures equality of power between Nationalists and Unionists on the Police Board. The rationale was that this system practically assures that the balance of representation would be tipped to favor larger political parties. This, the response explained, was contrary to the express Patten objective of reflecting a comprehension spectrum of political opinion and cultural perspective. [76] (Throughout the GFA negotiations, Alliance voiced its displeasure with this approach, staunchly adhering to a strict principle of democratic choice.)

Ulster Unionist Party (UUP)

The UUP deplored the Patten Commission Report in general, coming to the front in denouncing any proposed change of name of the RUC. First Minister David Trimble described the document as "full of recommendations unsubstantiated by good argument" and as "treat[ing] the RUC, its members and members of their fallen comrades shoddily."[77] Moreover, he attacked Chris Patten individually as having "based his recommendations on a flawed interpretation of the Belfast Agreement [GFA]."[78]

In particular, Trimble maligned the proposal as undermining the underlying human rights [principles]…[but] infring[ing upon] them with regard to its own members."[79] Additionally, he aligned himself and his party with Alliance in its strong oppositions to any hiring quotas.

Democratic Ulster Party (DUP)

It is difficult if not impossible to read anything into the DUP's response to Patten which even implies agreement. Prepared by Ian Paisley, Jr., and Gregory Campbell, the DUP reaction to the proposed change of name and symbol and prohibition of flying the Union flag at police stations was closer to a retort than a response. These party spokesmen wrote that these proposals were inserted solely "to appease those who have supported the decimation of the RUC… [an approach which]…only worsens an already diabolical set of proposals."[80]

The DUP view of an unarmed police force was that it was the "stuff of fantasy…," explaining that "[u]nder no circumstances should the RUC be disarmed while there is a terrorist capability in existence."[81] The same reaction was expressed with regard to any decrease in the number of police officers and phasing out the presence of British Army troops.[82]

Finally, the DUP soundly decried any use of a quota program in hiring, but argued rather for a continued use of a strict merit system.[83]

Sinn Féin

The 100-page reply from *Sinn Féin* epitomizes the attitude in the old adage of "give-him-an-inch-and-he'll-take-a-mile." That is, the more concessions one gets, the more difficult he is because he did not acquire yet more.

Although Patten in many respects virtually obliterated what had been the RUC, *Sinn Féin* criticized it for not having gone far enough. The conclusion of this more extreme of the two nationalist parties was that the Patten Commission had literally been "subverted" by U.K. government "secureocrats."[84] Even though its official response was basically positive, the post-submission public statements were accusations that the British government had engaged in "political chicanery."[85]

Contrary to *Sinn Féin's* obstinate insistence that the RUC title must be relegated to history books, hard-line Unionists threatened to boycott the New Northern Ireland Assembly (which would have led to its suspension, an event which was to occur nonetheless, but over another issue) unless the RUC name was retained.

Meanwhile, Chief Constable Flanagan proceeded to establish a Change Management team to prepare for what appeared certainly to be the future of what had been the RUC. Bombarded by criticism from both camps, poor Chris Patten likely had that sinking feeling that his Commission had succeeded in offending everyone in the British Isles.

The Police Bill

The Patten Report had instigated a minor battle, but during the days awaiting the first publication of the proposed legislation, a veritable political war erupted. After all, this would be statutory law enforceable in the courts, whereas Patten was merely a set of recommendations on which the Parliament would reflect.

Many felt that an inordinate amount of energy was being expended on the symbolic proposals, such as change of name and symbols. But the removal of the British flag from one segment of governmental buildings, police stations, was indeed puzzling. This recommendation seemed to evoke more amazement than anger.

To the same degree that Nationalists were elated over the prospective name change, Unionists were bitterly opposed. A compromise measure emerged to incorporate the existing title of RUC into the new name so that the complete title would be "The Police Service of Northern Ireland incorporating the Royal Ulster Constabulary." The entire name including the parenthetical would be used for official and documentary purposes, and "The Police Service of Northern Ireland" would be used for operational purposes.[86]

Offered by Ken Maginnis, this mid-way move only served to add incendiary fuel to an already burning fire. Nationalists had praised Patten for the recommendation of a complete name change, and Unionists insisted that any move toward compromise would concede defeat. Thus, this suggested amalgam of a mixture of the two offended both sides.[87]

The bill was made available to the public on July 13, 2000. The very first section designated the official name as "The Police Service of Northern Ireland incorporating the Royal Ulster Constabulary." [88] (Interestingly, although this title was to have become official on September 21, 2001, according to RUC sources, it was not yet in use a month following that date, but did become the formal name on November 4, 2001.[89]) Arguably, the compromise measure would allow sentimentalists accurately to continue to refer to the police service as the RUC.

The statute adopted the Patten Commission's recommendation that a Police Board replace the then-existing Police Authority. Enigmatically, the statute expressly stated that the Board would "not be regarded as the servant or agent of the crown." [90] It would be composed essentially according to the Patten recommendation, using the d'Hondt system to insure equal representation between the two communities.[91] The nineteen members would be appointed by the Secretary of State and would serve terms of a maximum of four years.[92] The Board would appoint (with the approval of the Secretary of State) and hold accountable the

Chief Constable,[93] a vast increase of its powers over those of the former Police Authority. (Existing law provided for this appointment to be by the Secretary of State alone.)

The Secretary of State then would appoint the Board. Its powers now would include appointment of and holding accountable the Chief Constable. The Board itself serves under the Secretary of State. The new hierarchy was to be as follows:

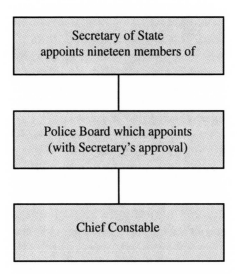

This modified structure clearly increases the Board's powers and duties over those of the former Police Authority. And in one sense, the Secretary of State's powers are diluted. He now has only an advisory role in the appointment of Board members, whereas the Secretary appointed Police Authority members.

The quota system, as unionists had feared, would be a pivotal part of the legislation,[94] and new hires would be 50% Catholic and 50% Protestant.

Unexpectedly, the bill addressed neither downsizing the police force nor removal of British troops from Northern Ireland.

Reactions to Police Bill

Assessment of the bill ran the gamut. Ken Maginnis of the UUP (the initiator of the proposed compromise on the new title of the police force) stated that the bill had "serious deficiencies, and *Sinn Féin*'s Gerry Adams accused the British government of having "defeated the objectives set by that same government," warning that neither the Irish government nor the major parties—in particular, those supporting the "broad republican/nationalist position"—would endorse this type of policing.[95]

The British government then announced that it would limit debate on the bill to seven hours, prompting Jeffrey Donaldson of the UUP to redress the legislation for having "dealt with the future [of the RUC] in such a shoddy way." [96] William Ross, another UUP spokesman, described the House of Commons as having acted as though it were "running some sort of little commercial business where…management decide[s] on a course of action and then they go ahead with it." [97] From the extreme Unionist party, DUP, Peter Robinson chided the Commons as "demeaning the government" to lend the perception that it is not sufficiently confident of its position to subject to a full debate.[98] His colleague, the Rev. Ian Paisley, described the bill as an effort to "demoralize and destroy the RUC." [99]

Andrew Mackay, Conservative Member of Parliament and shadow Secretary of State,[100] publicly stated that the bill was "fundamentally flawed" and thus in need of full debate for some substantial amendments.[101]

The proposed statute drew marked criticism even from both camps' more moderate parties. Second Minister Seamus Mallon (SDLP) accused First Minister David Trimble (UUP) of having falsely spread rumors that Mallon had threatened to resign along with Trimble were this bill to become law. Nonetheless, Mallon stated his opinion that the British government had "failed to meet up to its obligations to implement Patten."[102] Mallon seemingly had overlooked the purpose of Patten, which was not a legislative body, but merely one to study the issue and to forward its findings and recommendations to the body which would ultimately adopt a statutory measure. The U.K. Parliament was free to comply with Patten's suggestions in their entirely, or to disregard the Patten Report as inadvisable.

The proposed change of name continued to magnify the polarities between Unionists and Nationalists. Barbs flew back and forth between UUP's John Taylor and both Nationalist parties over his statement that the name change would crumble the Assembly and the Executive. They deemed such remarks as over-reactionary and duplicitous. However, these same Nationalists reminded that their own community's confidence that Westminster would implement the GFA's call for a "new beginning" for policing was quickly fading.[103]

Only the Alliance Party approved the bill as having accurately reflected the broad intent of Patten. Party leader Sean Neeson recalled the role of the Patten Commission's task to make recommendations to the Parliament which would then enact legislation as it concluded was best.[104] The major criticism from Alliance was its repeated objection to the hiring quota.

In reality, a scrutiny of the bill reveals little which is basically incompatible with the Patten recommendations other than the compromise on the change of name,[105] an evident move to placate both sides. Characteristic of Northern Ireland, an appeasement effort generally results in antagonism rather than pacification, surely the case on the name issue. Moreover, the Parliament had not enacted a definitive measure with respect to retention of the badge and symbol and flying the British flag at police locales. Rather, the bill simply authorized the Secretary of State (after consultation with the Police Board, Chief Constable and the Police Association) to make these determinations in the form of regulations.[106]

Summary

There is an old Irish poem entitled "The Cork Accent," part of which tells the story of an officer's "looking the other way" and thus not making an arrest of one who had clearly committed a crime in his presence. The poet Barry describes this preferential treatment : "The sergeant saw, and heard, and smiled…[there would be] no more reports…."[107] This—and its antithesis—embody the complaints by Catholics against the RUC in the past. According to those on this side of the problem, the proverbial "cheek is turned" when the violator is a Unionist, but a Nationalist Catholic in the same situation would be arrested, even brutally so. Part of the Patten Commission's charge was to recommend how to "fix" this predicament.

Neither side of the division in Northern Ireland has seriously contended that the pre-GFA police force was not in need of some substantial reform. Even the Chief Constable welcomed in principle some of the Patten Commission's recommended changes. The contention has been with regard to some precisely what any ultimate changes should be and the extent of any restructure.

For the neutral observer, the "Northern Ireland syndrome"—*i.e.,* inability to agree upon anything other than the status of the weather—is never more clearly evident than with the policing issue. An analysis of the rationales, however, shows a good deal of logic in both camps' arguments. The very sincere belief within the Catholic community that both the police force and the British Army have treated their people as second-class citizens is founded in fact, despite a dedicated and determined current leadership. To them, the "new beginning" as promised by the GFA necessarily requires a completely new façade, including renaming the police force and dispensing with all insignia and symbols which might bring that body to mind. On the other hand, symbols are a part of tradition, and to those who have served proudly with the RUC—or to those who have lost family members through its service—tradition must be retained as a part of what gives them an understandable and merited pride in this service.

Imposing a quota program on new hires is a provision abhorrent to those who support genuine equal opportunity. Yet, it is being implemented. And the downsizing and disarming possibilities invoke fear among those for whom terror is still a reality. Probably there is much in the Patten Report and the subsequent law to offend everybody, and, possibly, to please few.

The official name has now been changed, as likely will be the case with the symbol (which on its face evidences both "Irishness" and "Britishness"). Both sides hope for the eventual departure of British military troops, but differ only with regard to when the security situation safely permits their departure. Disarming the police service is perhaps a futuristic goal, but one on which Nationalists are determined. There will indeed be fewer officers, and the police service will ultimately be more representative of both sides of the community.

Will the newly enacted police statute be the panacea the lawmakers envision? The proverbial jury is still out as to whether this law will succeed in constructively revising pre-GFA policing in Northern Ireland for the good of both communities. It is indisputable that the human rights principles which prevail in all the post-GFA legislation will clearly influence this revision.

Bishop James Moore of the Church of Ireland was perhaps not overly simplistic when he pointed out that "we [citizens of Northern Ireland] learned to live with the violence. It's the peace that we find more difficult to handle."[108]

Endnotes to Chapter 7

[1] Linda Moore, *Policing and Change in Northern Ireland: the Centrality of Human Rights*, 22 FORDHAM INTERNATIONAL LAW JOURNAL 1577 (1999).

[2] *Sir Ronnie Flanagan as quoted in Ulster: The Deal; why I Want to See Real and Improved Police Changes*, THE BELFAST TELEGRAPH, April 30, 1999.

[3] Fionnuala Ní Aolain, THE POLITICS OF FORCE, at 91. (Blackstaff Press, Belfast, Ireland, 2000). The remaining 4% were categorized as "religion unknown."

[4] *Id.* at 248. Again, the remaining 4% were listed as "religion unknown."

[5] *See* Chief Constable Sir Ronnie Flanagan's Forward to RUC's Response To The Report Of The Independent Commission On Policing For Northern Ireland, 2000.

[6] Constabulary Act of 1822.

[7] HISTORY OF THE ROYAL ULSTER CONSTABULARY, published by the RUC Museum, RUC Headquarters, Belfast (September 1999).

[8] Indeed, the term "constabulary" is defined as "an armed police force of the civil government of a country organized along military lines." WEBSTER'S NEW COLLEGIATE DICTIONARY (2d ed. 1959).

[9] HISTORY OF THE RUC, *supra* note 7.

[10] *Id.*

[11] REPORT OF THE INDEPENDENT COMMISSION ON POLICING FOR NORTHERN IRELAND (the Patten Commission Report) at 75. (Crown Copyright, Norwich, England, 2000).

[12] *Id.* at 82.

[13] This report is summarized in John Conroy, A BELFAST DIARY (Beacon Press, Boston, Massachusetts, 1995), at 47-48.

[14] Policing–a New Service for a New Future, SDLP's (pre-Patten Report) Submission to the Independent Commission on Policing—1999, at paragraph 39, at 10.

[15] *Supra* note 8.

[16] Report of the Chief Constable, 1998-1999, at 119.

[17] Information obtained from Central Statistics Unit, RUC Management Support Department, July 20, 2000.

[18] The Chief Constable's Foreward to the Royal Ulster Constabulary Response To The Report Of The Independent Commission On Policing For Northern Ireland, summer 2000.

[19] Interview with Chief Constable Sir Ronnie Flanagan, RUC Headquarters, Belfast, July 21, 2000.

[20] Diplock Report 1972, promulgated into statute in 1973, later in Northern Ireland (Emergency Provisions) Act 1991 (EPA, and currently in the Terrorism Act 2000).

[21] John Jackson and Sean Doran, JUDGE WITHOUT JURY (Oxford University Press, Oxford, England, 1995) at 1. Professors Jackson and Doran are generally regarded as the preeminent experts on Diplock trials, and their book is intriguing reading for both the legal professional and the layperson.

[22] W. L. Twining, RETHINKING EVIDENCE: EXPLORATORY ESSAYS (Northwestern University Press, Evanston, Illinois, 1990), at 157.

[23] U.S. CONST. amend. VI.

[24] U.S. CONST. amend. VII. In British and Irish courts, the jury in civil trials has waned, being limited to defamation actions. All other civil trials are heard and decided by a judge.

[25] *See supra*, note 20. This 1973 law was amended in 1990, but the substantive portions remain unchanged.

[26] Prevention of Violence (Terrorism) Act 1938.

[27] Prevention of Terrorism (Temporary Provisions) Act 1984, ch. 8 (Eng.).

[28] Section 2(2) EPA, *supra* note 20, now Terrorism Act 2000. Professor Jackson reminds that a magistrate may hear the case, circumventing the Crown (criminal) Court, if the offense (although a scheduled one) is minor.

[29] Section 1 EPA, *supra* note 20. This list includes some common law offenses, *viz.*, murder, manslaughter, riot, kidnapping, false imprisonment, and assault; and statutory crimes, *viz.*, wounding with intent to cause grievous bodily harm, robbery and aggravated burglary, arson, and aggravated criminal damage.

[30] *See* Jackson and Doran, supra note 21, at 21.

[31] *Id.* at 35, Table 2.2

[32] These cases include the Guildford Four, the Birmingham Six, the Maguire Family, and the Cardiff Three. All were trials involving multiple convictions and later releases which provide sufficient material for an entire book.

[33] Section 18 EPA, *supra* note 20.

[34] U.S. CONST. amend. V.

[35] Miranda v. Arizona, 384 U.S. 436, 86 S.Ct. 1602 (1966).

[36] Article 4 Criminal Evidence (Northern Ireland) Order 1988.

[37] Amendment to article 4 of the Order accompanying Criminal Justice and Police Order Act 1994, section 10, paragraph 1.

[38] Article 5 Criminal Evidence (Northern Ireland) Order 1988 as amendment.

[39] The author thanks Professor John Jackson for this typical wording for the warning. He added that other special warnings may be given under Articles 5 and 6 of the 1988 Order in which a suspect is asked to explain marks or substances on his person, or his presence at the crime scene.

[40] Section 11(3) EPA, *supra* note 20.

[41] *See* R. v. McCormick and Others (1977), 105, 111 (McGonigal, J.).

[42] Section 11(2)(b) EPA, *supra* note 20.

[43] Unreported 1988 case discussed in Jackson and Doran, *supra* note 21, at page 37.

[44] Section 76 Terrorism Act 2000. Article 74 of the Police and Criminal Evidence (NI) Order (PACE) abrogated this common law voluntariness test in non-scheduled (jury) trials, essentially rendering a confession inadmissible if it had been obtained oppressively or in circumstances making it unreliable. According to Professor Jackson, a 2000 government study of Diplock trials recommended this same exclusionary rule (the PACE rule) for confessions in scheduled (non-jury) trials. However, the wheels of justice often turn slowly, and at this writing this recommendation has not been followed.

[45] Civil Authorities (Special Powers) Acts (NI) 1922-33, the precursors to the EPA. This policy is explained in Chapter 8 on Human Rights.

[46] Moore, *supra* note 1, at 1578.

[47] *Id.* at. 1579-1580.

[48] GFA at 22-24.

[49] *Id.* at 22, paragraph 1. (Emphasis added.)

[52] A New Beginning: Policing in Northern Ireland, The Report of the Independent Commission on Policing for Northern Ireland (hereafter "Patten Report"), part 2.1, page 10.

[53] Vincent Brown, *Political prophet, but not in his own country*, THE IRISH TIMES, Mar. 10, 2001, at 12, col. 1-6.

[54] Patten Report, *supra* note 50, part 2.3, at 11.

[55] SDLP Submission to the Independent Commission on Policing (1999), at 5, paragraph 16.

[56] *Id.* at 33, paragraph 189.

[57] Northern Ireland Women's Coalition Preliminary Submission to the Independent Commission on Policing in Northern Ireland (1999), at 2-3, Part 3(a).

[58] *Id.* at 7, Part 9.

[59] Report of the Advisory Committee on Police in Northern Ireland (Hunt Commission), 1969.

[62] European Convention for the Protection of Human Rights and Fundamental Freedoms (1950).

[63] Human Rights Act 1998 (HRA).

[64] Patten Report, *supra* note 50, at 2.

[65] Forward to The Royal Ulster Constabulary Response to the Independent Commission on: Policing for Northern Ireland.

[66] *Id.* at 75, response to recommendation 150.

[67] SDLP response to the Independent Commission on Policing, Nov. 1999, 125/15.13, at 53-54.

[68] SDLP Response to the Independent Commission on Policing, Nov. 1999, at 53-54.

[69] *Id.* at 8 and 8-9.

[70] Response of the SCLP to the Independent Commission on Policing, Nov. 1999, at Part I. G.

[71] *Id.*, Part II, *Guide to Implementation*, Chapter Four: *Human Rights,* paragraph 3/4.8.

[72] *See, e.g.*, Bakke v. Regents v. University of California, 438 U.S. 265 (1978) (program rejected), Weber v. Kaiser Aluminum/United Steelworkers, 443 U.S. 193 (1979) (program approved), and U.S. v. Paradise, 94 L.Ed.2d 615 (1987) (program approved.).

[73] SDLP response to Patten, *supra* note 65, at 5.

[74] Response of the Alliance Party to the Independent Commission on Policing, at paragraph 1.3.

[75] *Id.* at paragraphs 11.1(2); and 12.2-12.5.

[76] *Id.* at paragraph 3.2.

[77] *Patten plan 'a shoddy document,'* BELFAST NEWS LETTER, July 29, 2000, at 9, col. 1-3.

[78] *Id.*

[79] *Id.*

[83] *Id.* at 1.

[84] Chris Ryder, *Patten: The inside story on what the police reforms really mean*, BELFAST TELEGRAPH, July 21, 2000, at 13, col. 1-4.

[85] *Id.*

[86] Desmond McCartan, *Unionists win police force name concession*, BELFAST TELEGRAPH, July 7, 2000, at 8, col. 5-8.

[87] Frank Miller, *SDLP enraged by new British concession on retaining RUC title*, THE IRISH TIMES , July 7 at 9 col. 1-4.

[88] HL Bill (on Policing) 102, Part I, 1(1), enacted into law on November 23, 2000, as Police (Northern Ireland) Act 2000.

[89] October 10, 2001, fax from Christine Marks, RUC Change Management, informed that the original title was as of then still in use. On November 4, 2001, the change became official.

[93] *Id.*, Part VI, section 35(1) and Part II section 3(3), respectively.

[94] *Id.*, section 45(1).

[95] Joe Carroll, *Adams accuses Mandelson of emasculating Patten recommendations*, THE IRISH TIMES, July 11, 2000, at 6, col. 1-8.

[96] *Limit on debate in Commons 'deeply insensitive,'* THE IRISH TIMES, July 12, 2000, at 7, col. 6-8.

[97] *Id.*

[98] *Id.*

[99] *Id.*

[100] A "shadow" cabinet member is actually a non-member. He/she is a member of the minority party in Parliament who stands to assume this position in the event the

current majority party (Tony Blair's Labor) becomes the minority party. Andrew McKay is in the Conservative (Tories) party.

[101] THE IRISH TIMES, *supra* note 96.

[102] Noel McAdam and Desmond McCartin, *Mallon denies quit threat over Police Bill*, BELFAST TELEGRAPH, July 14, 2000, at 1, col. 3-5.

[103] Noel McAdam, *Anger over Taylor and RUC*, BELFAST TELEGRAPH, July 20, 2000, at 4, col. 7.

[104] *Alliance defends Police Bill*, BELFAST NEWS LETTER, July 18, 2000, at 6, col. 1-3.

[105] *See, e.g., Viewpoint* (editorial): *Leaders revisit the Policing Bill*, BELFAST TELEGRAPH, July 31, 2000, at 10, col. 1-2.

[106] Police Bill, *supra* note 85, Part VI, section 52.

[107] *See* A TREASURY OF IRISH FOLKLORE, Padraic Colum, editor, Wings Books, 2nd revised edition, 1992, at 454, in section entitled "The Tavern, crediting the poem to P. Barry.

[108] Interview with the Right Reverend James Moore, Bishop of Connor, Diocesan Officer in Belfast, August 7, 2000.

Chapter 8

Human Rights and Equality

"[The GFA is] conspicuous by the centrality it gives to and human rights.....concerns around fairness and justice are a recurring theme."

Mary Robinson
United Nations High Commissioner for Human Rights[1]

"Human rights" is not the household phrase in the U.S.A. that it is in western Europe. Indeed, it is most often used among Europeans in reference to the American states in a negative way, referring to the widespread legality of capital punishment (thirty-eight states among the fifty).[2] Just as those in Northern Ireland typically view the American administration of the death penalty as barbaric, the average American surely perceives the violence in the province with a jaundiced eye. Routine killings of people because they are of a different political or religious persuasion are indeed a prime example of abuse of basic human rights.

I had a good friend and colleague at the School of Law at Queens during part of my time on the faculty. He is a brilliant man, one who has almost a majestic control over a tense situation, and small setbacks or difficulties do not affect his resolve. The faculty and secretaries all had the utmost respect and admiration for this colleague. However, even this wonderful man who generally is able to function throughout times of tension does not have fond memories of 1970s Belfast.

During his time as a law student at Queen's, he lived with his parents in a stylish South Belfast home near the prominent Presbyterian Church his family attended, as he still does today. He told me that he generally took the Lisburn

245

Road bus, the street perpendicular to the law school, to his home in the early evenings. (Lisburn is a rather long street, full of trendy restaurants, churches, and shops—a "neutral" area, where one should feel safe.) Belfast is, however, a small city, and the "safe" and "not-so-safe" parts adjoin one another in close proximity. My friend told me that the constant sounds of shots and hand grenades from nearby Sandy Row (solidly Loyalist) at first terrified him as he waited for his bus to arrive. Almost sadly, he continued by saying that what had initially been so horrible to him soon became so routine that he scarcely would notice the noise. His sadness reflected the fact that we never want horror to become the routine. My friend in Derry, Caoimhghín O'Murchadha, phrased this reality in a way I have not forgotten: "The abnormal becomes normal."[3]

It is, then, somewhat contradictory that those in the province think of American killings by the state as inhumane, while we in the states are incredulous over the metaphorical bone marrow of daily life in which violence has become the norm for those in Northern Ireland. The primary goal of the GFA was to change this acceptance that killings in Northern Ireland are inevitable.

Assurance of human rights permeates throughout the GFA. This chapter will view the law as it existed prior to the signing of the document and will continue with the human rights and equality of treatment language in the GFA and supplementary legislation.

Human Rights Law Prior to the GFA

Nearly forty years before the GFA, the European Convention on Human Rights (ECHR)[4] was accepted by some forty[5] European countries, including the United Kingdom. All members of the European Union[6] and several Eastern European countries comprise this group of nations. This treaty lists basic human rights which all signatories are obligated to respect, including freedom of speech, religion, and opinion.[7] It also prohibits discrimination in general.[8]

This 1950 convention (or treaty) created two legal entities, the Council of Europe, the legislative arm, and the European Court of Human Rights (hereinafter "HR Court"), the judiciary that sits in Strasbourg, France and hears charges of violations of the convention. This court, however, is large on principle but quite limited with regard to power. To be sure, it can issue orders which are subject to political supervision by a Committee of Ministers,[9] but this Committee has no real powers of enforcement. Actual compliance is essentially voluntary,[10] making the ECHR a "feel-good" document and the HR Court a somewhat toothless tiger. Nonetheless, the Court has enjoyed wide respect within Europe, and its influence on European Communities [11] law has been considerable indeed.

The significance of the ECHR for the European Union in general (both the United Kingdom and Ireland are member states) is its recent promulgation into European Communities law.[12] For Northern Ireland in particular, the significance is the subsequent adoption of the ECHR into domestic law in the United Kingdom,[13] effective October 2, 2000. The first recorded failed attempt to incorporate the ECHR into British law had been in 1968,[14] but it was in response to the GFA that these efforts finally came to fruition.

Interestingly, despite its relatively negative reputation on human rights in Europe, the U.S.A. might claim some modicum of pride in this area. The first chair on the United Nations Commission on Human Rights—charged with submitting proposals for an International Bill of Rights—was former First Lady Eleanor Roosevelt. This appointment followed the signing of the United Nations charter in San Francisco, California in June, 1946.[15] Apparently, Mrs. Roosevelt was not aligned with her husband's suspension of *habeas corpus* for those suspected of espionage and his administration's lawful internment of all persons who were of Japanese descent living in World War II California.[16]

In Northern Ireland, the Standing Advisory Commission on Human Rights (SACHR) was created by Westminster legislation in 1973. This body was vested with the express duty of advising the Secretary of State on human rights issues.[17] SACHR was severely criticized during its tenure (The New Northern Ireland Human Rights Commission has taken the place of SACHR), however, for its mere advisory role and lack of real powers.

Why was it necessary for Westminster to adopt the ECHR even though the United Kingdom was already committed to convention principles, as a signatory nation? Some distinctions between British and American law clarify this seeming anomaly.

Although traditional English legal and political theory establish the courts as independent and essential in order for common law principles to be maintained, the same distinct separation-of-powers doctrine which is so basic to American constitutional law is nonexistent in the United Kingdom. The judiciary is always subordinate to the executive (which is a part of Parliament, according to the parliamentary system of government)[18] and is by no means the equal branch of government which the United States Supreme Court is. In British law, the Parliament is always supreme, and this includes supremacy over supranational law such as ECHR law.

Moreover, one of the general legal principles in the United Kingdom is that a treaty is not part of domestic law until Westminster Parliament has adopted it as legislation.[19] This illustrates the "top gun" role of Parliament, a reality to which Lord Hailsham of St. Marylebone has referred as "elected leadership."[20] The application of this doctrine can be extreme, since no rights are recognized as so fundamental that they are not subject to interference by Parliament.[21]

British jurists invariably point with pride to their "checks and balances" system, but relative to American constitutional law, the British model is weak indeed. In the U.S.A. the powers of each of the three branches of government—legislative (Congress), executive (the president) and judicial (the courts)—truly "balance" and "check" one another, a system probably unique in the world. Significantly, as far back as 1803 the Constitution was held by the U.S. Supreme Court to empower the Court to declare an act of Congress unconstitutional.[22] In contrast, in the United Kingdom, the courts do not have the power to declare an act of Parliament unconstitutional. This supremacy of Parliament prevails even if a statute at issue is viewed as being inconsistent with a provision of a convention or treaty to which the United Kingdom has subscribed.[23]

The U.S. Congress also has a "check" on the courts' power to construe acts of Congress. It might then enact a statute altering such a judicial interpretation that was contrary to the intent of the legislators. With regard to the executive branch, the Court also might declare an act of the president (or an Executive Order) unconstitutional, and the Congress has the constitutional right to impeach the president.

The executive's "check" on the courts under the American system is the president's power to appoint all federal judges. A further "check" on the president—and on these aspiring judges—is the Senate's later necessary confirmation of such appointments.[24]

This comparison between U.S. and U.K. constitutional law indicates the reason for the British domestic statute incorporating the ECHR, even though the European Commission's earlier adoption of this convention as law for the EU. One further practical importance of the British legislation relates to the possible forum for trial on charges of a violation. Whereas the only situs prior to passage of the law in the U.K. was the HR Court in Strasbourg, the new statute permits a citizen of the U.K. to use British courts (including those in Northern Ireland) to enforce these human rights.[25]

The U.K.'s track record before the HR court in Strasbourg has been far from sterling. There have been fifty judgments against the British government for charges of violation of ECHR rights. One such adverse decision was for the inhumane treatment of terrorist suspects in Northern Ireland. In *Brogan et al. v. U.K.*,[26] human rights lawyers successfully challenged the legitimacy of the seven-day detention rule before being charged. (This principle is discussed in connection with the Diplock trials in Chapter 7.) However, the U.K. was able to skirt this judgment by exercising its option to derogate from—*i.e.*, exempt itself—the applicable provision of the ECHR.[27] Although the derogation itself was then appealed to the HR Court in Strasbourg,[28] the U.K. prevailed on procedural grounds. With the 1998 statute, this side-stepping will not be an alternative for the British government in charges of abuse of human rights.[29]

Additionally, the government of the U.K. had been the target of a deluge of criticism from the United Nations Human Rights Committee and the Committee Against Torture between 1991 and 1995.[30] The new law should reverse that trend.

As of November, 2001, a bill was pending in the *Dáil* (parliament of the Republic of Ireland) to take the same step of enacting domestic law adopting the ECHR, but no final action had been taken. Somewhat anachronistically, this leaves

Ireland rather than the province of Northern Ireland (as a part of the U.K.) as the only member state of the EU which has not adopted the ECHR as the law of the land.[31]

The GFA and Human Rights and Equality

The GFA called for the creation of two administrative bodies, the Human Rights Commission and the Equality Commission. Although they are two separate entities, substantively, their concerns overlap considerably.

Northern Ireland Human Rights Commission

The Northern Ireland Human Rights Commission (HR Commission) was formally established on March 1, 1999 by the comprehensive statute which implemented the GFA. Its ten members are collectively accountable to the Secretary of State, who reports to Westminster Parliament. The only nexus of the HR Commission to the Northern Ireland Assembly is its funding of 750,000 pound sterling (in excess of $1 million) for each of its first two years of existence. There are nine regular members and one Chief Commissioner who serves as chair, all appointed by the Secretary of State for maximum periods of five years for the Chair and three years for the other nine regular members. Of these ten Commissioners, four are to be Catholic, and six Protestant (keeping in line with the power-sharing principle embodied in the GFA).[32] Chief Commissioner Brice Dickson explained to me that some perceive two of the Protestants as Nationalists.

The law lists seven duties of the Commission,[33] perhaps the most significant of which are two: (i) advising the Assembly on the compatibility of a proposed bill with the concept of human rights; and (ii) assisting and advising those who have applied for help regarding legal procedure involved in the protection of their human rights. Among its non-obligatory powers is the right to investigate allegations of human rights abuses. Chief Commissioner Dickson explained to me that this investigatory power is rather an empty one, however, since the HR Commission has no powers to issue subpoenas. He bemoaned this as "our greatest impediment."[34]

Regardless of this limitation, the law vests the new HR Commission with far more powers than its predecessor, SACHR, had. Whereas SACHR's areas included only political and religious rights, the HR Commission's authoritative arm extends to a panorama of areas, including all human rights in general.

I had known Brice Dickson since my semester in Belfast in 1998, when I gave a guest lecture to his class at University of Ulster Jordanstowne in Newtownabbey, just north of Belfast., where he was Professor of Law. During summer 2000, I was fortunate to have been able to talk with him about his new role as Chief HR Commissioner. Moreover, we would intermittently cross paths during that same summer at the Queen's University Physical Education Center. (Brice is a runner, I am a swimmer.)

A kind and gentle man, he seems ideally suited for this non-academic role, although he had the reputation of having been a superb law teacher. I had been struck by the comments about Brice from folks at the School of Law at Queen's, where he had been on the faculty prior to his work at Ulster. Each time anyone would mention Brice's name, the inevitable remark was that he was "such a *nice* man." A brilliant but soft-spoken and completely non-adulatory man, his commitment to leading the human rights agenda in the right, and effective, direction is evident from his zeal in talking about this task. He reminded me somewhat embarrassingly of America's sparse formal record in the area of human rights when he informed me that only the U.S.A. and Somalia from among all nations in the world had not ascribed to the 1989 United Nations Convention on Rights of the Child.

He spoke at length about the prospects of a bill of rights for Northern Ireland, one of the HR Commission's primary projects. As a non-devolved issue, if enacted into legislation this will be the task of the Westminster Parliament rather than the Northern Ireland Assembly.

A major item on the Commission's agenda has been the preparation of a draft for this bill of rights for the province. The U.S. Constitution's 10-article Bill of Rights has been with us since 1791, only four years after the adoption of the Constitution itself. Thus, Americans may marvel at the absence of a bill of rights in the British constitution, at least in the modern sense. One simplistic answer as to the reason is the fact that the United Kingdom does not have a written constitution at all. The British "constitution" is comprised of selected statutes—*i.e.*, acts of the Westminster Parliament—that the courts from time to time have deemed so fundamental as to embrace the concept of "constitutional rights." The only such statute considered a bill of rights was enacted by Parliament in 1688. However, this document delineates the rights of Parliament and the crown, rather than those of the people as individuals, whereas the American Bill of Rights protects the people from any overriding and excessive governmental authority. David Baugh, one of my friends in Richmond who is a constitutional lawyer, has referred to our Bill of Rights as a "fence" which protects the people on one side from the despotism of the government on the other. David designates the people of one side of the fence as "us," and the federal government on the other side as "them." The 17th century British version seems to be the reverse and to protect "them" from "us," rather than "us" from "them."

This archaism of the British version is somewhat of an anachronism in western Europe. The Republic of Ireland, for example, has had a bill of rights since its Constitution was adopted in 1937, and German's 1949 Constitution contains a list of "basic rights." [35]

Politicians in Northern Ireland often compare the peace for which the GFA aspires to the end of apartheid in South Africa. Most voters were probably unaware that the full photograph on the cover of the copy of the GFA distributed to every mailbox in Northern Ireland prior to the referendum was not taken in the province, but rather in South Africa. This photograph shows a family of four, walking with their backs to the camera, into a beautiful and glowing sunset, presumably, a metaphor for the bright and lovely ending which was the demise of apartheid and which the drafters hoped the GFA would also signal for Northern Ireland. Those in power in South Africa insured that the 1996 constitution which became law upon integration contained a bill of rights section.[36] Perhaps because of the prevalence of human rights abuses on Northern Ireland soil, the principals are eager to catch up with the province's counterparts throughout the world, independent from any document which Westminster might (or might not) approve for Northern Ireland (or Scotland or Wales, for that matter).

What then, is the role of the Northern Ireland Human Rights Commission with regard to a bill of rights? Part of the Commission's task is to advise the Secretary of State as to what specific rights in addition to those more general ECHR principles should be included in such a document. This duty is not an altruistic and voluntary one, but one which the GFA expressly imposed upon the H.R. Commission.[37] In 2000, the Commission presented its final proposed draft to the Secretary, a proposal which has taken the prudential direction of recommending a return to jury trials in all criminal cases, including those where the accused is suspected of terrorism. If ultimately enacted into law, this would abolish the Diplock system. (See Chapter 7 for a discussion of Diplock trials.) Significantly, the ECHR assures the right to a fair trial,[38] and it is conjunction with this guarantee that the H.R. Commission made this recommendation.

Why is a special bill of rights necessary for Northern Ireland? That is, why cannot Westminster simply adopt a U.K.-wide document equally applicable to all regions? And why is this even an issue, given the adoption of the ECHR into British domestic law? The H.R. Commission lists numerous reasons. This explanation is prefaced by the reminder that Northern Ireland has already won charges of human rights violations against the United Kingdom, a government which has usually avoided compliance. Moreover, the ECHR secures general rights, whereas the uniqueness of the Troubles merits more specificity in listing of fundamental rights. For example, the ECHR ensures equality in a public setting, but does not extend to private sector. This is particularly important in the area of employment.

Another reason that a bill of rights is needed for the province is that the ECHR gives very limited protections to parents regarding governing the schooling of their children. The division in Northern Ireland with respect to schools has no parallel in any other part of the U.K. and should be dealt with accordingly. The religious division in Northern Ireland virtually begs for a more equitable distribution with respect to funding for schools, both Protestant (public) and Catholic.

Additionally, the ECHR does not address any right to use a minority language, such as Irish Gaelic or Ulster Scots, nor does it prohibit the government from requiring that only one language (*i.e.*, English) be used in dealing with public bodies. Wales has been given the statutory right to use the Welsh language in court proceedings, if one or more parties would be unfairly and unduly prejudiced otherwise.[39] The H.R. Commission's rejoinder to those who regard this as a frivolous claim is that this same right granted in Wales should be extended to Northern Ireland. This is a rather heated issue in Northern Ireland, but one which would never arise in England. This demand might be compared with the same difficulty in the U.S.A. with those who charge that making English an official language is discriminatory, especially against the many persons of Hispanic origin residing in large part in southern Florida, Texas, and southern California. The difficulty with permitting alternate languages would be the anomalous result of confusion because most of the parties involved would not understand the minority language being used.

Final concerns which point to the need for a bill of rights that are confined to the province are two: (i) genuine concern over the current lack of enforceability of the cultural, economic, and social rights of one segment (*i.e.*, Catholics); and (ii) the special need in Northern Ireland to assure the rights of victims of inter-community conflict.[40]

One potential problematic issue for the H.R. Commission is the right to abortion, particularly in view of the precarious Protestant-Catholic balance. In July, 2000, a British House of Commons session indicated confusion even among MPs as to whether abortion reform is a matter devolved to the Northern Ireland Assembly or one properly within the domain of Westminster. Clearly it is not devolved, so it is a knotty question with which Westminster must grapple.

The same lack of comprehension as to jurisdiction over this volatile issue was evidenced in a debate at Stormont a month earlier when DUP (Unionist) Jim Wells sponsored a motion which would prohibit any move to extend the English abortion statute of the late 1960s to Northern Ireland.[41] This law provided a woman with the right to an abortion if she had become pregnant as a result of rape or incest. The current status of law in Northern Ireland is that a very limited right to abortion is judicially recognized, *only* if the woman presents a physician's written statement that the pregnancy, if not terminated, would present a "grave risk" of danger to her (not the child's) life or health. This is irrespective of how she became pregnant, so incest or rape would be irrelevant under Northern Ireland law.

It is generally recognized that adoption of a bill of rights which would apply solely to Northern Ireland would be enacted by Westminster, rather than the Northern Ireland Assembly. It seems primarily in the area of abortion that both Westminster and the Assembly have acted somewhat like Pontius Pilate and King Herod in trying to "shift the buck" regarding a determination of a controversial question onto the back of another. News columnist Eamonn McCann termed this a "combination of irrational fundamentalism and political cowardice [which] has produced a moral and legal mess."[42]

It is axiomatic that the human rights conflict lies in the interests of the mother versus those of the unborn child. The first discussion on the H.R. Commission's proposed bill did not mention abortion, a fact for which groups such as the Society for the Protection of Unborn Children (SPUC) soundly criticized the Commission. Chief Commissioner Dickson reportedly confirmed that the right to abortion, as contrasted with any rights of an unborn child, would indeed be among those in the final presentation to the Secretary of State. A compounded fear has trickled down into the heavily Catholic Republic of Ireland pro-lifers because of the assumption that any broadening of abortion rights in Northern Ireland would pressure the *Dáil* (Irish Parliament) to follow suit.[43]

Because of the division in Northern Ireland—if one must generalize, Catholics in opposition to abortion and Protestants (for the most part) in favor of the expansion of this right—the only certainty about a bill of rights provision which specifically would address abortion would displease a significant number on one side whichever way it might tilt.

Equality Commission

The Equality Commission is the twin sister of the Human Rights Commission, with which it works in tandem. Similar to the Human Rights Commission, its members—a minimum of fourteen and a maximum of twenty—are appointed by and responsible to the Secretary of State. Also like the Human Rights Commission, its Chief Commissioner (now Joan Harbinson) is appointed for a five-year maximum term, and the remaining Commissioners, for three-year terms.[44] The GFA had defined the role of this Commission broadly: to "advise on, validate and monitor the statutory obligation [not to discriminate] and [to] investigate complaints of default."[45]

The implementing statute obligates "all public authorities" in Northern Ireland to have "due regard" to the need to promote equality of opportunity between persons with respect to any differences in religious beliefs, political opinion*, racial group, age, marital status*, or sexual orientation*; between men and women; between persons with or without a disability; and between persons with dependents and those without dependents*.[46] [Those marked with an asterisk (*) indicate areas where the U.S.A. has no parallel federal anti-discrimination laws.[47]]

The listing in the statute of "public authorities" is so exhaustive as to leave the reader wondering whatever could have been omitted.[48] Moreover, the duty to "promote" equality rings much like the affirmative action principles which were replete throughout the GFA.

This "due regard" phrase merits some comment. The intent of the Westminster Parliament was to use a term stronger than simple "regard." This is compounded by the legislative "need" to promote equality of opportunity and the "desirability" to promote "good relations" between those persons in the various listed categories within the population. This is powerful terminology which connotes active rather than passive efforts on the part of public authorities in order to assure that inter-group relations are "good." The word "due" reflects the perception that minorities have an entitlement to such regard. Former Secretary of State "Mo" Mowlam designated the "equality" and "good relations" duties as complementary rather than conflicting,[49] arguably equating equal opportunity and affirmative action. This section of the law imposes a significant obligation on all public authorities.

The law also mandates that covered entities prepare equality impact assessments and include a policy-making consultation process with all persons affected by the required "promotion" of equality.[50] This is a duty comparable to virtually none under American federal law, with the possible exception of the affirmative action plan requirements in the 1973 Rehabilitation Act and the 1965 Executive Order. (Notably, these laws apply only to U.S. federal offices and private businesses which contract with the federal government.) Such "impact assessment statements" required under the new law in Northern Ireland are more similar to the cumbersome "environmental impact statements" required under U.S. federal environmental statutes than to employment law.

The required impact assessment is a detailed one. The statutory schedule establishes a two-stage duty, the (i) preparation of an Equality Scheme which is to address a lengthy catalogue of areas listed in the law, and (ii) actual implementation of this Scheme.[51] This is somewhat akin to a "14th Amendment-plus" duty from an American constitutional perspective: *i.e.*, to provide more than simple equality of protection. The procedure then requires the Equality Commission to approve the Equality Scheme and to refer those unapproved to the Secretary of State [the Northern Assembly is notified]. The Secretary might approve (essentially overruling the Commission), remand to the public authority for revision(s), or revise the Scheme himself.[52]

The Equality Commission functions much like its American counterpart, the Equal Employment Opportunity Commission (EEOC).[53] One major difference is that statutes administered by the EEOC cover both public and private sectors, rather than only the "public authorities" to which the Northern Ireland law applies. The statute of limitations—twelve months[54]—is somewhat longer than the 180-day (six months) statute in its American parallel. (This 180-day period is lengthened to 300 days, or ten months, in those states with approved state agencies where the process is first diverted.[55]) In either case, the time during which a complaint might be filed is longer in Northern Ireland than in the U.S.A.

The Equality Commission as an entity replaced several existing bodies, including the Fair Employment Commission for Northern Ireland, the Equal Opportunities Commission for Northern Ireland, the Commission for Racial Equality for Northern Ireland, and the Northern Ireland Disability Council.[56]

Also phased out was the 1973 Standing Advisory Committee on Human Rights (SACHR) which had been charged with handling complaints of discrimination on grounds of political or religious beliefs.[57] The Fair Employment Agency had been established in 1976[58] to handle charges of race and sex discrimination.

Some revisitation of the earlier comment on the history of SACHR is significant, since Parliament wanted to avoid its shortcomings when it created the new Equality Commission. SACHR was relatively mild-mannered, taking the approach that compliance should be voluntary. Parliament did strengthen this body in 1989[59] to make enforcement compulsory with mandatory monitoring and affirmative action regulations.[60]

One non-statutory document created by regulations in 1993, the Policy Appraisal and Fair Treatment (PAFT) Guidelines,[61] was also discontinued by the new legislation. The PAFT Guidelines had added age, ethnic origin, marriage and family status, and sexual orientation to those areas where discrimination was prohibited. The Equality Commission has swallowed all the separate agencies and offices and has comprehensive jurisdiction over discrimination charges on all grounds.

Housing Discrimination

Accusations of discrimination traditionally arose in several areas and was not limited to jobs (an area where discrimination had particularly been a problem in the public sector). There had been not only consistent claims of abuse of civil powers, allegedly with the aid of a sectarian police or policemen (addressed in Chapter 7), but also charges of discrimination in the allotment of public housing and voting districting.[62] Referring to problems with housing discrimination, two prominent British political scientists have written that the "UUP could rely on ingrained ethnic prejudices to sustain discrimination." [63] This stance points to the long-standing biases against Nationalists which have been passed from generation to generation, and which thus are impediments that are difficult to overcome.

Some scholars have referred to the Dungannon Rural District Council (population 25,000) in particular as having subjected Nationalists to housing discrimination. In 1964, a Catholic family named McKennan was evicted, and their house was allocated to Emily Beattie. Ms. Beattie was a single nineteen-year-old Protestant woman who worked as secretary to a local Unionist councillor.[64] [Author's note: A councillor is a member of the town, or city, council. American jargon would usually term these elected officials as "councilmen" or "councilwomen."]

The 1971 census revealed that of the 148,000 public housing units, only 45,000-55,000 were occupied by Catholics. This is perhaps a picture of what might be presumed to be anti-Catholic discrimination. However, it actually points to a disproportion that favors Catholics, since 30.7% of public housing was allocated to members of a group—Catholics—which comprised only 26.1% of all households in Northern Ireland. Nonetheless, one must look further to see a substantiation of the anti-Catholic premise. The U.K. allocation principle gives larger families housing priority, taking into account relative income and existing housing conditions.

Because the 1971 figures showed that 78% of families with six or more children were Catholic, the swinging statistics do indicate some evidence of anti-Catholicism in public housing.[65]

Housing in general in Northern Ireland does not meet the usual acceptable standards. In this same 1971 study, statistics show that as many as 30% of all houses in the province did not have sole use for residents of a unit of basic facilities such as water and indoor toilets.[66] This is a fact that has been cited as direct proof of housing discrimination in view of the proportion of large families which are Catholic.

DISCRIMINATORY GERRYMANDERING IN THE U.S.A.

The United States is no stranger to the coining of phrases, and "gerrymandering" is a term of American origin. In 1812, Massachusetts Governor Elbridge Gerry had approved a redistricting plan which would assure his Republican Party a safe control of the state legislature. Because one of the newly revised districts was so convoluted and misshapen as to resemble what one opposed legislator described as a salamander, the term "gerrymander" was born.[67]

To compare with the UK, the U.S. Supreme Court agreed with a constitutional challenge to a legislative reapportionment plan on grounds of racism. The case was *Baker v. Carr*,[68] the so-called "one-man-one-vote" decision, which prohibited race-board apportionment.

Then in a surprising 2001 decision, *Hunt v. Cromartie*,[69] the Court approved a North Carolina redistricting plan which resulted in dominant black districts, but which the state legislature had justified as having been based on *politics* rather than *race*. That is, the legislators' purpose was to assure a "safely Democratic district." The plan had been challenged under the Equal Protection Clause of the Fourteenth Amendment as having been crafted to concentrate black voters within the subject districts.

Polls showed that far more whites who had registered Democrat crossed over and voted Republican than did blacks. (Notably, blacks register and vote the Democrat ticket between 95% and 97% of the time.) This particular redistricting had resulted in a near solid-black/Democrat block. The Democratic legislature's strategy had been to achieve districting such that a normally black Democrat district would remain Democrat in such a manner that any newly created district would also be a "safe harbor" as a solid Democrat district. In other words, since most blacks were Democrat, to redistrict on party lines would necessarily involve the same concurrent effect on racial lines. The claim of the legislature was that party alone, not race, had determined the change of district lines.

A split (5-4) U.S. Supreme Court agreed with the North Carolina legislature and approved the plan which achieved racial gerrymandering by way of using political party segmentation as the rationale. Interestingly, the Court had held unconstitutional on Fourteenth Amendment grounds an earlier redistricting effort by this same state legislature because its "unconventional" and snake-like shape, together with past history, evidenced a deliberate attempt to create a majority black district.[70] The rationale of the 2001 Court's approval of the revised redistricting was that its purpose had been political rather than racial.

Using the *Hunt* decision as a sanction for redistricting, provided the purpose was political rather than racial, the 2001 majority Republican Virginia General Assembly adopted a controversial redistricting draft which would favor the Republican Party.[71] In the *Hunt* Court's approved manner, as long as an amalgamation of one party over the other is the aim of the legislature, it will meet constitutional muster, even though the major effect is to cluster population within a voting district according to race.

The new GFA-implementing statute for Northern Ireland would make this plan unlawful in the province. Since one of the "no-no" grounds of discrimination in Northern Ireland is political belief, such maneuvering would be unlawful gerrymandering on that ground. Moreover, since the majority of Nationalists are Catholics, and the majority of Unionists are Protestants, such redistricting, even if political gerrymandering *were* in fact lawful, would be futile. The religious-political affiliation is so conjoined that any effort to achieve political dominance would simultaneously achieve a religious dominance, also illegal.

Charges of anti-Catholicism via gerrymandering has overlapped into the area of housing. The claim has been that local authorities commonly build public housing which will be allotted to Catholics only in areas already predominantly Nationalist. This practice would contain this growing minority within a political division where they are already dominant, leaving the more populous Unionists to prevail in the more heavily populated areas. One example of such Catholic concentration is in Enniskillen, County Fermanagh. Political scientist Graham Gudgen has described this as "malpractice to maintain Union control." [72]

Committee on Administration of Justice

Any chapter on human rights law in Northern Ireland would be sorely lacking without mention of the Committee on Administration of Justice (CAJ). This civil liberties non-governmental organization (referred to in Northern Ireland by the acronym NGO) is clearly *not* Northern Ireland's version of the American Civil Liberties Union (ACLU).

Although the ACLU is largely concerned with violations of constitutional rights, that body's work takes a dramatically different direction than does the CAJ. The ACLU tends to focus primarily on the First Amendment right to freedoms of speech and religion and the Eighth Amendment's proscription of cruel and usual punishment. Using the latter as an argument, the ACLU is frequently a litigator in death penalty cases. Since capital punishment is not lawful in the United Kingdom, nor in Europe in general, this is not an issue for CAJ.

Moreover, the ACLU's involvement in religious issues more often broaches the issue of the non-establishment of religion clause of the First Amendment.[73] For example, the ACLU filed *amicus curiae* briefs[74] or provided assisting or even lead counsel for persons such as the convicted defendants in *Stone v. Graham.*[75] This was on behalf of the challengers of a Kentucky state statute which required the posting of the Ten Commandments in all public schools. The ACLU did the same for the plaintiffs in *Santa Fe Independent School District v. Jane Doe et al.*[76] The *Santa Fe* plaintiffs challenged the reading of a prayer, by vote of the student body, before each home football game at a Texas public school. The ACLU was on the victorious side in both cases, the Supreme Court holding that each of these practices constituted an unconstitutional establishment of religion.

Another such case was *Lamb's Chapel v. Center Moriches School District.*[77] In this case, the Supreme Court held that a public high school annual graduation ceremony which began with prayer by a local clergyman violated the non-establishment-of-religion-clause. These would be non-issues in Northern Ireland, where the primary complaint with regard to religion is discrimination against those belonging to the minority Catholic belief. Moreover, religion is inextricably intertwined in the fabric of Northern Ireland's schools, albeit two different approaches depending upon whether they are public (Protestant) or "controlled" (Catholic). (Chapter 9 discusses the sectarian school system in Northern Ireland.) Because of this, the American non-establishment clause is difficult for those in both Northern Ireland and the Republic of Ireland, and indeed, in most western European countries, to understand.

Another distinction between the concept of freedom of speech in the American sense and the GFA's treatment of what is appropriate is evident in the display and/or treatment of patriotic or secular symbols. In *Texas v. Johnson,*[78] a conviction under a Texas state statute that prevented desecration of designated objects, including the American and state flags, was overturned by the U.S. Supreme Court as an unlawful interference with First Amendment freedom of speech. The defendant in *Johnson* had burned a U.S. flag at a demonstration protesting the current administration's policies. The Court regarded this as an expression, however despicable or objectionable, and one protected by the constitution.

Also, in *R.A.V. v. City of St. Paul, Minnesota*[79] the Supreme Court struck down a city ordinance which prohibited the use of words that insulted or provoked violence because they were based upon race, color, creed, religion or gender. This defendant was a member of the Ku Klux Klan who had been convicted of burning a cross. This is one of the major activities of the Klan which represents hatred for persons belonging to certain racial or ethic groups such as blacks and/or Jews. The Court held that this activity, too, was constitutionally protected as an expression. The decisions in both *Johnson* and *R.A.V.* were close—5-4. The *R.A.V.* Court expressly stated that the First Amendment does not permit the imposition of limits or restriction on expressions just because they relate to sensitive or unfavorable subjects.

To the contrary, the language of the GFA is politically correct to the extreme. One result has been the prohibition of displaying the British flag at police buildings, and the change of the police badge so as not to reflect anything British (removal of the crown) or Irish (removal of the harp and shamrocks).[80] The GFA's direction was to dispense with all vestiges of symbols which might be hurtful or objectionable, or which might strike a nerve of ethnic or religious sensitivity. Such symbols would be routinely protected under the U.S. Constitution, regardless of whom may realistically be offended. Thus, it is important to keep in mind these two diametrically opposed mindsets. The "civil liberties" with which the CAJ is concerned, then, bear little resemblance to those that the ACLU upholds.

The CAJ devotes its efforts and resources to four areas: (i) reform of policing; (ii) repeal of the emergency laws (discussed in Chapter 7 on Policing); (iii) enactment of a bill of rights for Northern Ireland; and (iv) achieving equality. This office works closely with Amnesty International, especially with regard to allegations of mistreatment of prisoners and wrongful convictions.

The office's legal advisor is Paul Mageean, a young Queen's Law School educated barrister who evinces a sincere passion for his work. When Paul agreed to meet with me, he gave me explicit and detailed directions to CAJ's "hard-to-find" office. In the north of the city, the CAJ headquarters office is located quite near the Human Rights Commission offices. Both are just south of St. Anne's (Church of Ireland) Cathedral, on Donegall Street. (To the first-time visitor to Belfast, street names can prove quite confusing because of the repetition. There is a Donegall Pass, a Donegall Square, a Donegall Place, and a Donegall Street. Note the spelling which is different from the county, Donegal. Donegall with two "l"s is the surname of one of Northern Ireland's prominent families in the heyday of the linen industry.) Paul's directions were that one should turn into an alley off Donegall Street, behind a well-known pub which he named, diagonally across the street from another pub the latter marked with a large sign reading "Imbibing Emporium," a fact that still brings a chuckle. (The omnipresent pubs in Ireland and Northern Ireland provide many a landmark.)

Humble, unassuming, and small to the point of being cramped, the CAJ office resembled most of the governmental offices I visited. Indeed, except for the posh and sumptuous setting—exterior and interior—of Stormont and the Assembly members' offices, most were modest and unpretentious, but functional. One has the impression of a prevailing "let's-get-down-to-business" attitude, and fancy trappings seemed immaterial.

CAJ receives its financial support from about 400 members including British and American foundations such as a Quaker foundation in England and Ford Motor Company in the U.S.A. Although this office is not empowered to prosecute or to sue on behalf of anyone in Northern Ireland, it might do so at the European

Court of Human Rights in Strasbourg. Paul frequently appears in that forum in his role as barrister.

He spoke about his intense personal disdain for the Diplock trials and for the long-lasting "emergency" laws (both described in Chapter 7). "An 80-year emergency we've had!" he retorted. Paul seemed saddened when he told me that the first public contact which most of the youth in Northern Ireland have is with the police, whose harassment, according to Paul, "turns them into terrorists." A young father himself, his anxiety over this phenomenon was evident.

Paul remarked that he personally had "no great desire for a united Ireland," but that his primary hope with respect to the peace process is a curtailment of the need for the current abundance of security. Excitedly, he remarked that the "peace process has changed our way of working" and that people who had resisted any change had virtually "gone into overdrive," and had accepted the inevitability of real reform.

He was harshly critical of what he termed a failure to implement the "targeting-social-need" principles already adopted into statutory law, explaining that it usually is Nationalists who suffer because of a lack of enforcement of the law. ("Targeting Social Needs" program is referred to as TSN. The use of letters for offices or programs typical in Northern Ireland is reminiscent of the U.S. Army, which seems to have an acronymic language of its own.) Paul cited the "Catch-22" situation in largely Nationalist Strabane which has the highest unemployment rate in the province. He explained that, since the government built major roads and streets only in predominantly Unionist areas, no businesses would locate in Strabane, with its inadequate road system. Consequently, the Catholic unemployment problem is perpetuated. Paul said that a "Catholic man is two and one-half times more likely to be out of work in Northern Ireland than [is] a Protestant."

He seemed embittered over what he called a "hierarchy of victims." Paul described persons killed by paramilitaries as "first-class victims," while those killed by the British Army or the RUC were relegated to "second class." Quite clearly, he was not enamored with the then current security force situation.

Although CAJ had taken no stance on the release-of-prisoners issue ("there are no applicable human rights standards," Paul explained), he expressed that he had a "great deal of sympathy with *all* the victims." (By implication, he seemed to include the prisoners within the concept of "victims.") He insisted, however, that the "political reality" is that the GFA would not have been signed without the release of prisoners promise, a position which appeared to be consistent among most supporters of the GFA.[81]

CAJ might best be described as a non-governmental body with one foot in the Human Rights Commission's domain, and the other on the turf of the Equality Commission.

Counteract

Another NGO which tackles sectarian discrimination in the workplace is Counteract. An anti-intimidation group founded in 1990, this office is supported financially by the Irish Congress of Trade Unions (ICTU). The trade union connection is a natural one, since the all-Ireland ICTU has always taken an unwavering stand against both discrimination and the use of violence.

With a core staff of seven, the office is located on York Street in the northeast section of downtown and, fittingly for a union-oriented organization, near the docks. The director of Counteract is West Belfast born-and-bred Billy Robinson. He is a Catholic who revels in using his non-sectarian surname (Robinson might easily be either Protestant or Catholic) to make folks ponder over his religious affiliation. Before founding Counteract, Robinson was a union worker for British Telecom for some nineteen years, and he served another fourteen years negotiating on behalf of this same union. He extolled union members' fealty to one another, describing this togetherness as a "hands-off-my-mate" policy. According to Billy, most union members are irretrievably sectarian, and many have served as members of paramilitary organizations. (This fact caused me to take some issue with his "no-use-of-violence" statement.)

My meeting with Billy turned out to be both informative and fun. A nononsense and no-frills fellow whose conversation was peppered with mild (and at times not so mild) obscenities, he smiled constantly and laughed openly and freely. Billy Robinson is truly the epitome of the "what-you-see-is-what-you-get" model, and his genuineness and sincerity were refreshing. He explained that much of Counteract's work is in response to a request from a company's management for intervention in a labor dispute, a request which he said unfortunately comes as a rule after the dispute has reached nearly uncontrollable dimensions. Billy told me of one such large company which had faced a major problem with regard to workers' wearing of emblems. "Emblems," mused Billy, "are okay in themselves. It's how they're used that causes a problem."

The company in this instance was a large clothing manufacturer with approximately 3,000 factory workers in plants throughout the province. About 140 Catholic workers in one such factory with a workforce of 200 had worn black armbands to commemorate Bloody Sunday, a highly controversial 1972 Nationalist Catholic demonstration in Londonderry/Derry in which fourteen marchers were killed by British police. (This event is chronicled in Chapter 1.) Apparently, those in charge did not realize the potential of the fomenting strife, so the ensuing difficulty between the large segment of Catholic workers and their protesting Protestant counterparts was simply left to solve itself, so to speak. By the time Billy was contacted, the manager was frantic. A workers' riot had already erupted after Unionist workers participated in a sit-down strike in objection to this clearly Nationalist apparel. Management's impulsive reaction was a loudspeaker announcement that unless all workers had removed armbands within fifteen minutes, the factory would be closed. The intent was to quell the riot, but this move only further provoked both sides. Immediately following this announcement and realizing the compounded friction it had caused, management called Billy for help.

His approach was to call all Nationalist armband-wearers into a large room. He then explained to them his understanding and even empathy with their desire to honor those who had died in the tragedy that Bloody Sunday had been. In Billy's words, "Then I says, 'Do youse want to honor your dead by starting a battle? Is that what youse want? That ain't *honoring* them, that's *insulting* them!' And it worked." This explanation made eminently good sense to both sides of the dispute, and the Nationalist workers removed the armbands. Work resumed by both Nationalist and Unionist workers. In a simple manner that indicated his understanding of the reason for the wearing of the armbands as well as the reasons for the Unionist workers' objections to them, he was able to resolve this problem before it literally imploded.[82]

Billy continued, "You gotta promote the three concepts of equity, diversity and interdependence. Differences are not *wrong*," he said in a style reminiscent of Yogi Berra, but rather, "just *different*." Rather than using circuitous language to expand on the rationale for these deep-seated differences, Billy simply accepted them. Another of his observations related to the location of an unemployment center in a business park ("Northern-Irelandese" for a shopping center with several business offices). He boomed, "What's the first reaction of these businesses? To check security! And these are their potential employees! Lordy!" This was a man who felt it best to face a difficulty head-on, determined to reach a resolution by using simple common sense.

When asked his take on "political correctness," Billy called it a "negative." Regarding affirmative action, he seemed too opposed even to articulate anything printable (*i.e.*, without the spicy obscene words which clearly made his point).

I queried him about which questions might or might not be used during a job interview to indicate the religious affiliation of the applicant, questions which are "no-nos" since they are a discreet form of religious discrimination. Billy was now in his element, and he laughed out loud, saying, "Well, if the name or address doesn't give it away (the reader should keep in mind that most of Northern Ireland, in particular urban Belfast, is either a Catholic, or a Protestant, section of town), distract 'em and git 'em to spell a word with an 'h.' " For example, "I never can remember the spelling of Howth Street (a street which might be near to the applicant's address)—can you help me with it?" "If he says plain 'h,' " said Billy, "well, then, he's a Prod. If he says 'haytch,' he's a Catholic." (I later checked this one out, and he was correct.)

I then told Billy of another such interview question which I had been told would reveal one's religious preference in Belfast. This is something I had learned from Richard Steele, lecturer in labor law at Queen's University School of Law during my semester there in 1998. Richard took me to a seminar for training of human resource management professionals, and this question was mentioned. In Belfast, if the interview sways toward how the applicant uses his spare time, one might be asked, "Have you ever, by chance, done any pole-vaulting?" If the answer is in the affirmative, he is Catholic. Why? The only school in Belfast with pole-vault facilities is St. Malachy's Catholic School. Such questions enable the decision makers to refuse to employ a Catholic, provided a neutral reason is given for hiring another (a Protestant). This is what American discrimination lawyers refer to as "pretext" justification when charged with unlawful discrimination based on race or sex.[83] Or, in the Northern Ireland case with the pole-vaulting Catholic (!), the employer can simply fail to get back in touch with him about the position for which he had applied.

Billy continued by explaining that three elements are the root of all sectarian conflict: (i) fear, (ii) feelings, and (iii) lack of trust. He told another story of a group meeting in which one worker was a Muslim who apparently had been shunned by her colleagues. Billy, fascinated with a religion about which he knew little, bluntly asked her, "Hey, wudja explain that jewel in your head to me? I never did understand that." Conflict in Northern Ireland is caused by mere differences in people, whether based on religion, politics or culture. The worker responded to Billy's question, and her colleagues learned that she was not a horned toad. By pointing out that one could in fact learn something from others' differences—differences that did not make him or her "bad," but simply "different" and that these folks are therefore interesting—some of these heretofore unsolvable issues might disappear, or at least take on less significance.

Billy Robinson's "well, whatever" or "who-cares-what-your-religion-or-politics-is-because-it-doesn't-affect-me (but I'd sure be interested in hearing about it)" attitude may seem simplistic. But—in Billy's inimitable language—his, "I swear, by [expletive deleted], that it'll work" position seems at least a possibility of being one ultimate way to bring an acceptable degree of equality and respect for human rights in Northern Ireland, at least in the workplace.[84]

Conclusion

One of the trump cards of the GFA is the attention it lavishes on human rights and equality of rights. To be sure, even the most objective of observers would concur that in the past there has been an inordinate degree of governmental discrimination against Catholics. This has been evident in the allocation of public housing, the establishment of voting district boundaries, treatment by law enforcement officials, and employment. The human rights thrust of the GFA clearly acknowledges this as history and strives to present opportunities, indeed obligations, to remedy and alter this pattern. Westminster Parliament's efforts to adopt a bill of rights for Northern Ireland should make considerable inroads on achieving this goal.

Surely the Human Rights Commission and the Equality Commission must be given more legal artillery in the way of empowerment if they are to achieve the legislators' expectations. However, despite any portentous augmentation of their powers, realists know well that there can be no magic-wand readjustments which will abolish or neutralize inequality. Its vestiges will necessarily remain for some time, since housing allotments and residential divisions cannot be altered overnight.

Furthermore, the new affirmative action program favoring Catholics in police recruiting is an effort to achieve a "politically correct" balance within the force, whether or not one personally ascribes to such philosophy. And concerning any possible new "reverse gerrymandering," how quickly can a power-sharing government which has not yet been able even to function effectively within itself determine how to change voting districts in an equitable manner?

It took many years of determined and arduous discrimination for Northern Ireland to attain its current status of inequality. Quite plausibly, any undoing will also require much time and effort. The prayer of those who love Northern Ireland and its people is that they will be patient with the process. In time, it may prove fruitful.

Endnotes to Chapter 8

[1] Speech at Stormont Hotel, December 2, 1998. Mrs. Robinson, who was born and reared in County Mayo, was the first woman to serve as President of the Republic of Ireland (1990-1997).

[2] The death penalty is unlawful in Alaska, Hawaii, Iowa, Kansas, Maine, Massachusetts, Michigan, North Dakota, South Dakota, Vermont, West Virginia, and Washington.

[3] Telephone conversation with Caoimhghim O'Murchada, calling from Londonderry/Derry, September 20, 2001.

[4] European Convention for the Protection of Human Rights and Fundamental Freedoms (1950) [ECHR].

[5] Georgia, one of the former Soviet Socialist Republics, recently became a signatory to the Convention, increasing this number to 41. *See* Knut Ipsen, *Völkerrecht* (4th ed. 1999) at 693.

[6] Belgium, Luxembourg, the Netherlands, France, Germany Italy, Greece, Spain, Portugal, the United Kingdom, the Republic of Ireland, Denmark, Austria, Finland, and Sweden make up the European Union.

[7] Art. 9 ECHR.

[8] Art. 14 ECHR.

[9] Art. 46.2, Council of Europe Convention No. 5 (1950).

[10] "European Union" (EU) is the term used to the collective body formed by the 15 member states, and "European Community" (EC) refers to the bodies authorized to make and enforce European laws.

[11] *See* Theresia Degener and Gerard Quinn, *A Survey of International and Comparative and Regional Disability Law Reforms*, at 55, presented at "From principles to Practice: Symposium in Washington, D.C., October 22-26, 2000.

[12] Art. 6(2), ex Art. F.2, Treaty of Amsterdam. This clause amended Article 46 (now Art. 6(2)) by adding the language that the EU "shall respect fundamentals guaranteed by European Convention for the Protection of Human Rights and Fundamental Freedoms (Nov.4, 1950)."

[13] Human Rights Act 1998 (HRA).

[14] *See* HUMAN RIGHTS LAW AND PRACTICE (Lord Lester of Herne Hill and David Panrick, eds., Butterworths: London, Edinburgh, and Dublin, 1999), at 10, *citing* Anthony Lester, Democracy and Individual Rights, Fabian Tract No. 390, November, 1968.

[15] *Id.* at 3.

[16] *See* Korematsu v. U.S., 323 U.S. 214 (1944), in which the U.S. Supreme Court held this executive order and subsequent legislation constitutional. Many of those persons interned were second generation Japanese who were American citizens by birth, and many of their parents were naturalized citizens. Nonetheless the Court approved the measure as appropriate during this time of war. *See* Chapter 3 on Religion and Racism for more elaboration on *Korematsu*.

[17] Northern Ireland Act 1973 (Eng.)

[18] Lester and Panrick, *supra* note 14, at 2.

[19] *Id.* at 15.

[20] *Id.* at 1.

[21] *Id.* at 2.

[22] Marbury v. Madison, 1 Cranch 137, 5 U.S. 137 (1803).

[23] *See* Stephen Livingstone, *The Northern Ireland Human Rights Commission*, 22 FORDHAM INTERNATIONAL LAW JOURNAL 1465, 1466, at n. 4 (1999).

[24] This "checks-and-balances" principle is the result of Articles I, II, and III of the UNITED STATES CONSTITUTION which enumerated respectively the powers and duties the legislature, the executive, and the judiciary.

[25] Lester and Panrick, *supra* note 14, at 15.

[26] 145 Eur. Ct. H.R. (ser. B) 16 (1988).

[27] Art. 5 ECHR.

[28] Brann and McBride v. United Kingdom, 258 Eur. Ct. H.R. (ser. A) at 31 (1993).

[29] Lester and Panrick, *supra* note 14, at 9.

[30] Paul Mageean and Martin O'Brien, *From the Margins to the Mainstream: Human Rights and the Good Friday Agreement*, 22 FORDHAM INTERNATIONAL LAW JOURNAL 1499, 1509 (1999).

[31] E-mail conversation with Stephen Livingstone, Director of Institute for Human Rights Law, Queen's University School of Law, Belfast, November 5, 2001.

[32] Northern Ireland Act 1998 section 68(2); and Schedule 7, sections 2(2)(a), (b).

[33] *Id.* sections 69 and 70.

[34] Interview with Chief Commissioner Brice Dickson, July 24, 2000, Northern Ireland Human Rights Commission office, Belfast.

[35] *See* CONSTITUTION OF THE REPUBLIC OF IRELAND 1937, articles 40-44; and GRUNDGESETZ (Basic Law of Germany) 1949, articles 1-19.

[36] THE CONSTITUTION OF THE REPUBLIC OF SOUTH AFRICA of 1996, Act No. 108 of 1996.

[37] Rights, Safeguards and Equality of Opportunity, para. 4, GFA.

[38] Art. 6 ECHR.

[39] Westminster has indeed given Wales the statutory right to use Welsh in court proceedings. Welsh Courts Act 1942 (Eng.)

[40] "A Bill of Rights: Your Questions Answered," publication of the Northern Ireland Human Rights Commission (2000), available to the general public.

[41] Abortion Act 1967 (Eng.).

[42] Eamonn McCann, *Abortion law is in a moral and legal mess*, BELFAST TELEGRAPH, August 2, 2000, at 10, col. 3-7.

[43] Betty Gibson, *Cross-border fears over Rights bill*, PRO-LIFE TIMES, May 7, 200, at 1, col. 3-4. Ms. Gibson speaks on behalf of SPUC (Society for the Protection of Unborn Children).

[44] Northern Ireland Act 1998, section 75.

[45] Rights, Safeguards and Equality of Opportunity, para. 6, GFA.

[46] Northern Ireland Act 1998, section 75(1)(a)-(d).

[47] The major American federal anti-workplace discrimination statutes are the Equal Pay Act, 29 U.S.C. section 206(d)(1963), which prohibits pay disparity between the sexes for substantially equal work for the same employer; Title VII of the 1964 Civil Rights Act, 42 U.S.C. section 2000e, which prohibits discrimination in any form if based on the race, color, religion, national origin, or sex of the employee; the 1967 Age Discrimination in Employment Act (ADEA), 29 U.S.C. section 621 which makes unlawful any discrimination based on age if the plaintiff is 40 years of age or older; the 1973 Rehabilitation Act, 29 U.S.C. section 706, which prohibits discrimination against any person with a handicap in the federal sector, or by private companies with annual contracts with the federal government in a minimum amount of $10,000; and the 1990 Americans with Disabilities Act (ADA), 42 U.S. sections 12101 *et seq.* which essentially extends to the private sector the same protections to persons with disabilities which the Rehabilitation Act provided in the public sector.

[48] Northern Ireland Act 1998, sections 75(a)-(d).

[49] House of Commons Official Report, 27 July 1998, col. 109.

[50] Northern Ireland Act 1998, Schedule 9, para. 4(2)(2), (b); para. 5; and para. 9(2).

[51] *Id.* at Schedule 9, para. 4(2).

[52] *Id.* at Schedule 9, para. 6(1)(a), (b); and para. 7(3).

[53] The EEOC was established by Title VII of the 1964 Civil Rights Act, *supra* note 47. It is the administrative body which initially handles complaints of workplace discrimination under Title VII, the ADEA, and the ADA.

[54] 1998 Northern Ireland Act, Schedule 9, para. 10.

[55] Title VII, section 706. This 180-day period is lengthened to 300 days in deferral states with EEOC-approved state agencies which will first handle charges of discrimination. After the state agency has concluded its process, or 180 days after the charge was lodged with the agency without such a conclusion whichever comes first, the case is transferred to the EEOC.

[56] Northern Ireland Act, Part VII, para. 74(2).

[57] SACHR had been established in the Northern Ireland Constitution Act 1973 (Eng.), then replacing in part the Government of Ireland Act 1920.

[58] Fair Employment Act 1976 (Eng.).

[59] *Id.*

[60] *See* Christopher McCrudden, *Mainstreaming Equality in the Governance of Northern Ireland*, 22 FORDHAM INTERNATIONAL LAW JOURNAL 1698, 1706 (1999).

[61] CENTRAL SECRETARIAT CIRCULAR 5/93 Policy Appraisal and Fair Treatment, December 22, 1993.

[62] *See, e.g.,* Graham Gudgin, *Discrimination in Housing and Employment Under the Stormont Administration*, Chapter 5, THE NORTHERN IRELAND QUESTION: NATIONALISM, UNIONISM AND PARTITION (Patrick J. Roche and Brian Barton, eds., Avebury Press, Oxford, England, 1999).

[63] *Id.* at 28, n. 3, *quoting* Brendan O'Leary and John McGarry, THE POLITICS OF ANTAGONISM: UNDERSTANDING NORTHERN IRELAND, at 129. (Athlone Press, London, England.)

[64] *Id.* at 100.

[65] *Id.* at 101-102.

[66] *Id.* at 103.

[67] *See* "Gerrymandering," WORLD BOOK ENCYCLOPEDIA, Vol. 8 (1978), at 160.

[68] 369 U.S. 186 (1962). Note that the Court in *Baker* also announced the "political question" doctrine that some issues are purely political and within the domain of the legislature, and therefore not appropriate for judicial review. The *Baker* Court, however, did not deem this doctrine applicable in this instance, and thus decided the case.

[69] 532 U.S. 234, 121 S.Ct. 1452 (2001).

[70] Shaw v. Hunt, 517 U.S. 899, 116 S.Ct. 1894 (1996) (Shaw II).

[71] *See* Tyler Whitney, *Governor signs redistricting bills*, RICHMOND TIMES-DISPATCH, April 24, 2001, at A-1, col. 2-3.

[72] Gudgen, *supra* note 63, at 105.

[73] While the First Amendment assures freedom of religion, it also prohibits Congress from making any law that respects the establishment of religion.

[74] For the non-lawyer, *amicus curiae* is a Latin phrase meaning "friend of the court." A non-party might file such a brief with supporting legal authority for one party's position when the decision of the court would affect the non-party *amicus* in the future.

[75] 449 U.S. 39, 101 S.Ct. 192 (1981).

[76] 530 U.S. 290, 120 S.Ct. 2266 (2000).

[77] 113 S.Ct. 2141 (1993).

[78] 491 U.S. 397 (1989).

[79] 505 U.S. 377 (1992).

[80] *See* Recommendations 150, 151, and 152 in the Report of the Patten Commission.

[81] Interview with Paul Mageean, August 2, 2000, CAJ office, Belfast.

[82] This event and the Counteract philosophy and methodology are elaborated upon in Billy Robinson and Stevie Nolan, *Counteract: Working for Change*, 22 FORDHAM INTERNATIONAL LAW JOURNAL 1668 (1999).

[83] *See, e.g.,* Texas Department of Community Affairs v. Burdine, 450 U.S. 248, 101 S.Ct. 1089 (1981), where the (female) sex discrimination plaintiff had alleged the hire and subsequent promotion of a male rather than her was unlawful under Title VII. She challenged the employer's stated reason (*i.e.*, the male who had been chosen instead of her was better qualified and more closely met the employer's expectations) as being a mere pretext, and alleged that the real reason was her sex. If a plaintiff can prove that the actual reason for different treatment between the sexes was actually by reason of sex and that the company's stated legitimate reason was pretextual, the plaintiff will prevail. The plaintiff in *Burdine,* however, was not able to meet this burden.

[84] Interview with Billy Robinson, August 9, 2002, Counteract office, Belfast.

Chapter 9

Schools: *de facto* Sectarianism

"What's a Jew?" the West Belfast Catholic child asked, after having been told that Hitler hated Jews. "A Jew is someone who lives in Palestine. Jesus Himself was a Jew," answered her teacher. The child, appearing to understand, responded, "Then Hitler was an Orangie [Protestant]."

John Conroy [1]

American John Conroy's true account of living in West Belfast during the 1970's vividly illustrates the perception of the young that one must fall into one classification or the other—*i.e.*, a "*Fenian*" (Catholic) or an "Orangie" (Protestant). If Hitler hated Jews and Jesus was a Jew, then this young girl deduced that Hitler must have been Protestant. Children in Northern Ireland absorb such ideas almost by osmosis, being subtly taught to hate their denominational counterparts at the youngest of ages.

The screenwriters for the movie "South Pacific" added a song not among those Richard Rodgers and Oscar Hammerstein had written for the earlier stage musical of the same name. This song was a duet, "You've Got to be Carefully Taught." One of the singers was American Lieutenant Joe Cable, who had fallen in love with a young Polynesian woman while serving on a Naval base in the South Pacific, and he was torn by the looming cultural differences, should they ultimately marry. The other was Nellie Forbush, a Navy nurse from Little Rock, Arkansas, apparently Rodgers' and Hammerstein's exemplification of a backward and biased

Southern city. She had fallen for Emil Du Beque, a dashing Frenchman aiding American forces from his luxurious home near the base.

Nellie had just learned that Emil was a widower who had been married to a Polynesian. Further, he had two children, children who appeared Polynesian because of this genetic makeup. Joe and Nellie commiserated, struggling over their inescapable feelings of prejudice against these people who were "different," and they pondered the question of why these feelings persisted. Their conclusion was that the perception that blacks, Asians, and/or other ethnic groups simply were not as "good" as are Caucasians had been instilled in them since childhood and was as much a part of their upbringing and education as were correct manners. They had been "carefully taught."

Religious Discrimination in Northern Ireland Schools

Unfortunately, the quandary in which Nellie and Lieutenant Cable found themselves is not confined to a setting for musical fiction. Innate differences in groups of people often lead to discrimination, and this aptly describes Northern Ireland. This separation is, of course, on the basis of religion, and is reflected not only in residential segregation between Protestants and Catholics, but also in the sectarian-divided school system.

Unlike secondary schools in the Republic, in Northern Ireland one generally attends either a "Protestant" or a "Catholic" school. Although the national school system in all of Ireland had been established in 1831 to provide education for all, regardless of religious affiliation, this *de facto* segregated educational system was already the situation in the province in 1922, shortly after partition.[2]

Controlled and Voluntary Schools

This stark division of schools remains today. Schools in Northern Ireland are either "controlled" or "maintained" (also referred to as "voluntary"). "Controlled" institutions are state schools which are expressly open to all children, but which are nonetheless attended nearly exclusively by children of Protestants. "Maintained," or "voluntary," schools are owned by the Catholic church, and nearly all students are consequently Catholic.[3]

Once a child reaches the age of eleven, he or she has the opportunity to attend a "grammar school." [4] Entrance into such a school requires a successful performance on a competitive standardized examination from which only the top-scoring 33% are selected.[5] This, too, has been a major issue, since those children who gain admittance to grammar schools come predominately from controlled (*de facto* Protestant) schools.[6] Whether or not to alter, or even to retain, this selection process will be a major educational issue facing the New Northern Ireland Assembly.[7]

[An instant comparison to a similar issue in the U.S.A. comes to mind. Complaints that the Scholastic Aptitude Test (a standardized test usually required for admission to universities and which scores factor heavily in admission decisions into the more elite institutions), or SAT, is culturally biased against blacks have become a mantra.

This conclusion is one reached by inductive reasoning, one with which Walter Williams, a notable professor of economics at George Mason University in Virginia and a syndicated columnist, adamantly disagrees. He cites the 2000 California state average score on the math portion[8] of the SAT as 425 for black students, 530 for whites, and 565 for Asians and comments. Professor Williams, a black man who publicly opposes affirmative action programs, challenges one to identify any latent cultural bias in a question involving a square root of a number or the solution of a simultaneous equation problem.[9] His thesis is that a message to black students that the SAT is culturally discriminatory against them as a group is tantamount to telling them that preparation and/or a more serious approach toward school work played no role in their test outcomes—an "it's-not-my-fault" stance.

The "voluntary" school system in Northern Ireland probably was a reaction to partition. The Catholic church's opposition to the separation of the six counties of the North from the Free State of Ireland was its attempt to defend minority rights,[10] since the majority of those in the counties to be separated from the soon-to-be Free State of Ireland were Protestants. Closely conjoined with Catholic doctrine is the education of Catholic children, regarded as a religious right,[11] perhaps even a duty, and much of the fear of partition centered on its effect on schooling.

Post-Partition Education Law in Northern Ireland

After partition became a reality, a series of statutes affected education in Northern Ireland. The first such law, enacted in 1922,[12] required a declaration of allegiance to the British crown from anyone who received pay from the British government,[13] including public school teachers. The Catholic Church showed its resistance by refusing to transfer ownership of its schools to local education authorities.[14] Naturally, this removed their teachers from this requirement, an exemption which was short-lived. In 1923, Parliament responded by enacting a statute requiring all teachers (regardless of the source of their compensation) to take the same oath.[15] That same year, a comprehensive statute established education committees, a reorganization of primary education, and teacher training.[16] The implicit purpose of this law was to combat the "backward state of Northern Irish education."[17]

The statutory education committees were of particular concern to the Catholic Church. These bodies would oversee the British Parliament's financial assistance to all schools, the accreditation of schools, appointments of teachers, and scholarship funding and food allowances for poor children. Such governmental control of schools grated against the Catholic nerve, for the church staunchly supported the principle of clerically managed education at the primary level.

The total reorganization of the educational system created three categories of primary schools, and this classification remains today. Since the government would have total financial obligation to support the "transferred" schools (*i.e.*, those which would transfer ownership of the schools to the government), it would, in turn, have complete control over the first class, hence, "controlled" schools. The second class of schools would indeed receive governmental financing, but only to the extent of one-half the costs of maintenance and an unspecified amount to be allotted to capital expenses. These schools were managed by boards of six persons (the so-called "four-and-two", four who were nominated by the school's earlier managers [or trustees], and two by the local education committees established by the statute). Few chose this classification because of the lack of definiteness as to the amount of capital financing. Moreover, the presence of the two local authorities on the managing body was a repellant for the Catholic Church.

Thus, the church opted for the third classification, *i.e.*, "voluntary" schools. They would have no governmental management, but the concession was that they would receive only one-half the costs of heat, lights, and cleaning.[18] This deepened the cleavage caused by the perception among most Catholics of being victims of discrimination. Even though they unquestionably constituted the poorer part of Northern Ireland's population, their taxes nonetheless contributed toward the upkeep of schools which they felt were unsuitable for their children on religious grounds.

How about higher education? The Queen's University in Belfast, as the name infers, was the namesake of its founder, Queen Victoria. Established in 1849, the university was open to students of all (or no) religious faiths. Nonetheless, the name of Queen's gave it the aura of being a Protestant entity. School authorities cooperated with Queen's to educate teachers, another irritant for the Catholic clergy.[19]

Despite this Protestant appearance, Queens' religious neutrality is especially notable when compared with Trinity College Dublin. Established in 1592 by Queen Elizabeth I as the first university in Ireland, Trinity is renowned as the situs of the Book of Kells, the medieval manuscripts hand-printed by Ionian monks in the 9th century. Oliver Goldsmith and Samuel Beckett were educated at Trinity, a virtual lawned haven in the middle of downtown Dublin, just south of the River Liffey. Actually, one of the reasons for creating Trinity was to advance and support the Church of England, Britain's official state church.[20] Neither the British nor the Irish Parliaments had enacted a statute forbidding Catholics to attend Trinity, but internal university regulations achieved this effect.

In 1634, the Archbishop of Canterbury, the highest authority for the Church of England, approved a series of statutes, including the requirement that Trinity graduates take an Oath of Supremacy to the Church of England and denounce transubstantiation, a doctrinal principal of Catholicism. Moreover, all students were required to attend Church of England services regularly.[21] Observing and devout Catholics, of course, could not do so, but those more lax, or at least more liberal, ones likely did. The effect was to eliminate from the student body all Catholics who insisted upon adhering to the tenets of the faith.

A 1792 statute eliminated these requirements so that it was possible for Catholics to obtain degrees from Trinity.[22] Before 1793, some Catholics indeed did attend the university, and their numbers increased substantially afterwards. Early statistics are difficult to locate, if not non-existent. By 1900, Catholics constituted about 5 % to 10 % of the student body, a figure which increased to about 22 % by 1950.[23]

Despite this gradually increasing toleration of Catholics by both law and university regulations, the church itself had great difficulty condoning its parishioners' attending Trinity, a place which had so traditionally discriminated against those of the Catholic faith. Thus, there were church mandates preventing the truly faithful from attending the university. The major reason that University College of Dublin existed, which yet has a Catholic chapel as the only on-campus church, was to provide a university education for Ireland's Catholics. My personal sense is that these two excellent universities are still perceived as "Protestant" (Trinity) and "Catholic" (UCD).

There were also some restrictions on Catholics' serving as faculty and staff at Trinity. A law adopted in 1873[24] dispensed with these impediments by providing that neither a religious test nor a declaration of faith would be required for any position at Trinity.[25]

Returning to the post-partition secondary school level in Northern Ireland, the proverbial bitter icing on an already foul-tasting cake was the 1930 amendment to the Education Act. Over the objection of Catholic bishops and clergy, the law provided for Bible education in state schools upon the request of parents of at least ten students. Because the instruction would not be from the Douay (Catholic) Bible, this would not be acceptable to parents of Catholic children. Moreover, the influence of former managers of controlled, or transferred, schools (classification #1) was augmented by the new provisions. This act left Catholics with no alternative other than to continue with the strapped-for-funding voluntary schooling that had been their fate since the statute was first enacted in 1923.[26]

The GFA and Northern Ireland's Educational System

The consensus is that the "controlled"-"voluntary" separation of schools will remain and that the GFA will not alter the existing segregated status.[27] There are, of course, exceptions, since some controlled schools have a token number of Catholic students (about 3 %), and some voluntary schools have a token number of Protestants (also about 3 %). With another 3 % attending schools which are integrated (see below), the head count points to a predominantly segregated system, since over 90% of children in Northern Ireland attend a school in which they are a member of a sectarian majority.[28]

Some mention should be made of this small number of schools which are not segregated. Interestingly, since 1981 there have been in the province some twenty-six primary and seventeen secondary so-called "integrated" schools. The first such school was Lagan College, established in Belfast in September 1981, by a voluntary body which had designated itself All Children Together. This effort has not been deemed a resounding success, however, since by 1998, only 3 % the school population of Northern Ireland attended one of the integrated schools.[29]

In conjunction with the integrated school program, however, are some notable projects from which the segregated schools also might well benefit. Jerry Tyrell, a faculty member at University of Ulster Londonderry/Derry, was instrumental in initiating a unified effort to understand conflict at the primary-secondary school level. Tyrell's response to the divided school reality was his founding in 1982 of the Education for Mutual Understanding-Promoting School Project at the University of Ulster Magee Campus (Derry), and he has implemented a novel method of involving students themselves in peer mediation of problems and issues.[30] Somewhat prophetically, he had foreseen the spirit of cooperation that would later be the beacon of the GFA.

Professor Tyrell is a tall, pleasant, soft-spoken man, one whom it easy to imagine in a conciliatory role. He and Lucia McGeady, one of his advisory teachers, laughed when I asked their religion(s) and political preference(s), explaining that it was refreshing to hear such an open question (typically American). Indeed, they confirmed that the so-called "cultural politeness" that characterizes Northern Ireland—a bit like the "don't-ask-don't-tell" policy for gays in the U.S. military—contributes to the problem. Fear and mistrust preclude the open discussions which are necessary to solve difficulties arising from human differences.[31] (Incidentally, Tyrell answered without any reluctance that he is a Quaker without any particular political party affiliation. Lucia is a Catholic member of the *Sinn Féin* party.)

Seamus Dunn, Tyrell's counterpart at the University of Ulster Coleraine, has termed the mentality in Northern Ireland a "culture of politeness,"[32] differing from Tyrell's "silent acquiescence" only by terminology. Professor Dunn maintains that most people on one side of the divide do not even know persons on the other side, and that there is an intentional avoidance of confronting one another to discuss the problems.

Billy Robinson heads Counteract, a labor-union founded association in Belfast, an office which works with companies to solve labor strife arising from the division. He concurs that this unwillingness to discuss the underlying causes of a dispute adds fuel to an already raging fire. Robinson states in no uncertain terms that "political correctness" is a negative and an impediment to problem solving.[33]

Even though the sectarian division of the vast majority of schools in Northern Ireland will probably remain at least for the next several years, Tyrell's approach is instructive with respect to how to teach children from both communities at an early age to respect the religious differences in the province. His Center for the Study of Conflict at the University of Ulster has sponsored workshops for adults in Northern Ireland, England, and the Netherlands on using peer mediation.[34] The purpose of these workshops is to equip these adult participants with some knowledge about teaching this method to children, and the hope is to achieve some of the spirit of cooperation and respect promoted in the GFA.

Professor Tyrell's experience is not fluff—he worked with the Shankill Butchers, a group whom only their mothers could love. They were convicted and sentenced to life in prison on February 20, 1979, for the murders of nineteen Catholics in Belfast. The Shankill Butchers' killings are usually considered among the most brutal, and the mere mention of this group evokes a shudder.[35]

Significant for primary education in Northern Ireland is the exemption of educational institutions from the post-GFA anti-discrimination legislation.[36] The law generally requires public authorities to promote equality of opportunity between persons of different religious belief or political opinion, among other areas.[37] This provision exempting schools by inference represented deference to the Catholic Church, which allows it to grant preferences to Catholic applicants for teaching positions.[38] Despite the probable retention of segregated schools, however, the ongoing theme of the GFA is for cross-community cooperation and mutual acknowledgment of differences. Among the basic principles of the GFA is "protection and vindication of the human rights of all...[and]...partnership, equality and mutual respect."[39] (One comment overheard by the author was that, if one squeezed a copy of the GFA and its implementing legislation, human rights would likely ooze out. This underlying theme of respect of human rights will necessarily carry over into school issues.)

Minister for Education

Both the GFA and the implementing legislation listed education as one of the devolved, or transferred, areas.[40] This means that the Westminister Parliament vests in the New Northern Ireland Assembly the exclusive power to legislate with regard to schools. The statute provides for no more than ten Ministerial offices,[41] and the New Northern Ireland Assembly chose the maximum. Although the parliamentary process cannot be directly compared with the U.S.' separation of powers principle whereby the legislative, executive, and judicial branches of government are distinct with a clear balance of powers among the three, the closest parallel would be the Cabinet. (Note that Ministers are actually members of the legislature in a parliamentary system, while the U.S. system places cabinet members under the executive department, appointed by the president, but requiring Senate confirmation.)

Interestingly, two of these ministerial slots are allotted to education, one for primary/secondary education (Department of Education for Northern Ireland) and the other, for higher education (Department of Further and Higher Education and Training and Employment).

The method of allocating these offices on a bi-partisan basis is quixotic, (the mysterious d'Hondt system is explained in Chapter 5) Essentially, there is assured proportional representation among the Ministers.[42] The choice for Minister of Education under this process fell to the extreme Nationalist Catholic party, *Sinn Féin*, and the party leader, Gerry Adams, would be in charge of selecting which MLA would receive this plum position.

Speculation was that Adams would choose Barbaire de Brun, who had been a teacher herself and who had no connections with the dreaded IRA. His choice of Martin McGuinness instead was a shock to all, Nationalists included. McGuinness had always been suspected (a suspicion which was later to be confirmed) of having been the IRA's Commander in Northern Ireland. Moreover, McGuinness had quit school at the age of fifteen, so his qualifications for this post were dubious, at best.[43] One might even compare this to the appointment of Adolph Hitler to the governing board of a synagogue. Why Adams chose McGuinness remains a subject of debate, but there was some conjecture that this was Adams' way of exacting some degree of revenge against the UUP's David Trimble for his insistence of a deadline on paramilitary decommissioning during the negotiations leading to the agreement.[44]

The general public reacted negatively to giving someone with terrorist connections the responsibility of their children's education. During this wave of controversy, it was reported that McGuinness had even withdrawn his own children from school when the RUC paid a visit.[45]

Immediately after appointments for all ministerial posts were announced to the Assembly, Sammy Wilson, Deputy Minister of Education from Ian Paisley's DUP, responded. He said to the gathering in general, but not to McGuinness specifically,[46] that apparently his role would be that of a "Doberman at McGuinness' heels." McGuinness' later indirect response to Wilson's remark, made to the entire Assembly in its January 31, 2000 session was that the "place for a Doberman is at the heel of the Master."[47] Was this was a prelude to the respect envisioned by the GFA drafters to be afforded members of the Assembly of opposite parties?

Statutory Curriculum

Issues of education in the U.S.A. are among those delegated to the states,[48] and curriculum may indeed differ substantially from one jurisdiction to another. In a smaller country, or a province such as Northern Ireland, however, the usual scheme is for standardization. My friend Laura Lundy of the School of Law at Queen's University Belfast, an expert on education law, has noted critical differences between curricum laws in Northern Ireland from those in other parts of the United

Kingdom. She makes a particular reference to the provision for inclusion of the Irish language in the general course of study in Northern Ireland.[49]

The GFA required the government to impose upon the educational office the duty to encourage and facilitate the promotion of Irish education.[50] Although this provision was generally considered a positive one for Nationalists, the GFA also refers to Ulster Scots, a language connected to the culture of those among the population of Ulster who are Protestant descendants of Scottish planter immigrants to the island. This preservation of languages in school curricula is now reflected in legislation.[51]

Before the first suspension of the New Northern Ireland Assembly, Minister of Education McGuinness had announced that *Comhairle Na Gaelscholaiochta* would receive 500,000 pound sterling in trust for each of the next two successive years to be used for the promotion of the Irish language in schools. (*Comhairle Na Gaelscholaiochta* is translated literally from the Irish as "the organization for Irish language scholarship," *i.e.*, teaching completely in the Irish language. This term has now taken on a particular meaning in Northern Ireland as the name of an establishment which provides an opportunity for organizations involved in the Irish-medium education sector to work together. There is currently a progressive effort to establish an Irish-medium trust fund, *Iontaobhas na Gaelscolaiochta*, to support the development of this cohesive effort.[52]) Ms. Lundy, commenting on the current absence in Northern Ireland schools of any teaching of the Ulster Scots language, says that this will mandate some curriculum changes. In her words, "The agreement demands '*eeksie peeksie*'" (Ulster Scots for equality of treatment).[53]

Moreover, Ms. Lundy credits the GFA[54] with having provided the impetus for the Westminster Parliament to ratify the European Charter for Regional or Minority Languages. She predicts some far-reaching effects of this ratification, not only for Northern Ireland on other devolved governments in the U.K., Wales and Scotland. In Northern Ireland, she notes that the second most frequently used language in Northern Ireland is Chinese, due to the influx of immigrants from China. (Jean Jones, my landlady in Belfast, made an observation with which I have found no exceptions: "Every town or village in Northern Ireland has at least one Chinese restaurant"[55]) Ms. Lundy's opinion is that this statute should have an impact upon a system that currently requires only the teaching of French, Spanish, Italian, and German, in addition to English.

Surprisingly, civic education has not been required in the curriculum within the province. Ms. Lundy bemoans this, concluding that children who are a part of a setting with a history of violence might well be ignorant of the structures of political and government structure. She deems incorporating this study into the statutory curriculum as essential if devolution is to succeed.[56]

Cultural Identities and Programs for
Children Beyond the School Setting

Commingled with the religion factor which has bred separate schools is that of cultural pride. People speak in Northern Ireland only occasionally of "Britishness," but frequently of "Irishness." Some even dispute the existence of any culture in the province that is "British" other than the "indisputably British complexion in the primary and secondary schools."[57]

However, in more recent years, there has been a sense of a culture unique to Unionists in Northern Ireland, differentiating them from those across the Irish Sea. The Belfast Festival at Queen's University has been held each fall since 1964, the same year of the opening of the Ulster Folk Museum in Omagh. The Ulster Museum in Botanic Gardens at Queen's University and the Linenhall Library in Belfast focus on the history of Northern Ireland. In 1971, the Arts Council in Belfast (established in 1962) published *Causeway: The Arts in Ulster*, edited by poet Michael Longley, an account of artistic achievements in Northern Ireland including poetry, architecture, jazz and traditional Irish music (although the latter is generally associated with a culture which is strictly Irish).[58] Yet, there is rarely, if ever, any mention of political independence for Northern Ireland, and most would readily concede that this would be an economic impossibility.

There are many indicators that, despite their strong opposition to a united Ireland, even a sizeable constituency of Unionists still do not truly identify with the United Kingdom. For example, Mark Robinson, DUP member of the Assembly, told me that Tony Blair (British Prime Minister) and Peter Mandelson (immediate past Secretary of State for Northern Ireland) speak for the Labour government's general policy on Northern Ireland, and that the British government simply wants to do "whatever is necessary to appease Nationalists" and to assure that there are "no more bombs on the mainland."[59]

One apolitical figure, but one with much wisdom on political affairs, is a prominent judge in Northern Ireland. He told me that his opinion was that many persons feel that the only reason *Sinn Féin* is a part of the new government of the province is "because Tony Blair gave in to them." The judge's sense is that people simply do not believe Blair, whom he compared in this regard to former U.S. President Bill Clinton.[60] (Clinton suffered from a critical loss of credibility resulting from his many blatantly false public statements to the people.[61])

Thus, there is the feeling of a "Northern-Ireland-culture-by-default" among Unionists, one that is removed from anything truly "British." The zeal for Irish culture among Nationalists is dramatic by contrast, but there is no doubt that historical events separate the two in a cultural sense. These variant cultures ease into a child's psyche, and the separate schools strengthen the differences.

There have been distinct efforts toward reconciliation by both Protestants and Catholics, and one such ecumenical program was founded by a former prisoner of war in World War II Germany, Rev. Ray Davey. A Presbyterian minister in the Republic, Davey founded the Corrymeela Community at Ballycastle in County Antrim, Northern Ireland in 1965. The purpose was to provide a forum where people of all faiths might discuss the process of reconciliation.[62]

Notably, there have been many volunteer programs which sponsor summer stays for children from Northern Ireland in the United States. The one in the author's home city of Richmond, Virginia began with a program in which a family would be asked to house one child for the designated period, usually a month, and to participate with him or her in the group projects with other children from both Protestant and Catholic homes. The Richmond program, like similar ones, has evolved into one which asks that a family house two children, one from each background. The everyday-family setting interface has proven a successful way to show children that their counterparts are actually "pretty cool," and many interdenominational friendships have thus been formed. The unspoken hope is that some of this revelation will be passed on to their parents.

Even commendable programs such as these are attacked with the distrust prevailing in Northern Ireland, and a personal story is an example. The night before I left Belfast in summer 2000, I went to White's Tavern, Belfast's oldest pub (established 1630). In White's, one can always hear typical Irish music, usually by a group known as the Smugglers. Conversation flows freely in Irish pubs, and three men in their early-mid thirties began to talk with me. We discussed my reason for being in Belfast, and they immediately identified themselves as laborers from Protestant North Belfast.

They were solidly Unionist, and they spoke of their admiration for Johnny "Mad Dog" Adair, the recently released Loyalist prisoner. Adair lived in their neighborhood. These were essentially good men, and they passionately endorsed Northern Ireland's continued unity with the United Kingdom. Each of them told me that they had young children, and the pride in their families was evident. When I told them about this American program and suggested that they consider it for their children, each immediately reacted negatively. The disbelief that their children would ever be permitted to participate in such an activity still rings in my ears. "What do yuz think? That *my* kid would be chosen? No way! These are just *Sinn Féin* political maneuvers, all manipulated by Gerry Adams, Martin McGuinness, and their ilk. I'd be stupid to apply for such a program for my kid, because the only Prods they'd choose are those who aren't involved and who kowtow to Taigs." ("Taig" is a derogatory reference to a Catholic unless used internally by one Catholic to another. When an "outsider" speaks of a "Taig," it is always taken as an offense.)

This is a personification of the saying that "no good deed goes unpunished," and of the reality that there is a predominant distrust of anything designed to promote cooperation between members of both sides. Even the most well intended of efforts are viewed with suspicion by hardliners in Northern Ireland.

RACE DISCRIMINATION AND AMERICAN PUBLIC SCHOOLS (WITH SOME COMPARISONS TO RELIGIOUS DISCRIMINATION IN THE NORTHERN IRELAND SCHOOL SETTING)

Just as Ireland was the site of traditional anti-Catholic treatment, the United States has suffered from race discrimination. The *Dred Scott* decision[63] marked the official stamp of an affirmation that American blacks were regarded as an inferior class, but this was not an attitude which spontaneously emerged from Justice Taney's pen in 1857. The recognition that the single function of blacks as a group was indentured servitude had long been a sort of tacit assumption. For example, Presidents George Washington and Thomas Jefferson owned slaves.

The Civil War (1861-1865) was fought primarily over states' right, and many claim that the only states' rights issue of any relevance was whether or not slavery might be lawful or not at each state's discretion. The Southern states' position was that the federal government was unnecessarily and unconstitutionally encroaching on these rights.

The end of the war in 1865 reunited a broken country. Three successive constitutional amendments freed the slaves and vested them with substantial rights not earlier recognized,[64] but it was the Fourteenth Amendment (1868) which ultimately gave rise to litigation over the constitutionality of racially separated public schools. The Equal Protection Clause of this provision assured to all "persons" the "equal protection" of the laws, and to all "citizens," now including former slaves, all "privileges and immunities" attendant to citizenship.

The pre-1960's South clung to the idea that equality did not require co-mingling of the races. *Plessy v. Ferguson*[65] upheld a Louisiana law requiring separate wagons for blacks and white on public transportation, assuming that the two facilities were equal in quality. It took nearly sixty years for the constitutionality of racially separate public schools to be challenged.

Racial Separation in the Public Education Setting

In *Sweatt v. Painter*,[66] the Supreme Court held that admission of a qualified black applicant to the University of Texas School of Law was constitutionally required, irrespective of any proven equality of physical facilities in an all-black Texas University that had admitted him. The Court reasoned that to limit him to the one-race law school would separate him from those students who belong to a group constituting 85 % of the state's population (*i.e.*, white). Since most lawyers, judges, jurors, and witnesses with whom the plaintiff would later deal as a member of the bar belong to this segment, the Court held that his education would be unequal to the one he might attain at the University of Texas.

Decided on the same day as *Sweatt* and addressing a similar, but not identical, issue, was *McLaurin v. Oklahoma State Regents*.[67] The plaintiff was a black student enrolled in the University of Oklahoma School of Education graduate program. He was required to sit in a separate part of the school cafeteria, and he was assigned a table in the library separated from the general area used by other (*i.e.,* white) students. He claimed this to be a violation of the Clause, and a unanimous Court agreed. Using the same rationale as in *Sweatt,* the Court pointed out that there are integral parts to one's higher education which go beyond physical facilities and held that among these are studying, discussing pertinent issues relating to his area of study, and exchanging views with other students. Depriving him of these opportunities was held to render his education unconstitutionally inferior.

Probably since both *Sweatt* and *McLaurin* addressed education at the law school and graduate study levels, the decisions were not directly applicable to public grammar and high schools. Then came *Brown v. Board of Education of Topeka.*[68]

After having granted certiorari, the Supreme Court revisited its reasons for the *Sweatt* and *McLaurin* decisions, in particular *McLaurin,* where there was no question but that physical provisions were equal. A unanimous Court held the same rationale to be applicable, even "with added force," at the grade and high school levels. Chief Justice Earl Warren's landmark opinion stated that separating children according to their races at this stage in their lives "generates a feeling of inferiority as to their status in the community that may affect their hearts and minds in a way unlikely ever to be undone."

Brown ended the separate-but-equal view of *Plessy,* at least in the area of public schooling, the Court holding that racially separate educational facilities are inherently unequal. Interestingly, in 1868, shortly after the Civil War, eight *northern* states permitted segregated public schools, and five other *northern* states actually excluded black children from public schools.[69] Thus, the idea that the races should remain separate was not confined to the South, but was indeed the usual consensus throughout the country.

Some Personal Vignettes

Growing up in a small Southern town, I never attended grammar or high school with a single black student. There were white schools, and black schools. My parents were fundamentally good, decent, and completely unprejudiced, but it likely never occurred to them or to any of their contemporaries that the separate schools violated federal law. Indeed, everything was separated by race.

I cannot recall any public water fountains in Big Stone Gap, Virginia, the little town where we lived, perhaps because it was small. However, Mama often took us to Kingsport (a small city in northwest Tennessee, thirty-eight miles from my little Virginia town) to shop, and in Kingsport there were always two fountains side-by-side—one marked "whites," and the other, "coloreds."

The sole remaining movie theater in our town—television was likely the reason for the demise of the other two theaters—had a single entrance, but separate seating. Inside the theater there was a stairway which led to a small (and probably less comfortable seating) section reserved for black patrons, *i.e.*, the "colored" section. In this upstairs section were also located the bathrooms, which were not for the use of black customers. Of course, they paid the same price for a ticket, but I never really thought of this separation as relegating them to a lower "class." However, in retrospect, my family and friends would probably agree that this was its effect.

If anyone was asked how many restaurants were in town, he or she would probably respond that there were two: Riley's and Carmine's (owned and operated by my delightful Uncle Carl and Aunt Carmine Murphy). In reality, there was a third, Ray's, owned by Ray Barnes. However, Ray was a "colored" man, a fact that did not bother my wonderfully unbiased father at all. Daddy would sometimes say, "Nobody can fry fish and make hush puppies like Ray," so he would call Ray's and place an order. We would drive across the river to Ray's and a waiter would bring the telephone order to the front door. *We did not go inside.* I remember that Ray's was always full, and neither Riley's nor Carmine's had any cause to complain for lack of business. However, there were no white people in Ray's, and no "coloreds" in Riley's or Carmine's.

Probably because of the costs of building new schools—primary, middle, and high schools—large enough to accommodate students of both races, the public school system placidly ignored the *Brown* decision and turned the other cheek until 1960. Although this post-dated *Brown* by five years, my senior class was the last to graduate from the all-white Big Stone Gap High School before the inevitable "new" and larger school opened, and the local governing body finally succumbed to the law of the land. Traditionally, there had been for several years a senior trip during the week of the spring break, funded by students' work on various school-sponsored drives throughout the year. My class had traveled the ten-hour drive to Washington, D.C., and after about a three-day stay, further on to New York City, the legendary "Big Apple." These wonderful trips, silently and without any resistance, simply terminated after integration. One of my former high school teachers told me that it was simply "too much" to expect parents to allow their high school age children to actually go an a trip—a *social setting*, for goodness' sake—with "coloreds."

The general residential trends throughout the country resembled most parts of Northern Ireland, except that rather than "Catholic" (generally poorer) and "Protestant" sections, there were black and white sections. Most black sections were economically poorer, so the parallel is fairly similar. Although this has gradually changed somewhat in contemporary America, it is still much the case in many areas.

My brother told me some years after we both had married and had children of our own of the disdain in which his former neighbors held him and my sister-in-law after they sold their house in a relatively upscale "white" section of the small city where they lived (not in the South, incidentally) to a professional black man and his family. Perhaps the same attitude persists, since the Archie-Bunker-"there-goes-the-neighborhood" mentality is alive and well in the Land of the Free.

Post-*Brown v. Board of Education*

Some states did not view with favor the idea of "mixed" schools, and thus did not accept the *Brown* mandate without a fight, and in many ways this is reminiscent of the inability, or refusal, to accept lawfully adopted changes in Northern Ireland. One extreme example was in my home state of Virginia.

The local school board of Prince Edward County, the county which had been one of the defendants in *Brown*, took an interesting, if enigmatic, approach. The lawsuit had actually begun in 1951, when black students literally boycotted the black R.R. Moton High School to protest inadequate conditions—*i.e.*, separate and *un*equal. (Prince Edward County is about sixty miles southwest of Richmond, a rural area quite similar to my home county of Wise in the far southwest corner of the state, near the Tennessee border. True racial strife was virtually non-existent, but people are resistant to change, particularly that which upsets their culture and values.) In 1959, the all-white county Board of Supervisors simply voted not to fund the county schools, effectively forcing all to close.

This act was a blatant defiance of any order to integrate, one which became known as "massive resistance." A private foundation was established to fund the Prince Edward Academy, a school reserved exclusively for white students, regardless of ability to pay or academic merit. Subsequently the General Assembly (the state legislature) actually funded this private school. In *Griffin v. County School Board of Prince Edward County*[70] the U.S. Supreme Court ordered a resumption of state funding and reopening of public schools on an integrated basis.

A revisit of the R.R.Moton High School conditions in 1951 is instructive. The black high school was built in 1939, designed to accommodate 180 students. By April 23, 1951, the date the student boycott began, over 450 students were crammed into the building later described by one of them as having a "lack of educational material" and "falling apart." [71] The two-week student "strike" triggered the Virginia legal action that was to reach the U.S. Supreme Court in 1954 (*Brown*). Some black students left Prince Edward County when the public schools were officially closed and lived with relatives to attend school elsewhere. There were, of course, many who did not have this option. Thus, they were simply left with no education at all. This latter group is still known as the "Lost Generation."[72]

What did this blatant refusal to comply with a Supreme Court decision accomplish for the white population of Prince Edward County? One black resident who was a participant in the 1951 school strike, Willie Shepperson, said in 2001 that he "still [has] that hate in me...and I will take it to my grave." [73]

On a comparative note, how many Catholics in Northern Ireland can forget the Penal Law era when Catholic children were not entitled to education? And how many can forget the post-partition essential elimination of public schooling for their children by the enactment of statutes rendering them institutions unacceptable to Catholics on religious grounds? The only characteristic of residual bitterness is continued polarization. The resulting divide is difficult, if not impossible, to expunge.

On April 23, 2001, Prince Edward County officially recognized the Fiftieth Anniversary of the 1951 student walkout at R.R. Moton High School. The Robert Russa Moton Museum was opened on that date in the renovated building where the old school had been housed. One participant in the 1951 event who attended the ceremony, John Watson, is now an award-winning talk-show host in Wilmington, Delaware. Referring to the event's three-fourths mile march from the old school to the courthouse, Watson's telling comment is rhetorical: "What do you think would have happened if we had all tried [in 1951] to walk down here?" [74]

Voiced at the anniversary event was a Christian plea for racial reconciliation in Prince Edward County, again similar to what has become usual in Northern Ireland. These had indeed been shameful days in Virginia's history, and the local government's 1950s actions were unquestionably racist. One local Baptist minister, the Rev. David Upshaw, recognized this, but stated that he "believe[s] that God wants us to be together...[W]e have to forgive and heal...There is so much that divides us, but in Christ, we are reunited." [75]

Immediate Effects of *Brown*

Brown left localities with the problem of how effectively to integrate public schools. It is axiomatic that an across-the-board razing of small schools and rebuilding larger ones to accommodate students of both races would be financially impossible. Nonetheless, the concept of neighborhood schools—*i.e.*, a child attended the public school in the district where he or she lived—presented a roadblock to integration. Since racial patterns were reflected in housing, areas were either substantially white or black. This left a *de facto* (existing as a matter of fact), although not a *de jure* (enforced by law), segregation in most public schools.

The so-called "magic words" in the *Brown* opinion were that integration should be achieved "with all deliberate speed." One solution was a court-ordered busing requirement of children of both races into districts where the predominate race was other than their own. There were veritable nightmare stories of small children being deposited onto buses before dawn to travel two hours and pass by several other schools to reach the school where they were assigned.

The "granddaddy" of these busing decisions was *Swann v. Mecklenburg County*[76] involving public schools in the Charlotte, North Carolina area. The *Swann* litigation bounced back and forth through the federal court system over the issue of whether or not the degree of integration had been adequate enough to terminate the practice of busing children into districts other than their own.

Swann has been a litigation with a seemingly perpetual lifespan. The latest progeny was *Belk v. Charlotte-Mecklenburg County Board of Education*,[77] which partially reversed a federal trial court's holding[78] that the school system had achieved a "unitary" (nonracially discriminatory) status. The U.S. Court of Appeals for the Fourth Circuit remanded the case to the federal district court with a list of detailed instructions. The determination of "unitary" status achievement would require some consideration of the school board's remedial action taken during the current year, in the midst of litigation. The appellate court was particularly concerned over the imbalance between blacks and whites in student assessments. The trial court was asked to review the extent of progress by revisiting both student achievement and transportation of students, two factors which the Court of Appeals saw as "intertwined." The lower court's finding that unitary status was proven with regard to composition of faculty and extra-curricular activities was affirmed by the appellate court, so the North Carolina school system can take some solace for its thirty-year-old efforts.

The forced desegregation via busing of students which was the progeny of *Swann* has nearly the same longevity as the "official" onset of the Troubles – 1971 and 1969, respectively. It is an anachronism that the thrust in North Carolina has been to require racial integration of public schools. Conversely, the method in Northern Ireland has been to stabilize the separation-by-religion status of secondary education.

Progression or Regression?

Public education in Virginia (and in North Carolina, when the *Swann* litigation is reviewed) has reached the unenviable stage of appearing at times to be traveling backwards rather than forward with regard to race relations. In recent years in Richmond, for example, there have been protests over the retention of high school identifying names that refer to the Civil War, much of which was fought on Virginia soil. Black groups objected, to no avail, to the "Rebels" of Douglas S. Freeman High School (Freeman authored a multi-volume biography of Southern commanding Gen. Robert E. Lee) and the "Confederates" of Lee-Davis High School (Davis was Jefferson Davis, President of the Confederacy).

Moreover, Richmond was the capitol of the Confederacy, and much of Virginia history involves a study of the Civil War. The recently adopted statewide Standards of Learning tests to determine whether students have reached the desired level to permit them to move forward into the next grade (or to graduate) have been the topic of considerable debate as to their effectiveness, primarily the content.

Curriculum is generally arranged so as to teach students the material on which they are to be tested, and Civil War historians and defenders of Confederate heritage have been critical of a dearth in teaching of this significant part of Virginia's history. Only ninety minutes of instruction are required to be devoted to the Civil War, a situation leading several groups to lobby the state Board of Education. A particularly active group is the Sons of Confederate Veterans, but they were joined by facially neutral groups such as Parents Across Virginia United to Reform the Standards of Learning, which has the broad goal of insuring that students are provided a sufficient education, including history.[79] The point is that this adequacy-of-history issue has become a racial issue, a situation which has been common in Virginia and in some other states.

On the other hand, a 2000 film, "Remember the Titans," portrayed an actual account of the 1961 integration of the Alexandria, Virginia public schools in the aftermath of *Brown*, from the perspective of the Southern institution that is high school football. Racism had flourished, and the initial problems were predictably overwhelming. This was especially so on the football team, where competition of starting positions was already fierce, and no player was willing to give up his place for a "colored boy."

The white coach of the team had achieved winning records in recent years at the formerly all-white school and was consequently an icon. Not only were his stellar and successful white players faced with being joined by black teammates, but their coach was forced by school administration to be demoted to the level of assistant. The head coach was to be a black man, imported from a local formerly all-black school.

The school board reasoned that this would be convincing evidence of their good faith. The former (white) head coach was offered the choice of becoming an assistant to the black newcomer or transferring to another, less successful, football program. He chose to stay, and the two men developed a winning team and a lasting friendship. Together, they helped players of both races achieve this same respect and compatibility.

The story of Alexandria's Titans was in 1961, and the SOL racial squabble arose in 2001. One might reasonably conclude that Virginians were more forward-thinking with regard to racial reconciliation forty years ago than they are today.

Postscript

In the educational setting, religious division in Northern Ireland and racial strife—although not separation—in the U.S.A. still abound. Northern Ireland probably will retain segregated schooling by choice, and American public schools, though integrated by law, still face frequent issues of racial problems.

A haunting question about prejudices affecting public education applies both to Northern Ireland and to racial divisions in the U.S.A.: what is the reason that innocuous differences between groups of people are permitted to work to the detriment of our children? And why do we perpetuate our own biases by making them a part of what these children will become?

Divided schools are a fact in Northern Ireland, but divided minds persist not only in Northern Ireland, but also parts of the U.S.A.

Endnotes to Chapter 9

[1] John Conroy, A BELFAST DIARY at 102-103 (Beacon Press, Boston, Massachusetts, 1995).

[2] Jerry Tyrell, Brendan Hartop and Seamus Farrell, *Schools of Lessons from the Agreement*, 22 FORDHAM INTERNATIONAL LAW JOURNAL 1680, 1681 (1999).

[3] Laura Lundy, *Education Law under Devolution: the Case of Northern Ireland*, EDUCATION LAW JOURNAL 81, 82 (2000).

[4] This should not be confused with the American concept of "grammar school," which is a primary school. A "grammar school" in Northern Ireland is a parallel to a combined American middle and high school.

[5] Lundy, *supra* note 3, at 82.

[6] This was a bone of contention, which was subject to much public discourse when I worked in Belfast in summer, 2000. Lectures against the system were frequent, and posted throughout the city were signs reading, "Stop the 11-plus."

[7] Tyrell, *et al., supra* note 2, at 1681.

[8] There is also a verbal section with each of the two—math and verbal—having maximum scores of 800, with a perfect score thus being 1600.

[9] *See* Walter Williams, *SAT Charges Mask Education Fraud*, RICHMOND TIMES-DISPATCH, Feb. 28, 2001, at A-13, col. 1-3.

[10] An anomaly for the first time visitor to the Republic of Ireland is the fact that the official state church is Protestant, the Church of Ireland (counterpart to the Episcopal Church in the U.S.A), while more than 95% of the population is Catholic. *Ireland,* THE WORLD BOOK ENCYCLOPEDIA (1978), Vol. 10, p. 332b. [Note that this church is no longer the official state church. This is discussed in Chapter 3. The Church of Ireland as the state church was established in 1661, however, and retained this status until 1869. *See* Paul Johnson, IRELAND at 58 (Academy Chicago Publishers, 1980), and W.A. Phillips (ed.), HISTORY OF THE CHURCH OF IRELAND, 3 volumes (London, 1933-34).

[11] Mary Harris, *The Catholic church, minority rights and the founding of the Northern Irish state*, NORTHERN IRELAND AND THE POLITICS OF RECONCILIATION at 62 (Dermot Keough and Michael H. Haltze, eds., Woodrow Wilson Center Press and Cambridge University Press, Cambridge, England, 1994).

[12] Local Government Act (N.I.) 1922.

[13] *Cf. with* similar requirement of oath for certain public servants under U.S. constitutional law, U.S. CONST. Article VI section 3.

[14] Harris, *supra* note 11 at 72.

[15] Promissory Oaths Act 1923.

[16] Education Act (N.I.) 1923.

[17] Harris, *supra* note 11 at 73.

[18] *Id.*

[19] *Id.* at note 42, *citing* IRISH CATHOLIC DIRECTORY (Dublin, 1924) at 602-606.

[20] *See* Séamas MacAnnaidh, MICROPEDIA IRISH HISTORY 93 (Parragon Publishers, 1999).

[21] Paul Johnson, IRELAND: A CONCISE HISTORY FROM THE TWELFTH CENTURY TO THE PRESENT DAY 45 (Academy Chicago Publishers, 1984).

[22] Catholic Relief Act 1792. *See* Johnson, *id.*, at 77.

[23] R.B. McDowell and D.A. Webb TRINITY COLLEGE DUBLIN 1592-1952, at 504 (Cambridge University Press, Cambridge, England, 1982).

[24] Faucett's Act 1873.

[25] My sincere thanks go to my wonderful friend and colleague, Norma Dawson, professor of law at Queen's University Belfast, for providing many of these sources.

[26] Education Act (N.I.) 1923, *supra* note 16.

[27] Lundy, *supra* note 3 at 90.

[28] *Id.* at note 4, *citing* P. Cumper, *Parent Power: Building Bridges in Northern Ireland*, 3 EDUCATION AND THE LAW 27 (1991).

[29] Tyrell *et al., supra* note 2, at 1682.

[30] *Id.* At 1683.

[31] Interview with Jerry Tyrell and Lucia McGeady, July 24, 2000, Magee Campus of University of Ulster, Londonderry/Derry. [Sadly, the author learned of Mr. Tyrell's death shortly before publication of this book.]

[32] Seamus Dunn and Jacqueline Nolan-Healely, *Conflict in Northern Ireland After the GFA*, 22 FORDHAM INTERNATIONAL LAW JOURNAL 1372, 1387-1388 (1999).

[33] Interview with Billy Robinson, August 8, 2000, Counteract Office, Belfast.

[34] *See* 1998-2000 Biennial Review, The EMU Prooting School Project, at 19-20.

[35] There is a paperback book about this small group of self-proclaimed terrorists for the not-so-faint-hearted entitled simply THE SHANKILL BUTCHERS (Routledge Publishing, New York City, New York, 1999). The author is Martin Dillon.

[36] The Fair Treatment and Employment (N.I. Order) 1998 (Sl 1998/3162), art. 71.

[37] Northern Ireland Act 1998 §75(1)(a).

[38] *Cf. with* similar exception for religious institutions under American employment discrimination law, Title VII of 1964 Civil Rights Act, 42 U.S.C. §2000(e).

[39] GFA, page 1.

[40] Northern Ireland Act 1998 §4.

[41] *Id.* §17(4).

[42] *Id.* §18.

[43] Lundy, *supra* note 3 at 83.

[44] *Id.* Note that the IRA's imperturbable refusal to comply with the end-of-May, 2000 date for total decommissioning (a "deadline" which Unionists maintain is part of the spirit of the GFA) provided the impetus for Trimble's resignation as First Minister on July 1, 2001.

[45] *Id.*

[46] Wilson, also currently Lord Mayor of Belfast, is among those Unionists who refuse to address any member of *Sinn Féin* directly. Mark Robinson, another DUP member of the New Northern Ireland Assembly, said to me, "How can a rational, clear thinking person sit with terrorists?" Interview with Robinson, DUP Headquarters, Belfast, August 3, 2000.

[47] Lundy, *supra* note 3 at 84, note 24.

[48] U.S. CONST. amend. X. The Tenth Amendment transfers all powers to the states which the Constitution does not expressly reserve to the federal government nor deny to the states.

[49] Lundy, *supra* note 3 at 91.

[50] GFA, Rights, Safeguards and Equality of Opportunity section, paragraph 4, at 20.

[51] Education (N.I.) Order 1998.

[52] The author's thanks go to Fergus Ryan of the Law Faculty at Dublin Institute of Technology for providing this information.

[53] Lundy, *supra* note 3 at 91.

[54] *Id., referring to* GFA, para 4, *Rights, Safegards and Equality of Opportunity:Economics, Social and Cultural Issues* section.

[55] My colleagues at Queen's University School of Law informed that Asians comprise the fastest-growing immigration population in Northern Ireland.

[56] Lundy, *supra* note 3, at 91.

[57] Terence Brown, *The cultural issue in Northern Ireland, 1965-1991*, NORTH-ERN IRELAND AND THE POLITICS OF RECONCILIATION, *supra* note 11 at 160. Brown, who teaches English at Trinity College, Dublin, contrasts this absence of British culture with the omnipresence of discussion on cultural issues in the Republic of Ireland. (Dermot Keough and Michael H. Haltze, eds., Woodrow Wilson Center Press and Cambridge University Press, Cambridge, England, 1994).

[58] *Id.* at 164.

[59] Interview with Mr. Robinson, August 3, 2000, DUP Headquarters, Belfast. The inference to be drawn from Robinson's words is that Westminster is not concerned with the carnage in Northern Ireland as long as it does not reach Great Britain's territory.

[60] I spoke with this judge on July 6, 2000. His request for anonymity is typical in Northern Irealand.

[61] Clinton's loss-of-public-confidence Waterloo was probably his adamant finger-pointing to a national (indeed, international) television audience in January, 1998, immediately following the eruption of the Monica Lewinsky scandal, when he tensely stated "I did not have sex with that woman...Ms. Lewinsky." He unequivocally denied any intimacy with her, a denial he was later forced to retract the following August after evidence clearly proved otherwise.

[62] Josiah Horton Beemar and Robert Mahony, *The institutional churches and the process of reconciliation in Northern Ireland: recent progress in Presbyterian-Roman Catholic relations,* NORTHERN IRELAND AND THE POLITICS OF RECONCILIATION, *supra* note 11 at 150-151. This chapter by Beemar and Mahony describes many such interdenominational ecumenical programs undertaken jointly by local churches in Northern Ireland. (Dermot Keough and Michael H. Haltze, eds., Woodrow Wilson Center Press and Cambridge University Press, Cambridge, England, 1994).

[63] 60 U.S.(19 How.) 393 (1857).

[64] The Thirteenth Amendment (1865) abolished slavery; the Fourteenth Amendment (1868) assured all persons the right to equal protection of the laws and all citizens to the privileges and immunities of citizenship; and the Fifteenth Amendment (1870) gave black men the right to vote.

[65] 163 U.S. 537 (1896).

[66] *Sweatt v. Painter*, 339 U.S. 629. 70 S.Ct. 848 (1950).

[67] 339 U.S. 637 (1950).

[68] 347 U.S. 483 (1954).

[69] R. Kluger, SIMPLE JUSTICE 633-634 (Random House, New York City, New York, 1976).

[70] *Griffin v. School Board of Prince Edward County*, 377 U.S.218, 84 S.Ct. 1226 (1964).

[71] Kathryn Orth, *Moton students' mission a success,* RICHMOND TIMES-DIS-PATCH, April 21, 2001, at A-1, col. 3-4.

[72] *Id.*

[73] Jamie C. Ruff, *It is not gone. It is still deep,* RICHMOND TIMES-DISPATCH, April 21, 2001, at A-15, col. 1-2.

[74] Kathryn Orth, *A Walk to Remember*, RICHMOND TIMES-DISPATCH, April 24, 2001, at A-1, col. 2-4.

[75] Ruff, *supra* note 72.

[76] *Swann v. Charlotte-Mecklenburg County*, 402 U.S. 1. 91 S.Ct. 1267 (1971).

[77] 233 F.3d 232 (4th Cir. 2001).

[78] A collateral issue involved whether there was any evidence of racial discrimination in the assignment of students to slots in so-called "magnet schools." Such schools focus on a particular subject area, such as math or science, and only those students who apply and who are selected are admitted.

[79] Jason Wermers, *Critics say SOLs slight Civil War,* RICHMOND TIMES-DIS-PATCH, March 22, 2001, at B-1, col. 5.

Epilogue

The island of Ireland is a lyrical, mystical, and almost musical place. There is lilt in the brogue—both North and South—and even the names of the towns seem melodic. There are countless villages beginning with "Bally" (Irish for village)— Ballyshannon, Ballymoney, Ballywater and the like, and there are Killarney, Inishmore, Killybegs, Castleblaney, Shannon, Glenarm, and Tullamore.

Of course, the leprechauns and fairies add their own fictional mystique, as well as delightful bases for many a tale. There is one particular example of how everything seems to evoke thoughts of an air, a jig, or a ballad. A mere mention of the lush and rolling Mountains of Mourne will be followed by the typical local's impulsive singing of Percy French's famous musical tribute.

The people—the wonderful people—of Ireland are perhaps what is instrumental in luring us back. As my younger son said on arrival in Belfast without his luggage (no fault of *Aer Lingus*, I might add, but that of the U.S.-based airline on which he traveled as far as New York City), "Mom, this happens every time I fly on this [unnamed American] airline. But these folks here are so nice. It's just impossible to be angry with these people!" Yes, indeed, 'tis.

What does the fortune portend for the six counties of Northern Ireland, the province which most definitely possesses these same fascinating traits as does the Republic of Ireland? Will it remain a part of the United Kingdom, or will it reunite with the twenty-six counties of the Republic as a political entity?

One of the anomalies of Northern Ireland is the disparity of responses from politicians and others who call the province home when asked the question, "Do you think there will be a united Ireland within the next twenty-five years?" This paradox is compounded when two different responses will be supported by the same rationale. Economics is one such reason. This recalls the similarly polar sides on the issue of capital punishment in the U.S.A. Proponents cite the financial burden on the public trough to absorb costs of lifetime imprisonment, which would be the alternative to the death penalty. Opponents in turn point to the protracted costs in funds, time, and manpower created by a seemingly endless process of appeals by those on death row.

Correspondingly, with regard to a single Ireland *vis-à-vis* keeping Northern Ireland in the United Kingdom, those on both sides refer to the economic factor as supportive of their respective positions. Unionists would only grudgingly surrender the $8 billion annual subsidy the region receives from the British government.[1] Moreover, this figure is used primarily for public sector jobs, which constitute nearly one-half the workforce. A collateral argument for this position is that this work would not be in existence if the British government were not in control.

On the flip side of the coin, advocates for a united Ireland cite the island's potential for tourism if the two parts were united. Frequently, visitors to Ireland purposely avoid Northern Ireland because it evokes fear of exposure to bombs, violence and hand grenades, despite the safety of most parts of the province, particularly for non-residents. (One of my friends in Belfast told me that "Americans seem to believe that we all walk around wearing flak jackets, with a gun in one pocket.") This is despite the safety of most places in Northern Ireland, particularly when it is apparent that one is a visitor.

What do those directly concerned say? One of my meetings was with Eoin O'Brion (pronounced "Owen O' Broyne"), born in Dublin, university-educated in England, and an adopted son of Belfast on the staff of *Sinn Féin*, the party with the staunchest of Nationalists. He looked incredibly young to me, my guess being that he probably is approaching thirty. We went to an Irish Gaelic café in the heart of the Falls Road, *Cúpla Focal* ("a few words"). This is the section where the tricolor Republic of Ireland flag adorns nearly every shop and/or home. Eoin explained that only Irish is spoken in this cafe, but added that "they'll understand, because you're an American." I am indeed, and they did indeed.

We spoke of his thoughts on the possibility of a single Ireland within the foreseeable future. (I had suggested the twenty-five-year time frame.) Eoin excitedly assured me that this would happen considerably before that length of time, at least during his lifetime.

Eoin's eagerness and enthusiasm are almost infectious. He explained that after the GFA, agriculture has regained its former dominance. Additionally, he saw a cohesiveness between the two Irelands with regard to tourism and business. "Even Unionists," said Eoin "want some cross-border linkages" in these respects. He mentioned that the United States is attracted to Ireland because of its available skilled labor and its position as the "gateway to Europe," and that Northern Ireland, too, has marvelous tourist sites (true) which would enhance the drawing power of the island.

Eoin added three more reasons to expect a united Ireland before very long. First, prior to the 1960s, the eastern part of the province was industrially connected to England, and the Belfast shipping industry was heavily engaged in commerce with Manchester and Liverpool. However, according to him, this economic trading connection of Northern Ireland with Great Britain is "nearly dead."

Secondly, he had noted from his days as a student in England that the British "look upon those from Northern Ireland as Irish," and the entire island as an entity connected by what he called "Irish things," such as Catholic banning of suggestive movies. He told me that a Northern Irelander in Great Britain is not regarded as a citizen of the United Kingdom, but simply as someone from Ireland.

Third, he stressed other items where consistency of policy would be desirable for residents of areas with contiguous borders, such as social policies and health problems. The North-South Council and the emphasis on assurance of human rights, he believes, will strengthen the possibility of unity.[2]

As expected, Eoin's *Sinn Féin* colleague, MLA Mitchel McLaughlin, concurred. "We[*Sinn Féin*] created space which Unionists could accept for the inevitable [a united Ireland]," he told me. "This [the GFA] was all about managing the process [of ultimate unification]. [W]e know there'll be a united Ireland," he continued, and, to *Sinn Féin*, the GFA laid the groundwork for an "irreversible change." He seemed to view the GFA as both easing and expediting a union which *Sinn Féin*ers believe is certain to occur. McLaughlin added that he saw a "hemorrhaging" within Unionists, among whom the fear is that they will be "treated as we [Nationalists] were in the past." (McLaughlin is alluding to the anti-Catholic laws and historical discrimination against Irish Catholics in general.) He sincerely believes that many Unionists recognize the inevitability of a single Ireland, calling the cross-border body a "timely development in this phase of Ireland." Moreover, he told me that G-7 chair Sir George Quigley of Ulster Bank, traditionally a Unionist, had begun to advocate a united Ireland.[3]

Sinn Féin leader Gerry Adams has been unambiguous about his feelings. He has written that the political objective of his party is to attain "a united Ireland free of British interference. Everything that we do is intended to advance that entirely legitimate and realizable goal. We see a 32-county republic as the best way to eradicate the range of political, social, economic, and other inequalities that effect [sic] the people of this island."[4]

Womens Coalition's Monica McWilliams was clearly less positive, stating only that there "possibly" would be a single Ireland. Contrary to those who rely on economic factors, she opined that "what helps business does not necessarily affect politics in Northern Ireland," something she regarded as a difference from American politics.[5] As a social worker, her innate interest in social ills probably is akin to Eoin O'Broin's feeling that common health and social problems are desirable for North and South.

Outside politics, there are those less impassioned but who nonetheless predict a united Ireland. Among those is Bishop James Moore (Diocese of Connor, Northern Ireland, Church of Ireland), who told me that "inevitably and in due course, there'll be an all-Ireland."[6] This comes from a man of the cloth who regards himself as a Unionist, so this view is particularly telling.

Martin Mansergh, a scholar who is Special Advisor to the *Taoiseach* in the Republic of Ireland, did not give an immediate answer to this question, but rather, reflected a bit before he responded, "There could be [a single Ireland]...I don't know." He appeared to me to lean objectively toward such an outcome, presenting two oft-cited, but slightly differing, thoughts on demographics. One is that the Catholic population of Northern Ireland will increase until there is parity, at which time such increase will stop. The other is that not only will the Catholic sector increase in numbers (many base this upon church doctrine opposing contraception usage and abortion), and that this rise will continue until Catholics comprise the majority.[7] The effect of the latter would tip the vote in favor of unification.

From academia comes Professor Brendan O'Leary's rationale underlying his belief that a single Ireland looms in the future. He has rhetorically asked whether the GFA is a document which "simply fall[s] within the rubric of devolution within a centralized unitary state." Answering his own question in the negative, Professor O'Leary sees two critical distinctions between the devolved governments of Scotland and Wales and that of Northern Ireland. He explains first that the GFA is an agreement between two sovereign states, the Republic of Ireland and the United Kingdom, one founded on the principle of national choice on the island in addition to convention which is British in nature. Scotland and Wales have no such characteristics which would permit a consolidation with another country. Significantly, the United Kingdom has recognized through the GFA the right of Northern Ireland to secede and to join the Republic, provided a majority so desires. Probably Professor O'Leary is implying that this recognition is a big step toward a "letting go" of Northern Ireland by the British.

Secondly, Professor O'Leary stresses the additional factor in Northern Ireland's devolution. Unlike those of Scotland and Wales, both which have no relationship to any other sovereign than the United Kingdom, the North-South institutions within the island of Ireland borne of the GFA evidence an independent element regarding international law. According to him, this component is federal in nature, pre-empting the British government from unilaterally exercising power over the province which is not consistent with the GFA.[8]

Lest the reader is convinced otherwise, rest assured that the "no" side is not devoid of representatives. Probably foremost is First Minister David Trimble of the Northern Ireland Assembly. When asked whether a single Ireland was likely, his answer was curt: "No."[9] In classic Trimble fashion, he did not elect to elaborate.

MLA Mark Robinson of the DUP repeated the economic argument for continuance of political affiliation with the United Kingdom. He told me that the EU "handouts" to the Republic have been substantial, but that this bounty is "burning itself out." Robinson added the religious issue. The Republic is sparse on Protestants, and "we [DUP] don't like that." He added that people in Northern Ireland are becoming more "liberal," and that they abhor the church and state link in the Republic. "Unionists want freedom of religion," he insisted.[10] Presumably, he was referring to the Catholic majority in the Republic, although the Irish Constitution expressly guarantees freedom of religion.[11] He also did not address the fact that the same queen who is the crown over Northern Ireland is head of the Church of England—an official state church within the United Kingdom of which his province is a part.

PUP's David Ervine told me he did not think there would be a united Ireland for yet two other reasons. He mused that "there'll be a different Ireland," and a "different Europe." Ervine's long-range view relates to a European Union amalgamation, and he simply sees no constructive reason to reunite the two Irelands. He also explained a political reason for his position. *Sinn Féin* now has eighteen elected representatives to the 108-member Assembly. Realizing this party's increasing popularity, he hypothetically assumed that this would increase to twenty-five members. To the contrary, *Sinn Féin* is a very small party in the Republic. These combined factors led Ervine to reason that *Sinn Féin* would eventually prefer to stay where they are stronger. "Would they give up this large representation [in the Northern Ireland Assembly] for only five members in the much larger *Dáil* [in the Republic]?"[12] He feels unequivocally that in reality they would remain where they are most significant. (Having heard from many *Sinn Féin*ers on this issue, I was not convinced by Ervine's reasoning.)

It is worthwhile to consider the informed opinion of Dr. Dennis Kennedy who, like O'Leary, is an academic. A delightful man, he has worked in Ethiopia as a Lutheran missionary, served as Deputy Editor of *The Irish Times* and on the editorial staff of *The Belfast Telegraph*, and has spent six years as the European Commission's representative in Northern Ireland. Astute in many respects, he was dubious of most of the claimed positive attributes of the GFA, which he termed a "sort of apartheid solution." His undergraduate degree is from Queen's, but his Ph.D. from Trinity College came during his eighteen years in Dublin. Thus, he has lived on both sides of the border.

Regarding the likelihood of a united Ireland, Dr. Kennedy's response was "probably not." His rationale was reminiscent of David Ervine's. "I think of myself as European, and Irish in [only] a cultural sense." He sees no real sense of a national identity on the island, and his opinion is that "nationalism" should have had its demise following World War I.[13]

So, there you have it, as the English say. Will there be a united Ireland? "Yes" and "no," according to the experts. More important than the future political status of Northern Ireland, however, is that its people might finally attain the peace they so genuinely deserve.

University of Alabama coaching great Paul "Bear" Bryant said that "[w]hen you win, there's glory enough for everybody. When you lose, there's glory for none,"[14] a philosophy which could well be applicable to Northern Ireland. As long as tensions are so high and emotions so intense, one side—either Unionists or Nationalists—will be dissatisfied, even though each has endorsed deferring to the desires of the majority.

The news at time of publication of this book is not encouraging. On October 14, 2002, the British government suspended the provincial government in Northern Ireland for the third time and resumed direct rule once again. The IRA remained alive and well, and the issue of decommissioning by paramilitaries appeared to be the Rasputin of the anti-GFA movement.

Will this most recent hiatus in the devolved government be a long-lasting one, or will the residue of the hopes initially aroused by the GFA re-energize a new commitment to peace and self-rule? Does sufficient common ground between Nationalists and Unionists remain to revitalize the peace movement which led to devolution negotiated in 1998? Has the power-sharing government met its demise, or is it only temporarily dormant?

This book ends much as it began. The self-government which the GFA created for Northern Ireland was tenuous from its inception, and this latest redux has it yet again. On hold. The attainment of genuine peace in Northern Ireland seems destined too be an arduous and prolonged process, and whether it will finally be a reality is a toss-up.

An oft-cited quotation is that of Bobby Sands, Republican hunger striker (over conditions for inmates) in the Maze Prison who died in 1981 during this fast. Sands said, "our revenge will be the laughter of our children." A better world—a world in which they might laugh more freely and openly—should be, to be sure, one of the great motivators for striving for peace and putting an end to the violence. I wish, however, that he had refrained from using the word "revenge." The tenacity of those who yearn for vengeance is the misguided inciter of the tragedy which still envelops Northern Ireland.

"I'm so pleased that you haven't given up on Northern Ireland," one of my good Belfast friends, Judge John Martin, said to me when I returned in Summer, 2000, for work on this book. Be assured, Judge John, that I never will. Whatever the years to come bode for Northern Ireland, I yearn and pray for lasting peace in this province which became a true second home to me. I am certain that when I left Northern Ireland, my heart became smaller. A significant portion of this heart remained there forever.

> "I have spread my dreams under your feet.
> Tread softly because you tread on my dreams."
>
> William Butler Yeats, 20th century Irish poet

Endnotes to Epilogue

[1] This figure comes from the fiscal year 1995. See Northern Ireland: a Special Report, WORLD BOOK ENCYCOPEDIA YEARBOOK (1996), at 316.

[2] Interview with Eoin O'Broin, coffee house in West Belfast, July 7, 2000.

[3] Interview with Mitchel McLaughlin, Sinn Féin Constituency Office, Londonderry/Derry, July 26, 2000.

[4] Gerry Adams, To Cherish a Just and Lasting Peace, 22 FORDHAM INTERNATIONAL LAW JOURNAL 1179, 1180 (1999). Adams points out in this same article that his party is both "radical" and "innovative."

[5] Interview with Monica McWilliams, her office in Stormont, Belfast, July 21, 2000.

[6] Interview with the Right Reverend James Moore in his diocesan office, Belfast, August 7, 2000.

[7] Interview with Dr. Martin Mansergh, in his office in Dublin, July 10, 2000.

[8] Brendan O'Leary, The Nature of the Agreement, 22 FORDHAM INTERNATIONAL LAW JOURNAL 1628, 1646-47 (1999).

[9] Interview with David Trimble, in his office at Stormont, Belfast, July 21, 2000.

[10] Interview with Mark Robinson, DUP Constituency Office, Belfast, August 3, 2000.

[11] *Bureacht na hÉireann*, Constitution of Ireland (1937), Article 44. This somewhat disputes the appellation in the preamble to "the Most Holy Trinity, from Whom is all authority and to Whom, as our final end, all actions both of men and State must be referred." This preamble continues with a virtual prayer, where "[w]e the people of Eire, Humbly acknowledge all our obligations to our Divine Lord Jesus Christ...."

[12] Interview with David Ervine, in his office at Stormont, Belfast, July 3, 1000.

[13] Interview with Dr. Dennis Kennedy, in his office at Queens University Belfast, July 19, 2000.

[14] THE WISDOM OF SOUTHERN FOOTBALL (Criswell Freeman, editor) (1995), at 77.

A "Reader's Digest Condensed Version" of Irish-British Animosities
(with apologies and disclaimers to Irish historians everywhere)

1366: Statutes of Kilkenny prohibited use of the Gaelic language or the wearing of Gaelic dress, or adoption of other "undesirable Gaelic attributes." (For the most part, these laws were ignored by the Irish.)

1494: Poynings' Law made all acts of the Irish Parliament subject to British approval.

1541: King Henry VIII became King of Ireland and took control of the Catholic Church in Ireland. His daughters, Queen Mary and later Elizabeth I, shortly thereafter introduced the "plantation" system in Ireland, the "planting" of English settlers throughout the island who later not only displaced the Irish and dominated the country politically, but also stripped Irish Catholics of any rights (See also 1641, Cromwell, below).

1601: End of Nine Years' War. At the Battle of Kinsale, British Lord Mountjoy defeated Irish Hugh O'Neill and his Spanish allies, effectively terminating what had been Gaelic Ireland; pro-English Dublin government forfeited all the O'Donnell (Donegal) and O'Neill (Tyrone) properties to the British government.

1641-1658: Reign in Britain of military leader Oliver Cromwell. He massacred Drogheda and Wexford and took control of Munster and ultimately the whole of Ireland; every Catholic landowner in Ireland was displaced by Cromwell, who refined and empowered the plantation system.

1689 (April): Troops of Protestant (Dutch) William of Orange (husband of Queen Mary, Catholic King James II's daughter) defeated his father-in-law James' Catholic troops at Derry after James' 105-day siege of the city.

1690 (July): William of Orange defeated James II at Carrickfergus near Drogheda (north of Dublin) in the Battle of the Boyne. Usually regarded as the most important battle in Irish history, this is the precursor to Northern Ireland's Protestant marching season, culminating the week of July 12 each year and led by the all-male "Orangemen" established in the 1790's. The defeat at the Battle of the Boyne officially established British Protestantism as controlling in Ireland. Opponents included the Ulster Protestant Dissenters as well as Catholics.

Early 1700's: Enactment by British government of penal laws in Ireland, which stripped all Catholics of the rights to hold public office, bear arms, and practice law.

1798 (May): Dublin lawyer Protestant and Dissenter Wolfe Tone led a localized Irish rebellion throughout the country, the largest being in Wexford, Down, and Antrim. About 30,000 Irish were killed in these British victories.

1803: Dublin uprising organized by Robert Emmet aborted. Emmet escaped, but was captured and executed.

1829: Later Member of British Parliament (MP) Daniel O'Connell achieved statutory Catholic Emancipation in Ireland.

1845-49: The Great Famine resulted from failure of the potato crop (the main food staple of Ireland) because of deadly fungus which led to typhus, dysentery and scurvy. Thus, the Irish were impoverished and evicted from homes they "rented" from British who had taken control of their land. Moreover, the British government, though continuing to export food to foreign countries, did not send relief staples to Ireland. The population of Ireland decreased from 8 million to 4.5 million (about 2 million died, and a near-equal number immigrated in so-called "coffin ships," many having died enroute to Australia, the U.S.A. and England).

1870's: Fenian movement revived nationalism, energizing Home Rule efforts. Protestant MP Charles Stewart Parnell established Irish Parliamentary Party. Conciliatory statutes benefiting the Irish followed.

1905: *Sinn Féin* ("ourselves alone") political party formed; promoted Home Rule for Ireland.

1916: Easter Rising in Dublin—Irish volunteers and Fenians organized rebellion against British rule, taking over the General Post Office in Dublin. After a week-long battle, they were defeated, and sixteen of the leaders were summarily executed at Dublin's Kilmainham Jail, without trial.

1919-21: Irish Civil War.

1921: Irish Civil War ends with the Anglo-Irish Treaty. Although the Civil War did not result in an Ireland completely independent from Britain, leader Michael Collins did achieve Home Rule. However, the treaty partitioned Ireland into the present two divisions: the now-Republic of Ireland (twenty-six counties) and Northern Ireland (six counties), the latter which remained subject to direct British rule.

1949: Ireland became a Republic, an independent country which had already adopted its own constitution in 1937.

January 30, 1972: Bloody Sunday. Fourteen civilians in Derry (Londonderry) were killed by British troops, allegedly in self-defense. Riots between Catholics (Nationalists) and Protestants (Unionists).

1972: Westminster Parliament disbanded Northern Ireland's Parliament, and Northern Ireland became entirely subjected to the British crown. British troops were brought into Northern Ireland.

1973: Sunningdale agreement was to re-establish Northern Ireland's parliament, but the new government lasted only from January until May, 1974, because of a Protestant strike opposing the shared Protestant-Catholic government the agreement established.

1995-1998: Peace negotiations in Northern Ireland, brokered by former U.S. Senator George Mitchell.

April 10, 1998 (Good Friday): Peace Agreement signed in Belfast by all major political parties in Northern Ireland.

May 22, 1998: Vote on peace agreement passed in the Republic of Ireland by a 95% margin and in Northern Ireland by nearly 72%.

June 25, 1998: 108-member Northern Irish Parliament was elected, appointing UUP (Unionist) party chair David Trimble First Minister.

October 19, 1998: Trimble and John Hume, SDLP (Nationalist) party chair, awarded Nobel Peace Prize.

Chart Indicating Major Political Parties
(and Leaders) in Northern Ireland

Note: Top row designates Nationalists (pro-united Ireland), and bottom row indicates Unionists (pro-remaining part of the United Kingdom), listing major leaders at the time the GFA was signed. The more extreme of each of the two sides are indicated at the ends.

Middle section divides the two sides, indicating the two parties which are not aligned "U" or "N."

NATIONALIST	*Sinn Féin*	*Gerry Adams, Martin McGuinness*	Political wing of Irish Republican Army (IRA)
	SDLP (Social Democratic & Labour Party)	*John Hume*	
NON-ALIGNED	**Alliance** Party	*Lord Alderdice*	
	Women's Coalition		
UNIONIST	**UUP** (Ulster Unionist Party)	*David Trimble*	
	PUP (Progressive Unionist Party)	*David Ervine*	Political wing of Ulster Volunteer Force (UVF)
	DUP (Democratic Unionist Party)	*The Rev. Ian Paisley*	

POLITICAL PARTIES
(Beginning with largest in each sub-group)

<u>Nationalist (Catholic) Political Parties:</u>

      Social Democratic and Labour Party (SDLP)

      Sinn Féin ("ourselves alone")

<u>Unionist (Protestant):</u>

      Ulster Unionist Party (UUP)

      Democratic Unionist Party (DUP)

      United Kingdom Unionist Party (UKUP)

      Progressive Unionist Party (PUP)

      Ulster Democratic Party (UDP)

(Note: The UDP did not have a sufficient number of votes for membership in the Northern Ireland Assembly, but its representatives participated in the peace talks.)

<u>Neutral on Unionist/Nationalist Issue:</u>

      Alliance Party

      Women's Coalition

MAJOR PARAMILITARY GROUPS
(and affiliation with political party, where appropriate)

* asterisk denotes most prominent, and "x" denotes that group is not currently observing a ceasefire.

Republican (Nationalist)

*   Irish Republican Army (IRA) (political wing is Sinn Fein)

Provos (splinter group which left the IRA in 1970)

x   "Real" IRA (more recent splinter group which advocates continued violence)

Irish National Liberation Army (INLA, generally referred to as "Irps," derived from name of its originating political wing, the Irish Revolutionary Socialist Party)

Loyalist (Unionist)

*   Ulster Volunteer Force (UVF) (political wing is PUP)

Ulster Defense Association (UDA) (political wing is UDP)

Loyalist Volunteer Force (LVF, splinter group from UVF)

x   Ulster Freedom Fighters (UFF)

x   Red Hand Commandos

A Brief Glossary of Terms

Anglo-Irish: Anglo-Normans who took over Ireland in the 17th century.

Anglo-Norman: English, coupled with Scandinavian conquerors of England, in the 11th century.

Apprentice Boys: Group of young men and boys who successfully closed the gates of the city of Derry to protect Protestant William of Orange against the Catholic forces of James II in the 1689 Siege of Derry.

baton round: Weapons used by security forces which fire rubber and/or plastic (*i.e.*, non-lethal) bullets.

British-Irish Council: So-called "Council of the Isles," the island of Ireland/ island of Great Britain council which will discuss cross-island affairs of mutual interest, per the Good Friday Agreement and supplementary legislation.

cross-community principle: the assurance-of-equal-representation in the Northern Ireland Assembly, per terms of the Good Friday Agreement and supplementary legislation.

Crown Court: Appellate court in Northern Ireland in criminal matters. See "High Court" below.

Dáil: Primary body in the Irish Parliament, a term often used in reference to the collective body. See "*Oireachtas*," below.

decommission: (verb) To disarm, particularly with reference to a paramilitary body in Northern Ireland, more specifically, the Irish Republican Army (IRA). Note the use of the root word "commission." This gives an appearance of legitimacy to the paramilitary body that was unlawfully constituted.

devolved matters: Areas transferred to a newly created legislative body of a province (in this context, Northern Ireland), which areas will thereafter be "off-limits" for the parent legislature (i.e., Westminster, or British, Parliament).

d'Hondt: A complicated formulatic principle used in achieving a cross-community (see above) balance within a legislative body (in this context, the Northern Ireland Assembly). Named for the Belgian mathematician who devised this system.

Diplock Trial: Trial without jury for terrorist-related charges in Northern Ireland. Created by Westminster statute in 1972 in response to the 'Troubles.'

direct rule: Resumption of control over a province (in this context, Northern Ireland) by its parent political head (i.e., the United Kingdom).

Drumcree: Church of Ireland parish church in outlying area of the County Armagh (Northern Ireland) town of Portadown. Used to refer to the parade which has traditionally caused the most difficulty for security forces during the Protestant July 12 marches, because the Portadown Orange Order (Protestant) march traverses a Catholic section.

Éire (**or** *Éireann*): Official (Gaelic) title for the Republic of Ireland.

Fenian: Originally a term referencing a revolutionary group in the U.S.A. which promoted the independence of Ireland. Also a generic reference to a Catholic.

First Minister: Party leader of the strongest party in the Northern Ireland Assembly (currently David Trimble of the Ulster Unionist Party [UUP]).

High Court: Appellate court for civil matters in Northern Ireland. See "Crown Court" above.

House of Lords: Hereditary peerage body in Westminster (British) Parliament, and the court of last resort in criminal matters throughout the United Kingdom (which includes the province of Northern Ireland).

"involved": Adjective describing one in Northern Ireland who is engaged in activities regarding the political affiliation (*i.e.*, to remain with the United Kingdom, or to reunite with the Republic of Ireland for a single Ireland).

Loyalist: paramilitary group of one of the Unionist political parties (see "Republican" below). Paramilitaries believe in the use of violence to achieve their desired goals.

Nationalist: Northern Irelander who aspires to a united Ireland of all thirty-two counties and an end to the province's present affiliation with the United Kingdom. See "Unionist" below.

NGO: Acronym for "non-governmental organization," referring to a body which performs some functions usually assigned to the government, but also assumes other duties.

"North of Ireland": Term usually spoken by Nationalists in Northern Ireland to refer to the region, which is officially Northern Ireland. This infers that they think of themselves as the northern section of the Republic of Ireland, which in reality is not accurate.

North-South Ministerial Council: Intra-island body created by the 1998 Good Friday Agreement and supplementary legislation which agrees upon policies for all-Ireland matters.

Northern Ireland Assembly: Title of the legislative body for the devolved government of Northern Ireland, post-Good Friday Agreement in 1998.

Northern Ireland Parliament: Title of the legislative body for Northern Ireland from 1922 until 1972.

Oireachtas: collective name for both bodies of the Irish Parliament.

paramilitary: Wings of either sector in Northern Ireland—Nationalist and Unionist—which use violence as a means to achieve their desired goal. Note the use of the root word "military," which lends some degree of legitimacy to these groups that are actually unlawful.

partition: Official 1920 legislative separation of the island of Ireland into the six counties in the northeast (now Northern Ireland) and the twenty-six counties in the south and northwest (now the Republic of Ireland).

plantation: Land area established through the program begun by Queen Mary ("Bloody Mary") and continued by her sister, Queen Elizabeth I in the 16th century, by which lands owned by the Irish were "taken" and supplanted by English landlords.

Prime Minister: Head of ruling political party in a parliamentary governmental legislative body (for purposes of this book, referring to Westminster, or British, Parliament).

Quango: Acronym for "quasi-non-governmental organization," indicating an organization which is partially financed, and probably owned, by the government, but privately operated.

Republican: Paramilitary wings of Nationalists. See "Loyalist" above.

reserved matters: Areas expressly deferred to the U.K. government, cross-border or inter-island governance per the Good Friday Agreement and supplementary legislation. See "North-South Council" and "British-Irish Council" above.

Royal Irish Constabulary (RIC): British police in control of security in Ireland prior to partition. After partition, this body became the *Garda* (Gaelic for police department) and (in Northern Ireland) the Royal Ulster Constabulary (RUC).

Royal Ulster Constabulary (RUC): Successor to the RIC in post-partition Northern Ireland (since November, 2001, the Police Service of Northern Ireland, per terms of the Good Friday Agreement and supplementary legislation).

Saorstát Éireann: Gaelic for "Free State of Ireland," dominion status of Ireland from 1922 until full independence and republic status in 1949.

Secretary of State for Northern Ireland: Member of Westminster (British) Parliament assigned by the Prime Minister to Northern Ireland.

Stormont: Building which housed the first Northern Ireland Parliament, 1922-1972 and which currently houses the Northern Ireland Assembly (1998-). The legislative body of Northern Ireland is often referred to simply as "Stormont." It is also the name of the section of East Belfast where the building is located.

Sunningdale: Short (four-month) revival of self-government for Northern Ireland in 1974. Sunningdale is the location in England where the negotiations for this plan took place.

Taig: A somewhat derogatory reference to a Catholic (*i.e.*, negative *unless* used by a Catholic referring to another Catholic).

Taoiseach: Prime minister of the Republic of Ireland ("high chief" or "*chieftain*" in Gaelic).

The 'Troubles': term referring to the political/religious strife and violence which has plagued Northern Ireland.

Unionist: Northern Irelander who favors continued political affiliation with the United Kingdom. See "Nationalist" above.

Westminster Parliament: British Parliament.

Table of Cases

Index

About the Author

Carol Daugherty Rasnic is Professor of Employment and Labor Law at Virginia Commonwealth University in Richmond, Virginia. She is licensed to practice law in Virginia as well as Tennessee and has engaged in private practice in both states. Professor Rasnic has taught each summer since 1991 at schools of law in Germany and Austria. In addition to this book, she is the author of more than eighty law journal articles and two other law-related books.

She was a 1992-93 Fulbright Lecturer-Researcher at Friedrich-Alexanders-Universitaet Erlangen, Germany, a 1998 Fulbright Distinguished Professor at Queen's University School of Law Belfast and a 2003-04 Fulbright Professor at National University of Ireland Galway.

She was born and grew up in the southwestern corner of Virginia and lives with her husband, Jack, in Richmond. She is the mother of two sons whom she describes as the "lights in my life."

The author with three young boys in Derry, July 2000.

Printed in the United States
85371LV00002BA/388-402/A